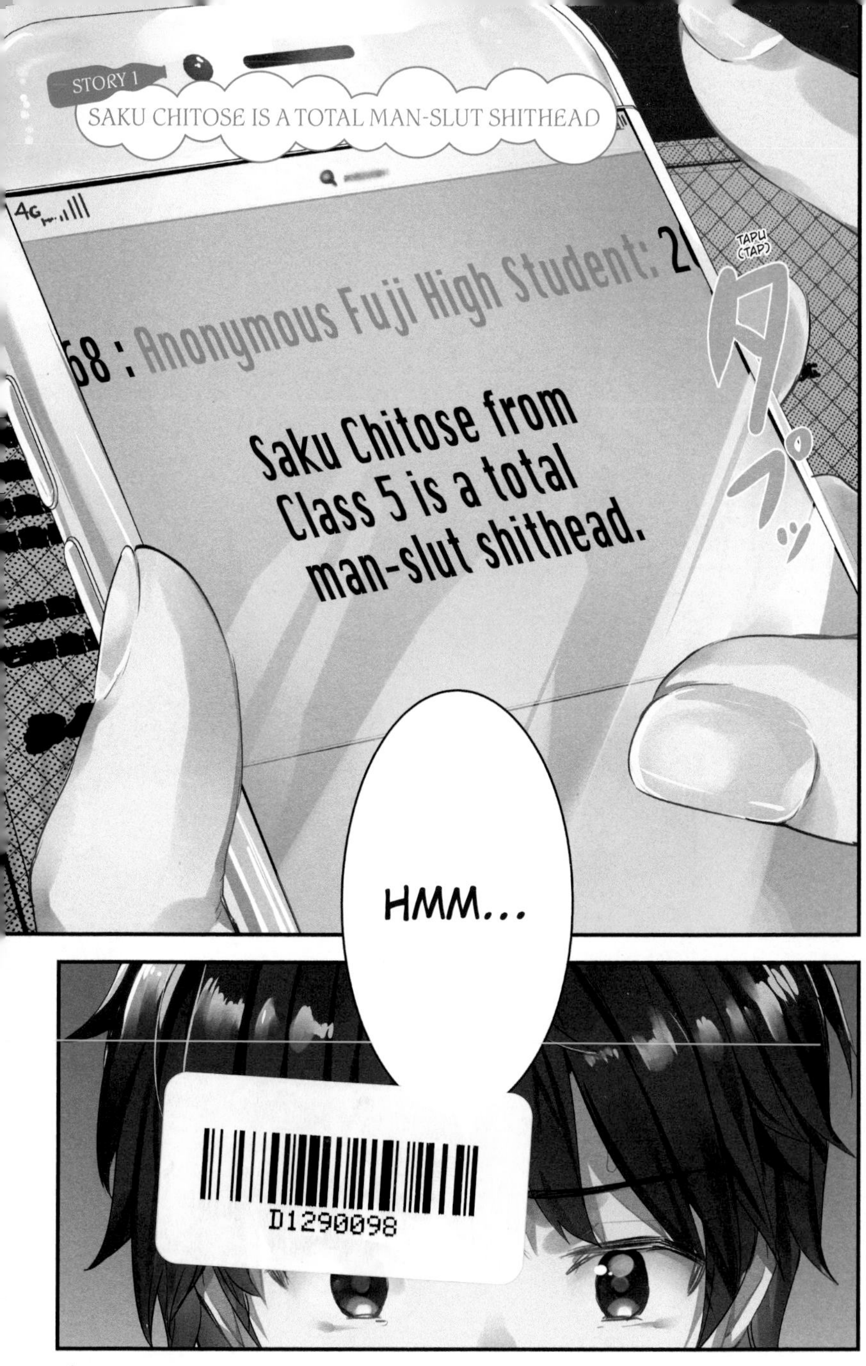
STORY 1
SAKU CHITOSE IS A TOTAL MAN-SLUT SHITHEAD
68 : Anonymous Fuji High Student: 2
Saku Chitose from Class 5 is a total man-slut shithead.
TAPU (TAP)
HMM...

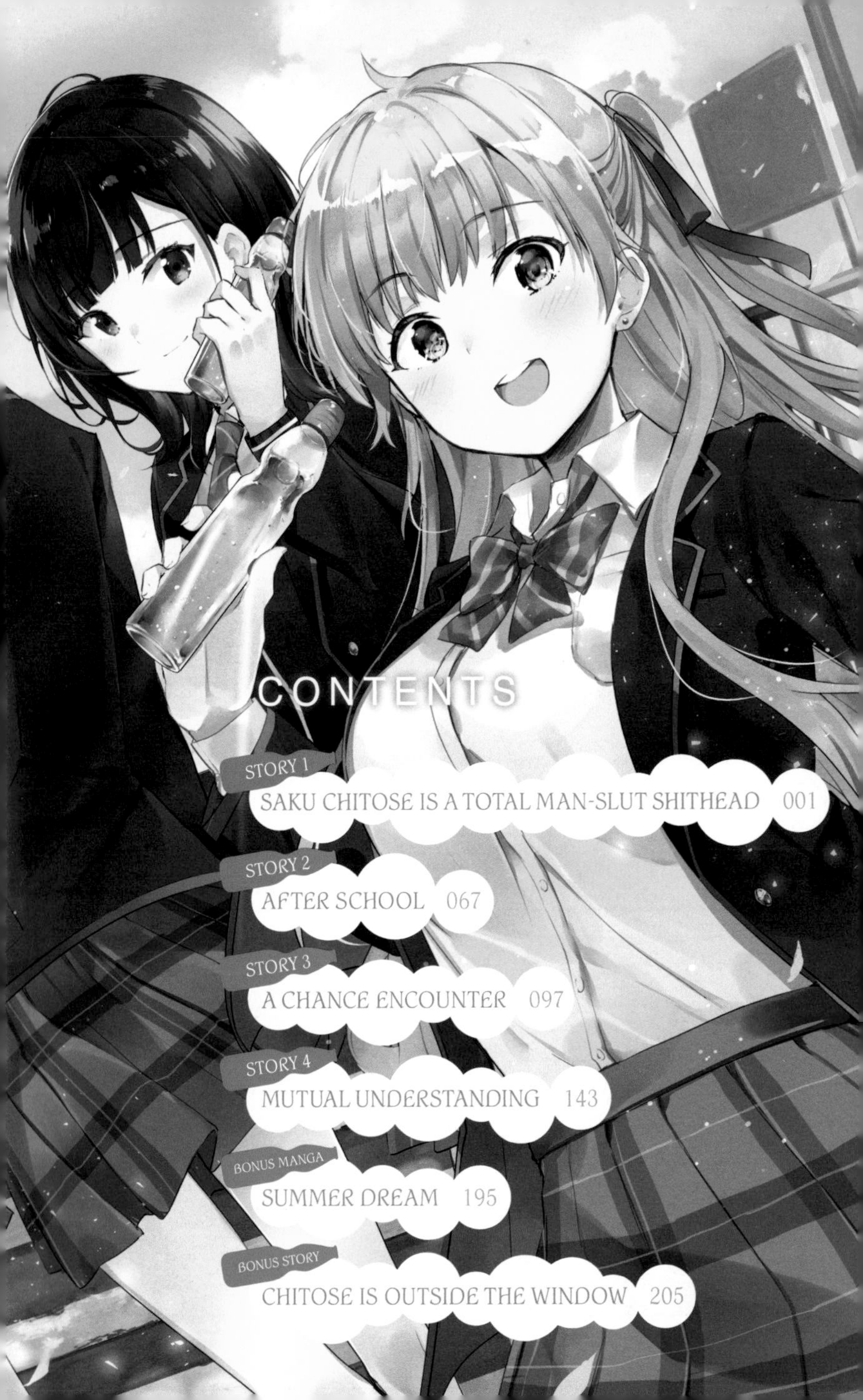

CONTENTS

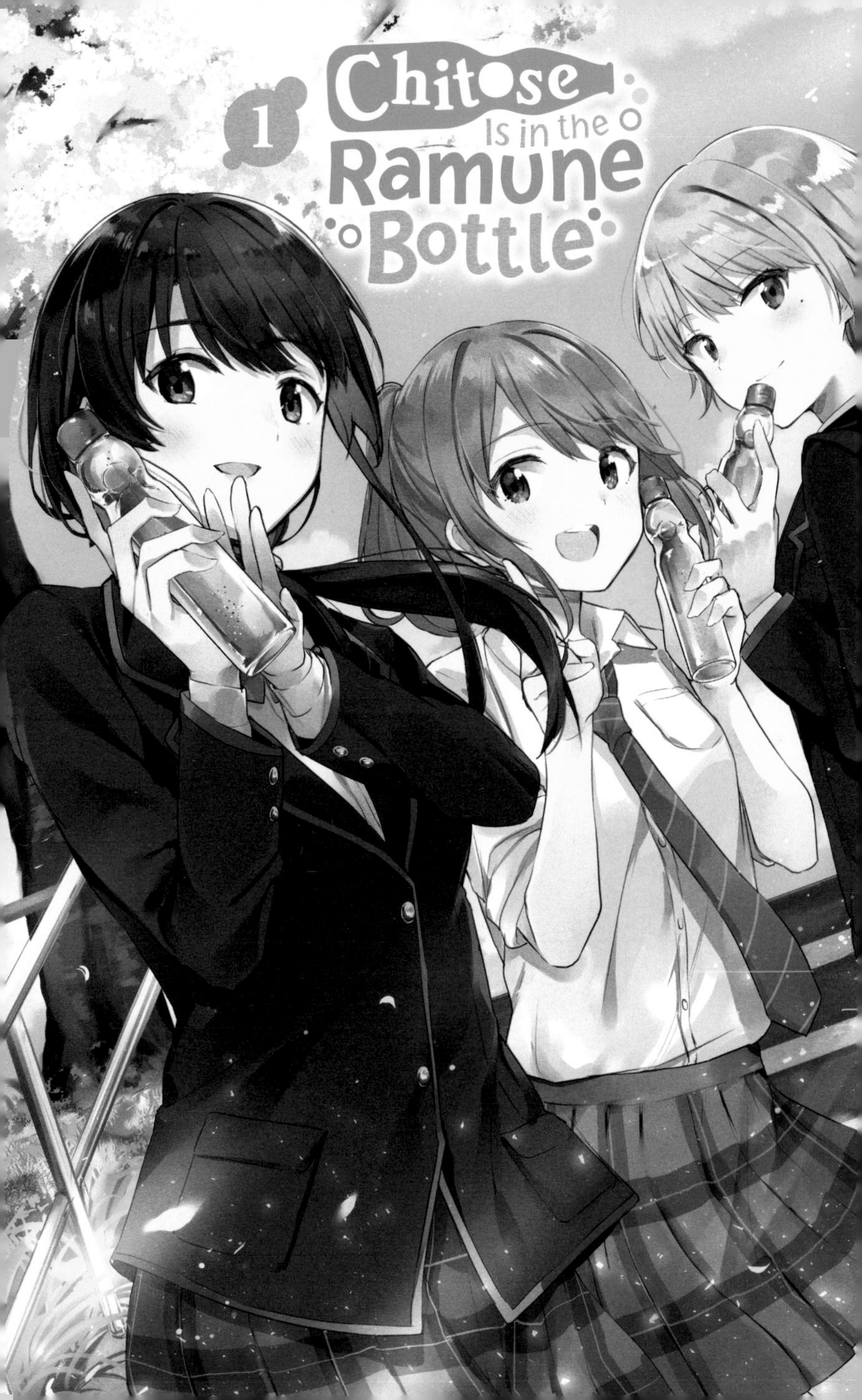
1
Chitose Is in the Ramune Bottle

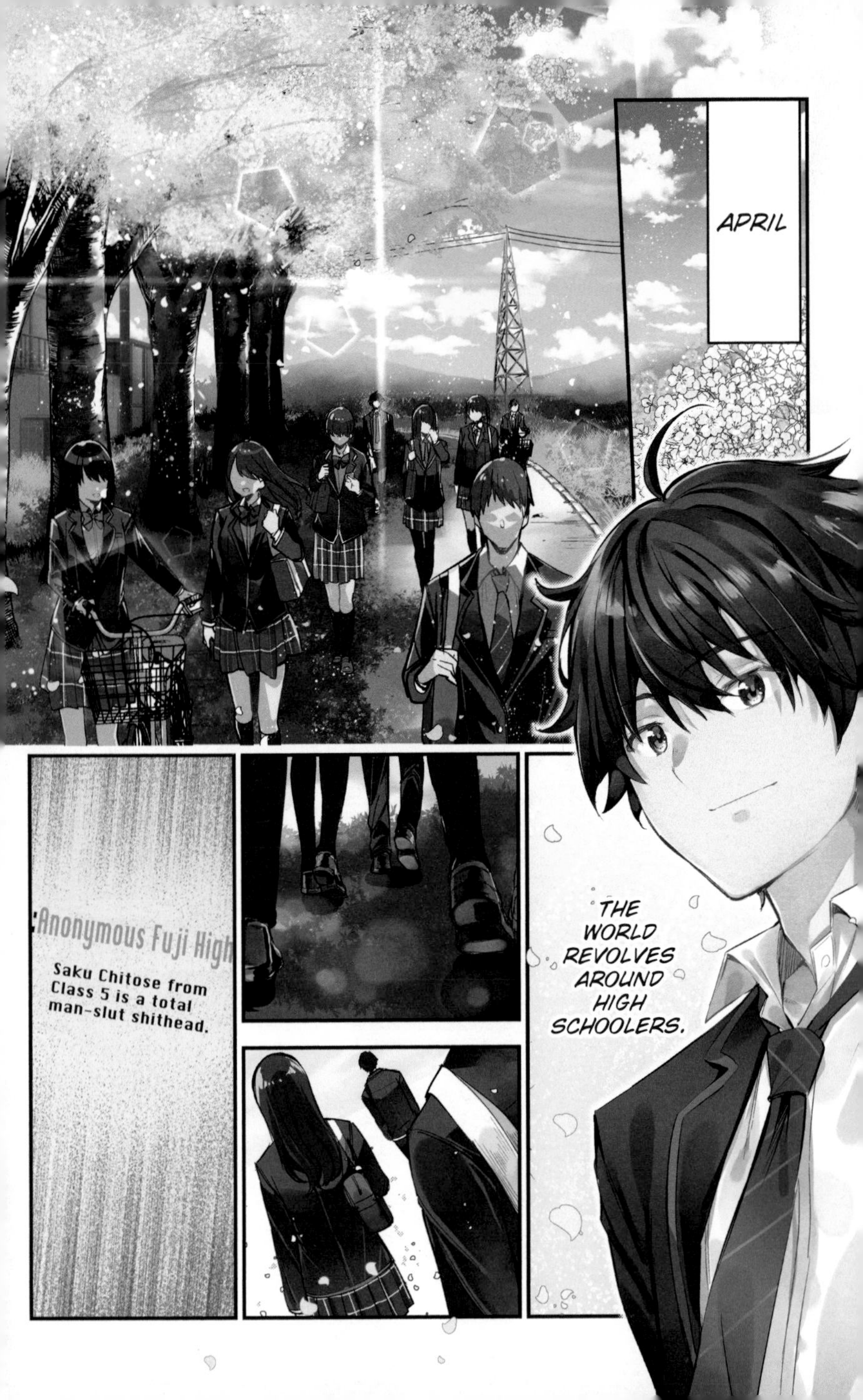
APRIL
THE WORLD REVOLVES AROUND HIGH SCHOOLERS.
:Anonymous Fuji High
Saku Chitose from Class 5 is a total man-slut shithead.

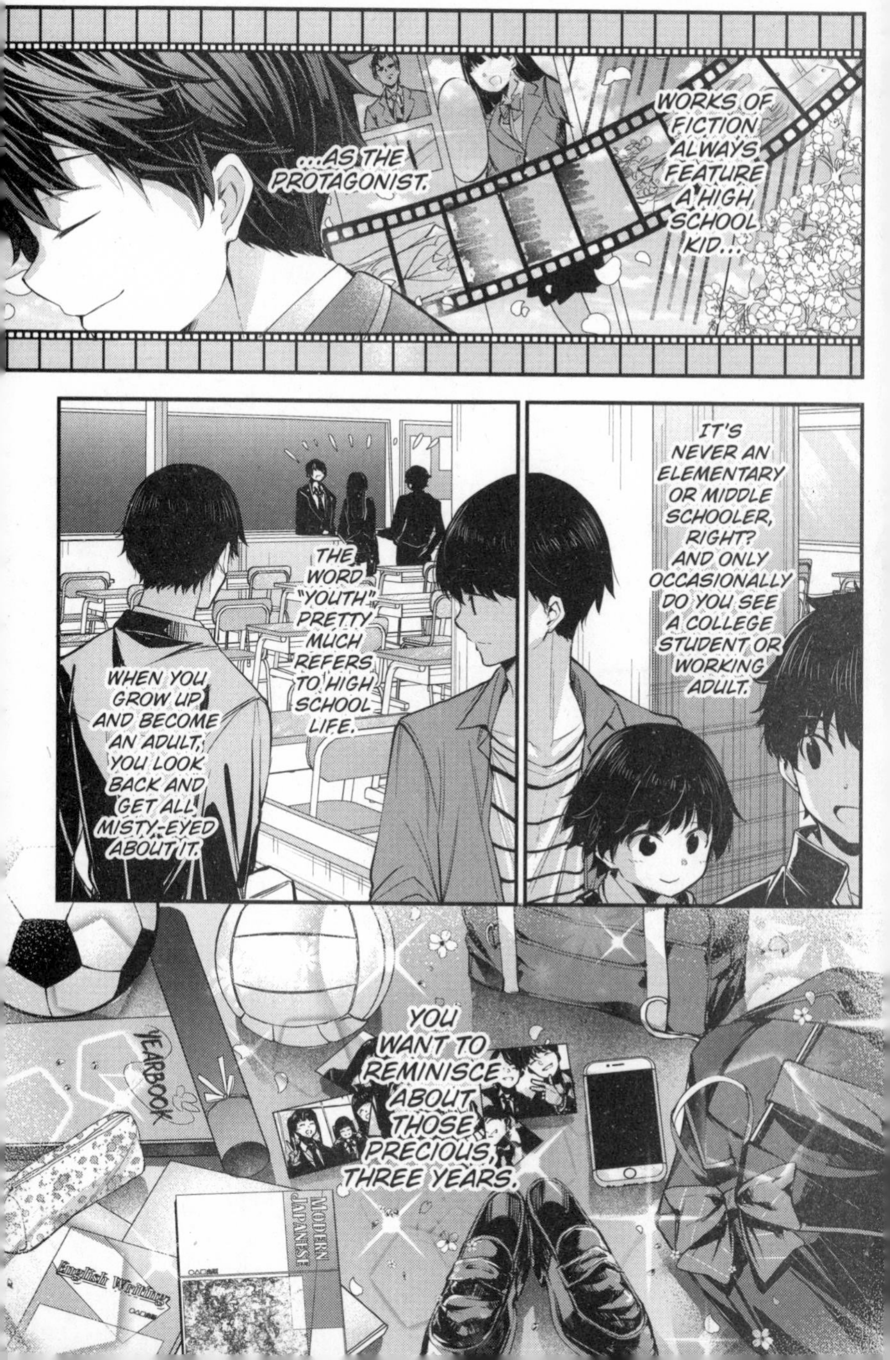
WORKS OF FICTION ALWAYS FEATURE A HIGH SCHOOL KID...
...AS THE PROTAGONIST.
IT'S NEVER AN ELEMENTARY OR MIDDLE SCHOOLER, RIGHT? AND ONLY OCCASIONALLY DO YOU SEE A COLLEGE STUDENT OR WORKING ADULT.
THE WORD "YOUTH" PRETTY MUCH REFERS TO HIGH SCHOOL LIFE.
WHEN YOU GROW UP AND BECOME AN ADULT, YOU LOOK BACK AND GET ALL MISTY-EYED ABOUT IT.
YOU WANT TO REMINISCE ABOUT THOSE PRECIOUS THREE YEARS.
YEARBOOK
MODERN JAPANESE
English Writing

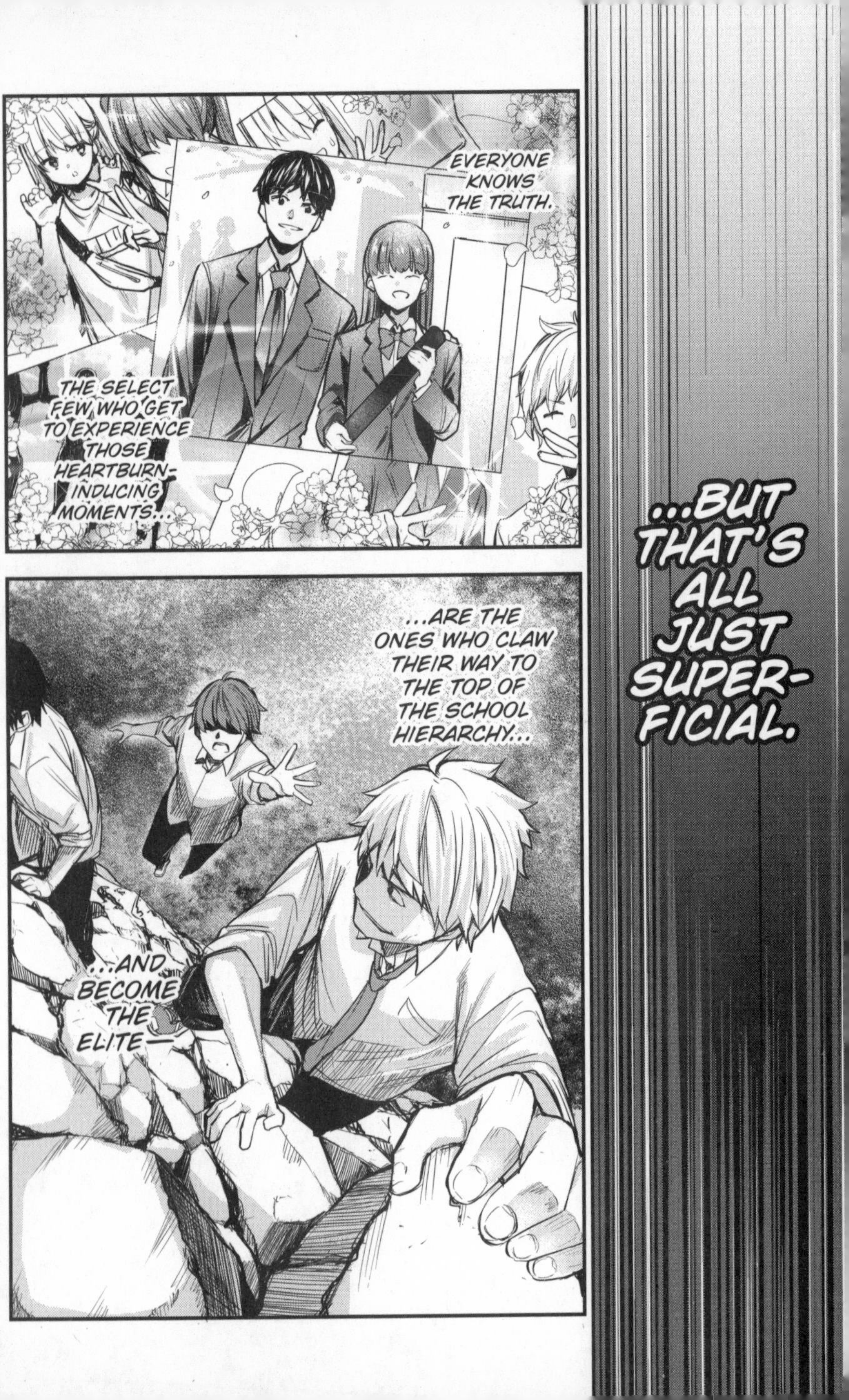
EVERYONE KNOWS THE TRUTH.
THE SELECT FEW WHO GET TO EXPERIENCE THOSE HEARTBURN-INDUCING MOMENTS...
...ARE THE ONES WHO CLAW THEIR WAY TO THE TOP OF THE SCHOOL HIERARCHY...
...AND BECOME THE ELITE—
...BUT THAT'S ALL JUST SUPER-FICIAL.

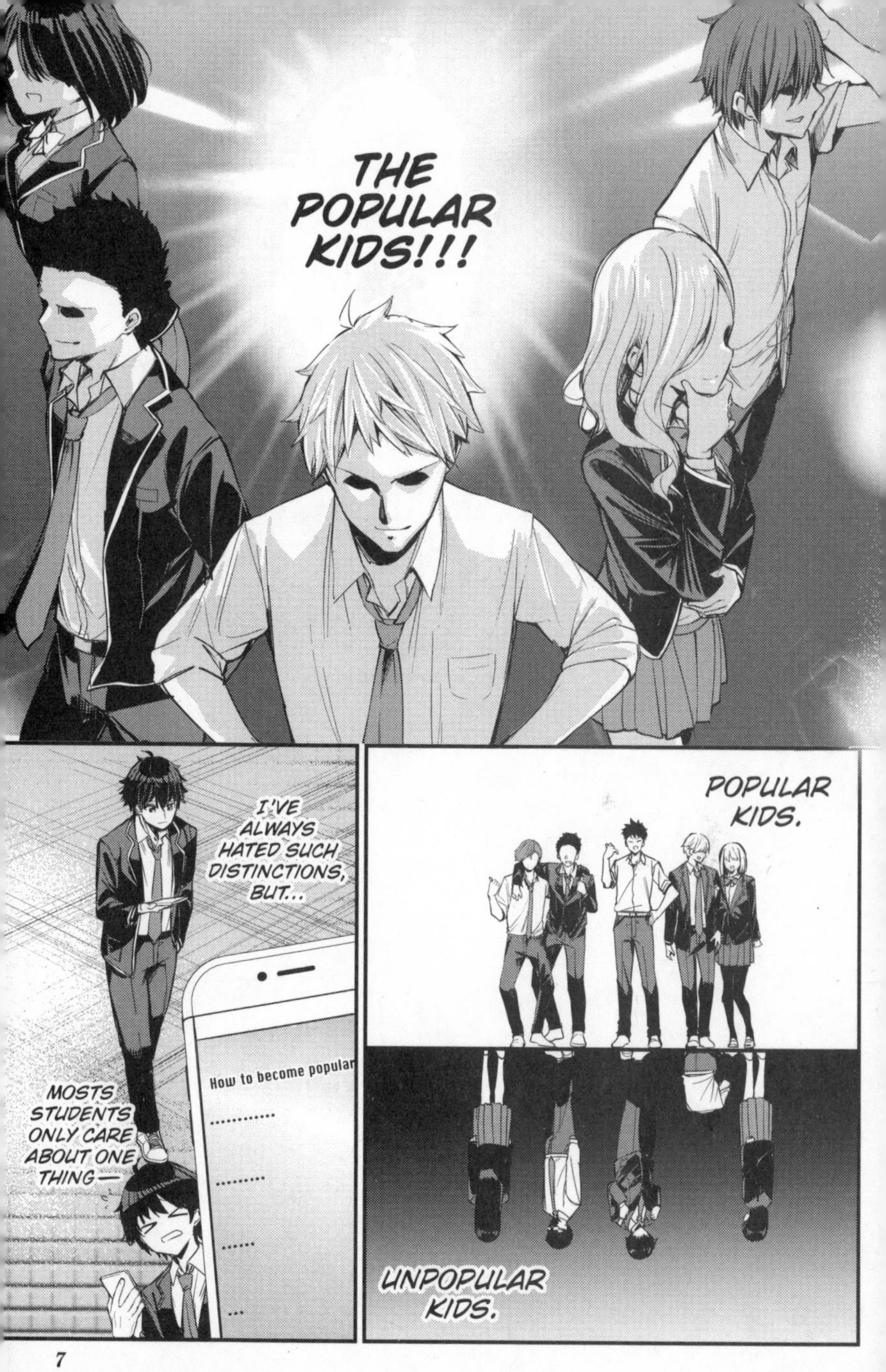
THE POPULAR KIDS!!!
POPULAR KIDS.
UNPOPULAR KIDS.
I'VE ALWAYS HATED SUCH DISTINCTIONS, BUT...
MOSTS STUDENTS ONLY CARE ABOUT ONE THING—
How to become popular

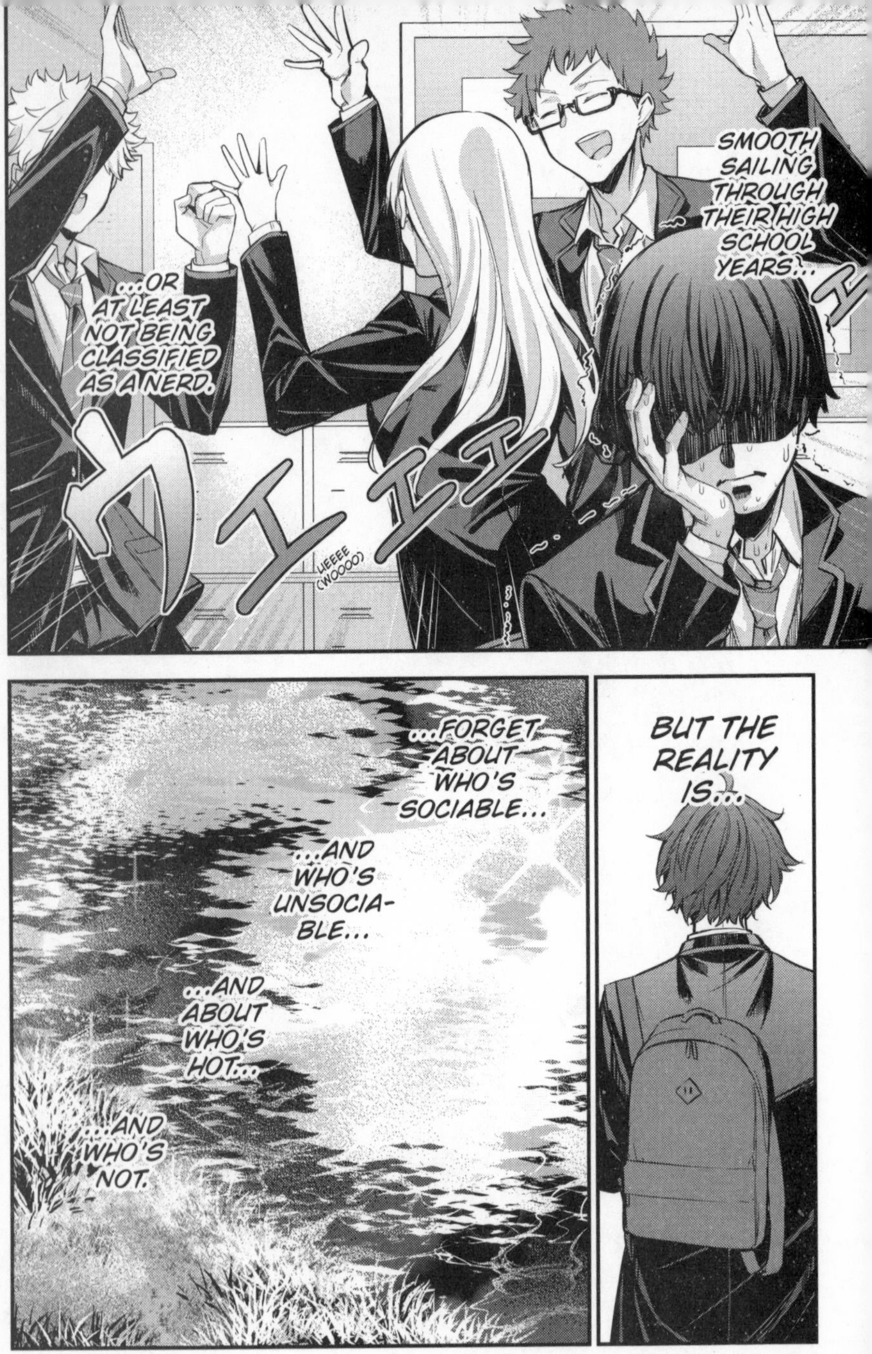
SMOOTH SAILING THROUGH THEIR HIGH SCHOOL YEARS...
...OR AT LEAST NOT BEING CLASSIFIED AS A NERD.
UEEEE (WOOOO)
BUT THE REALITY IS...
...FORGET ABOUT WHO'S SOCIABLE...
...AND WHO'S UNSOCIA-BLE...
...AND ABOUT WHO'S HOT...
...AND WHO'S NOT.

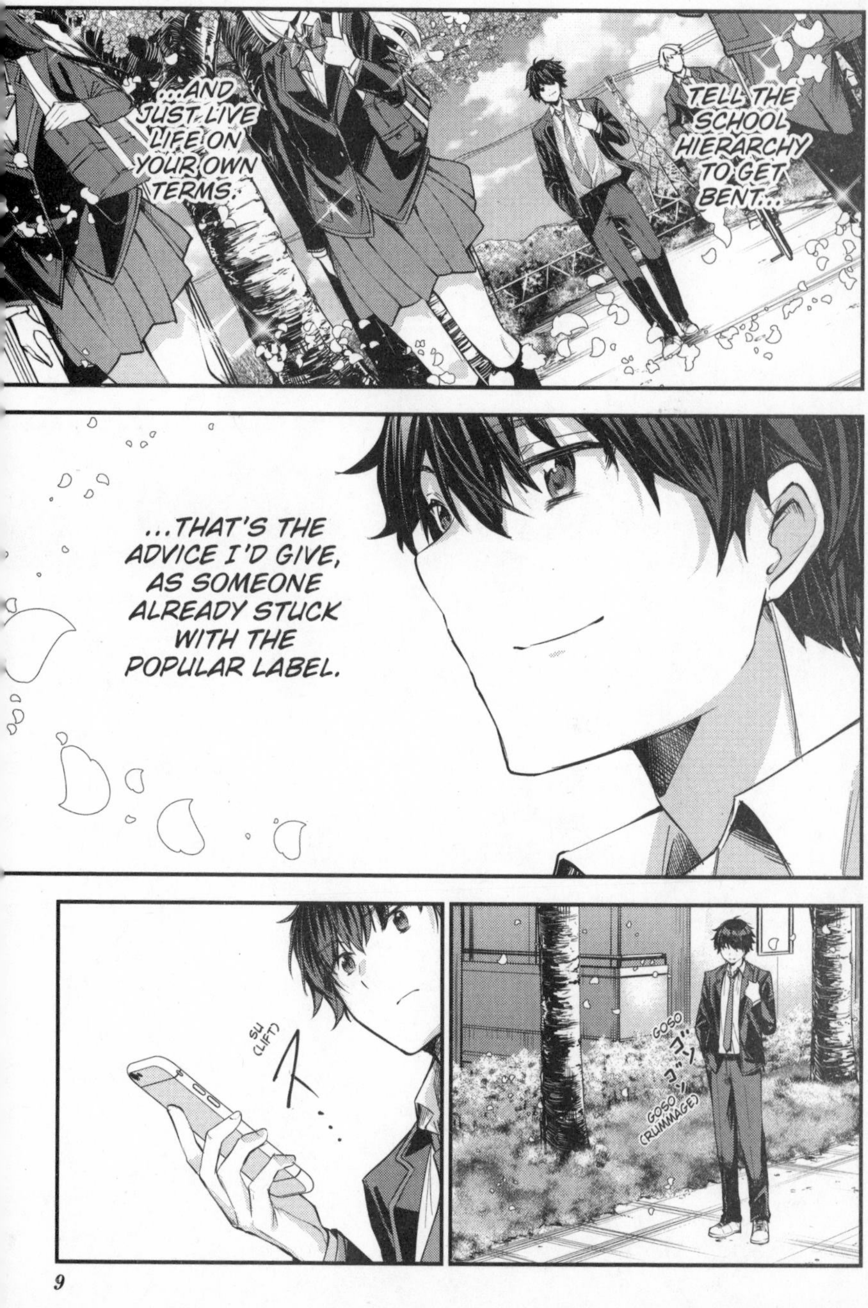
TELL THE SCHOOL HIERARCHY TO GET BENT...
...AND JUST LIVE LIFE ON YOUR OWN TERMS.
...THAT'S THE ADVICE I'D GIVE, AS SOMEONE ALREADY STUCK WITH THE POPULAR LABEL.
GOSO
GOSO (RUMMAGE)
SU (LIFT)
...

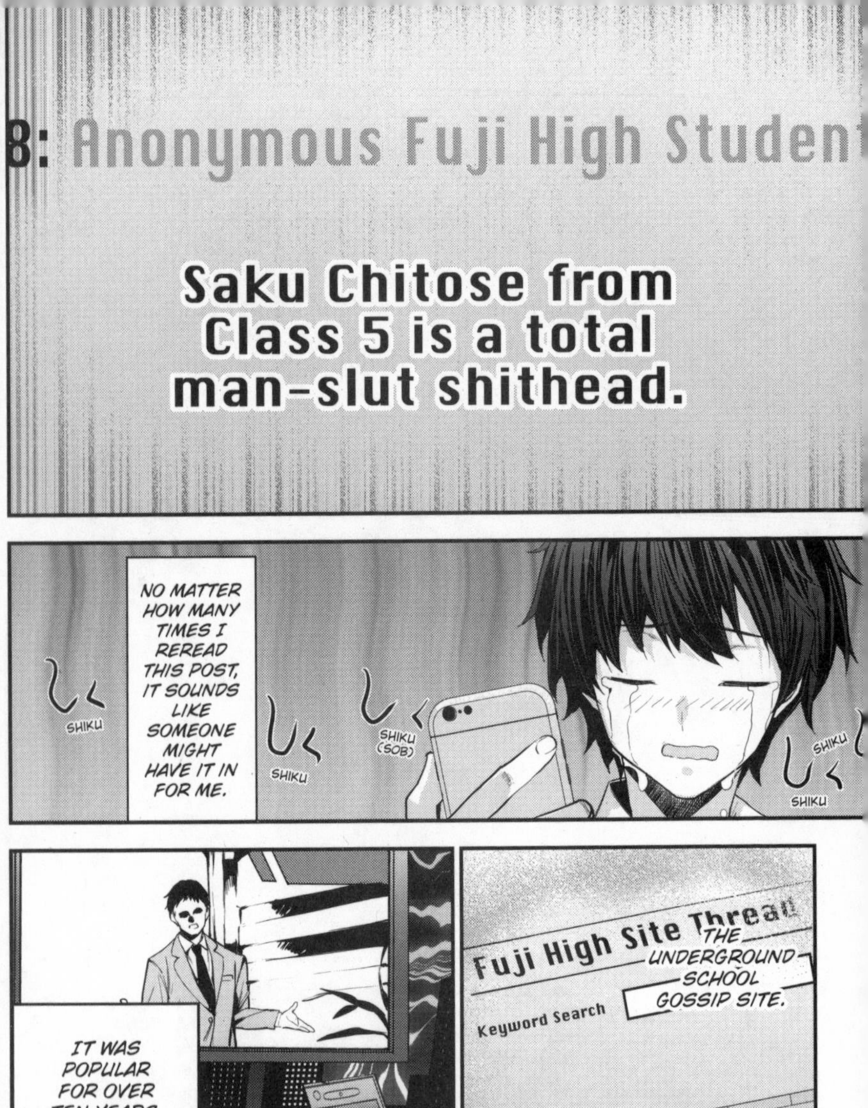

8: Anonymous Fuji High Studen
Saku Chitose from Class 5 is a total man-slut shithead.
しく SHIKU
しく SHIKU
しく SHIKU (SOB)
NO MATTER HOW MANY TIMES I REREAD THIS POST, IT SOUNDS LIKE SOMEONE MIGHT HAVE IT IN FOR ME.
しく SHIKU
しく SHIKU
Fuji High Site Threa
THE UNDERGROUND SCHOOL GOSSIP SITE.
Keyword Search
[Fuji High] Anti Saku Chitose Threa
IT WAS POPULAR FOR OVER TEN YEARS, BUT THEN IT BECAME THIS BIG "SOCIAL ISSUE" BECAUSE OF BULLYING AND WAS ABANDONED.

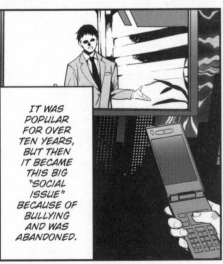

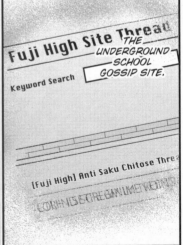

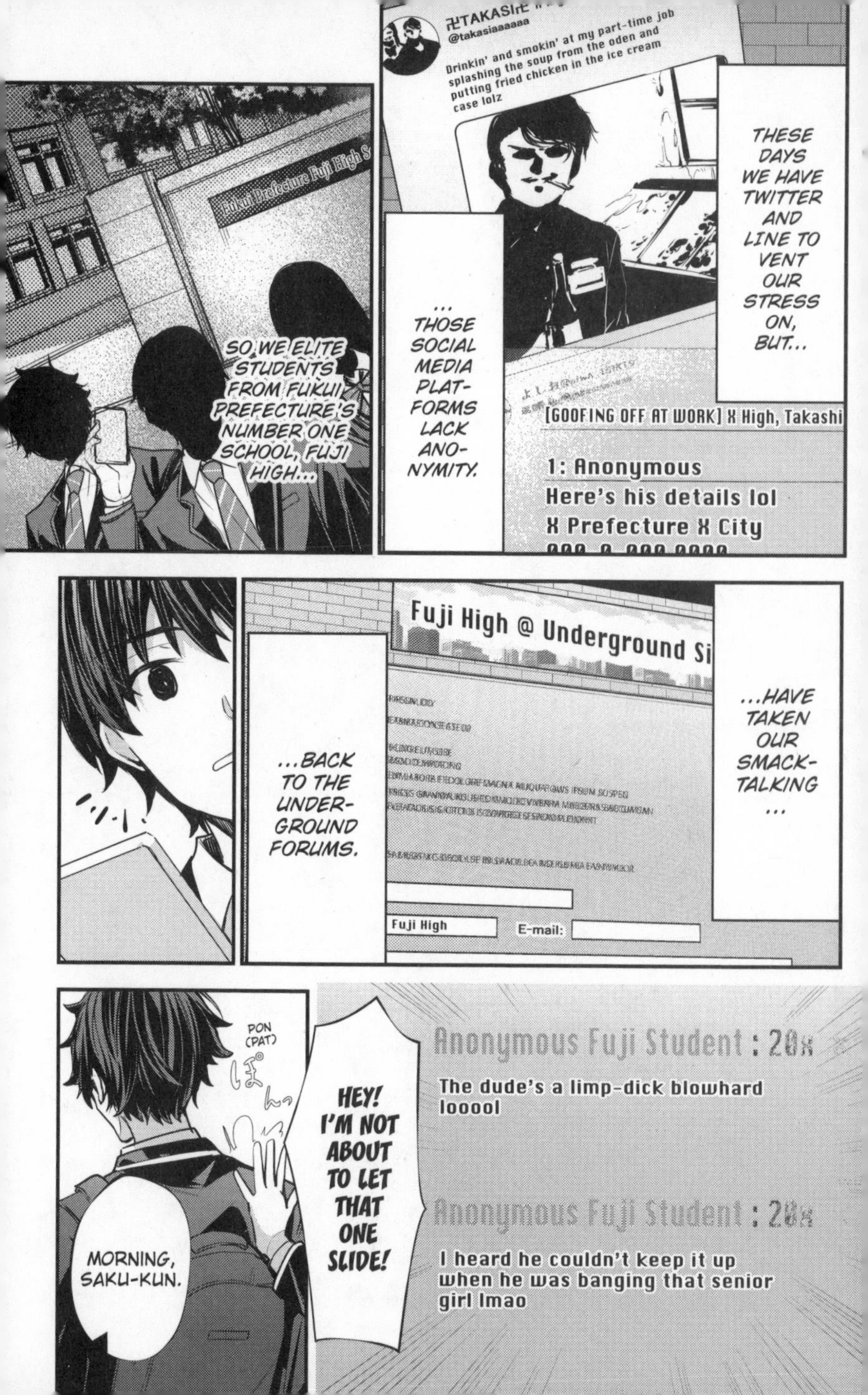

卍TAKASI卍
@takasiaaaaaa
Drinkin' and smokin' at my part-time job splashing the soup from the oden and putting fried chicken in the ice cream case lolz
THESE DAYS WE HAVE TWITTER AND LINE TO VENT OUR STRESS ON, BUT...
...THOSE SOCIAL MEDIA PLATFORMS LACK ANONYMITY.
[GOOFING OFF AT WORK] X High, Takashi
1: Anonymous
Here's his details lol
X Prefecture X City
Fukui Prefecture Fuji High S
SO WE ELITE STUDENTS FROM FUKUI PREFECTURE'S NUMBER ONE SCHOOL, FUJI HIGH...
Fuji High @ Underground Si
...HAVE TAKEN OUR SMACK-TALKING...
...BACK TO THE UNDERGROUND FORUMS.
Fuji High
E-mail:
Anonymous Fuji Student : 20X
The dude's a limp-dick blowhard looool
Anonymous Fuji Student : 20X
I heard he couldn't keep it up when he was banging that senior girl lmao
HEY! I'M NOT ABOUT TO LET THAT ONE SLIDE!
PON (PAT)
ぽんっ
MORNING, SAKU-KUN.

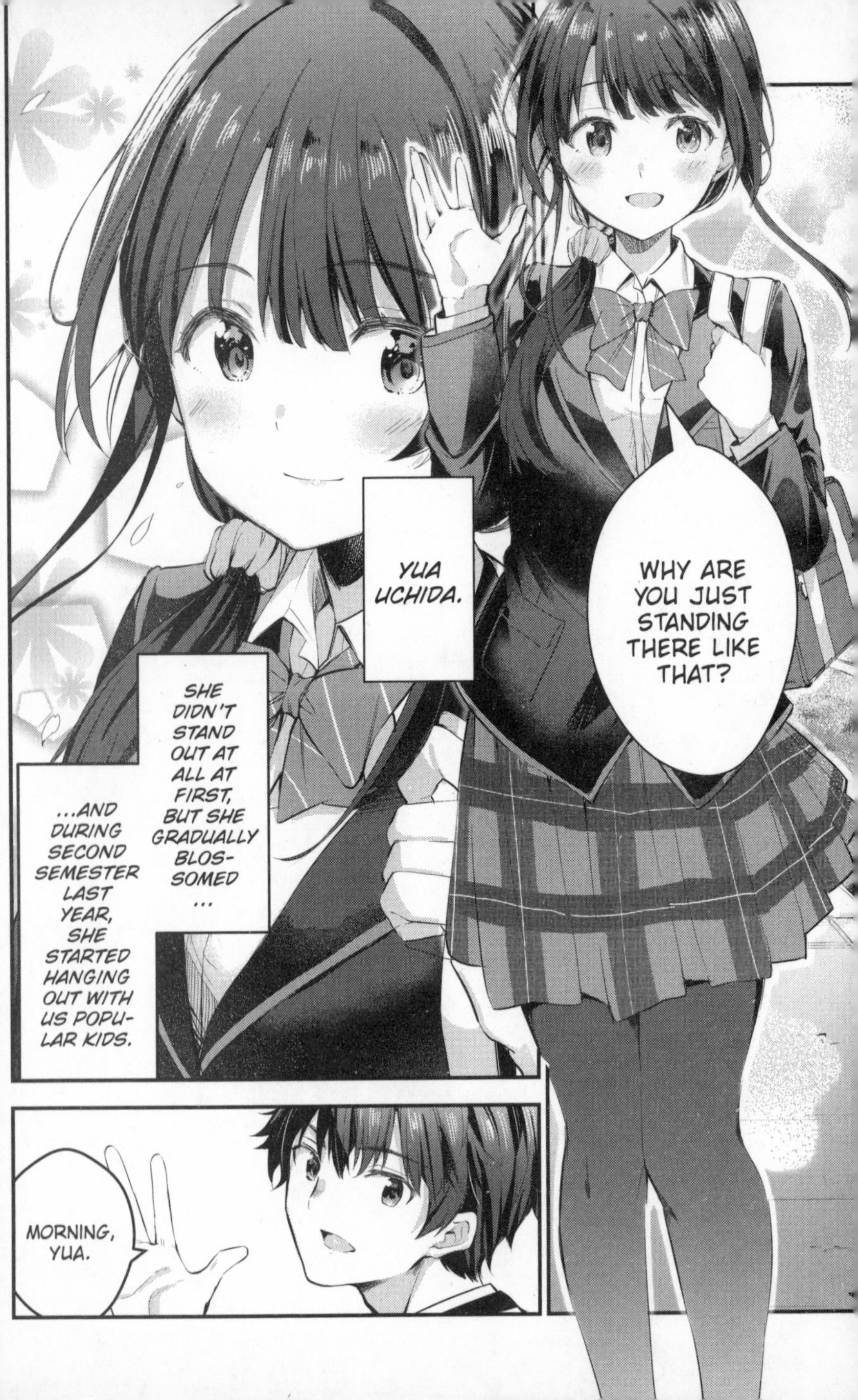
WHY ARE YOU JUST STANDING THERE LIKE THAT?
YUA UCHIDA.
SHE DIDN'T STAND OUT AT ALL AT FIRST, BUT SHE GRADUALLY BLOS-SOMED...
...AND DURING SECOND SEMESTER LAST YEAR, SHE STARTED HANGING OUT WITH US POPU-LAR KIDS.
MORNING, YUA.

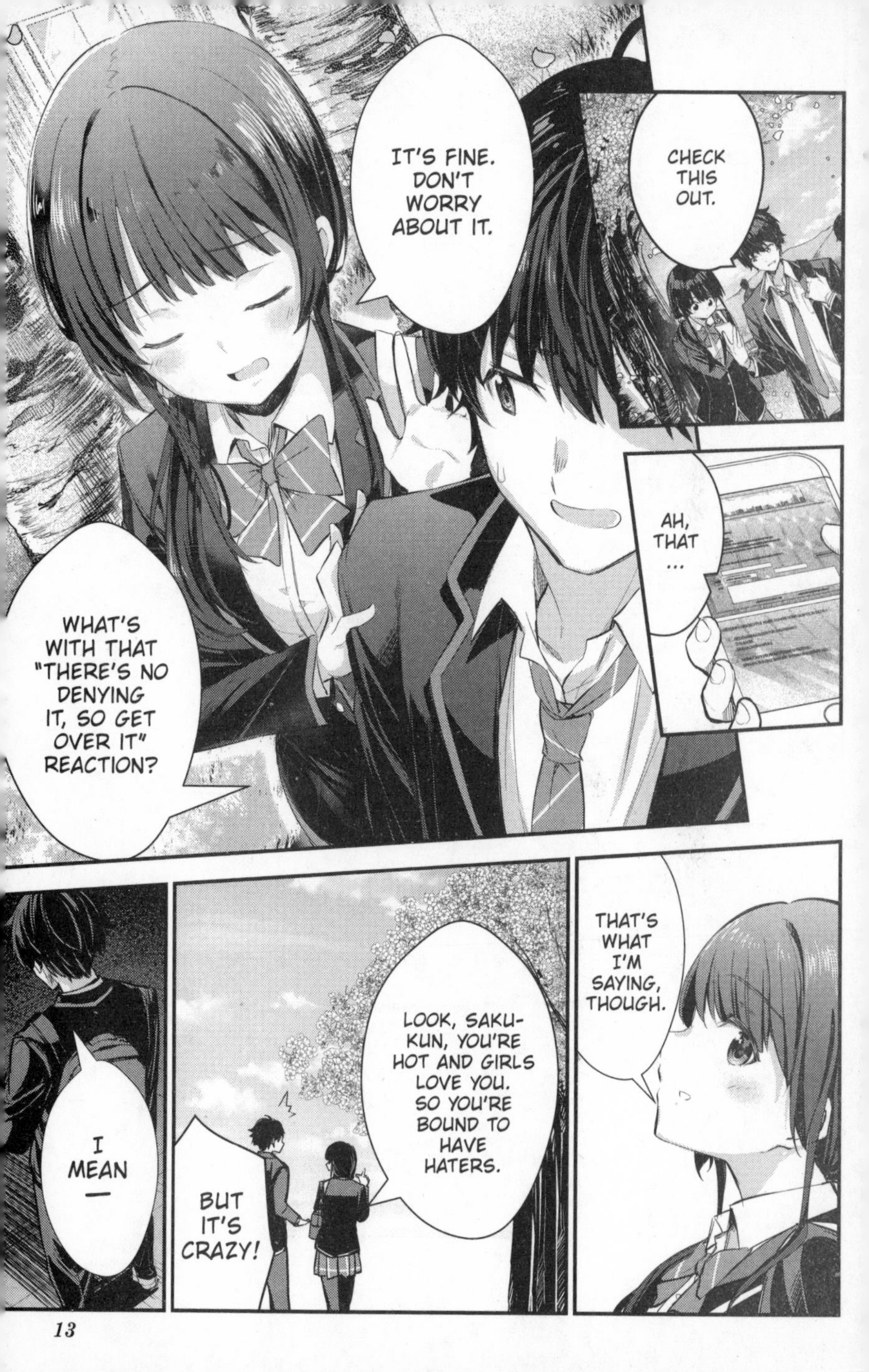
CHECK THIS OUT.
AH, THAT...
IT'S FINE. DON'T WORRY ABOUT IT.
WHAT'S WITH THAT "THERE'S NO DENYING IT, SO GET OVER IT" REACTION?
THAT'S WHAT I'M SAYING, THOUGH.
LOOK, SAKU-KUN, YOU'RE HOT AND GIRLS LOVE YOU. SO YOU'RE BOUND TO HAVE HATERS.
BUT IT'S CRAZY!
I MEAN—

PRETTY MUCH... ALL OF THE ABOVE?

HERE'S A SUPER-HOT, STYLISH GUY, WHO'S ATHLETIC, WITH TOP-NOTCH GRADES, GETS ALONG WITH EVERYONE, IS SUPER-NICE AND ALSO AN EXCELLENT LEADER WITH, I MIGHT ADD, A GREAT SENSE OF HUMOR FOR EVERYTHING FROM WITTY PUNS TO DIRTY JOKES. I'M GREAT! WHY DO THEY HATE ME!?

OH GOOD!

LOOKS LIKE THE CORE POPULAR KIDS FROM CLASS 5, LAST YEAR ARE ALL IN THE SAME CLASS ON THE HUMANITIES TRACK.

Student Number	Name	
1	青海 颯	Aomi, Haru
2	浅野 海人	Asano, Kaito
3	綾瀬 なずな	Ayase, Nazuna
4	上村 亜十夢	Uemura, Atomu
5	内田 優空	Uchida, Yua
6	川野 明日海	Kawano, Asumi
7	川端 英倫	Kawabata, Hanami
8	川村 昱	Kawamura, Tak
9	日下部 譲	Kusakabe, Fuk
10	久米美 紀子	Kume
11	小平 明菜	Kod
12	坂上月 希子	
13	滋賀 純子	
14	重松 一聡	
15	新保 裕斗	
16	杉山 守彦	
17	千歳 朗	
18	土居 滉生	
19	飛田 湊	
20	長崎日 日出	
21	七瀬 悠月	
22	西口 楽人	
23	柊 夕湖	
24	福山 陽日	
25	益子 昼	

14

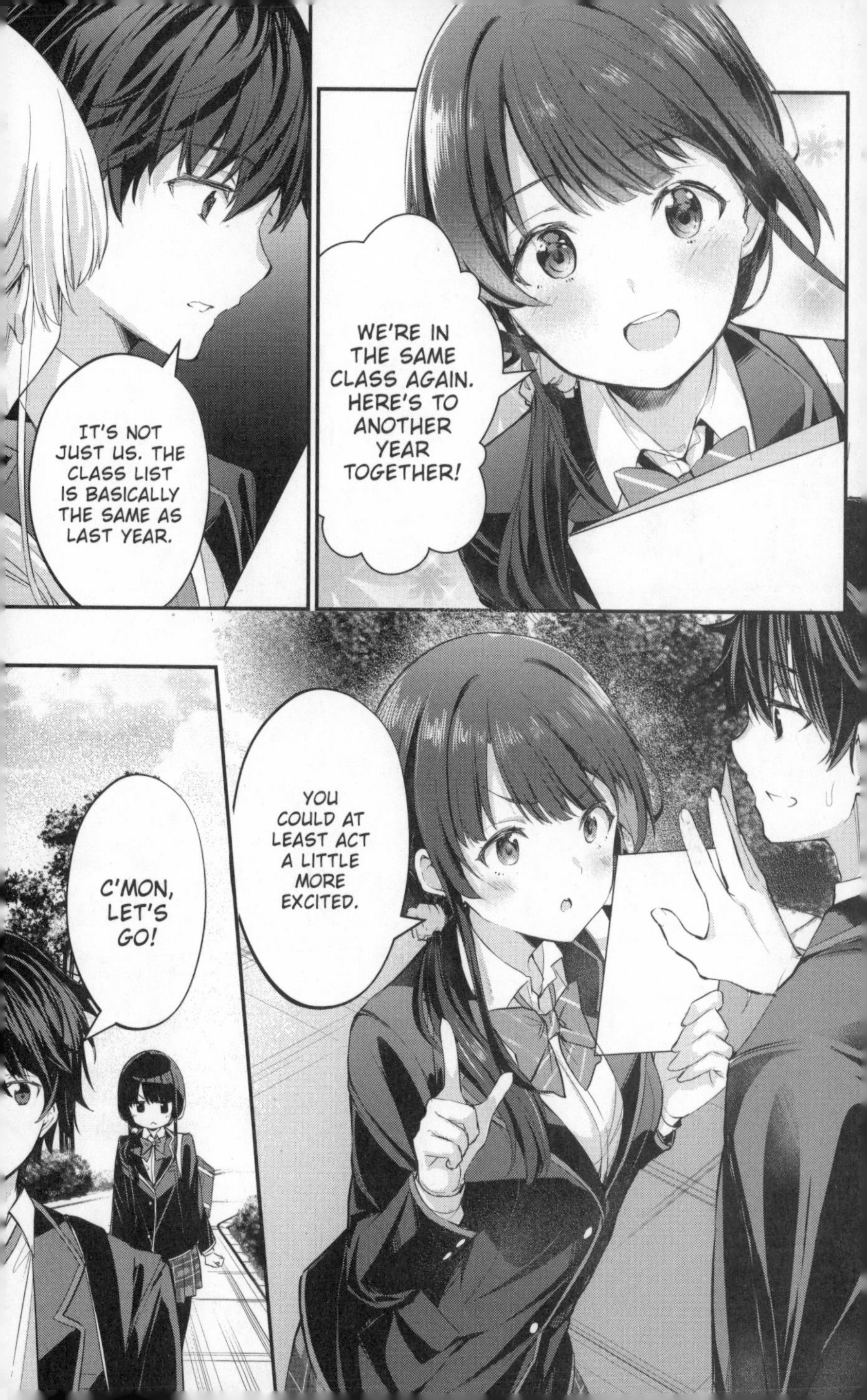
WE'RE IN THE SAME CLASS AGAIN. HERE'S TO ANOTHER YEAR TOGETHER!
IT'S NOT JUST US. THE CLASS LIST IS BASICALLY THE SAME AS LAST YEAR.
YOU COULD AT LEAST ACT A LITTLE MORE EXCITED.
C'MON, LET'S GO!

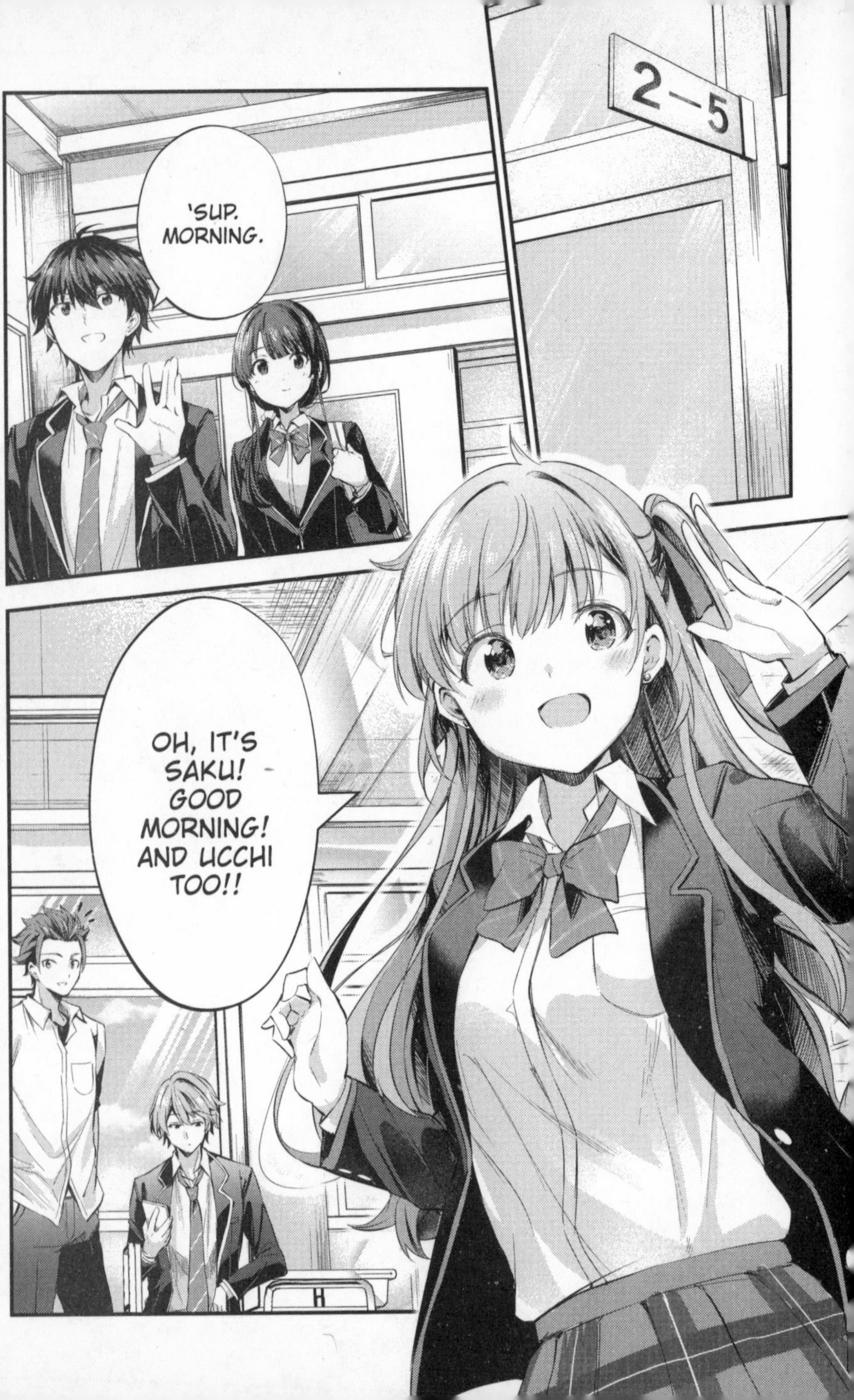
2—5
'SUP. MORNING.
OH, IT'S SAKU! GOOD MORNING! AND UCCHI TOO!!

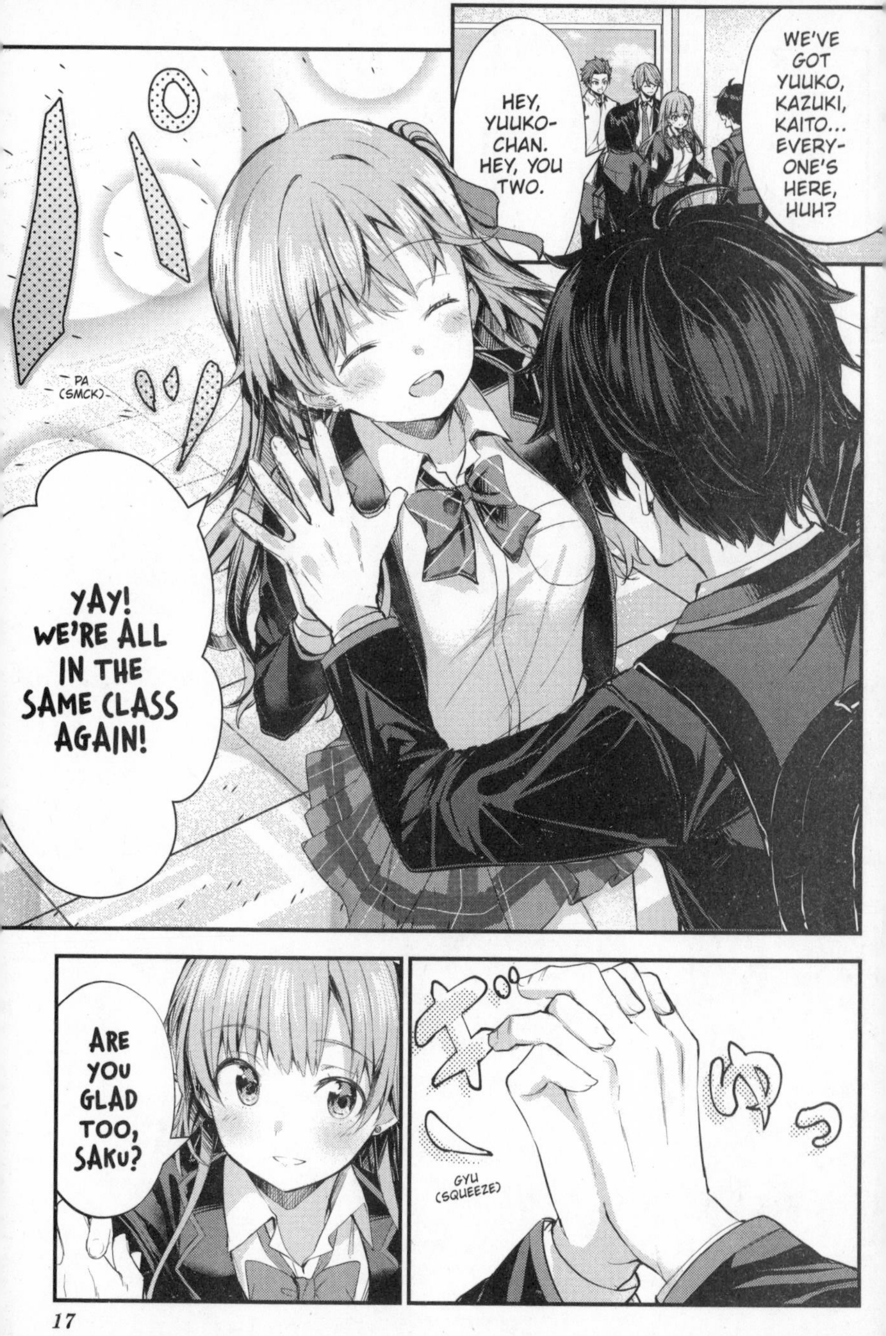
WE'VE GOT YUUKO, KAZUKI, KAITO... EVERYONE'S HERE, HUH?
HEY, YUUKO-CHAN. HEY, YOU TWO.
PA (SMCK)
YAY! WE'RE ALL IN THE SAME CLASS AGAIN!
GYU (SQUEEZE)
ARE YOU GLAD TOO, SAKU?

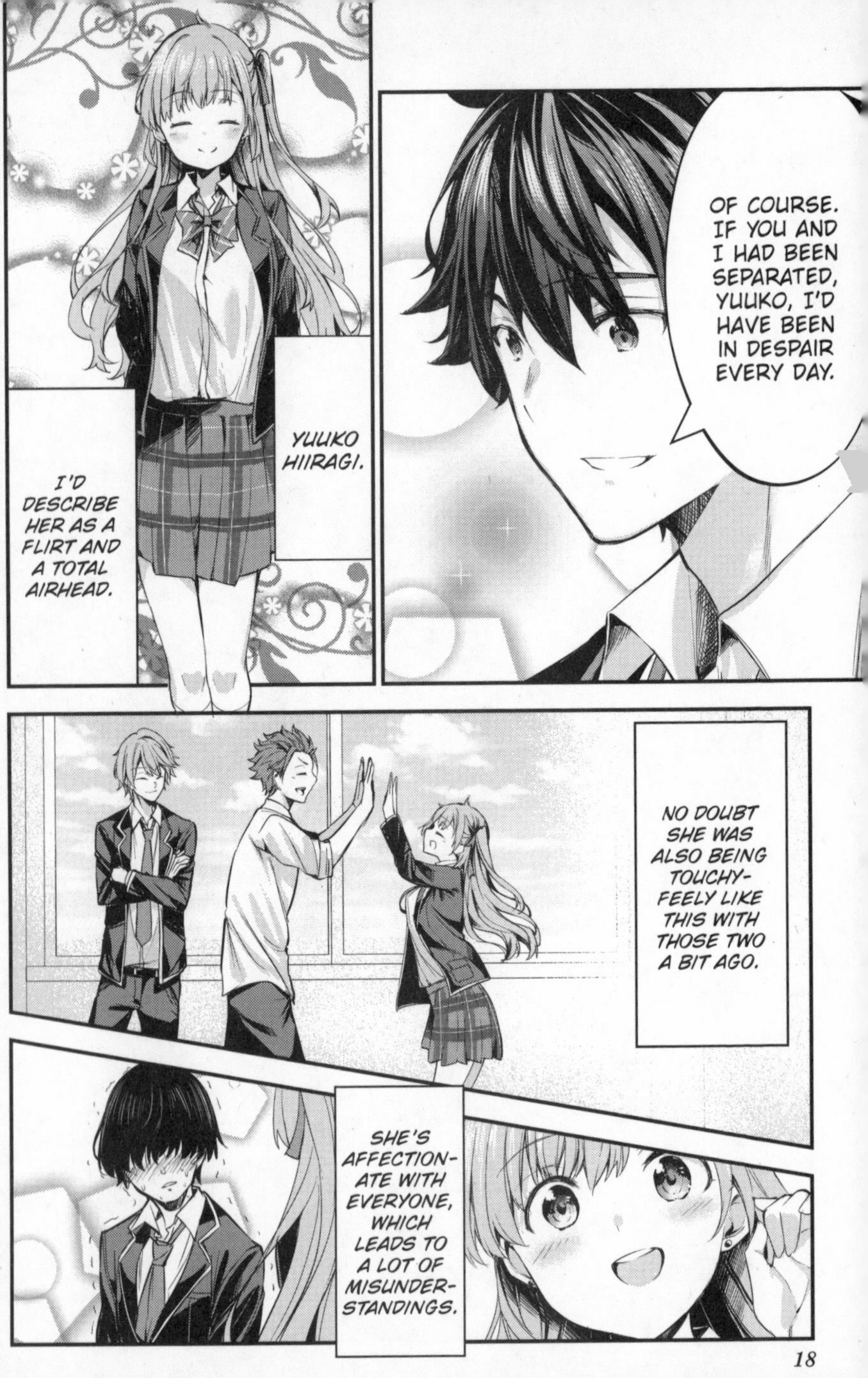
OF COURSE. IF YOU AND I HAD BEEN SEPARATED, YUUKO, I'D HAVE BEEN IN DESPAIR EVERY DAY.
YUUKO HIIRAGI.
I'D DESCRIBE HER AS A FLIRT AND A TOTAL AIRHEAD.
NO DOUBT SHE WAS ALSO BEING TOUCHY-FEELY LIKE THIS WITH THOSE TWO A BIT AGO.
SHE'S AFFECTION-ATE WITH EVERYONE, WHICH LEADS TO A LOT OF MISUNDER-STANDINGS.

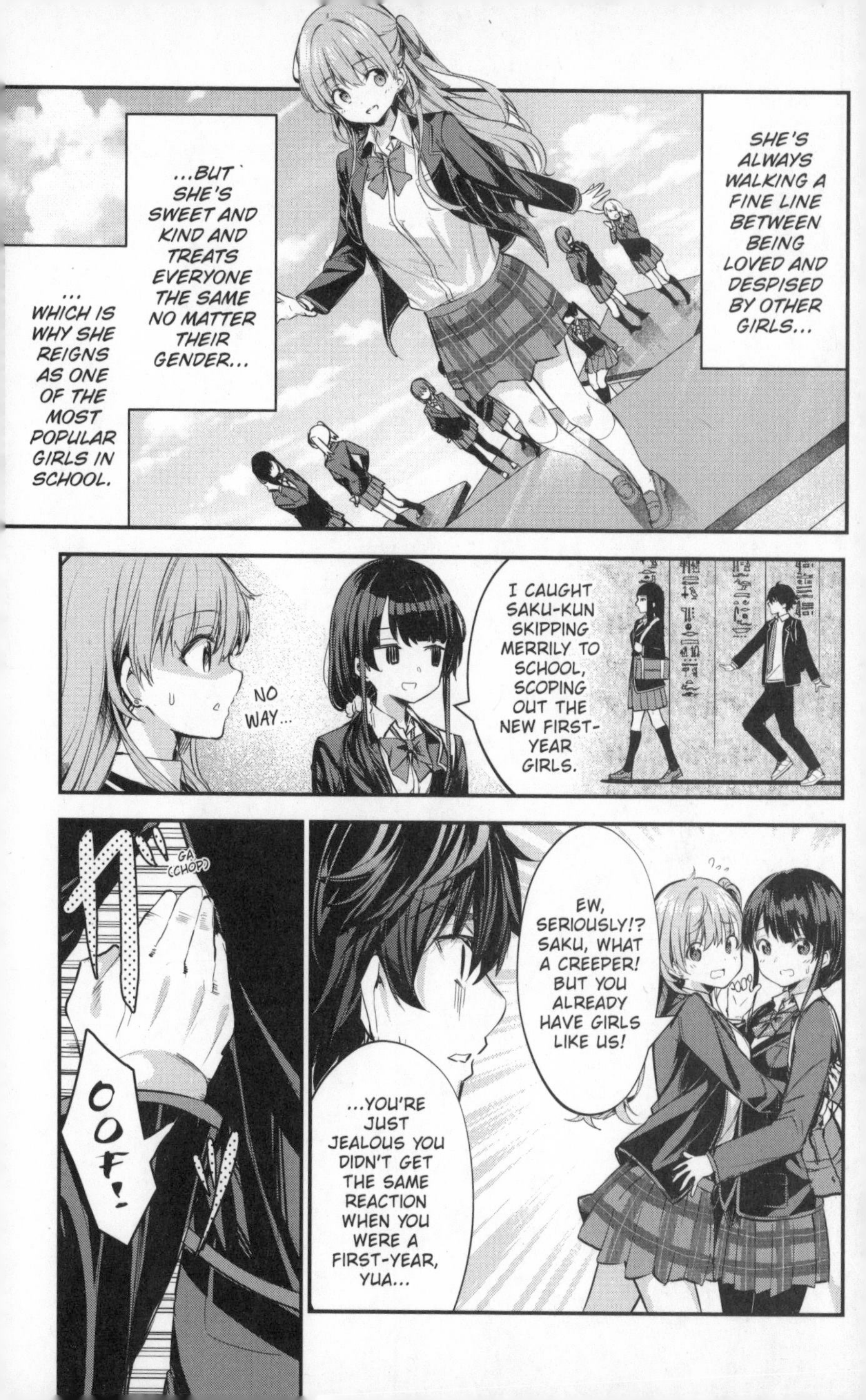
SHE'S ALWAYS WALKING A FINE LINE BETWEEN BEING LOVED AND DESPISED BY OTHER GIRLS...
...BUT SHE'S SWEET AND KIND AND TREATS EVERYONE THE SAME NO MATTER THEIR GENDER...
...WHICH IS WHY SHE REIGNS AS ONE OF THE MOST POPULAR GIRLS IN SCHOOL.
I CAUGHT SAKU-KUN SKIPPING MERRILY TO SCHOOL, SCOPING OUT THE NEW FIRST-YEAR GIRLS.
NO WAY...
EW, SERIOUSLY!? SAKU, WHAT A CREEPER! BUT YOU ALREADY HAVE GIRLS LIKE US!
...YOU'RE JUST JEALOUS YOU DIDN'T GET THE SAME REACTION WHEN YOU WERE A FIRST-YEAR, YUA...
GA (CHOP)
OOF!

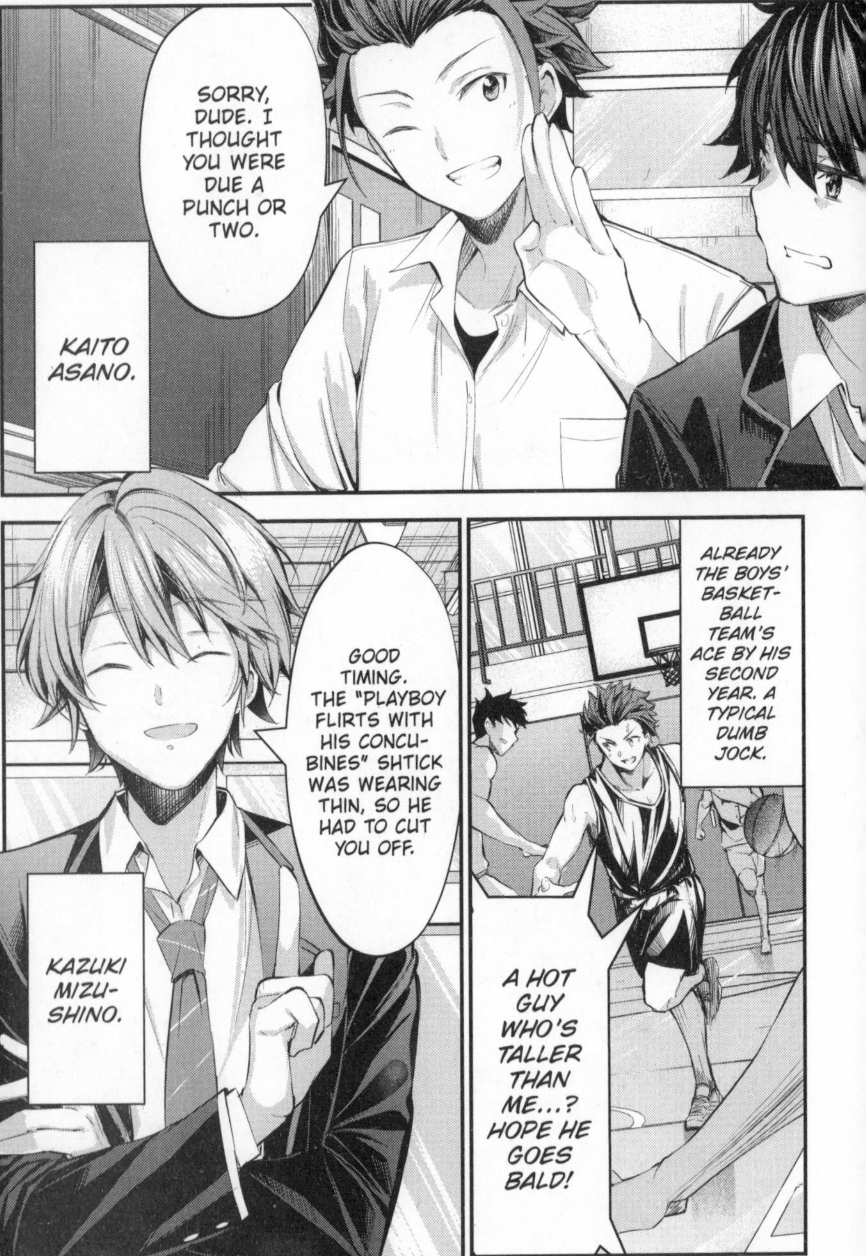
SORRY, DUDE. I THOUGHT YOU WERE DUE A PUNCH OR TWO.
KAITO ASANO.
ALREADY THE BOYS' BASKETBALL TEAM'S ACE BY HIS SECOND YEAR. A TYPICAL DUMB JOCK.
A HOT GUY WHO'S TALLER THAN ME...? HOPE HE GOES BALD!
GOOD TIMING. THE "PLAYBOY FLIRTS WITH HIS CONCUBINES" SHTICK WAS WEARING THIN, SO HE HAD TO CUT YOU OFF.
KAZUKI MIZUSHINO.

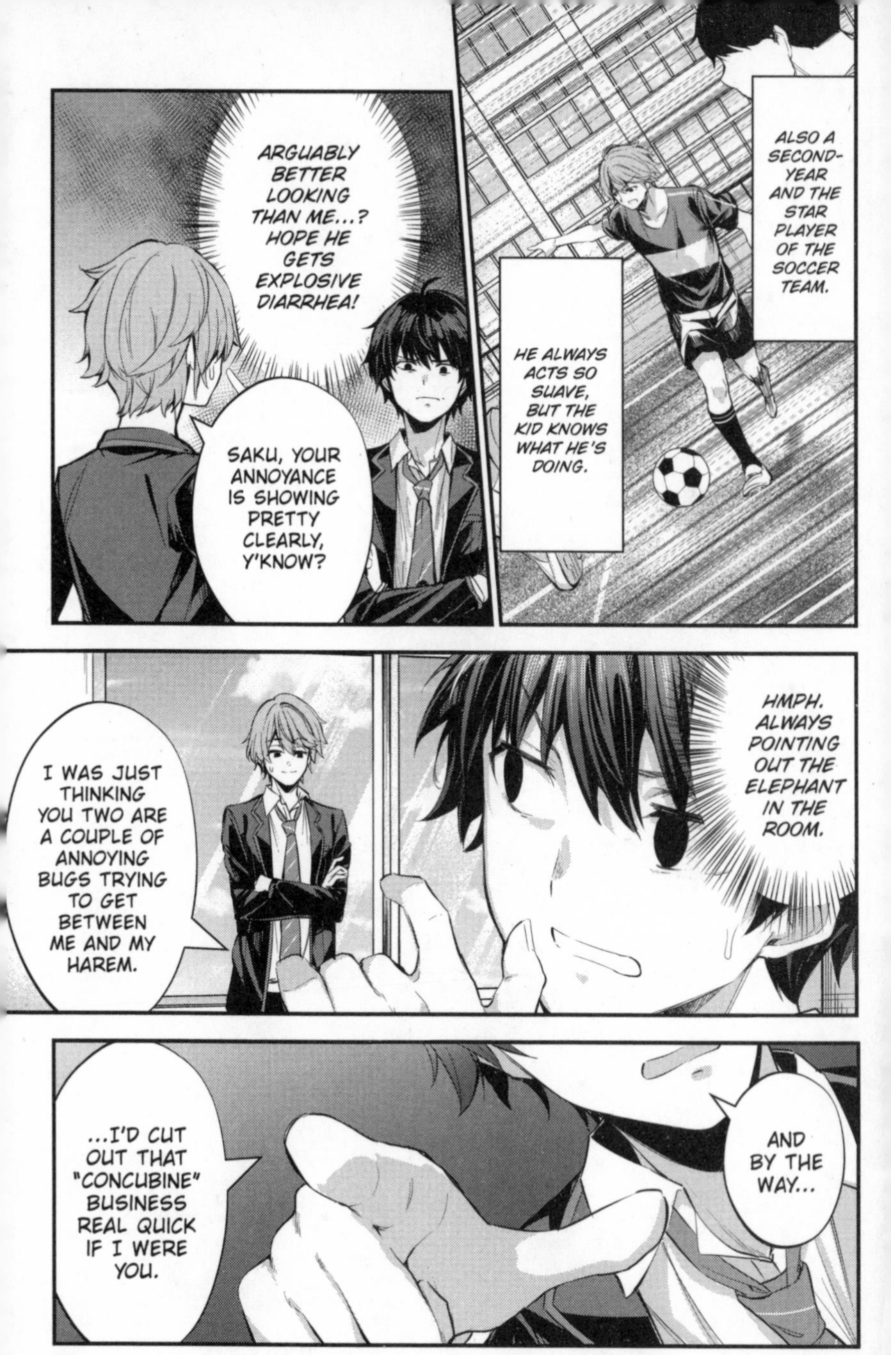
ALSO A SECOND-YEAR AND THE STAR PLAYER OF THE SOCCER TEAM.
HE ALWAYS ACTS SO SUAVE, BUT THE KID KNOWS WHAT HE'S DOING.
ARGUABLY BETTER LOOKING THAN ME...? HOPE HE GETS EXPLOSIVE DIARRHEA!
SAKU, YOUR ANNOYANCE IS SHOWING PRETTY CLEARLY, Y'KNOW?
HMPH. ALWAYS POINTING OUT THE ELEPHANT IN THE ROOM.
I WAS JUST THINKING YOU TWO ARE A COUPLE OF ANNOYING BUGS TRYING TO GET BETWEEN ME AND MY HAREM.
AND BY THE WAY...
...I'D CUT OUT THAT "CONCUBINE" BUSINESS REAL QUICK IF I WERE YOU.

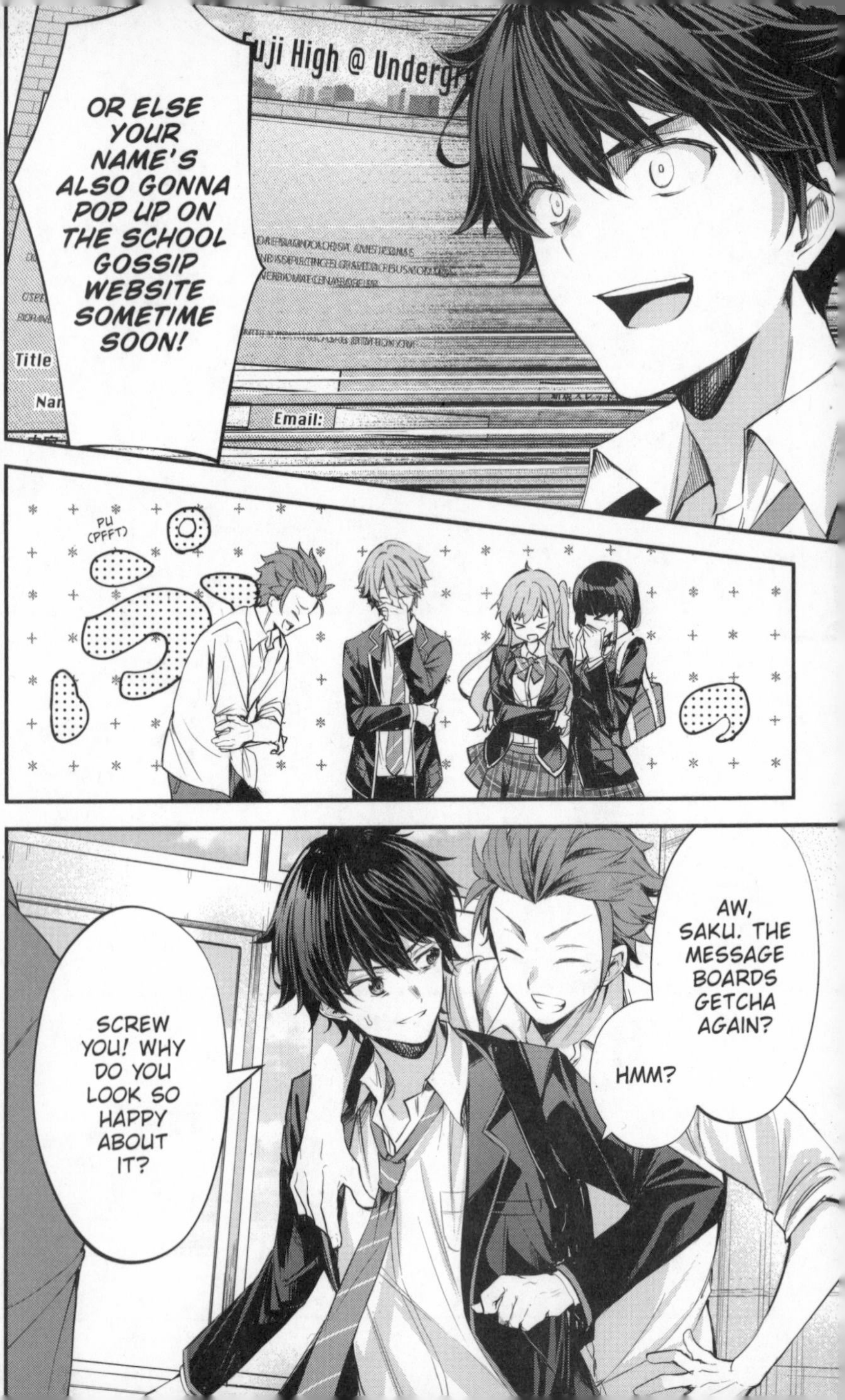
OR ELSE YOUR NAME'S ALSO GONNA POP UP ON THE SCHOOL GOSSIP WEBSITE SOMETIME SOON!
Fuji High @
Title
Email:
PU (PFFT)
AW, SAKU. THE MESSAGE BOARDS GETCHA AGAIN?
HMM?
SCREW YOU! WHY DO YOU LOOK SO HAPPY ABOUT IT?

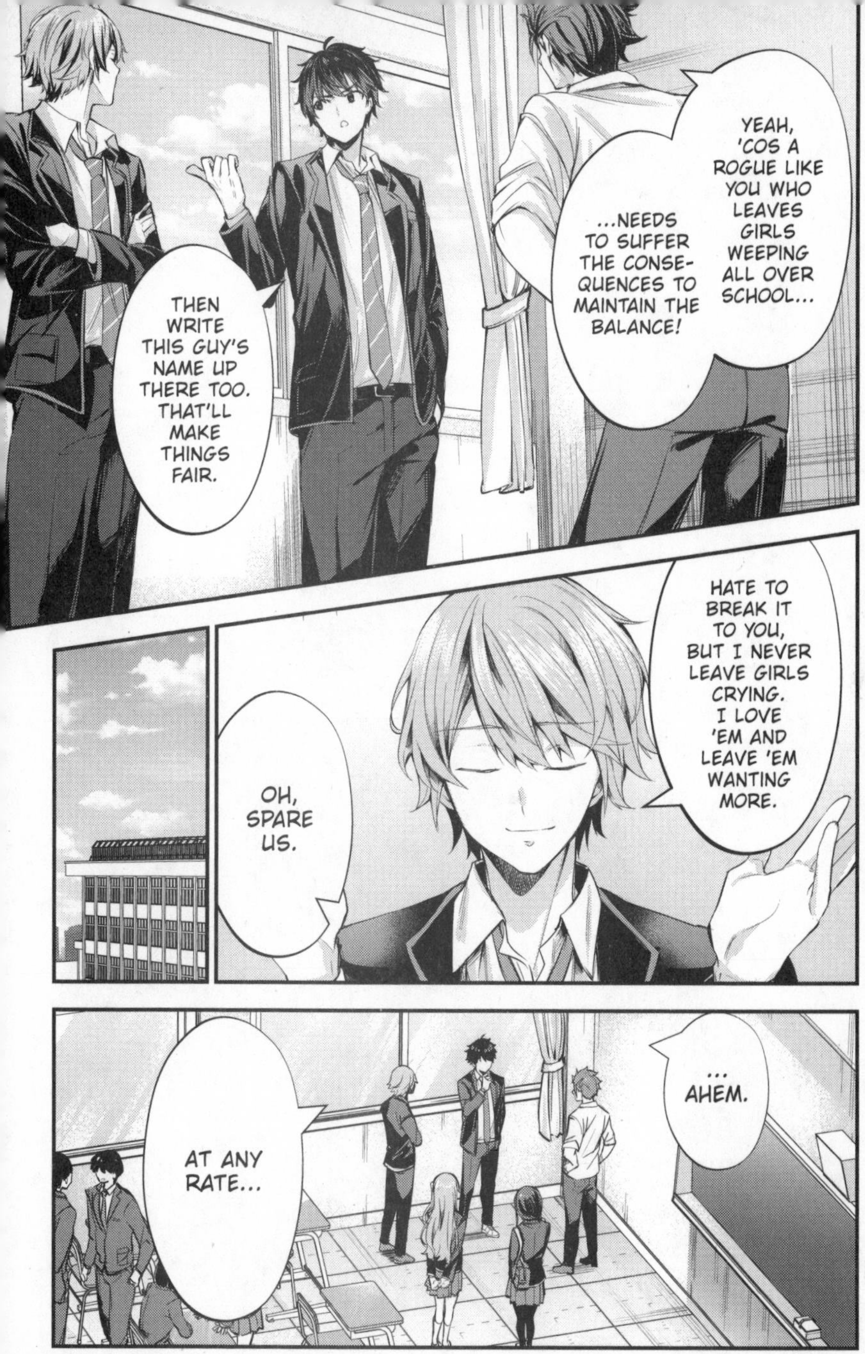
YEAH, 'COS A ROGUE LIKE YOU WHO LEAVES GIRLS WEEPING ALL OVER SCHOOL...
...NEEDS TO SUFFER THE CONSE-QUENCES TO MAINTAIN THE BALANCE!
THEN WRITE THIS GUY'S NAME UP THERE TOO. THAT'LL MAKE THINGS FAIR.
HATE TO BREAK IT TO YOU, BUT I NEVER LEAVE GIRLS CRYING. I LOVE 'EM AND LEAVE 'EM WANTING MORE.
OH, SPARE US.
...AHEM.
AT ANY RATE...

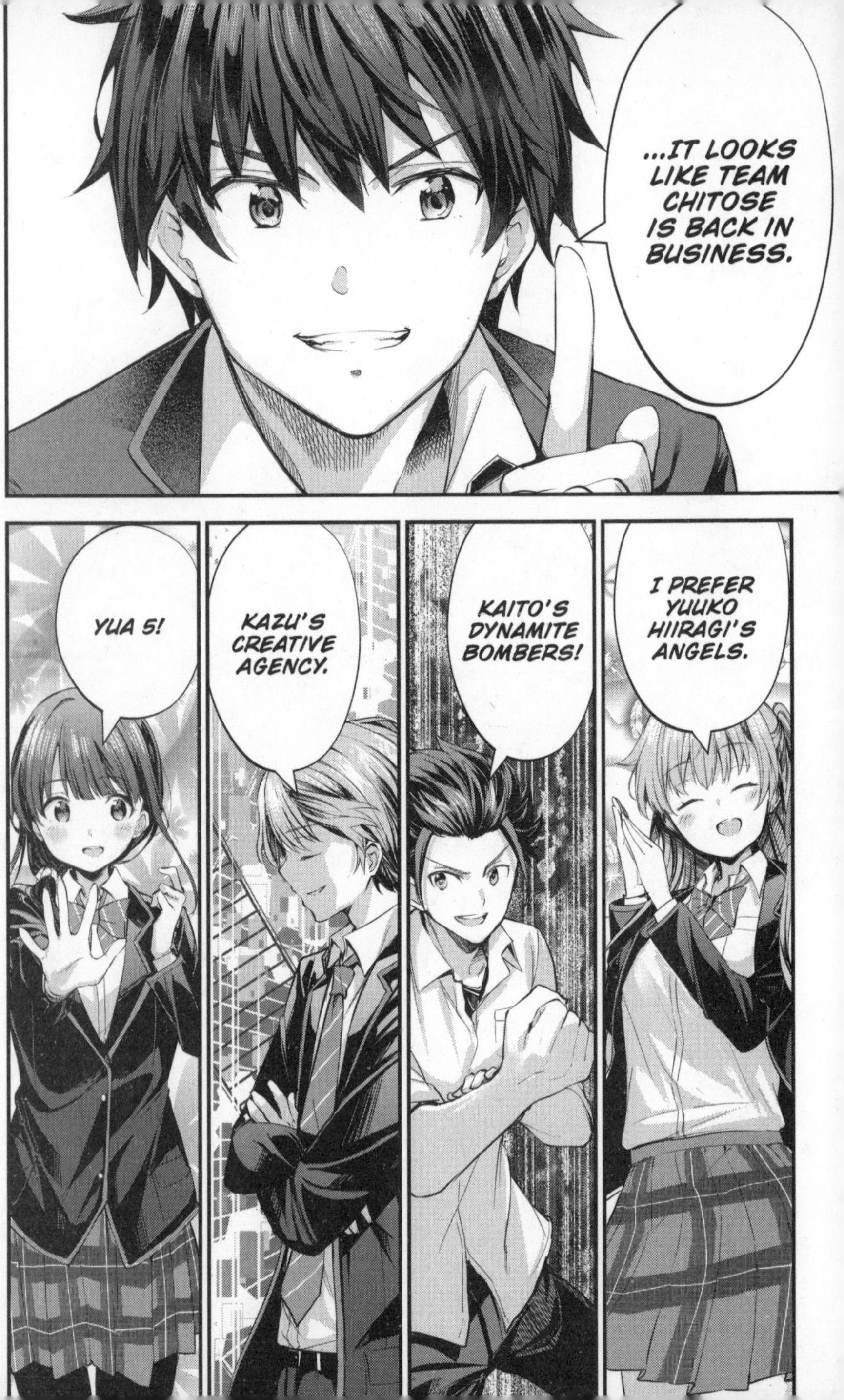
...IT LOOKS LIKE TEAM CHITOSE IS BACK IN BUSINESS.
I PREFER YUUKO HIIRAGI'S ANGELS.
KAITO'S DYNAMITE BOMBERS!
KAZU'S CREATIVE AGENCY.
YUA 5!

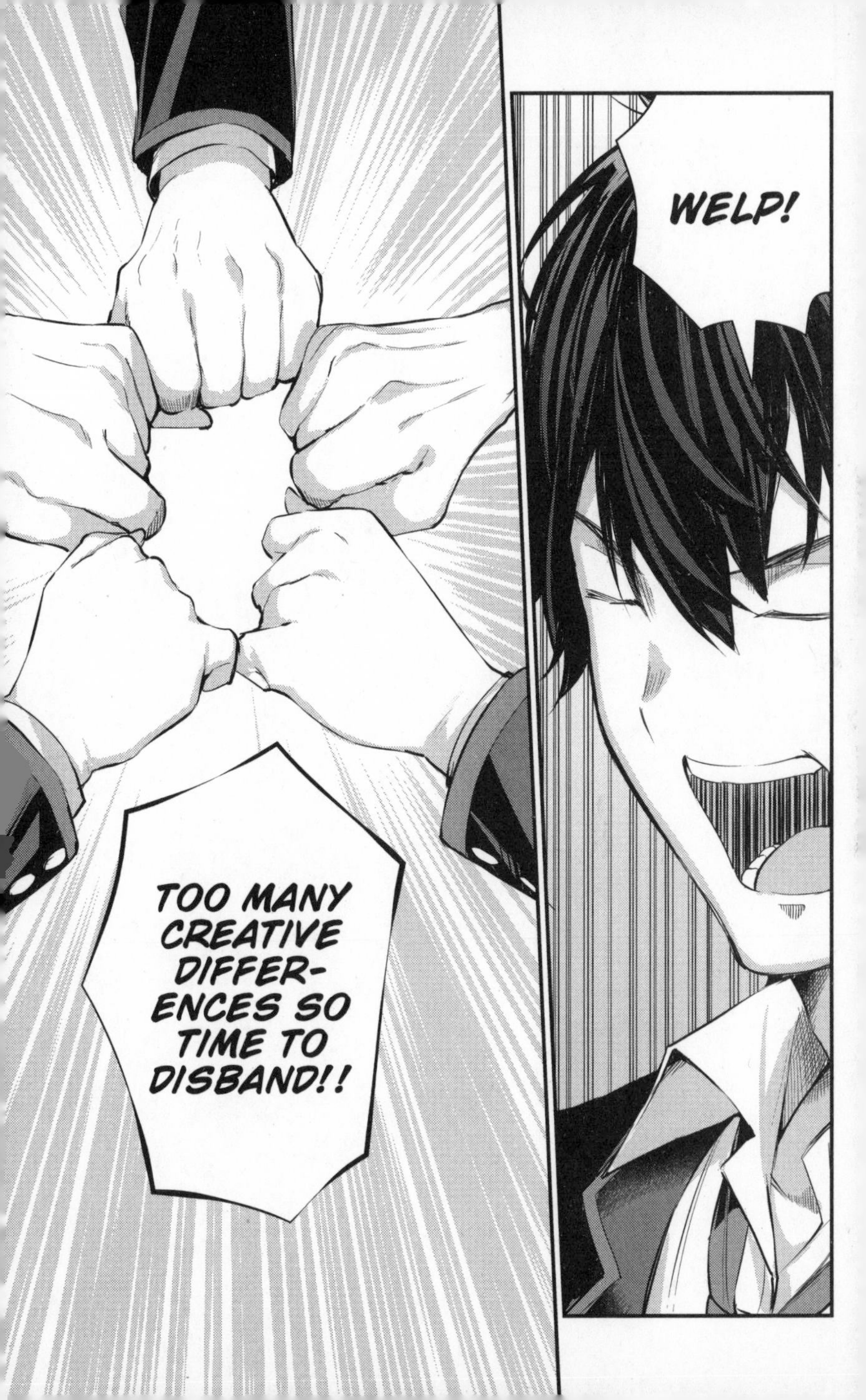
WELP!
TOO MANY CREATIVE DIFFER-ENCES SO TIME TO DISBAND!!

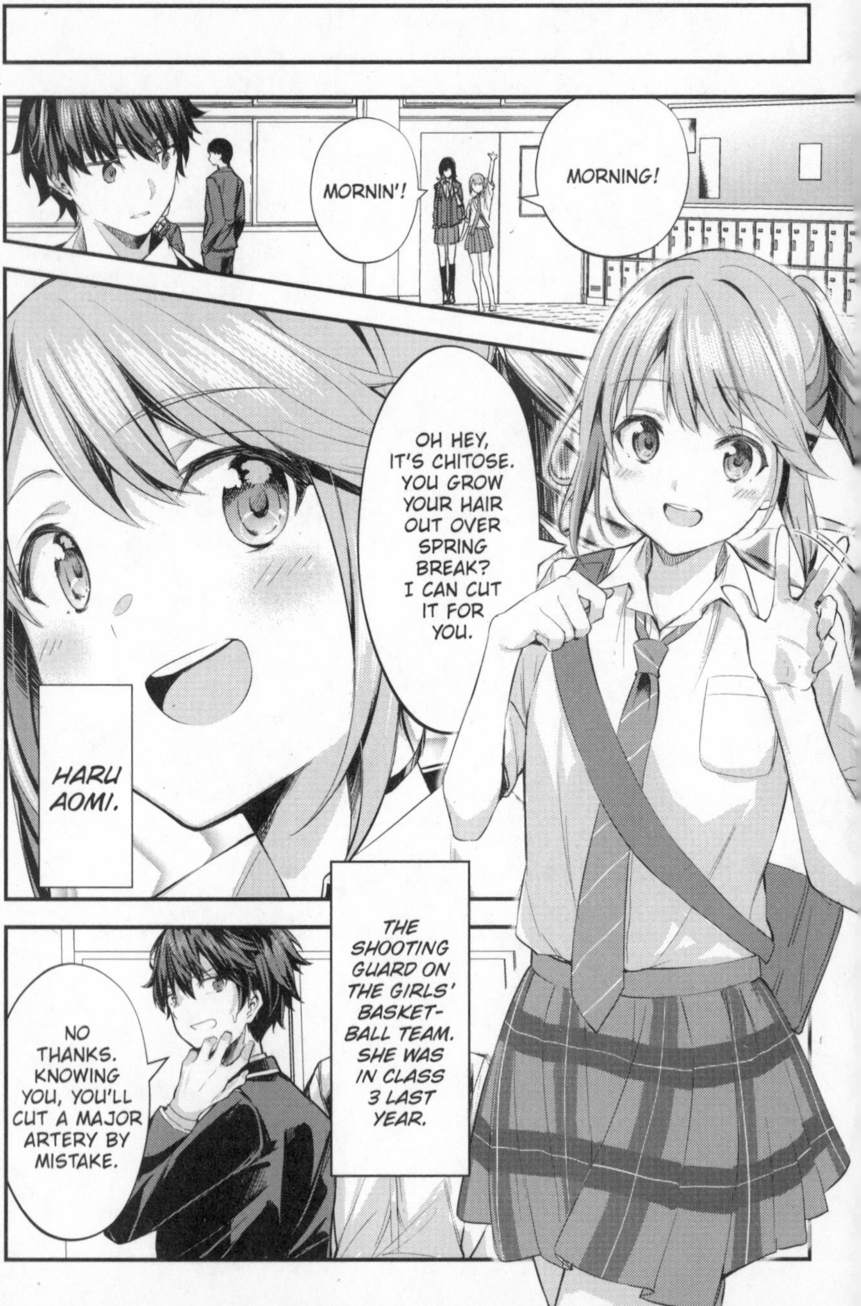
MORNING!
MORNIN'!
OH HEY, IT'S CHITOSE. YOU GROW YOUR HAIR OUT OVER SPRING BREAK? I CAN CUT IT FOR YOU.
HARU AOMI.
THE SHOOTING GUARD ON THE GIRLS' BASKET-BALL TEAM. SHE WAS IN CLASS 3 LAST YEAR.
NO THANKS. KNOWING YOU, YOU'LL CUT A MAJOR ARTERY BY MISTAKE.

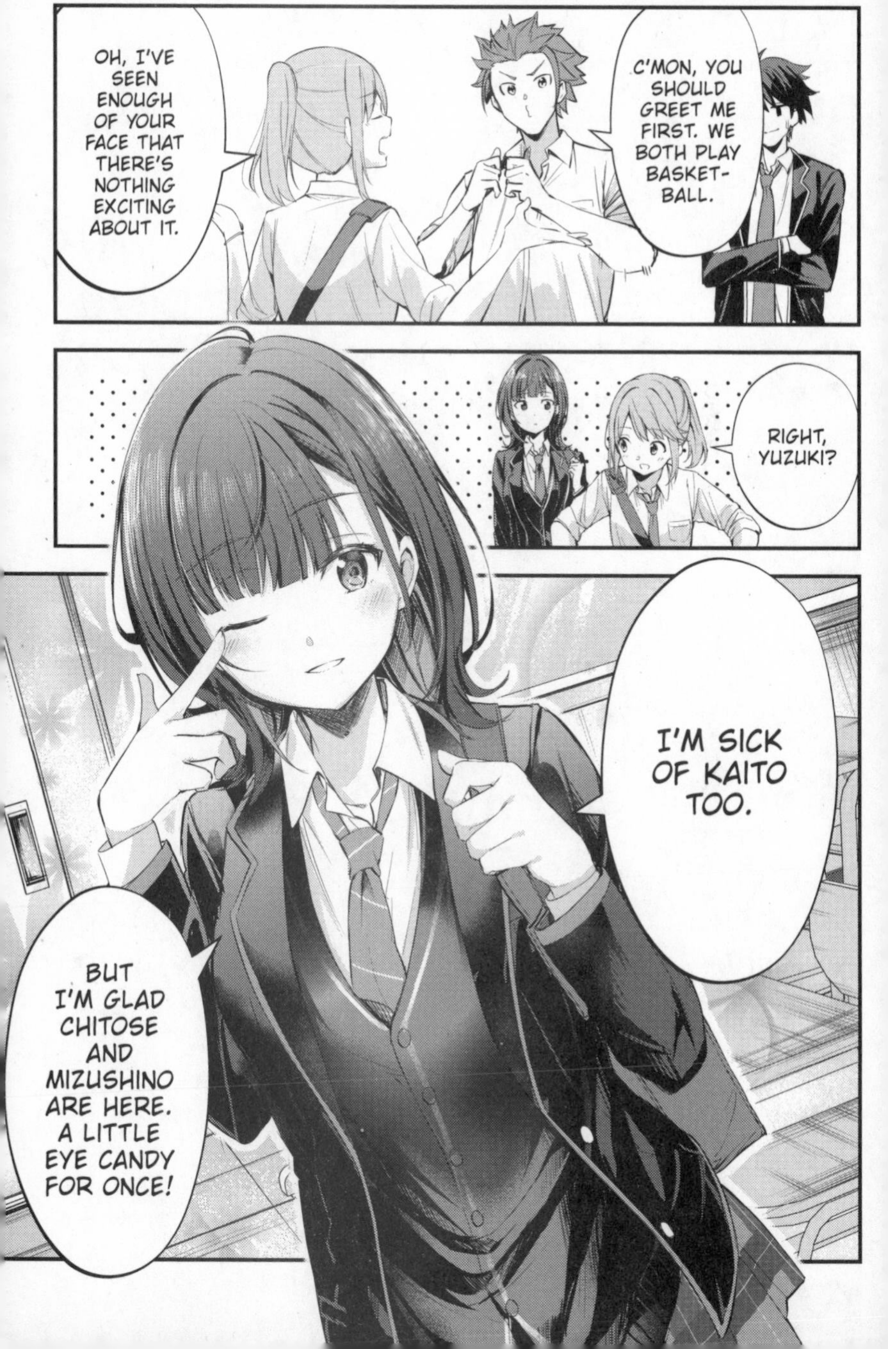
C'MON, YOU SHOULD GREET ME FIRST. WE BOTH PLAY BASKET-BALL.
OH, I'VE SEEN ENOUGH OF YOUR FACE THAT THERE'S NOTHING EXCITING ABOUT IT.
RIGHT, YUZUKI?
I'M SICK OF KAITO TOO.
BUT I'M GLAD CHITOSE AND MIZUSHINO ARE HERE. A LITTLE EYE CANDY FOR ONCE!

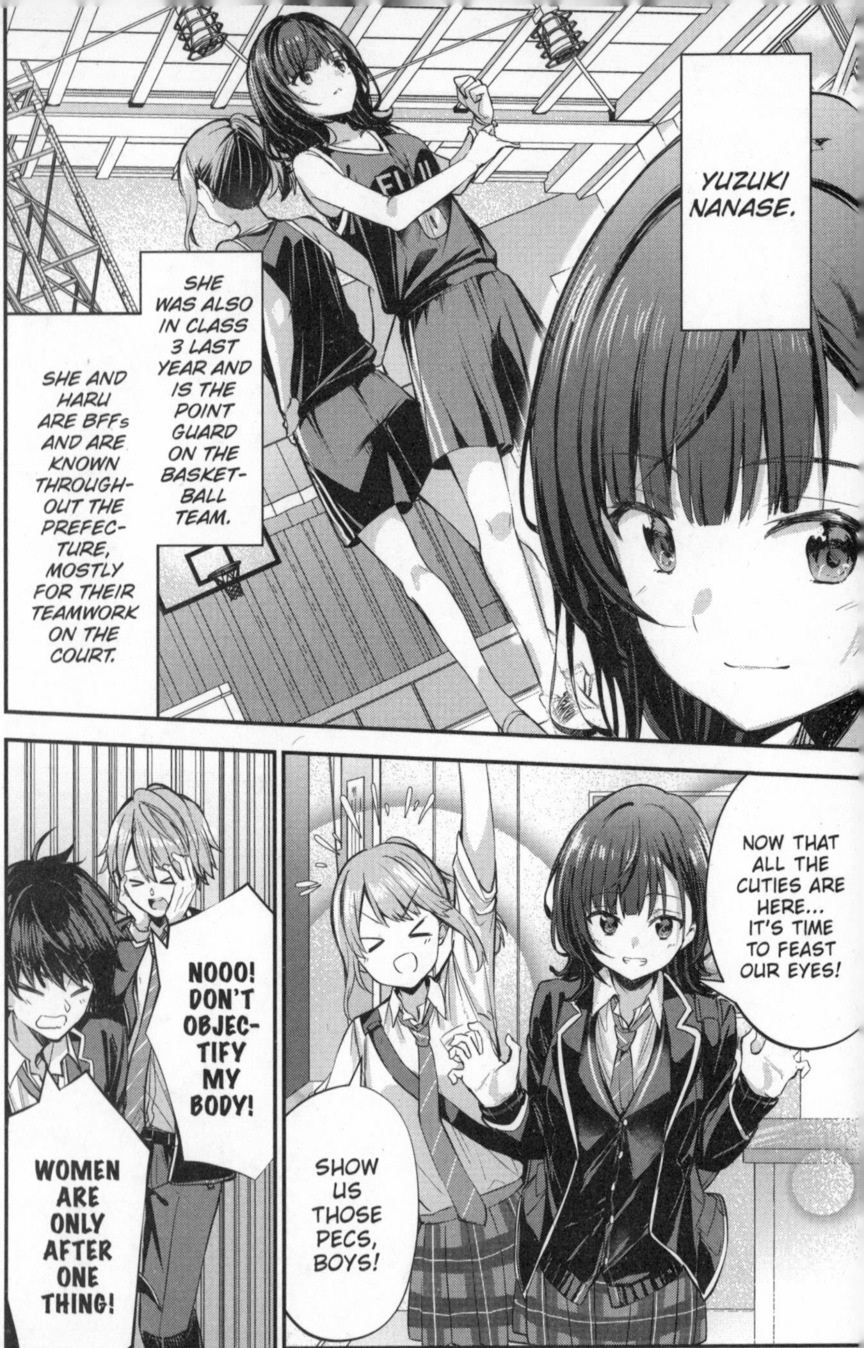
YUZUKI NANASE.
SHE WAS ALSO IN CLASS 3 LAST YEAR AND IS THE POINT GUARD ON THE BASKET-BALL TEAM.
SHE AND HARU ARE BFFs AND ARE KNOWN THROUGH-OUT THE PREFEC-TURE, MOSTLY FOR THEIR TEAMWORK ON THE COURT.
NOW THAT ALL THE CUTIES ARE HERE... IT'S TIME TO FEAST OUR EYES!
SHOW US THOSE PECS, BOYS!
NOOO! DON'T OBJEC-TIFY MY BODY!
WOMEN ARE ONLY AFTER ONE THING!

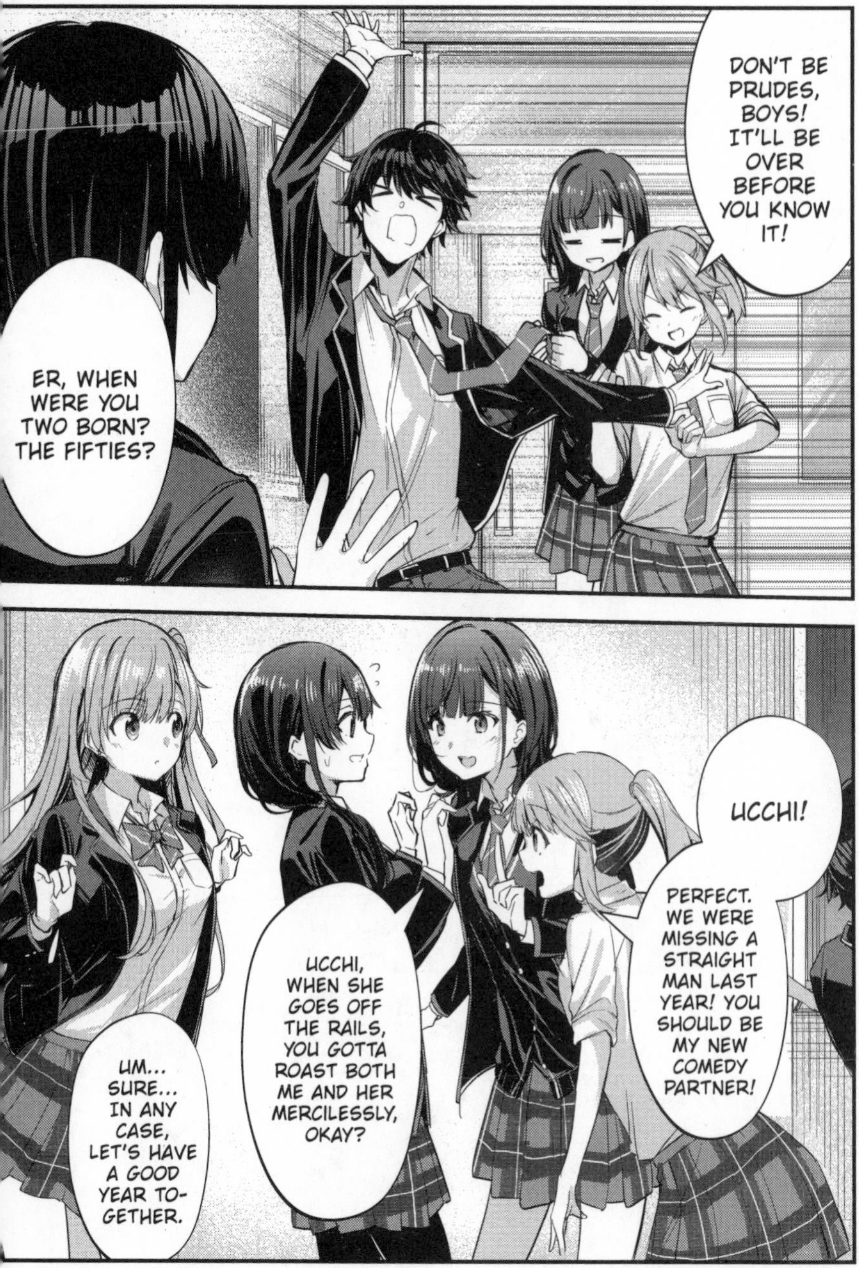
DON'T BE PRUDES, BOYS! IT'LL BE OVER BEFORE YOU KNOW IT!
ER, WHEN WERE YOU TWO BORN? THE FIFTIES?
UCCHI!
PERFECT. WE WERE MISSING A STRAIGHT MAN LAST YEAR! YOU SHOULD BE MY NEW COMEDY PARTNER!
UCCHI, WHEN SHE GOES OFF THE RAILS, YOU GOTTA ROAST BOTH ME AND HER MERCILESSLY, OKAY?
UM... SURE... IN ANY CASE, LET'S HAVE A GOOD YEAR TO-GETHER.

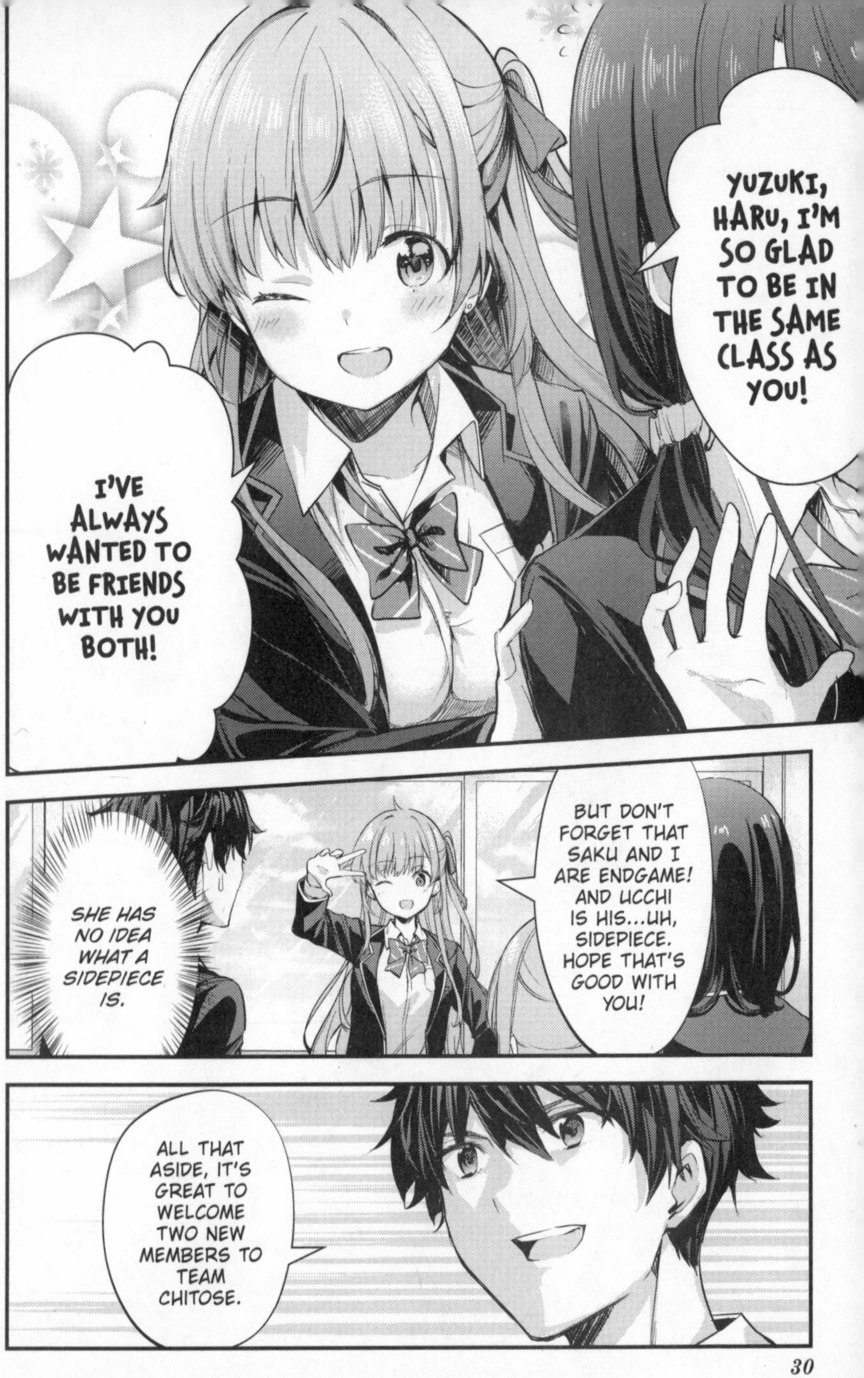
YUZUKI, HARU, I'M SO GLAD TO BE IN THE SAME CLASS AS YOU!
I'VE ALWAYS WANTED TO BE FRIENDS WITH YOU BOTH!
BUT DON'T FORGET THAT SAKU AND I ARE ENDGAME! AND UCCHI IS HIS...UH, SIDEPIECE. HOPE THAT'S GOOD WITH YOU!
SHE HAS NO IDEA WHAT A SIDEPIECE IS.
ALL THAT ASIDE, IT'S GREAT TO WELCOME TWO NEW MEMBERS TO TEAM CHITOSE.

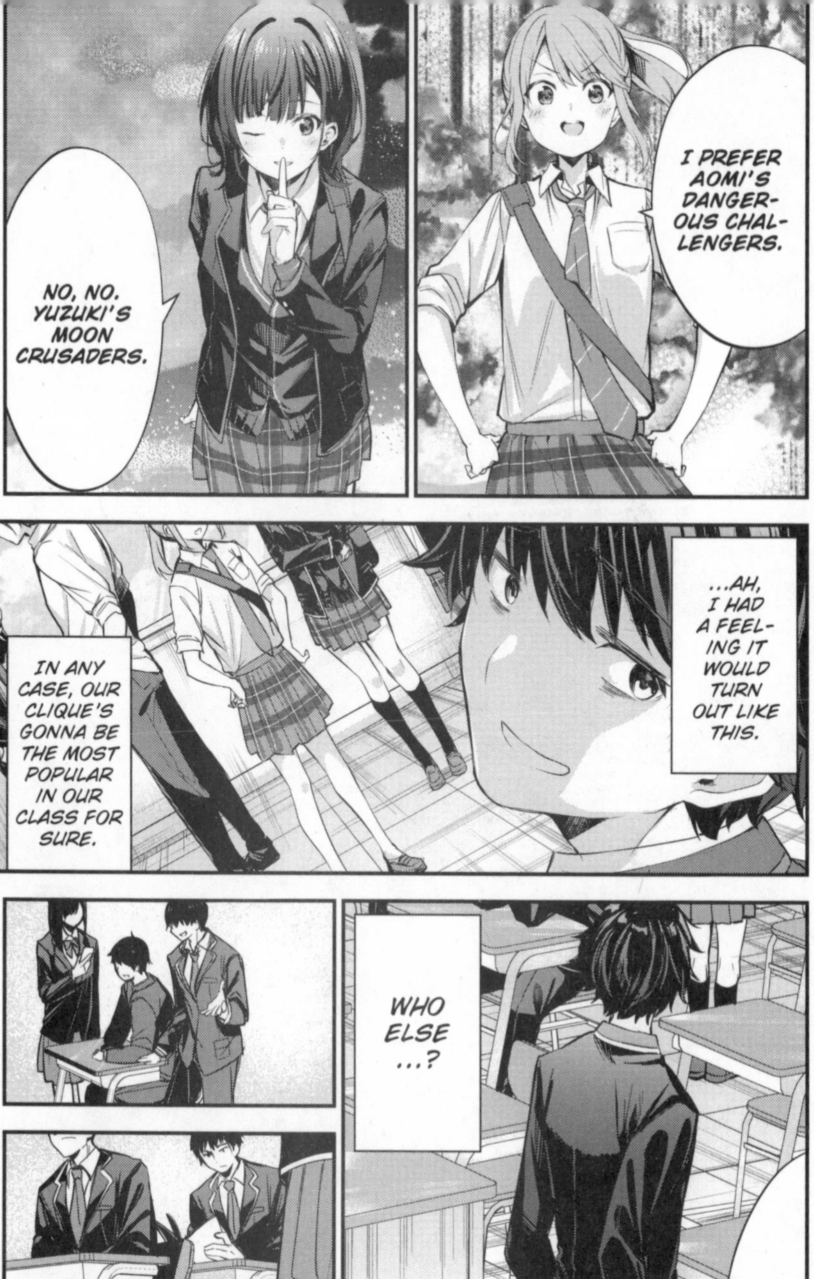
I PREFER AOMI'S DANGEROUS CHALLENGERS.
NO, NO. YUZUKI'S MOON CRUSADERS.
...AH, I HAD A FEELING IT WOULD TURN OUT LIKE THIS.
IN ANY CASE, OUR CLIQUE'S GONNA BE THE MOST POPULAR IN OUR CLASS FOR SURE.
WHO ELSE ...?

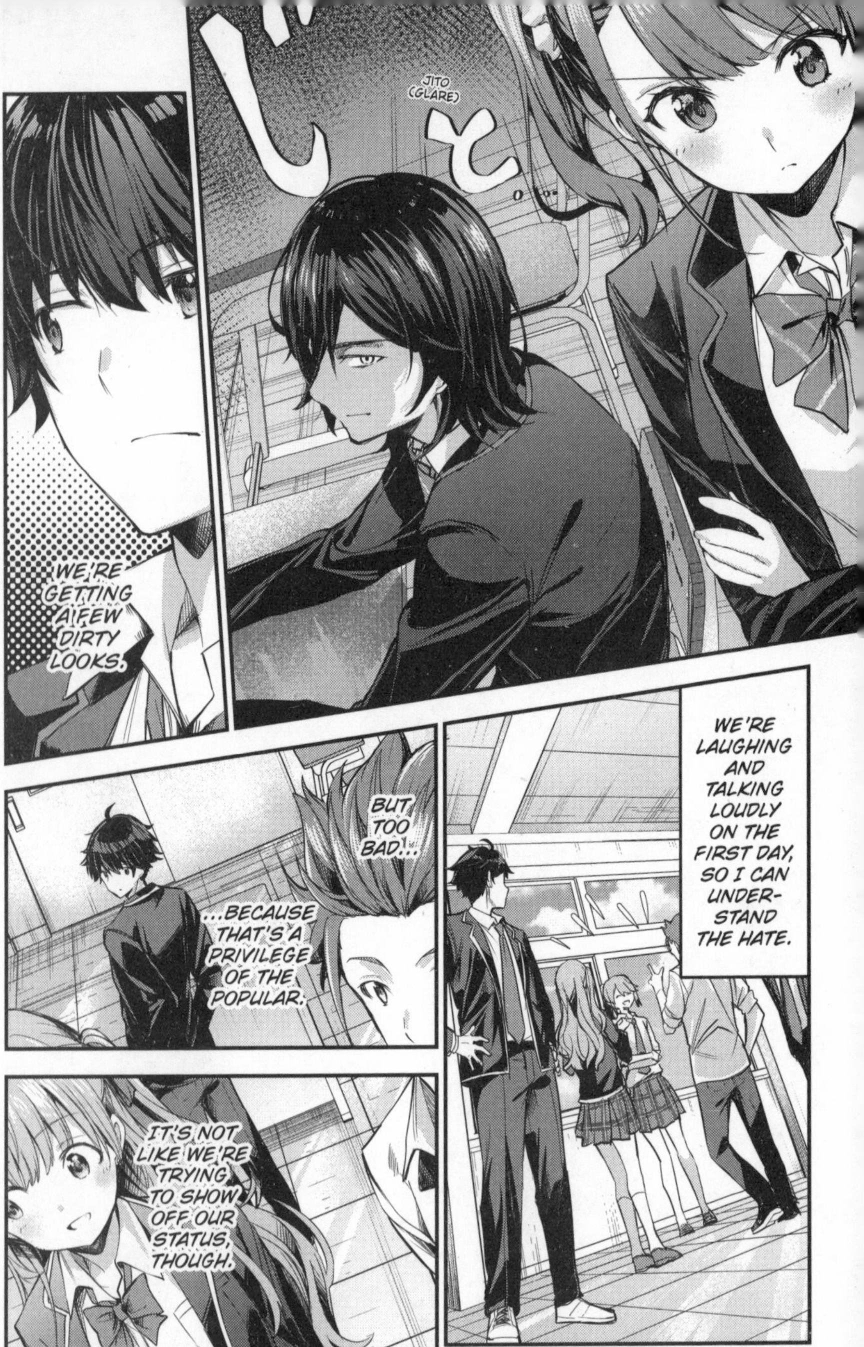
JITO (GLARE)
WE'RE GETTING A FEW DIRTY LOOKS.
WE'RE LAUGHING AND TALKING LOUDLY ON THE FIRST DAY, SO I CAN UNDER-STAND THE HATE.
BUT TOO BAD...
...BECAUSE THAT'S A PRIVILEGE OF THE POPULAR.
IT'S NOT LIKE WE'RE TRYING TO SHOW OFF OUR STATUS, THOUGH.

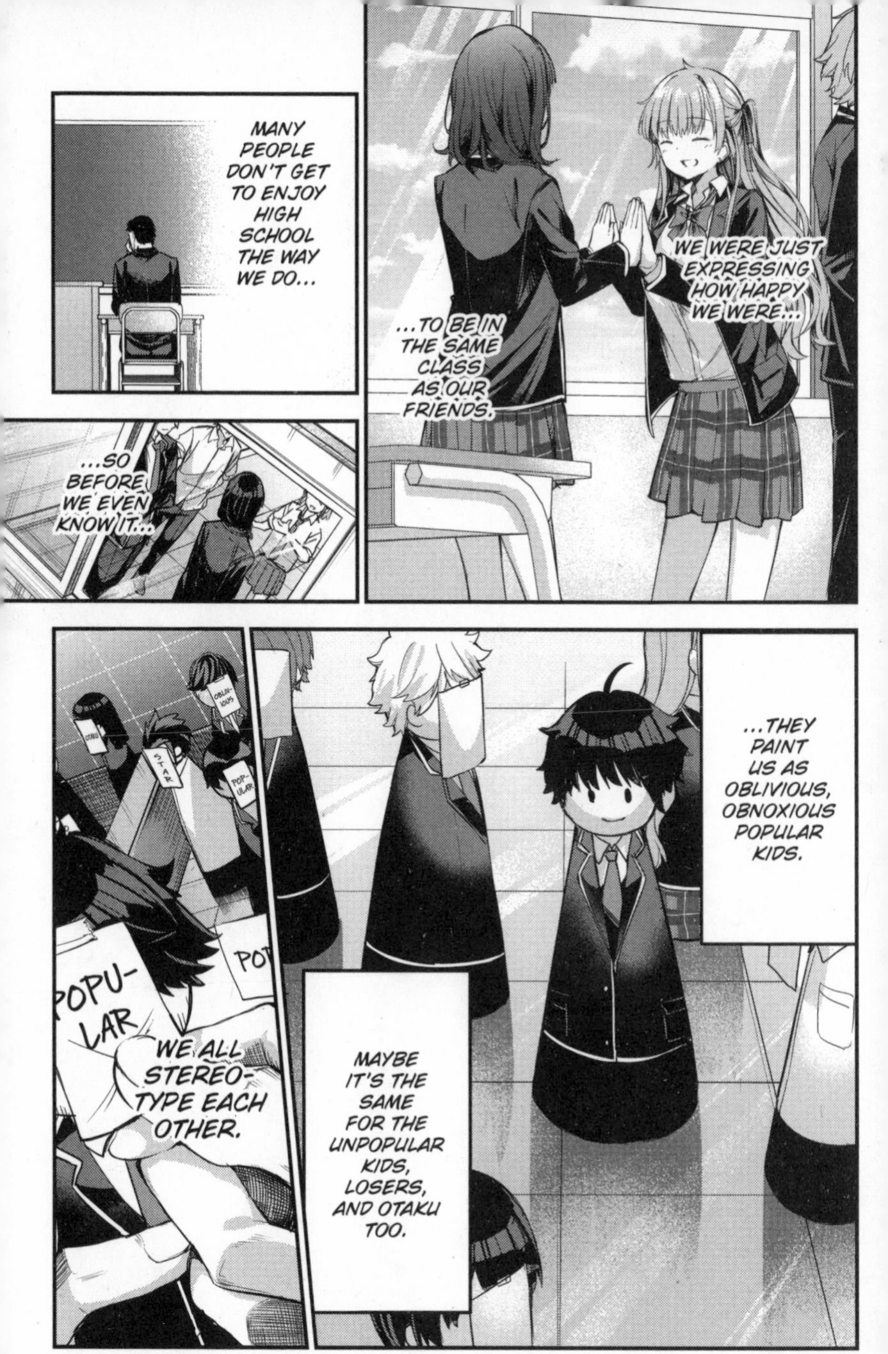
WE WERE JUST EXPRESSING HOW HAPPY WE WERE...
...TO BE IN THE SAME CLASS AS OUR FRIENDS.
MANY PEOPLE DON'T GET TO ENJOY HIGH SCHOOL THE WAY WE DO...
...SO BEFORE WE EVEN KNOW IT...
...THEY PAINT US AS OBLIVIOUS, OBNOXIOUS POPULAR KIDS.
MAYBE IT'S THE SAME FOR THE UNPOPULAR KIDS, LOSERS, AND OTAKU TOO.
OBLI-VIOUS
STAR
POP-ULAR
PO
POPU-LAR
WE ALL STEREO-TYPE EACH OTHER.

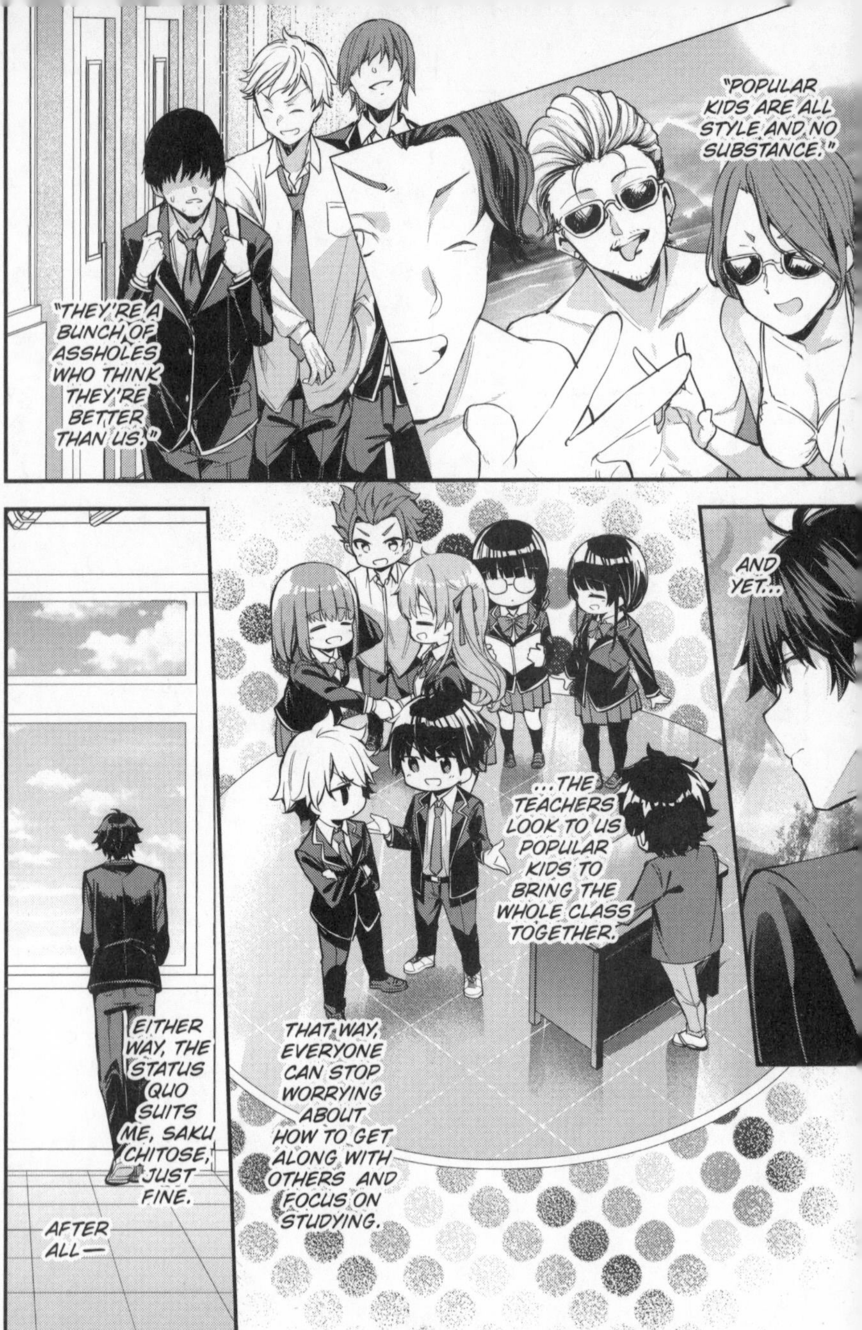
"POPULAR KIDS ARE ALL STYLE AND NO SUBSTANCE."
"THEY'RE A BUNCH OF ASSHOLES WHO THINK THEY'RE BETTER THAN US."
AND YET...
...THE TEACHERS LOOK TO US POPULAR KIDS TO BRING THE WHOLE CLASS TOGETHER.
THAT WAY, EVERYONE CAN STOP WORRYING ABOUT HOW TO GET ALONG WITH OTHERS AND FOCUS ON STUDYING.
EITHER WAY, THE STATUS QUO SUITS ME, SAKU CHITOSE, JUST FINE.
AFTER ALL—

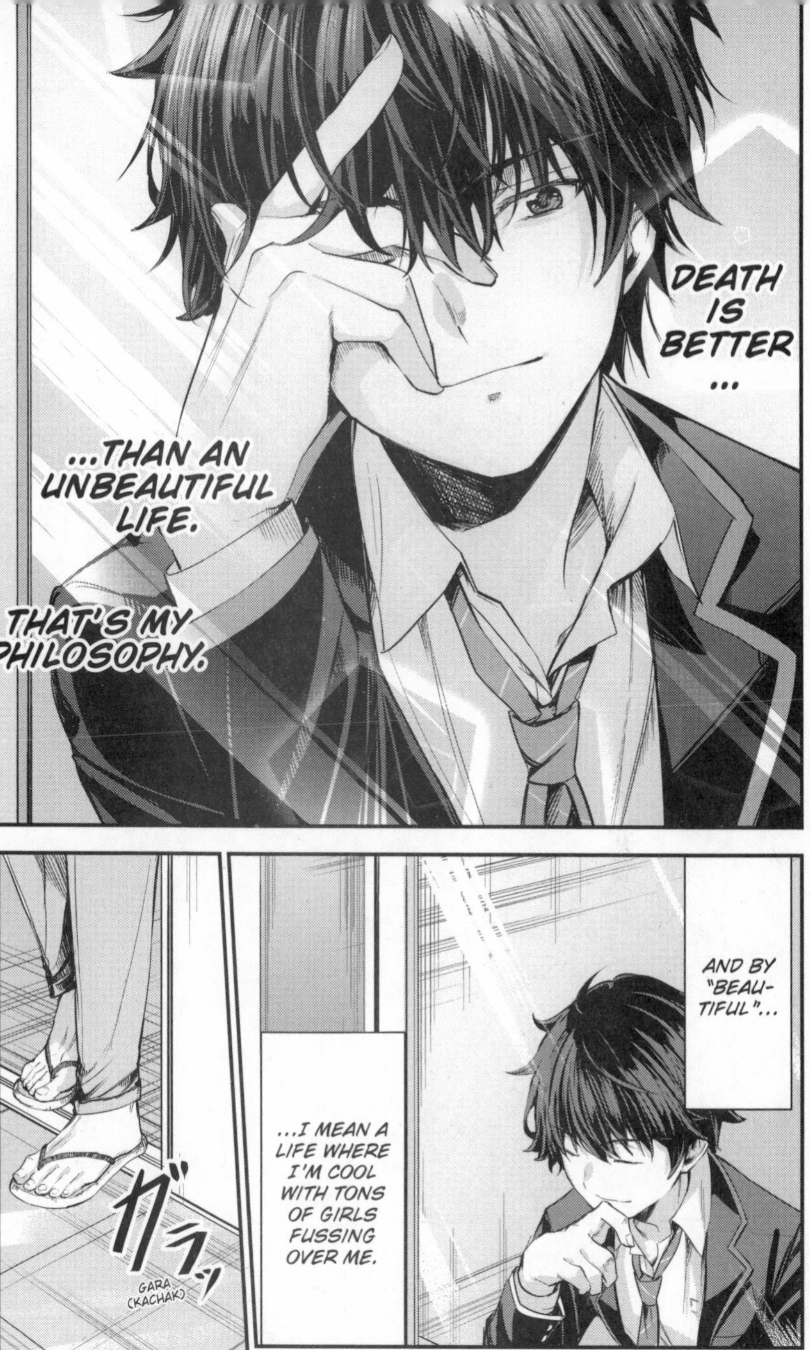
DEATH IS BETTER...
...THAN AN UNBEAUTIFUL LIFE.
THAT'S MY PHILOSOPHY.
AND BY "BEAU-TIFUL"...
...I MEAN A LIFE WHERE I'M COOL WITH TONS OF GIRLS FUSSING OVER ME.
ガラッ
GARA (KACHAK)

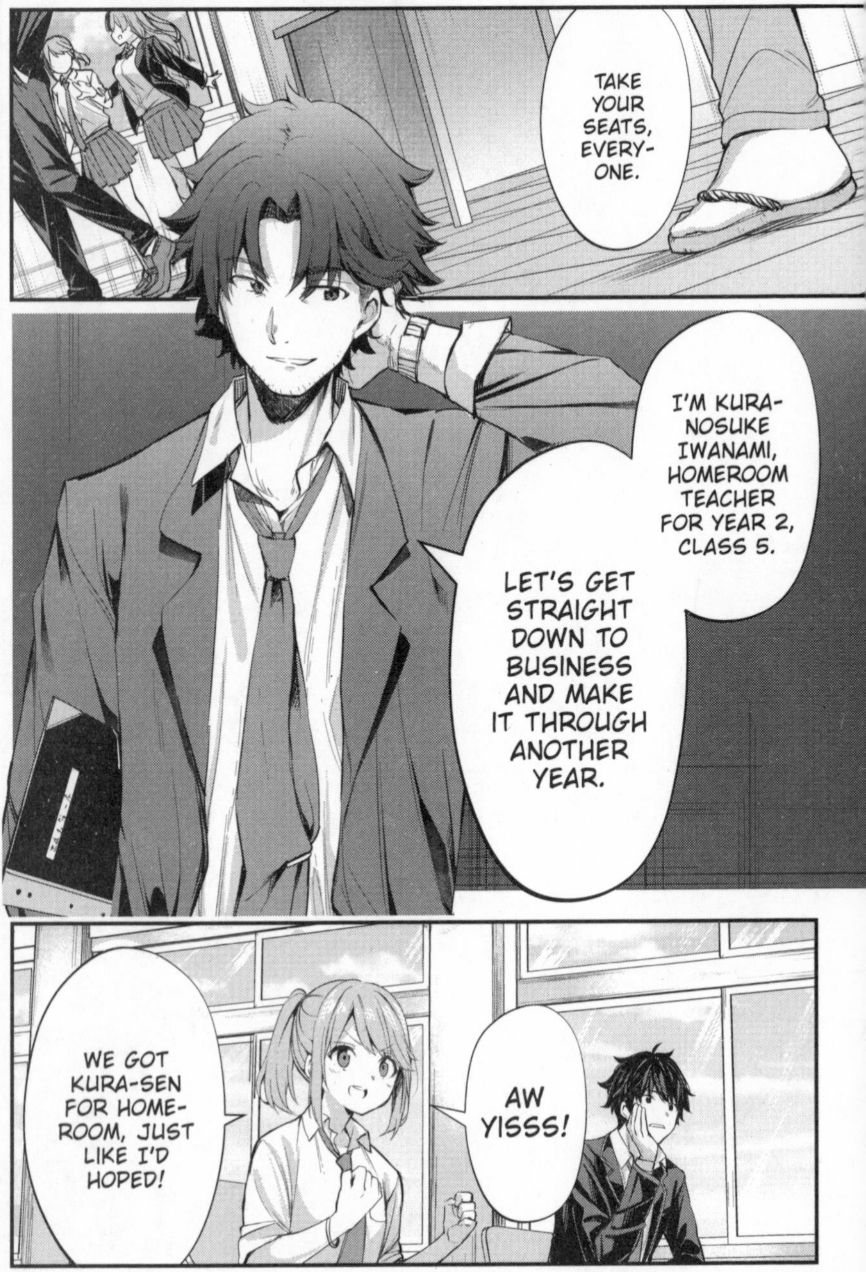
TAKE YOUR SEATS, EVERY-ONE.
I'M KURA-NOSUKE IWANAMI, HOMEROOM TEACHER FOR YEAR 2, CLASS 5.
LET'S GET STRAIGHT DOWN TO BUSINESS AND MAKE IT THROUGH ANOTHER YEAR.
AW YISSS!
WE GOT KURA-SEN FOR HOME-ROOM, JUST LIKE I'D HOPED!

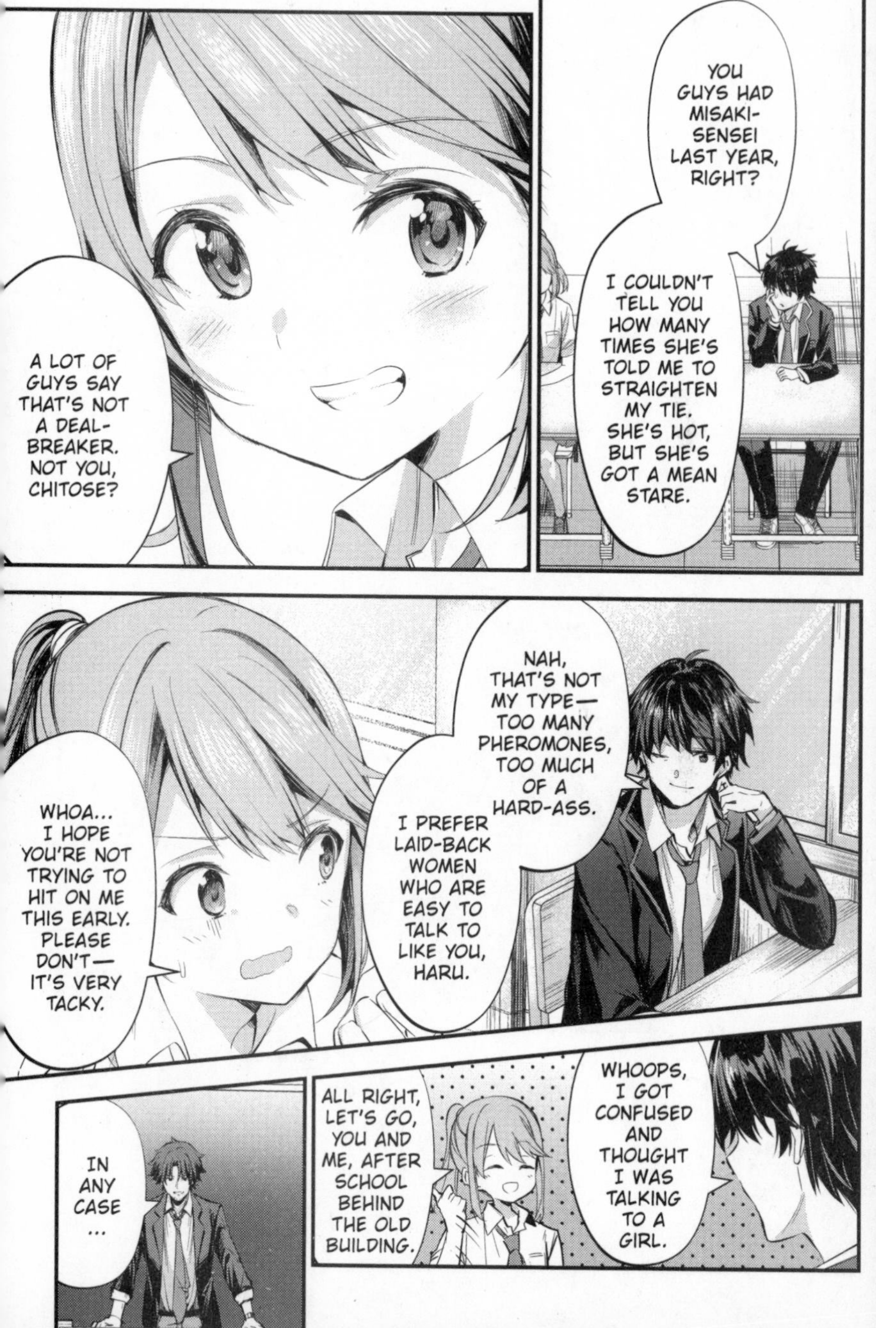
YOU GUYS HAD MISAKI-SENSEI LAST YEAR, RIGHT?
I COULDN'T TELL YOU HOW MANY TIMES SHE'S TOLD ME TO STRAIGHTEN MY TIE. SHE'S HOT, BUT SHE'S GOT A MEAN STARE.
A LOT OF GUYS SAY THAT'S NOT A DEAL-BREAKER. NOT YOU, CHITOSE?
NAH, THAT'S NOT MY TYPE—TOO MANY PHEROMONES, TOO MUCH OF A HARD-ASS.
I PREFER LAID-BACK WOMEN WHO ARE EASY TO TALK TO LIKE YOU, HARU.
WHOA... I HOPE YOU'RE NOT TRYING TO HIT ON ME THIS EARLY. PLEASE DON'T—IT'S VERY TACKY.
WHOOPS, I GOT CONFUSED AND THOUGHT I WAS TALKING TO A GIRL.
ALL RIGHT, LET'S GO, YOU AND ME, AFTER SCHOOL BEHIND THE OLD BUILDING.
IN ANY CASE...

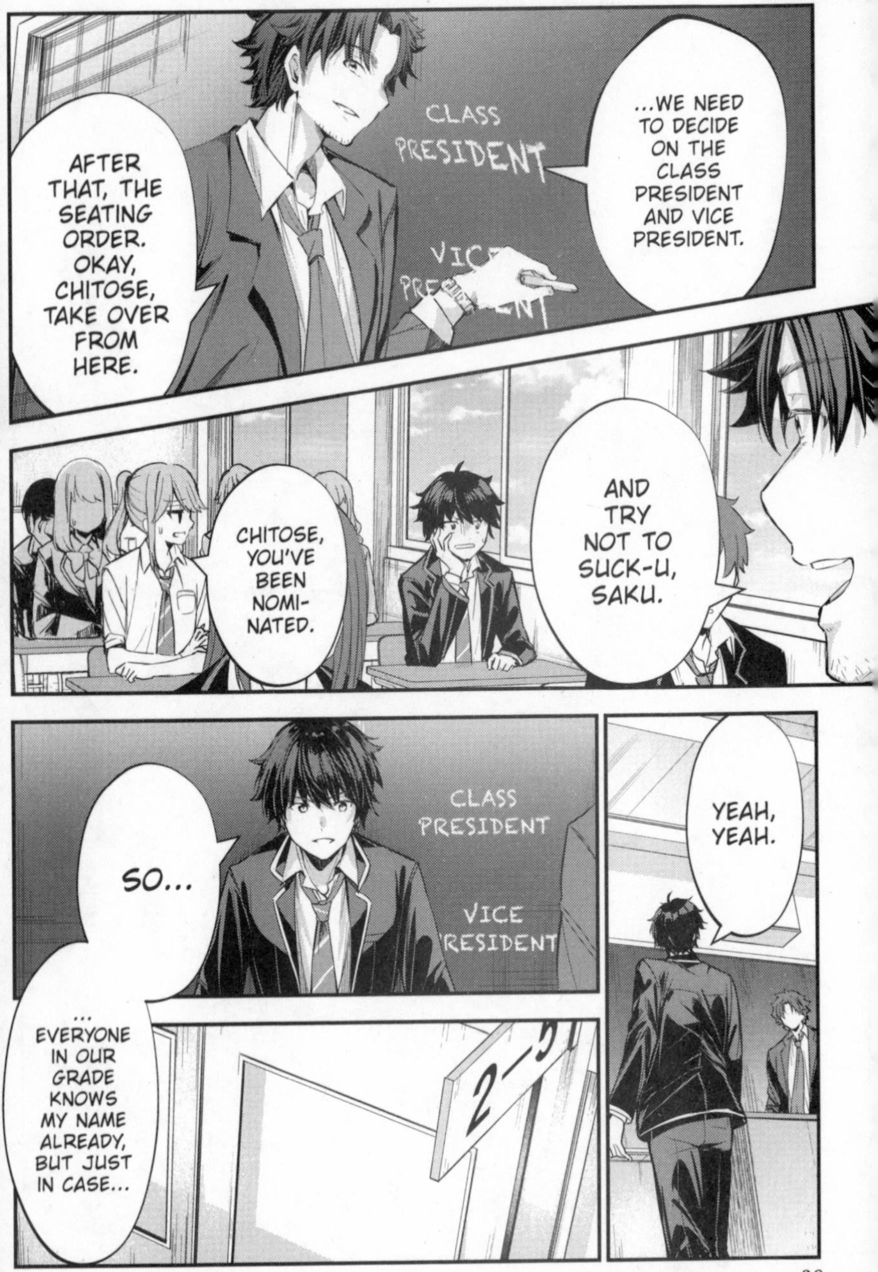
CLASS PRESIDENT
...WE NEED TO DECIDE ON THE CLASS PRESIDENT AND VICE PRESIDENT.
AFTER THAT, THE SEATING ORDER. OKAY, CHITOSE, TAKE OVER FROM HERE.
AND TRY NOT TO SUCK-U, SAKU.
CHITOSE, YOU'VE BEEN NOMI-NATED.
YEAH, YEAH.
CLASS PRESIDENT
SO...
... EVERYONE IN OUR GRADE KNOWS MY NAME ALREADY, BUT JUST IN CASE...

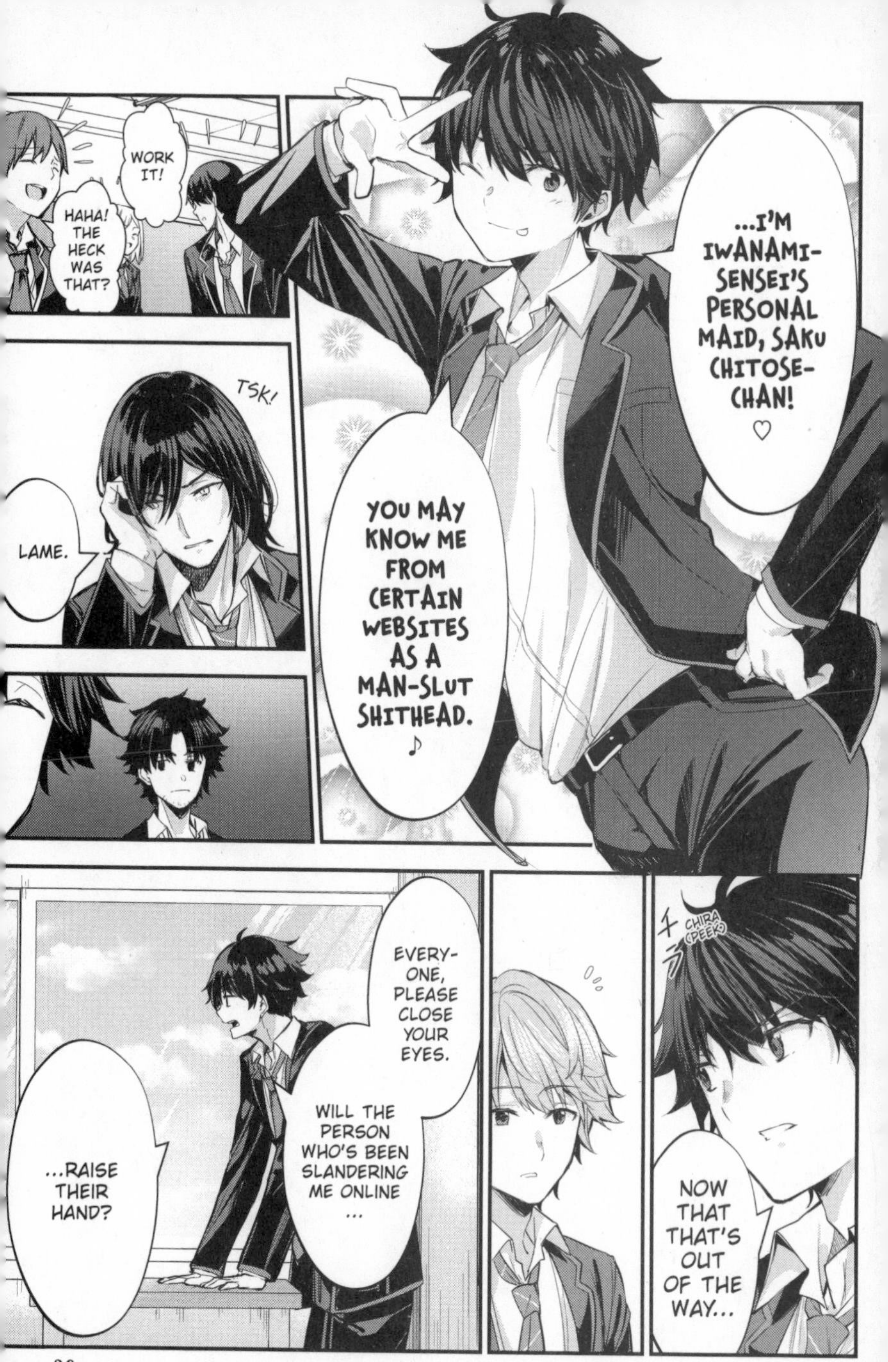
...I'M IWANAMI-SENSEI'S PERSONAL MAID, SAKU CHITOSE-CHAN! ♡
YOU MAY KNOW ME FROM CERTAIN WEBSITES AS A MAN-SLUT SHITHEAD. ♪
WORK IT!
HAHA! THE HECK WAS THAT?
TSK!
LAME.
CHIRA (PEEK)
NOW THAT THAT'S OUT OF THE WAY...
EVERY-ONE, PLEASE CLOSE YOUR EYES.
WILL THE PERSON WHO'S BEEN SLANDERING ME ONLINE ...
...RAISE THEIR HAND?

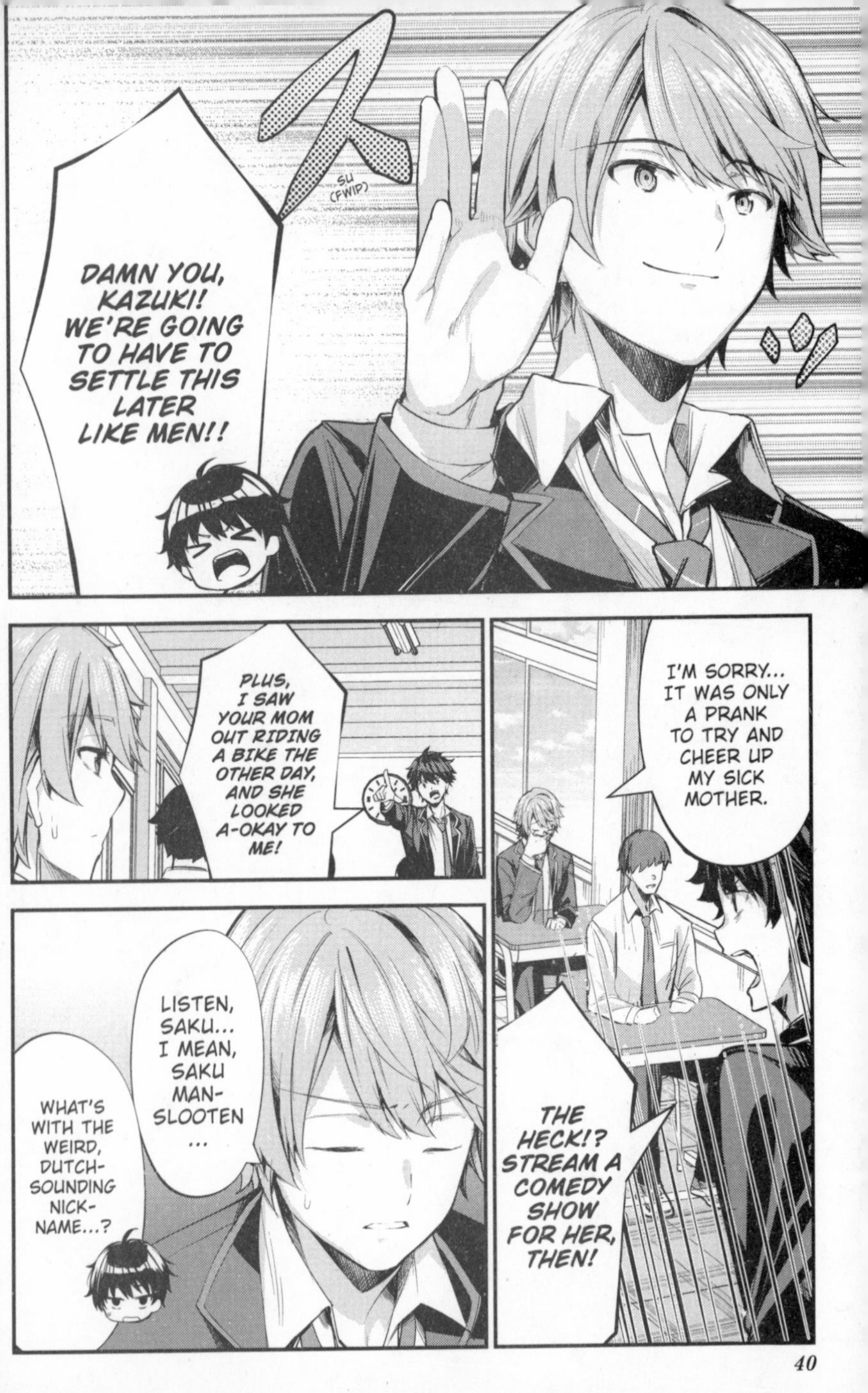
SU (FWIP)
DAMN YOU, KAZUKI! WE'RE GOING TO HAVE TO SETTLE THIS LATER LIKE MEN!!
I'M SORRY... IT WAS ONLY A PRANK TO TRY AND CHEER UP MY SICK MOTHER.
THE HECK!? STREAM A COMEDY SHOW FOR HER, THEN!
PLUS, I SAW YOUR MOM OUT RIDING A BIKE THE OTHER DAY, AND SHE LOOKED A-OKAY TO ME!
LISTEN, SAKU... I MEAN, SAKU MAN-SLOOTEN...
WHAT'S WITH THE WEIRD, DUTCH-SOUNDING NICK-NAME...?

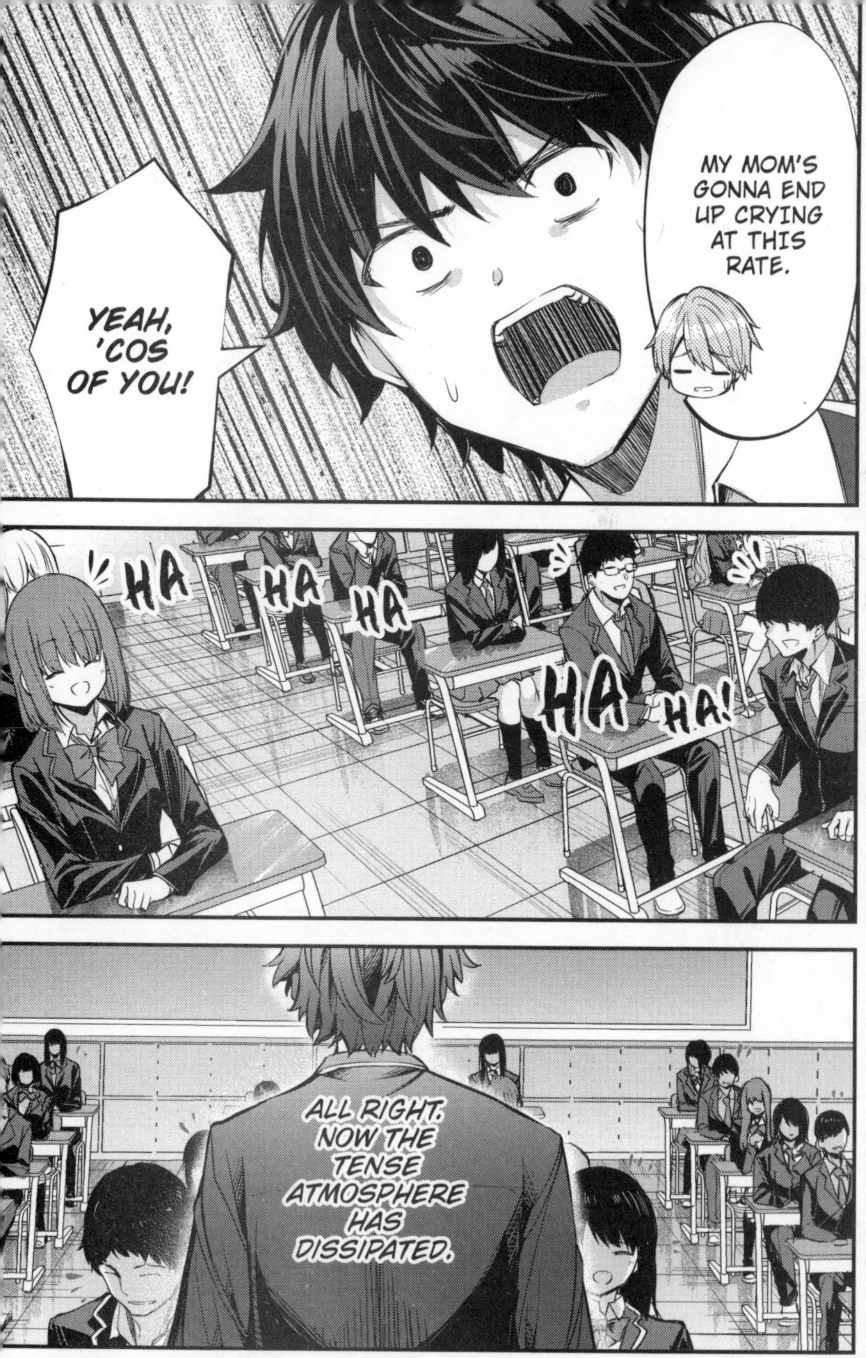
MY MOM'S GONNA END UP CRYING AT THIS RATE.
YEAH, 'COS OF YOU!
HA HA HA
HA HA!
ALL RIGHT. NOW THE TENSE ATMOSPHERE HAS DISSIPATED.

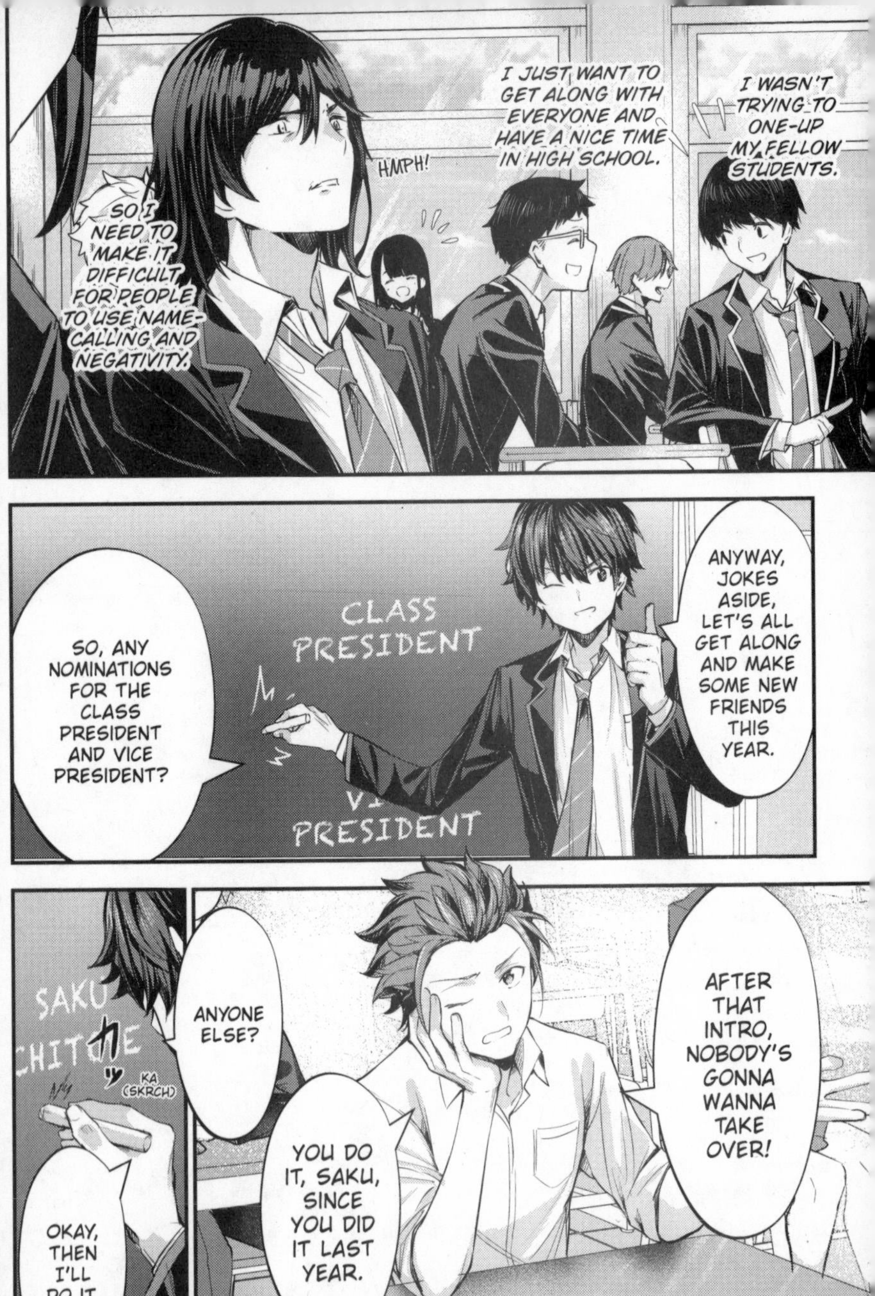
I WASN'T TRYING TO ONE-UP MY FELLOW STUDENTS.
I JUST WANT TO GET ALONG WITH EVERYONE AND HAVE A NICE TIME IN HIGH SCHOOL.
HMPH!
SO I NEED TO MAKE IT DIFFICULT FOR PEOPLE TO USE NAME-CALLING AND NEGATIVITY.
ANYWAY, JOKES ASIDE, LET'S ALL GET ALONG AND MAKE SOME NEW FRIENDS THIS YEAR.
CLASS PRESIDENT
SO, ANY NOMINATIONS FOR THE CLASS PRESIDENT AND VICE PRESIDENT?
PRESIDENT
AFTER THAT INTRO, NOBODY'S GONNA WANNA TAKE OVER!
ANYONE ELSE?
YOU DO IT, SAKU, SINCE YOU DID IT LAST YEAR.
SAKU
KA (SKRCH)
OKAY, THEN I'LL DO IT.

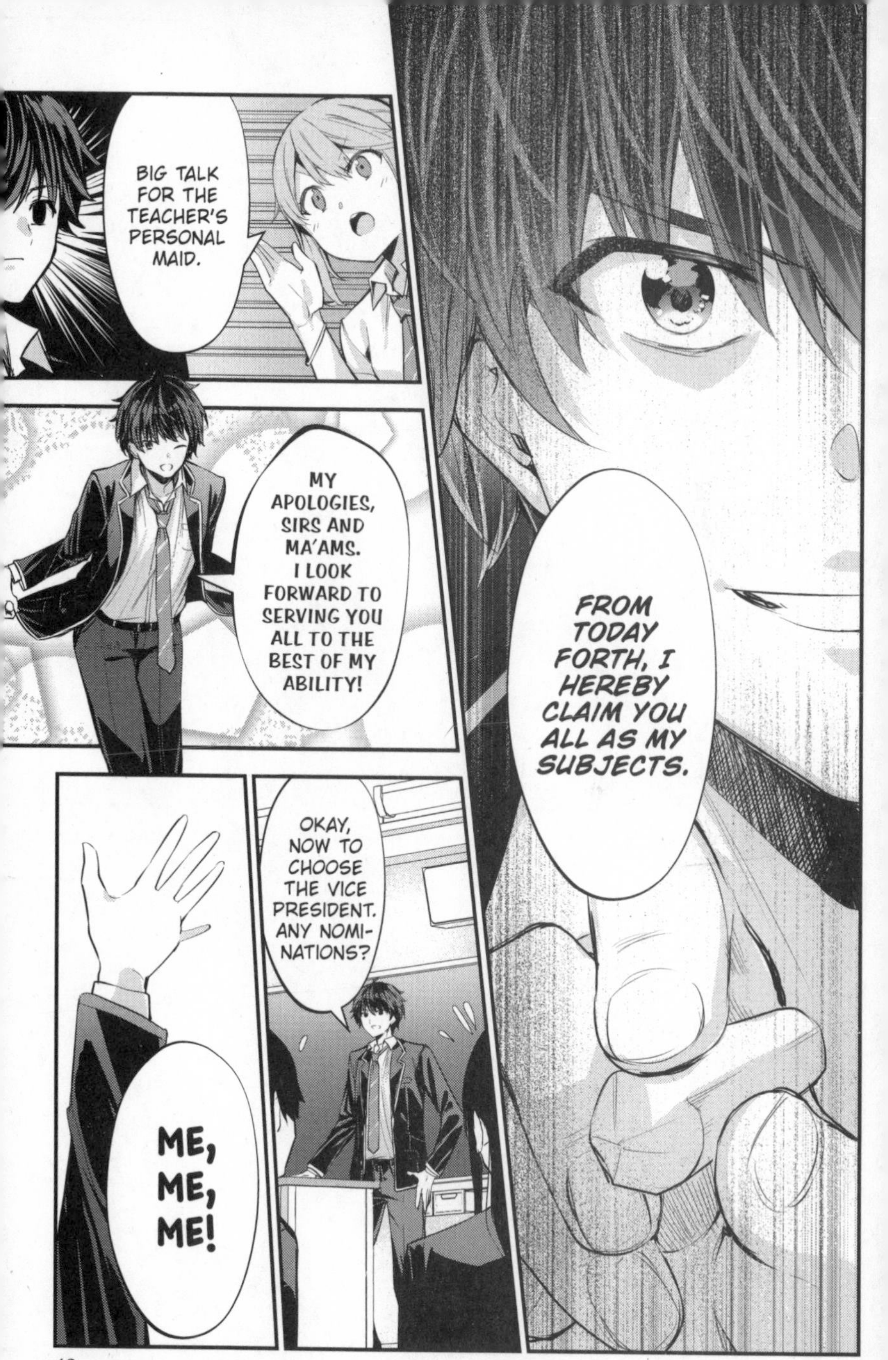
FROM TODAY FORTH, I HEREBY CLAIM YOU ALL AS MY SUBJECTS.
BIG TALK FOR THE TEACHER'S PERSONAL MAID.
MY APOLOGIES, SIRS AND MA'AMS. I LOOK FORWARD TO SERVING YOU ALL TO THE BEST OF MY ABILITY!
OKAY, NOW TO CHOOSE THE VICE PRESIDENT. ANY NOMI-NATIONS?
ME, ME, ME!

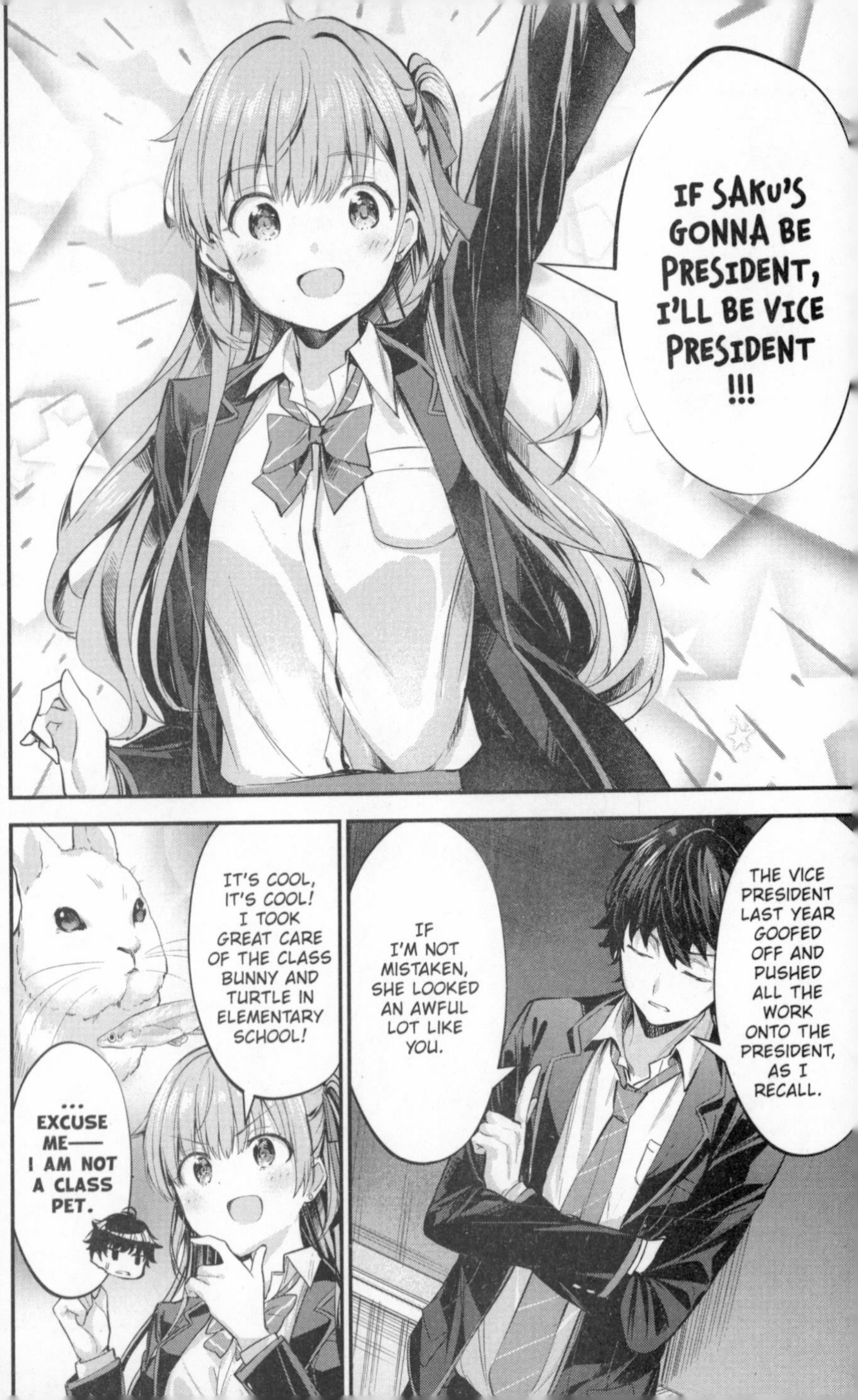
IF SAKU'S GONNA BE PRESIDENT, I'LL BE VICE PRESIDENT !!!
THE VICE PRESIDENT LAST YEAR GOOFED OFF AND PUSHED ALL THE WORK ONTO THE PRESIDENT, AS I RECALL.
IF I'M NOT MISTAKEN, SHE LOOKED AN AWFUL LOT LIKE YOU.
IT'S COOL, IT'S COOL! I TOOK GREAT CARE OF THE CLASS BUNNY AND TURTLE IN ELEMENTARY SCHOOL!
... EXCUSE ME—— I AM NOT A CLASS PET.

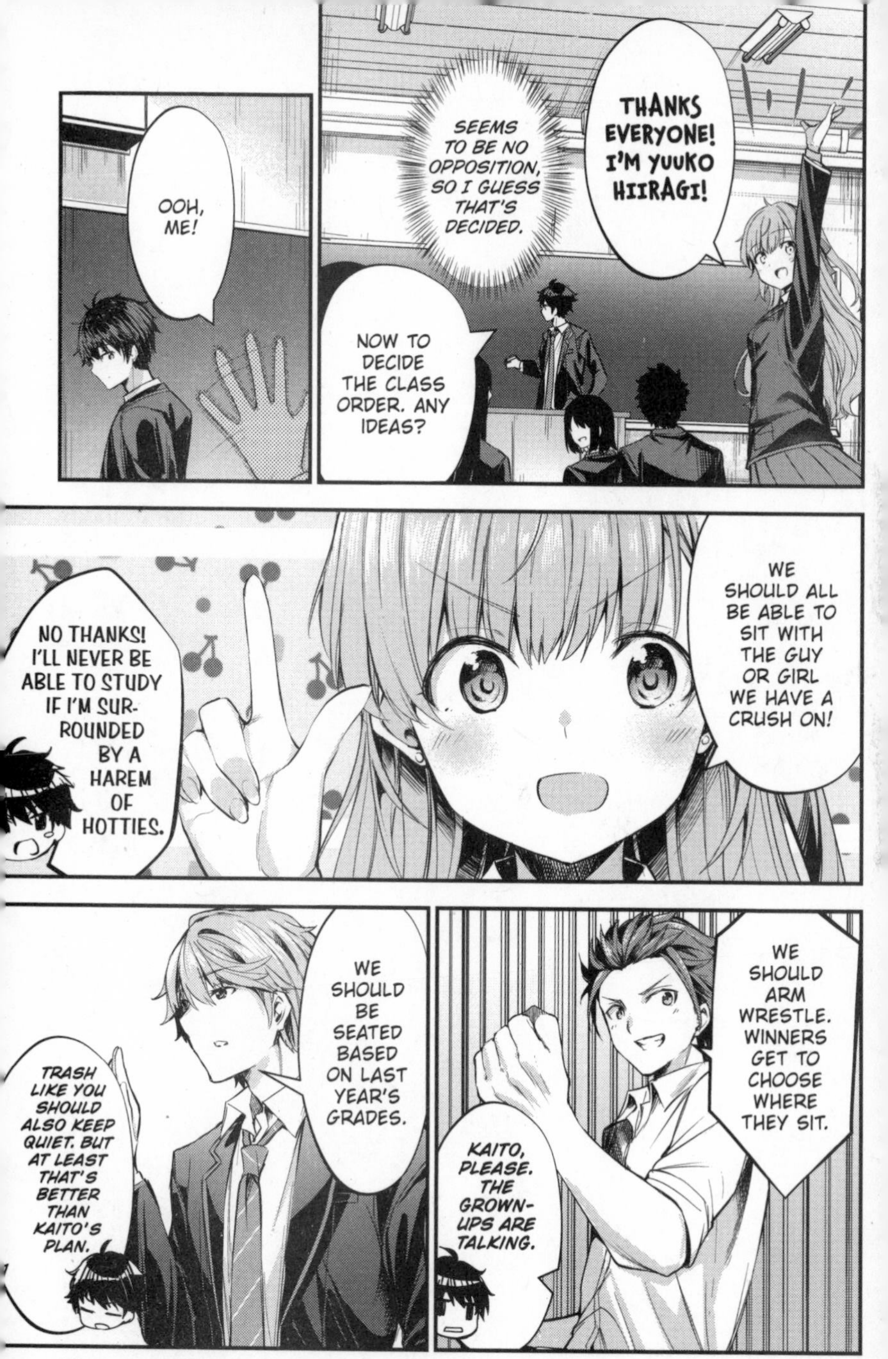
THANKS EVERYONE! I'M YUUKO HIIRAGI!
SEEMS TO BE NO OPPOSITION, SO I GUESS THAT'S DECIDED.
NOW TO DECIDE THE CLASS ORDER. ANY IDEAS?
OOH, ME!
WE SHOULD ALL BE ABLE TO SIT WITH THE GUY OR GIRL WE HAVE A CRUSH ON!
NO THANKS! I'LL NEVER BE ABLE TO STUDY IF I'M SURROUNDED BY A HAREM OF HOTTIES.
WE SHOULD ARM WRESTLE. WINNERS GET TO CHOOSE WHERE THEY SIT.
KAITO, PLEASE. THE GROWN-UPS ARE TALKING.
WE SHOULD BE SEATED BASED ON LAST YEAR'S GRADES.
TRASH LIKE YOU SHOULD ALSO KEEP QUIET. BUT AT LEAST THAT'S BETTER THAN KAITO'S PLAN.

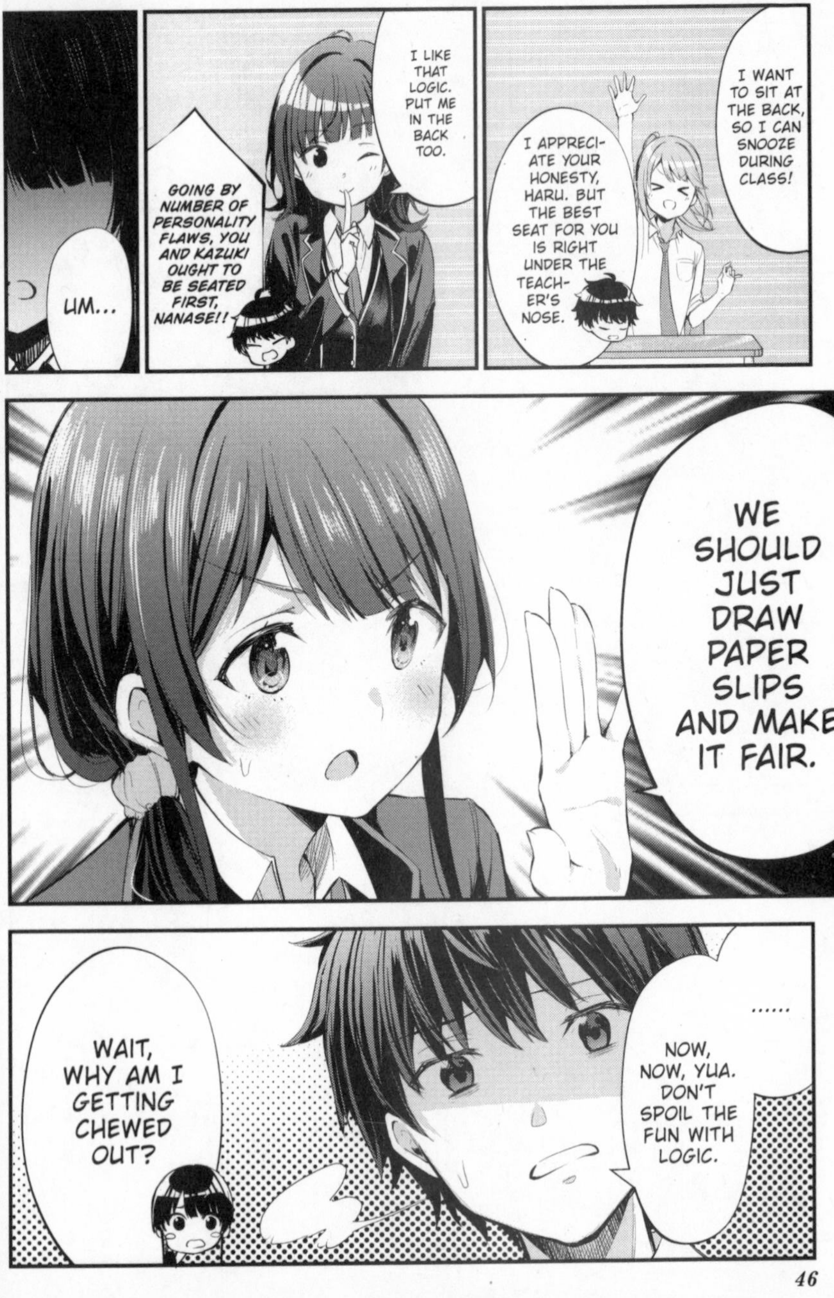
I WANT TO SIT AT THE BACK, SO I CAN SNOOZE DURING CLASS!
I APPRECI-ATE YOUR HONESTY, HARU. BUT THE BEST SEAT FOR YOU IS RIGHT UNDER THE TEACH-ER'S NOSE.
I LIKE THAT LOGIC. PUT ME IN THE BACK TOO.
GOING BY NUMBER OF PERSONALITY FLAWS, YOU AND KAZUKI OUGHT TO BE SEATED FIRST, NANASE!!
UM...
WE SHOULD JUST DRAW PAPER SLIPS AND MAKE IT FAIR.
......
NOW, NOW, YUA. DON'T SPOIL THE FUN WITH LOGIC.
WAIT, WHY AM I GETTING CHEWED OUT?

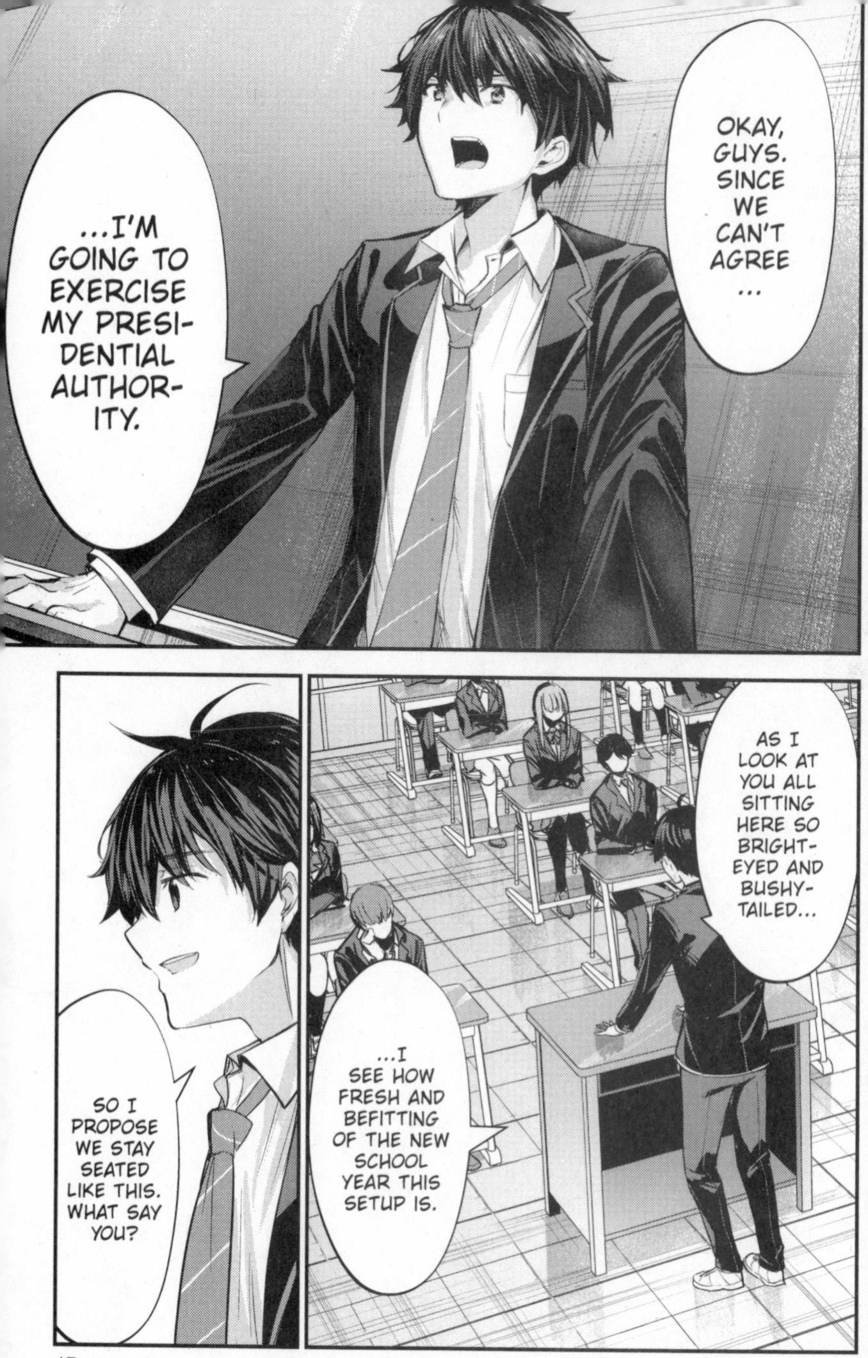
OKAY, GUYS. SINCE WE CAN'T AGREE...
...I'M GOING TO EXERCISE MY PRESIDENTIAL AUTHORITY.
AS I LOOK AT YOU ALL SITTING HERE SO BRIGHT-EYED AND BUSHY-TAILED...
...I SEE HOW FRESH AND BEFITTING OF THE NEW SCHOOL YEAR THIS SETUP IS.
SO I PROPOSE WE STAY SEATED LIKE THIS. WHAT SAY YOU?

FOR ANY ISSUES, LIKE NOT BEING ABLE TO SEE THE BOARD FROM THE BACK...

...COME TALK TO ME AND WE CAN DISCUSS IT, OKAY?

ALL RIGHT, SO EVERYONE SEEMS TO BE ON BOARD. THEN LET'S STAY LIKE THIS.

LET'S HAVE A GOOD YEAR.

WHAT A LAME ENDING. WHAT HAPPENED TO THE HUMOR?

AH, I'LL ALSO AGREE TO SEATING CHANGES IF THE SIGHT OF KURA-SEN PUTS YOU OFF YOUR SCHOOL-WORK.

48

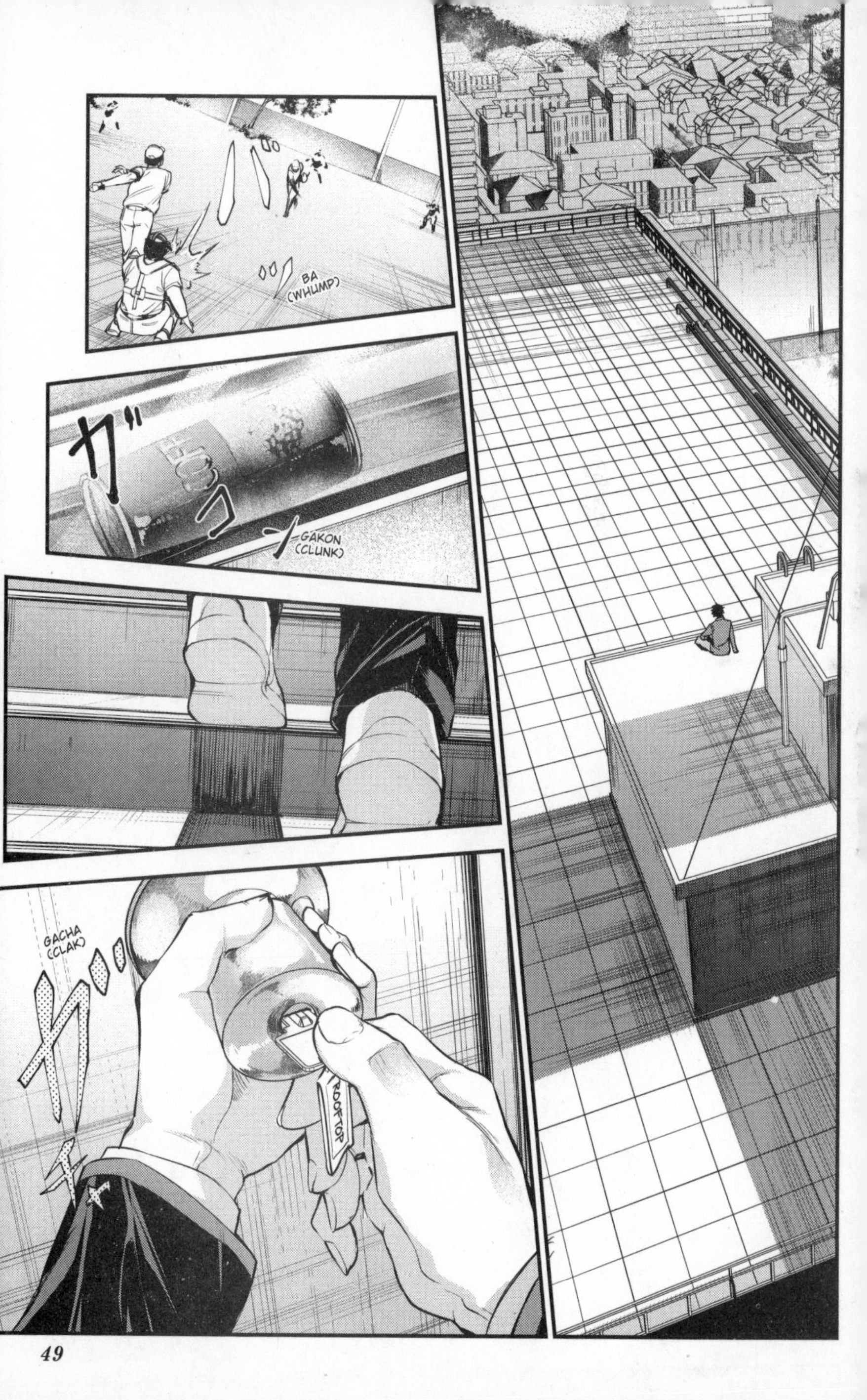
BA (WHUMP)
GAKON (CLUNK)
GACHA (CLAK)
ROOFTOP

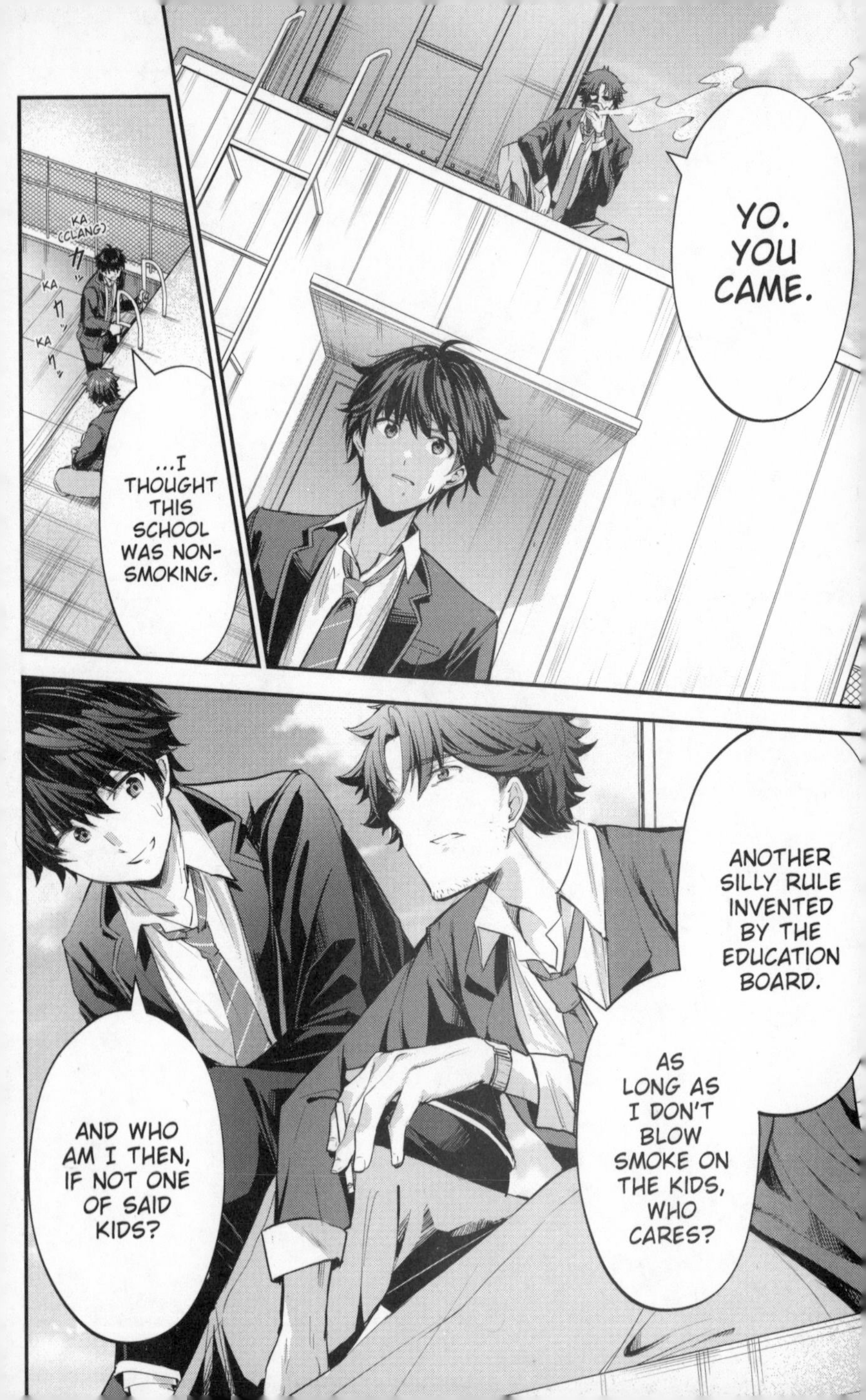
YO. YOU CAME.
KA (CLANG)
KA
KA
...I THOUGHT THIS SCHOOL WAS NON-SMOKING.
ANOTHER SILLY RULE INVENTED BY THE EDUCATION BOARD.
AS LONG AS I DON'T BLOW SMOKE ON THE KIDS, WHO CARES?
AND WHO AM I THEN, IF NOT ONE OF SAID KIDS?

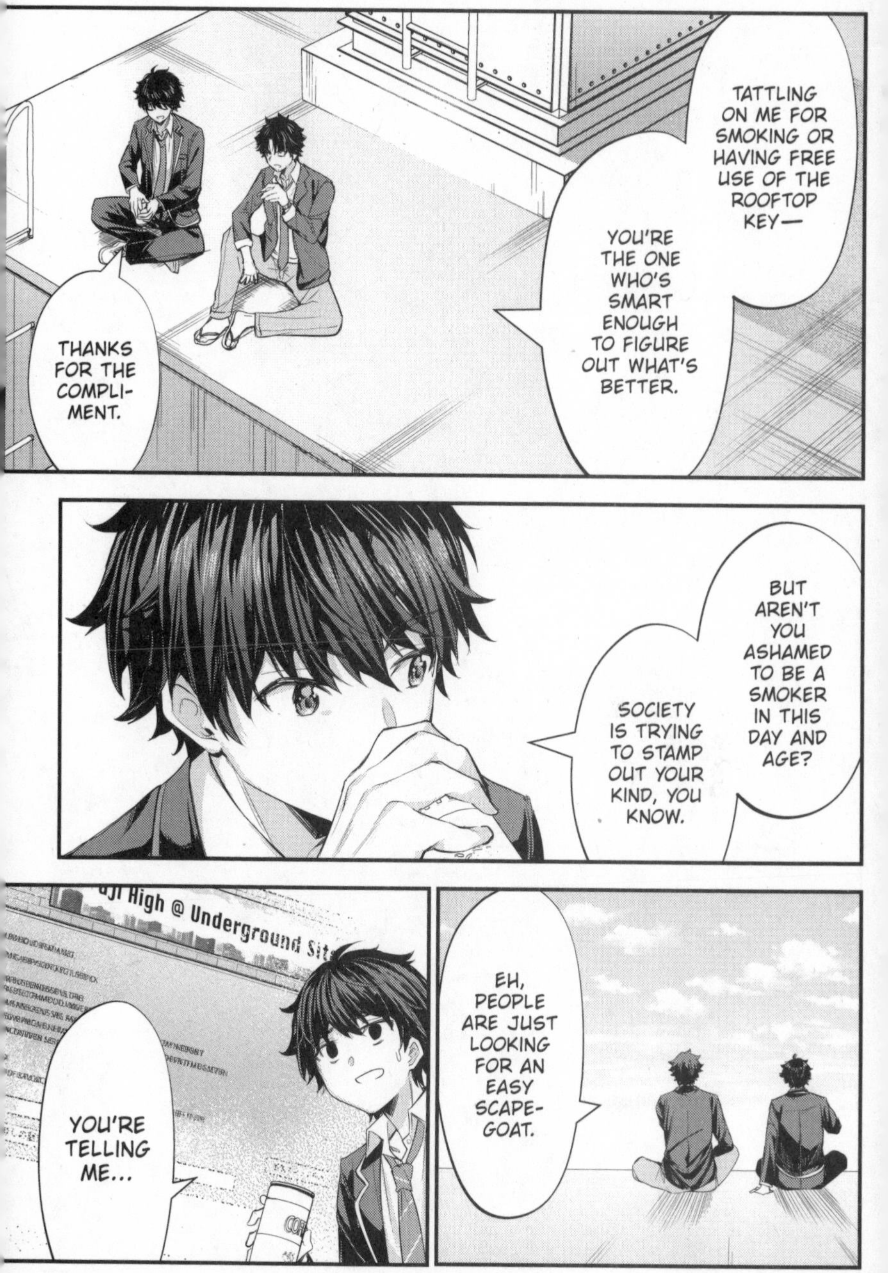
TATTLING ON ME FOR SMOKING OR HAVING FREE USE OF THE ROOFTOP KEY—
YOU'RE THE ONE WHO'S SMART ENOUGH TO FIGURE OUT WHAT'S BETTER.
THANKS FOR THE COMPLIMENT.
BUT AREN'T YOU ASHAMED TO BE A SMOKER IN THIS DAY AND AGE?
SOCIETY IS TRYING TO STAMP OUT YOUR KIND, YOU KNOW.
EH, PEOPLE ARE JUST LOOKING FOR AN EASY SCAPE-GOAT.
YOU'RE TELLING ME...

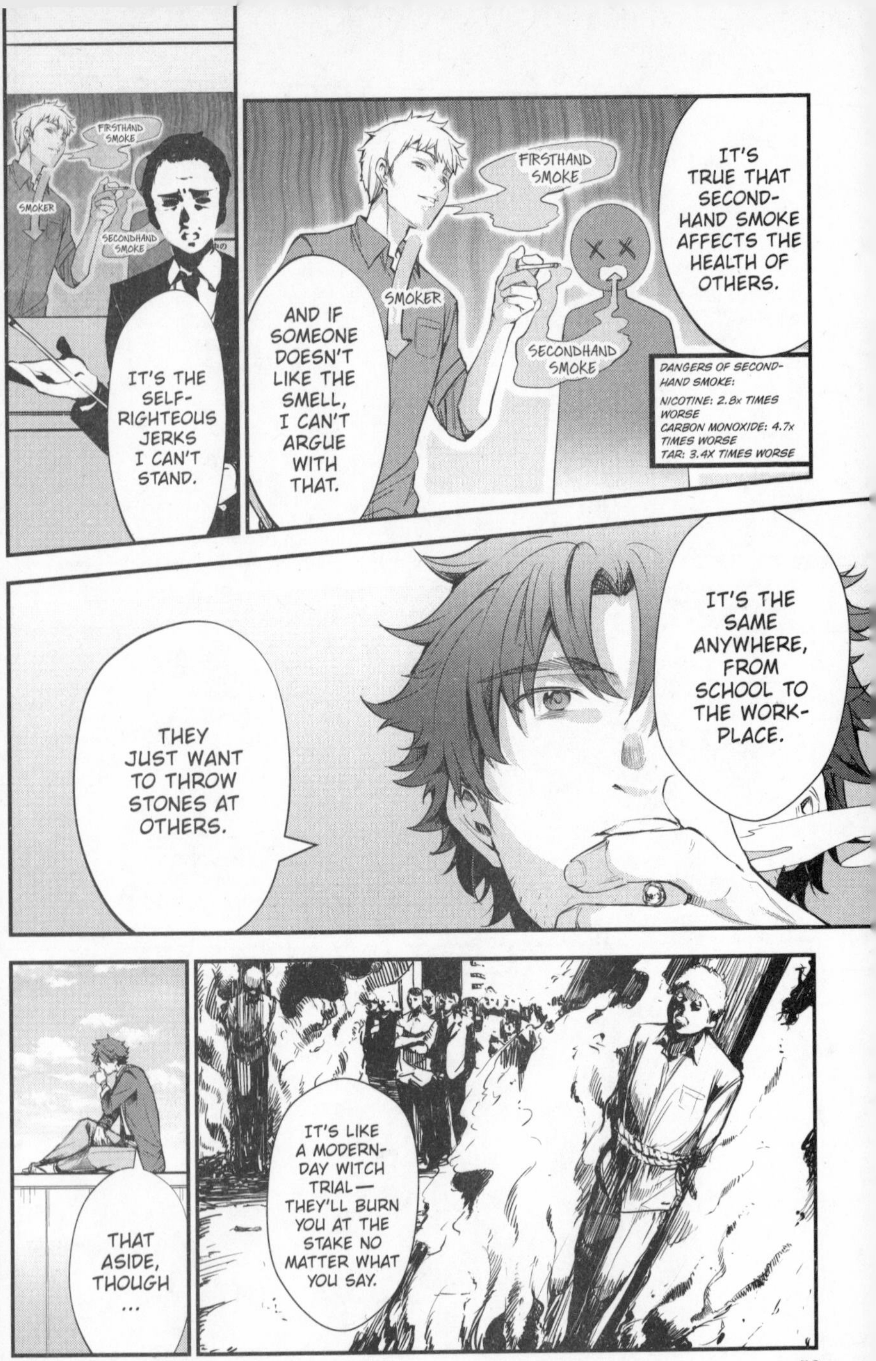
IT'S TRUE THAT SECOND-HAND SMOKE AFFECTS THE HEALTH OF OTHERS.
FIRSTHAND SMOKE
SMOKER
SECONDHAND SMOKE
DANGERS OF SECOND-HAND SMOKE: NICOTINE: 2.8x TIMES WORSE CARBON MONOXIDE: 4.7x TIMES WORSE TAR: 3.4X TIMES WORSE
AND IF SOMEONE DOESN'T LIKE THE SMELL, I CAN'T ARGUE WITH THAT.
FIRSTHAND SMOKE
SMOKER
SECONDHAND SMOKE
IT'S THE SELF-RIGHTEOUS JERKS I CAN'T STAND.
IT'S THE SAME ANYWHERE, FROM SCHOOL TO THE WORK-PLACE.
THEY JUST WANT TO THROW STONES AT OTHERS.
IT'S LIKE A MODERN-DAY WITCH TRIAL— THEY'LL BURN YOU AT THE STAKE NO MATTER WHAT YOU SAY.
THAT ASIDE, THOUGH...

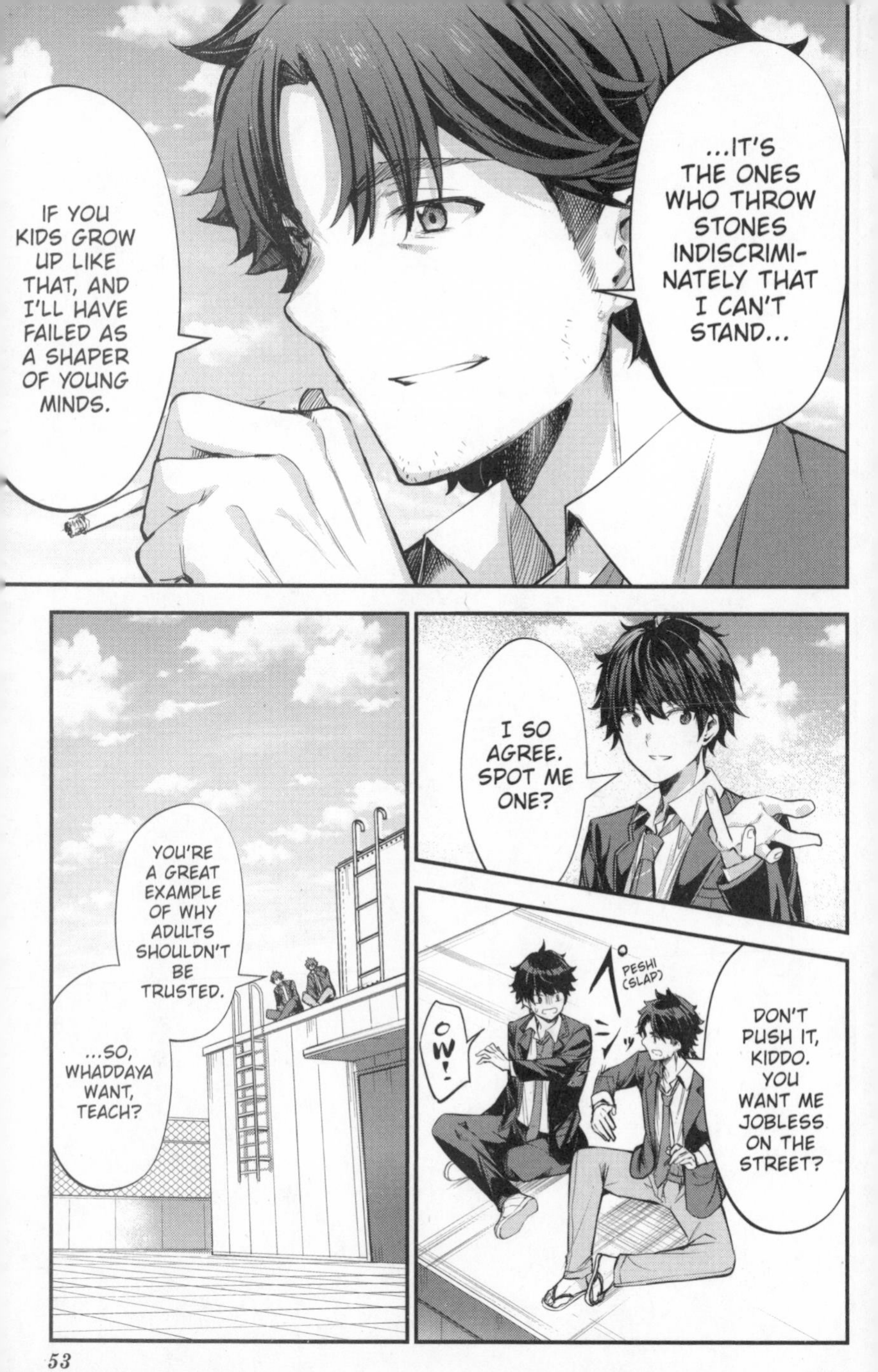
...IT'S THE ONES WHO THROW STONES INDISCRIMI-NATELY THAT I CAN'T STAND...
IF YOU KIDS GROW UP LIKE THAT, AND I'LL HAVE FAILED AS A SHAPER OF YOUNG MINDS.
I SO AGREE. SPOT ME ONE?
PESHI (SLAP)
DON'T PUSH IT, KIDDO. YOU WANT ME JOBLESS ON THE STREET?
OW!
YOU'RE A GREAT EXAMPLE OF WHY ADULTS SHOULDN'T BE TRUSTED.
...SO, WHADDAYA WANT, TEACH?

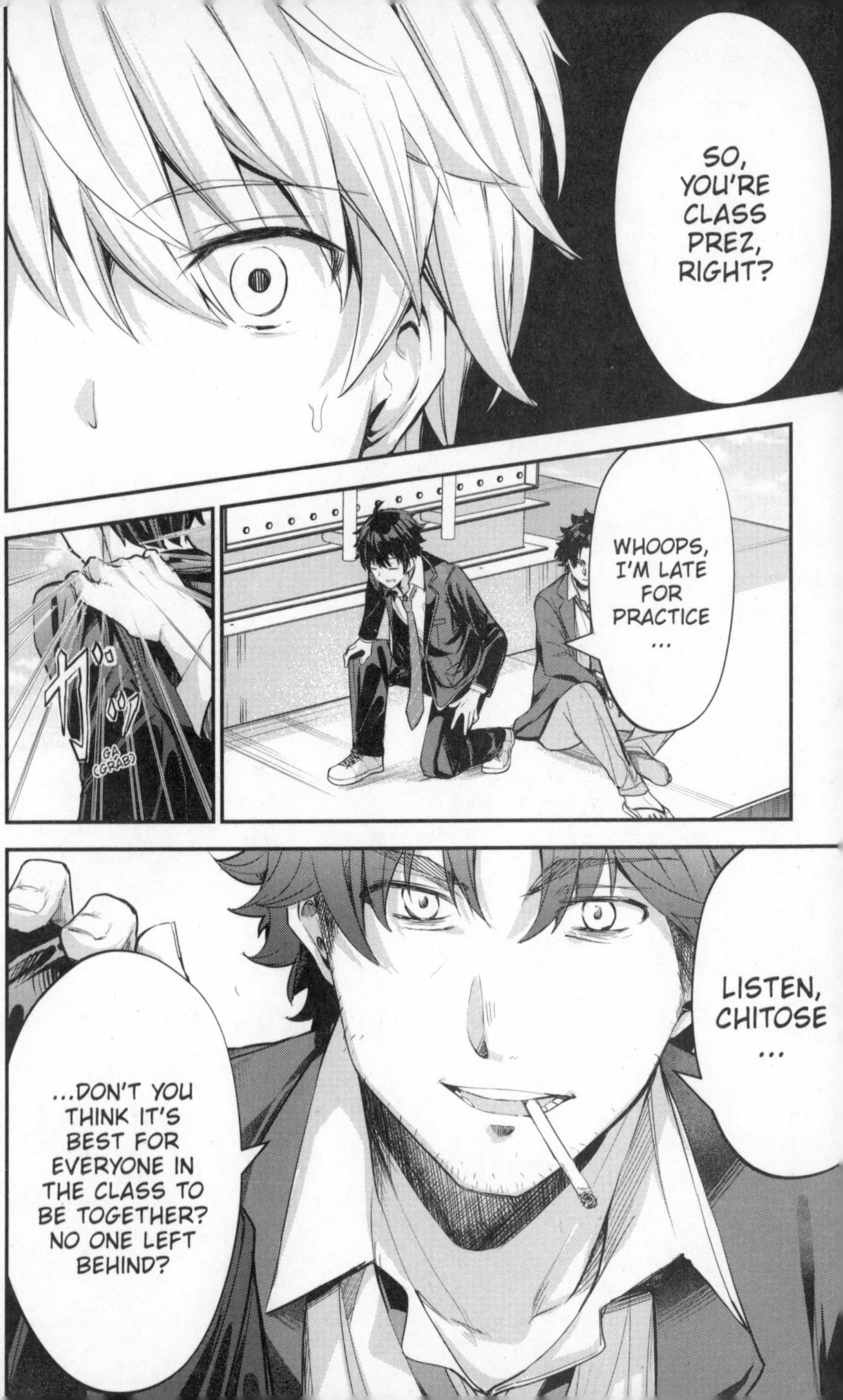
SO, YOU'RE CLASS PREZ, RIGHT?
WHOOPS, I'M LATE FOR PRACTICE ...
GA (GRAB)
LISTEN, CHITOSE ...
...DON'T YOU THINK IT'S BEST FOR EVERYONE IN THE CLASS TO BE TOGETHER? NO ONE LEFT BEHIND?

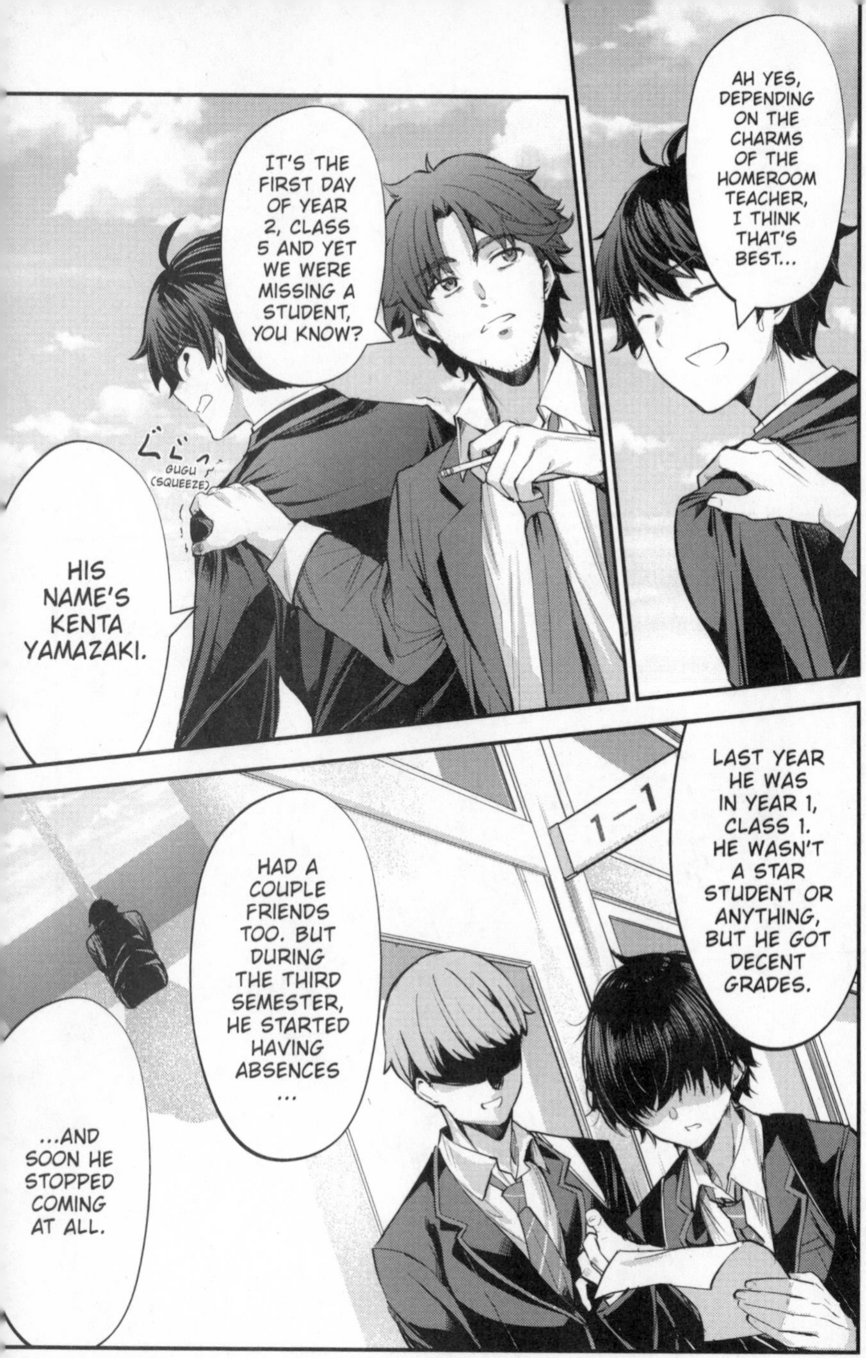
AH YES, DEPENDING ON THE CHARMS OF THE HOMEROOM TEACHER, I THINK THAT'S BEST...
IT'S THE FIRST DAY OF YEAR 2, CLASS 5 AND YET WE WERE MISSING A STUDENT, YOU KNOW?
ぐぐっ
GUGU (SQUEEZE)
HIS NAME'S KENTA YAMAZAKI.
LAST YEAR HE WAS IN YEAR 1, CLASS 1. HE WASN'T A STAR STUDENT OR ANYTHING, BUT HE GOT DECENT GRADES.
1—1
HAD A COUPLE FRIENDS TOO. BUT DURING THE THIRD SEMESTER, HE STARTED HAVING ABSENCES...
...AND SOON HE STOPPED COMING AT ALL.

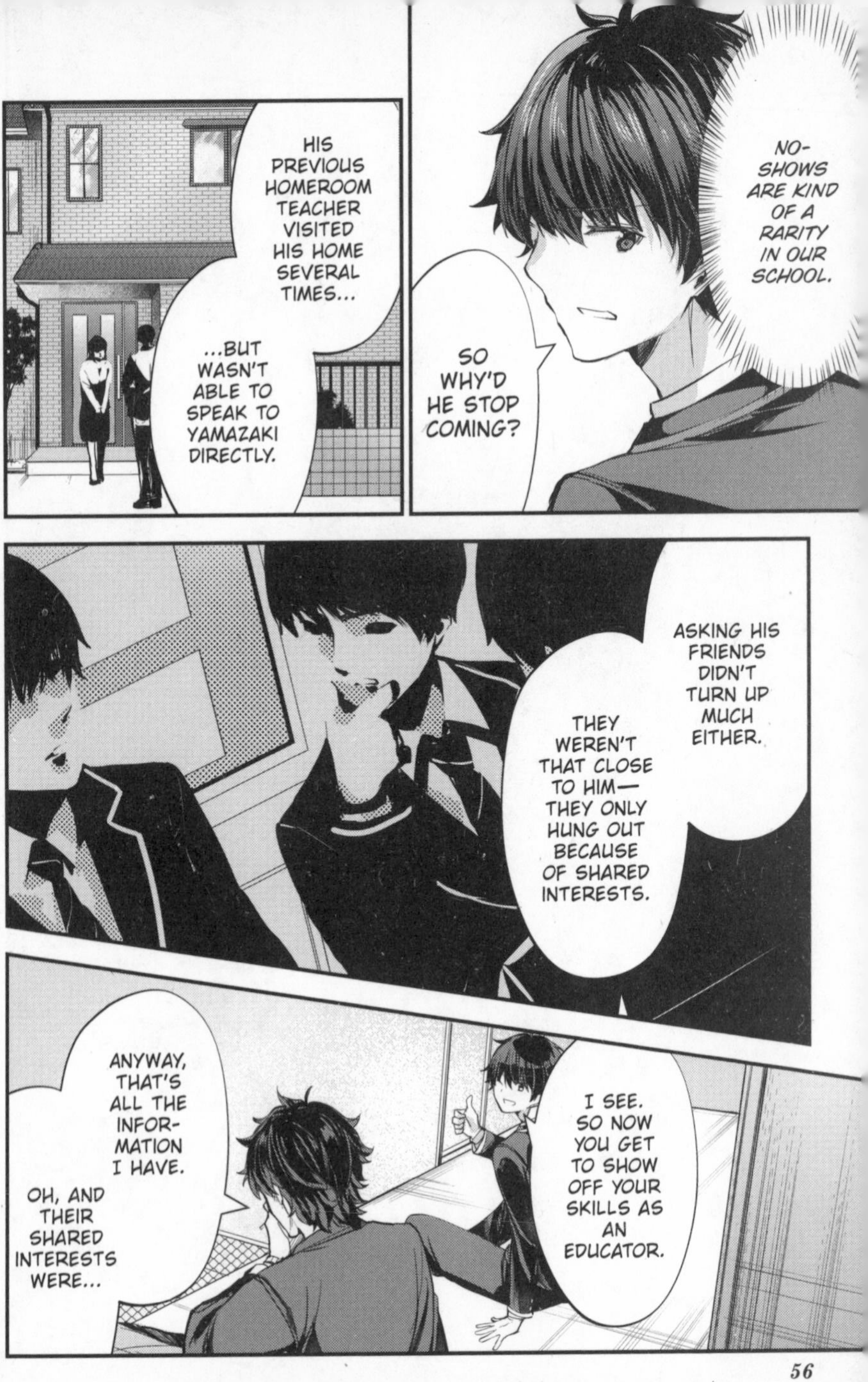
NO-SHOWS ARE KIND OF A RARITY IN OUR SCHOOL.
SO WHY'D HE STOP COMING?
HIS PREVIOUS HOMEROOM TEACHER VISITED HIS HOME SEVERAL TIMES...
...BUT WASN'T ABLE TO SPEAK TO YAMAZAKI DIRECTLY.
ASKING HIS FRIENDS DIDN'T TURN UP MUCH EITHER.
THEY WEREN'T THAT CLOSE TO HIM—THEY ONLY HUNG OUT BECAUSE OF SHARED INTERESTS.
I SEE. SO NOW YOU GET TO SHOW OFF YOUR SKILLS AS AN EDUCATOR.
ANYWAY, THAT'S ALL THE INFOR-MATION I HAVE.
OH, AND THEIR SHARED INTERESTS WERE...

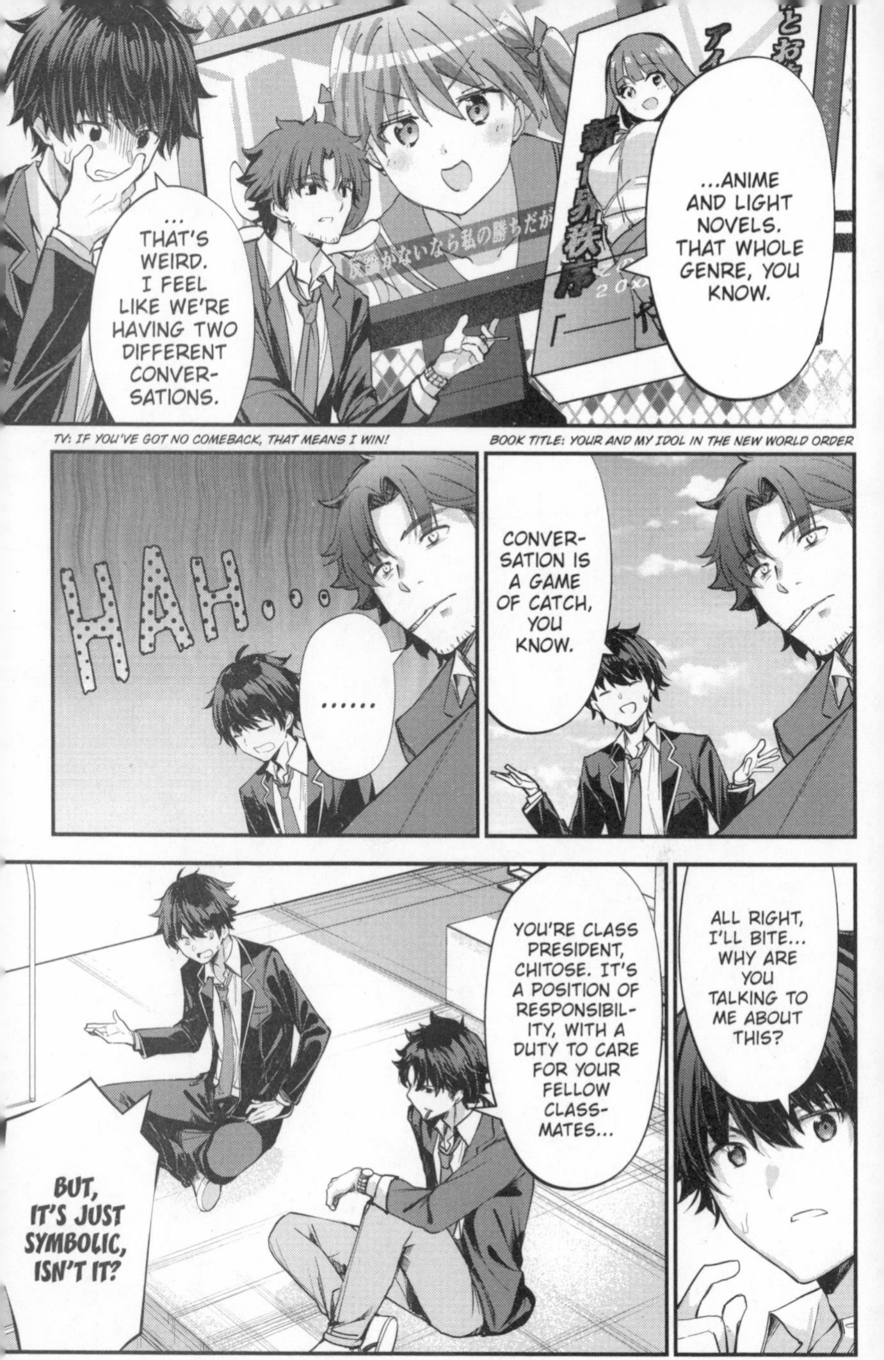

...ANIME AND LIGHT NOVELS. THAT WHOLE GENRE, YOU KNOW.
... THAT'S WEIRD. I FEEL LIKE WE'RE HAVING TWO DIFFERENT CONVER-SATIONS.
BOOK TITLE: YOUR AND MY IDOL IN THE NEW WORLD ORDER
TV: IF YOU'VE GOT NO COMEBACK, THAT MEANS I WIN!
CONVER-SATION IS A GAME OF CATCH, YOU KNOW.
HAH...
......
ALL RIGHT, I'LL BITE... WHY ARE YOU TALKING TO ME ABOUT THIS?
YOU'RE CLASS PRESIDENT, CHITOSE. IT'S A POSITION OF RESPONSIBIL-ITY, WITH A DUTY TO CARE FOR YOUR FELLOW CLASS-MATES...
BUT, IT'S JUST SYMBOLIC, ISN'T IT?

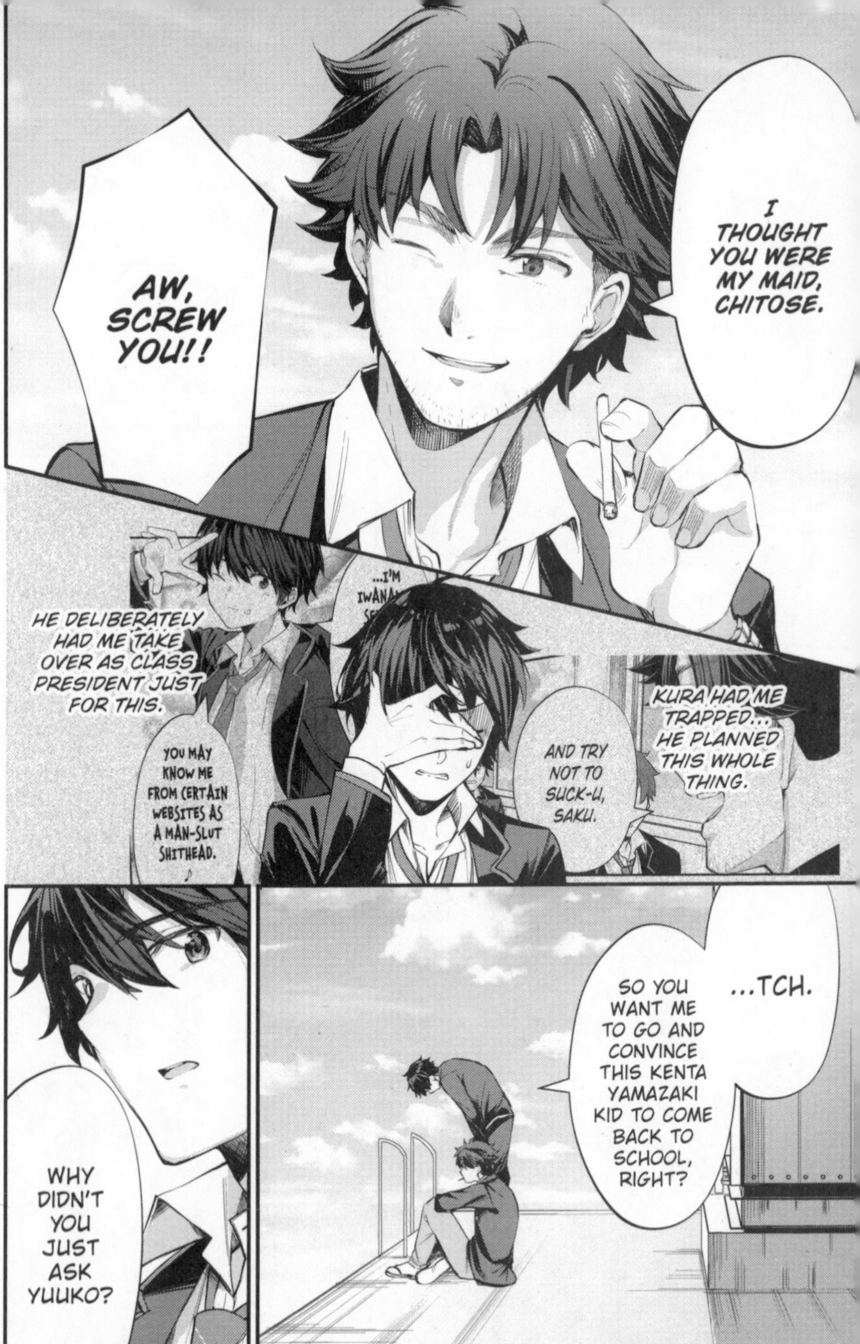
I THOUGHT YOU WERE MY MAID, CHITOSE.
AW, SCREW YOU!!
KURA HAD ME TRAPPED... HE PLANNED THIS WHOLE THING.
AND TRY NOT TO SUCK-U, SAKU.
YOU MAY KNOW ME FROM CERTAIN WEBSITES AS A MAN-SLUT SHITHEAD. ♪
HE DELIBERATELY HAD ME TAKE OVER AS CLASS PRESIDENT JUST FOR THIS.
...TCH.
SO YOU WANT ME TO GO AND CONVINCE THIS KENTA YAMAZAKI KID TO COME BACK TO SCHOOL, RIGHT?
WHY DIDN'T YOU JUST ASK YUUKO?

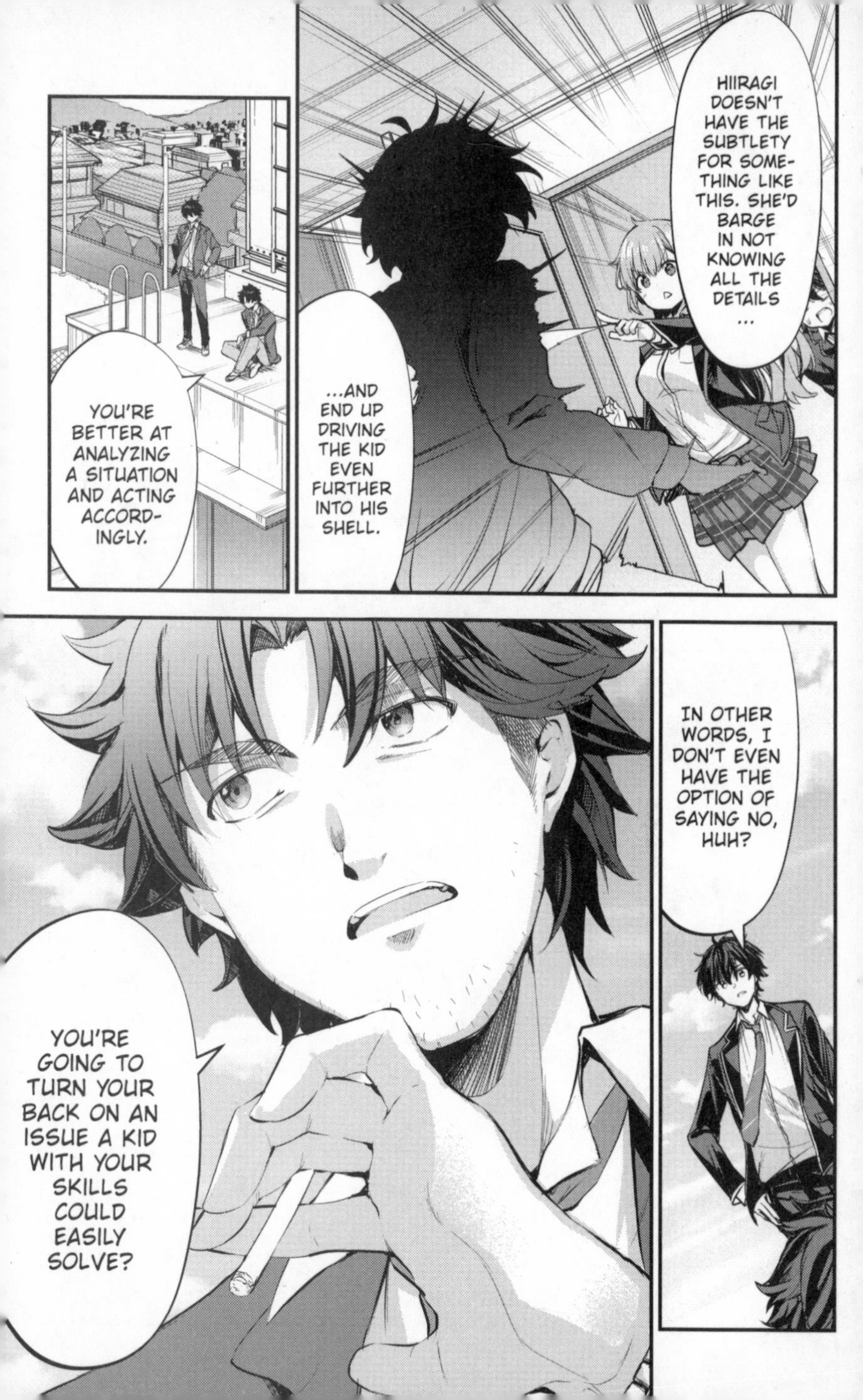
HIIRAGI DOESN'T HAVE THE SUBTLETY FOR SOME-THING LIKE THIS. SHE'D BARGE IN NOT KNOWING ALL THE DETAILS ...
...AND END UP DRIVING THE KID EVEN FURTHER INTO HIS SHELL.
YOU'RE BETTER AT ANALYZING A SITUATION AND ACTING ACCORD-INGLY.
IN OTHER WORDS, I DON'T EVEN HAVE THE OPTION OF SAYING NO, HUH?
YOU'RE GOING TO TURN YOUR BACK ON AN ISSUE A KID WITH YOUR SKILLS COULD EASILY SOLVE?

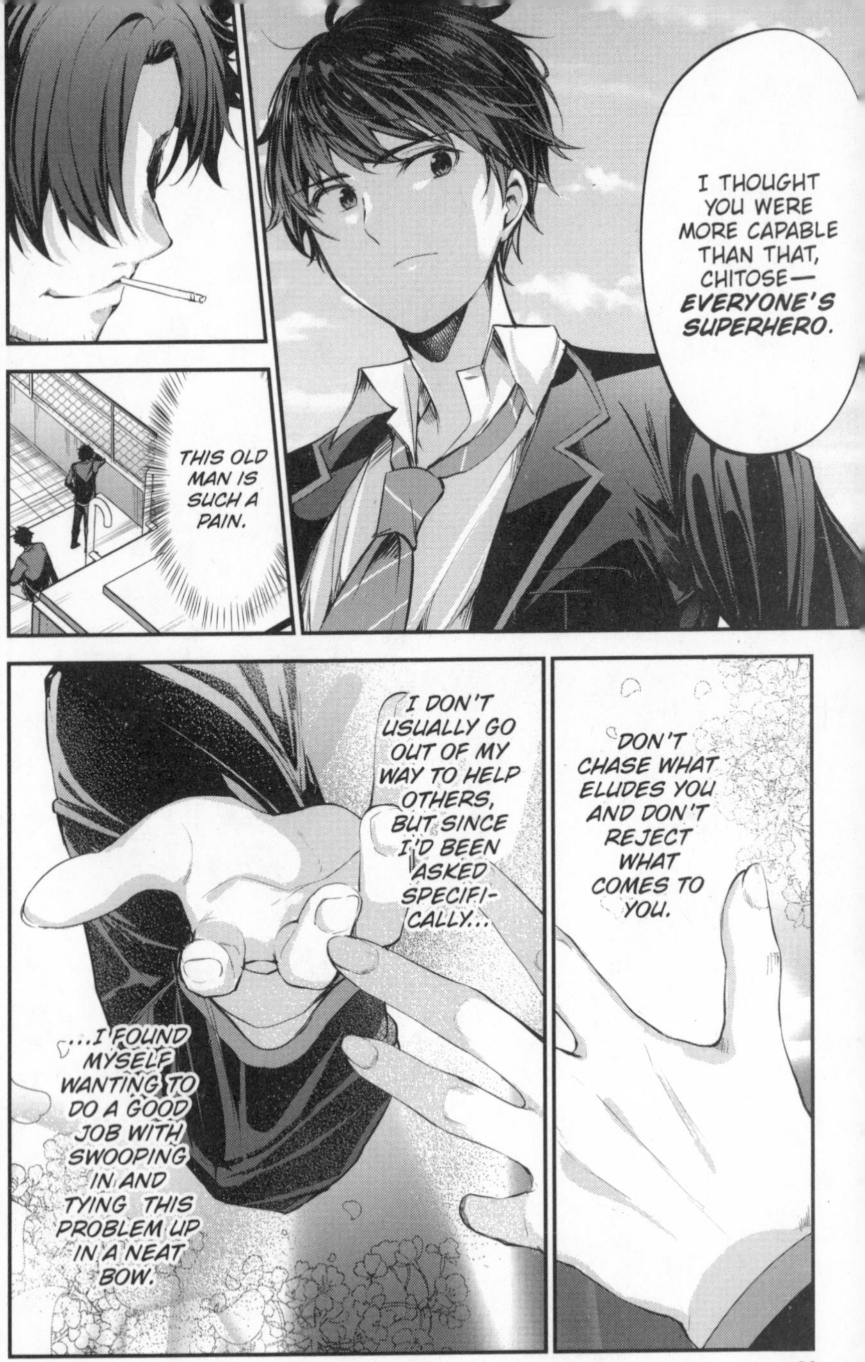
I THOUGHT YOU WERE MORE CAPABLE THAN THAT, CHITOSE—**EVERYONE'S SUPERHERO.**
THIS OLD MAN IS SUCH A PAIN.
DON'T CHASE WHAT ELUDES YOU AND DON'T REJECT WHAT COMES TO YOU.
I DON'T USUALLY GO OUT OF MY WAY TO HELP OTHERS, BUT SINCE I'D BEEN ASKED SPECIFI-CALLY...
...I FOUND MYSELF WANTING TO DO A GOOD JOB WITH SWOOPING IN AND TYING THIS PROBLEM UP IN A NEAT BOW.

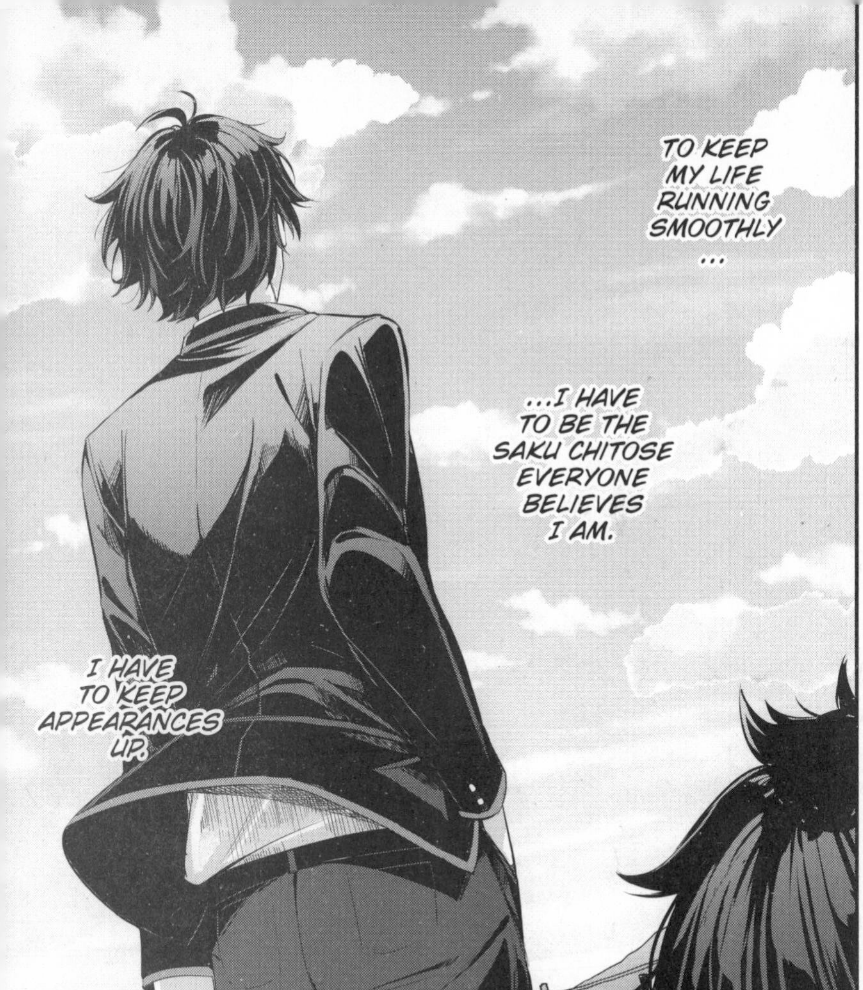
TO KEEP MY LIFE RUNNING SMOOTHLY ...
...I HAVE TO BE THE SAKU CHITOSE EVERYONE BELIEVES I AM.
I HAVE TO KEEP APPEARANCES UP.

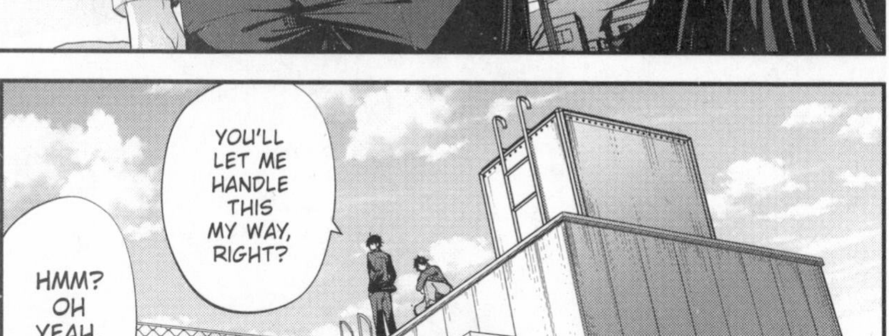
YOU'LL LET ME HANDLE THIS MY WAY, RIGHT?
HMM? OH YEAH.

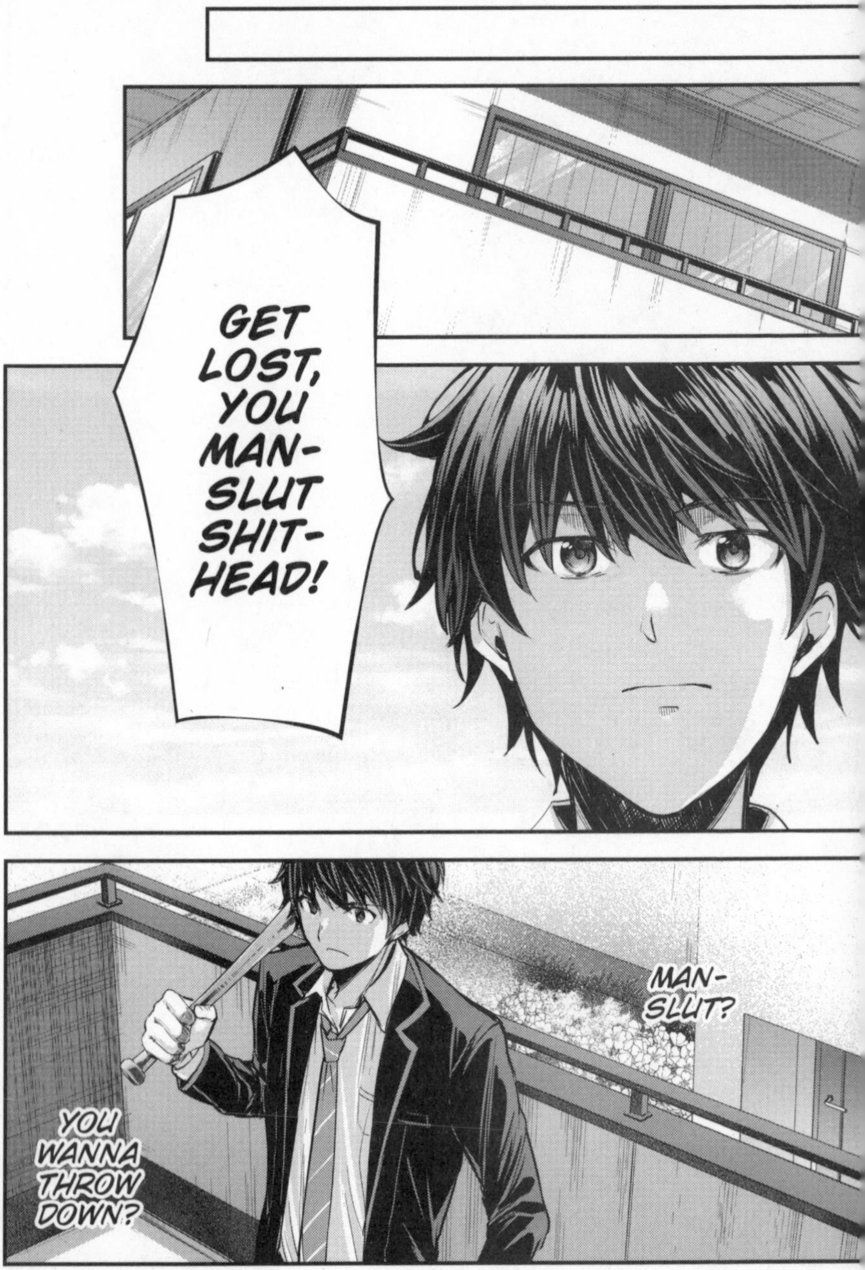
GET LOST, YOU MAN-SLUT SHIT-HEAD!
MAN-SLUT?
YOU WANNA THROW DOWN?

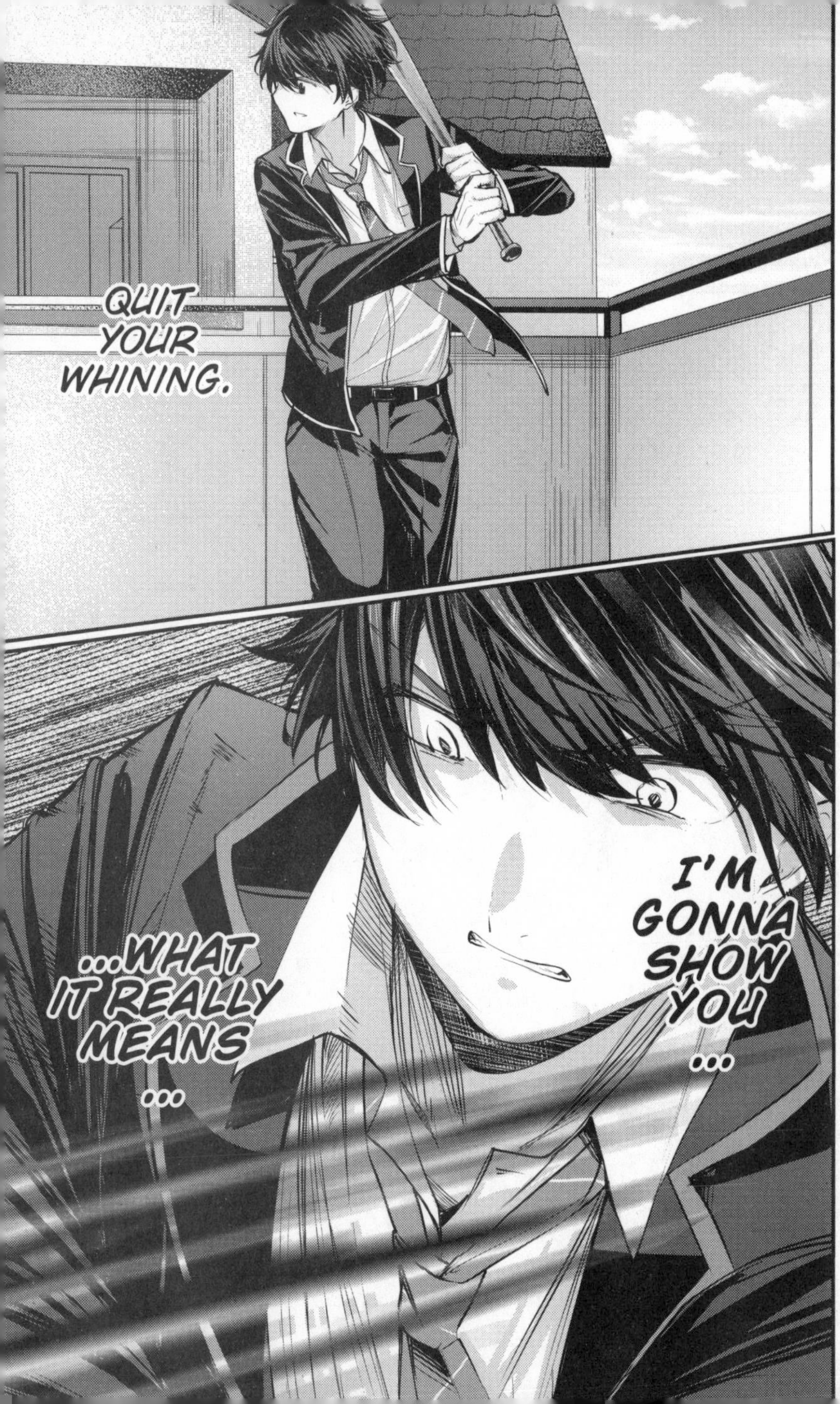
QUIT YOUR WHINING.
I'M GONNA SHOW YOU ...
...WHAT IT REALLY MEANS ...

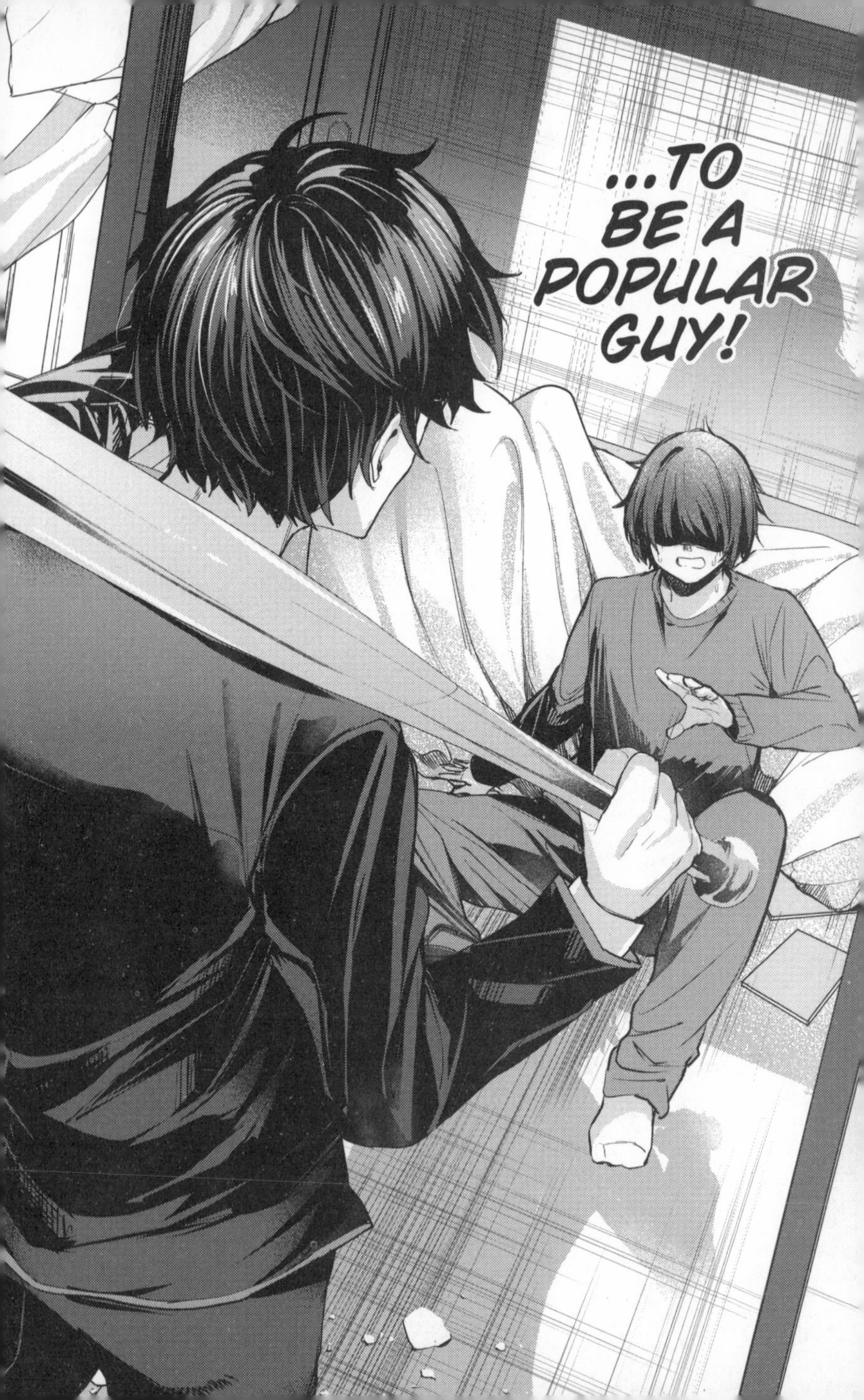
...TO BE A POPULAR GUY!

CHARACTER PROFILE

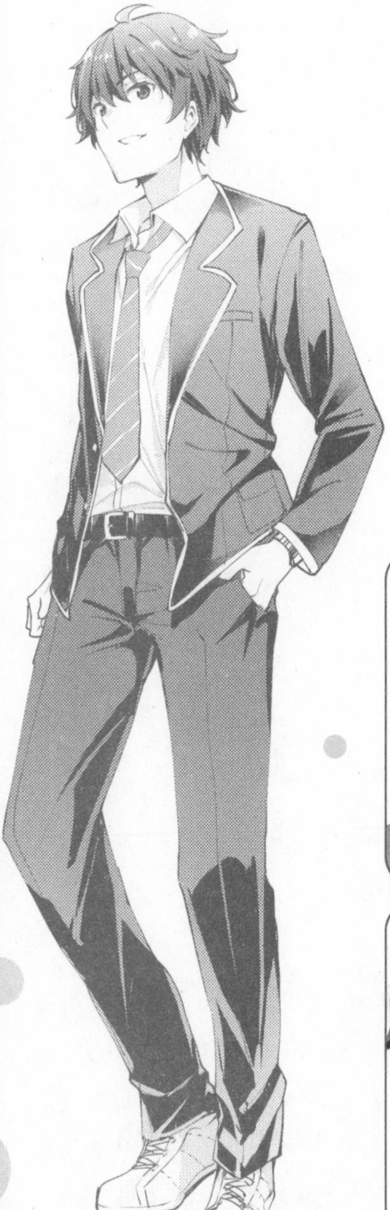

Saku Chitose

Age: 16 years old

Height: 5’9” (175 cm)

School Club: Going Home Club (formerly baseball)

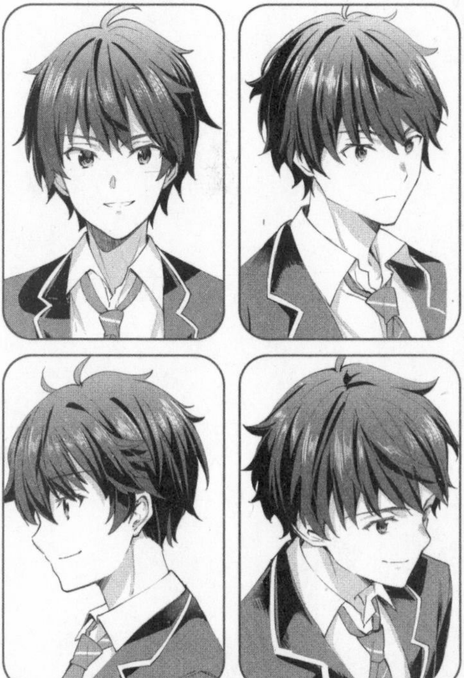

Chitose Is in the Ramune Bottle

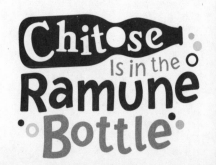

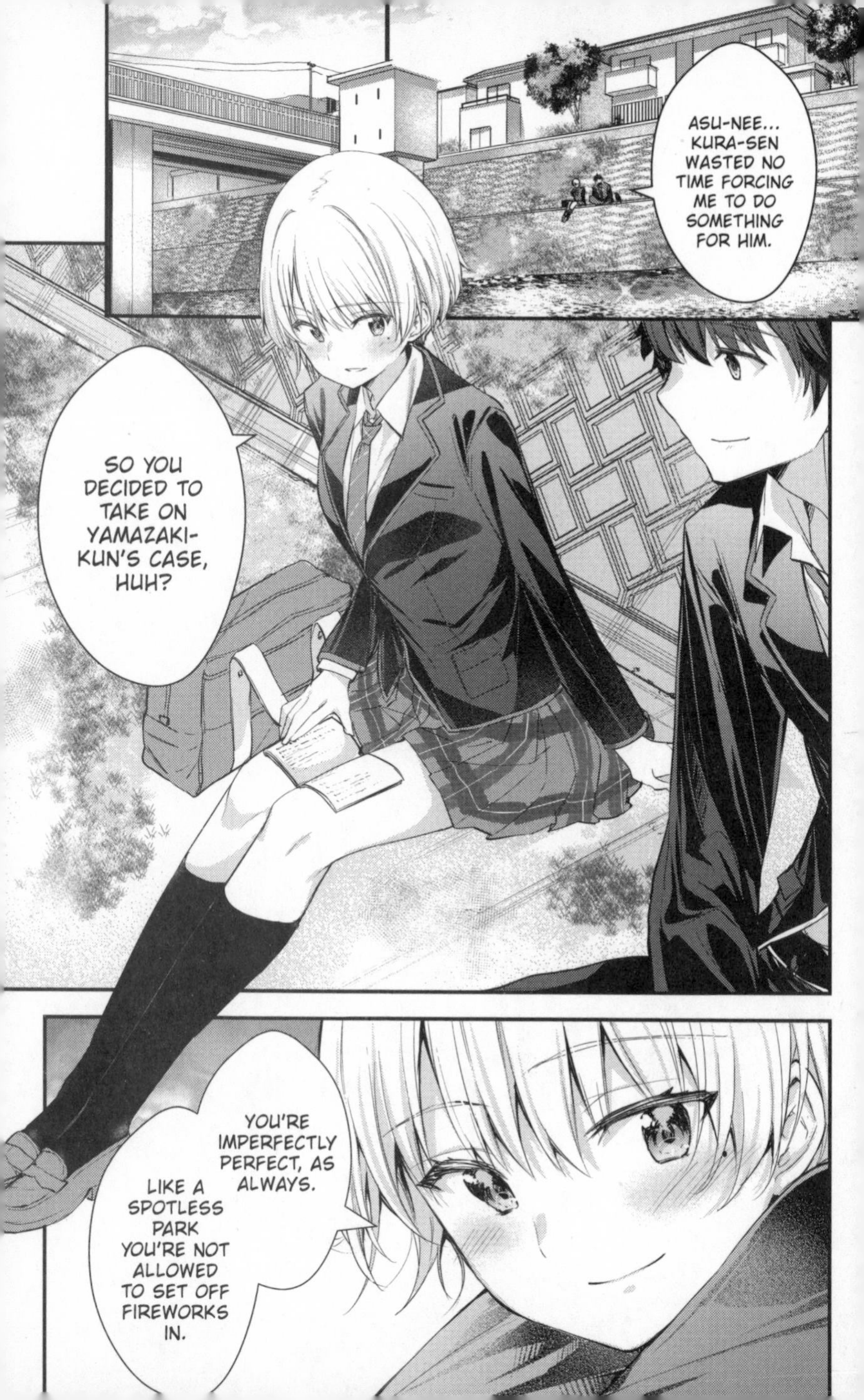
ASU-NEE... KURA-SEN WASTED NO TIME FORCING ME TO DO SOMETHING FOR HIM.
SO YOU DECIDED TO TAKE ON YAMAZAKI-KUN'S CASE, HUH?
YOU'RE IMPERFECTLY PERFECT, AS ALWAYS.
LIKE A SPOTLESS PARK YOU'RE NOT ALLOWED TO SET OFF FIREWORKS IN.

STORY 2: AFTER SCHOOL

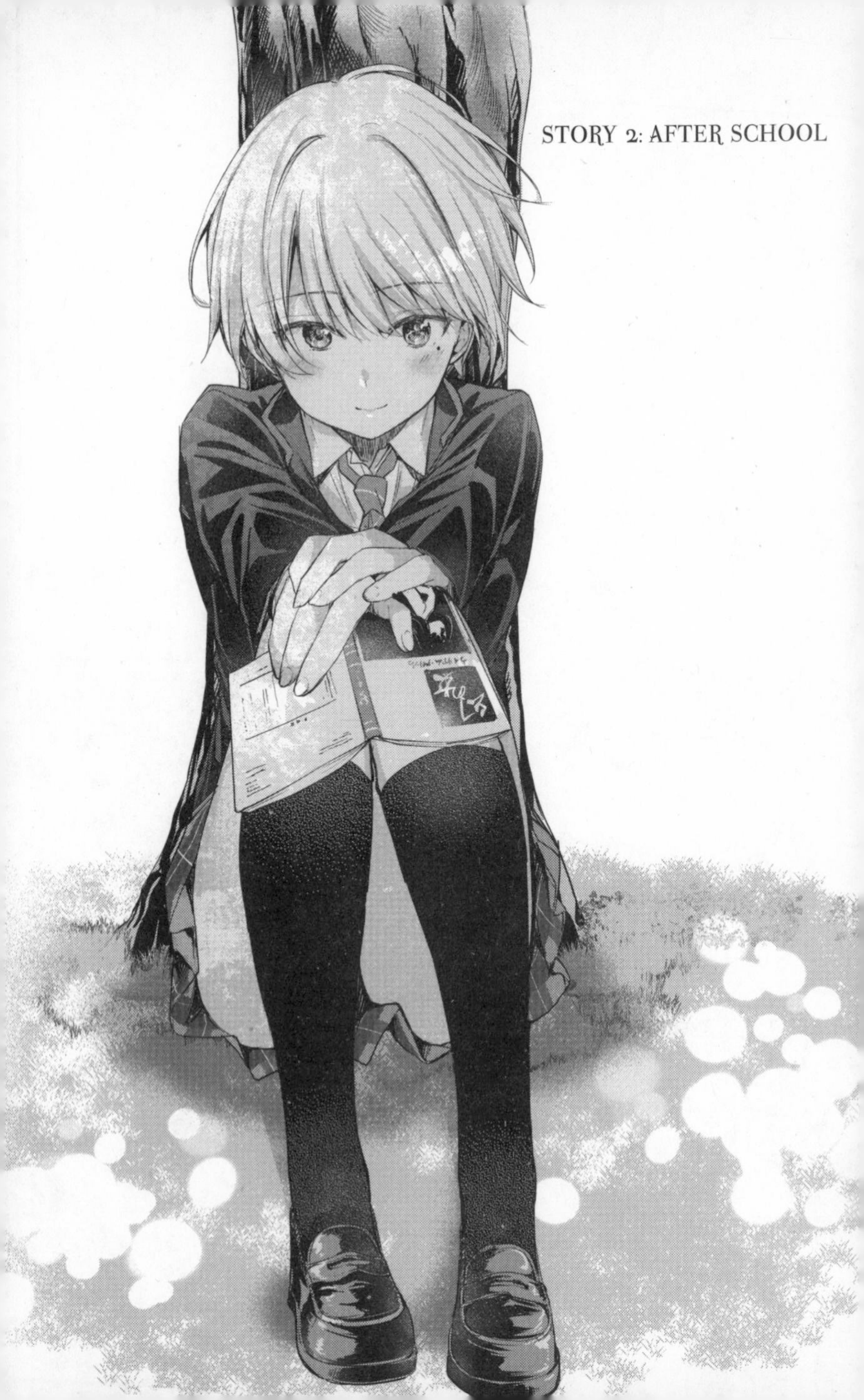

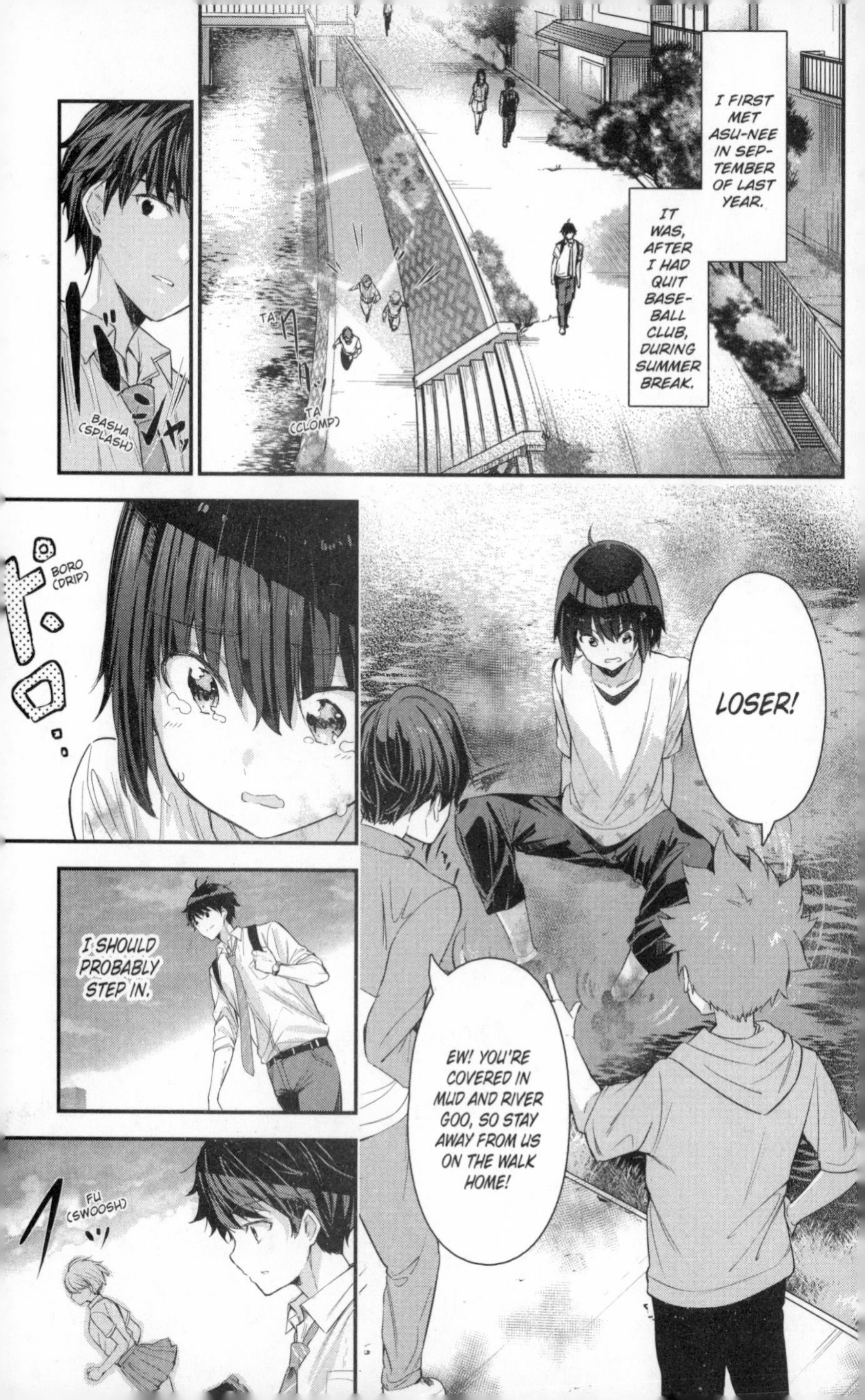
I FIRST MET ASU-NEE IN SEPTEMBER OF LAST YEAR.
IT WAS, AFTER I HAD QUIT BASEBALL CLUB, DURING SUMMER BREAK.
TA
TA (CLOMP)
BASHA (SPLASH)
LOSER!
EW! YOU'RE COVERED IN MUD AND RIVER GOO, SO STAY AWAY FROM US ON THE WALK HOME!
BORO (DRIP)
I SHOULD PROBABLY STEP IN.
FU (SWOOSH)

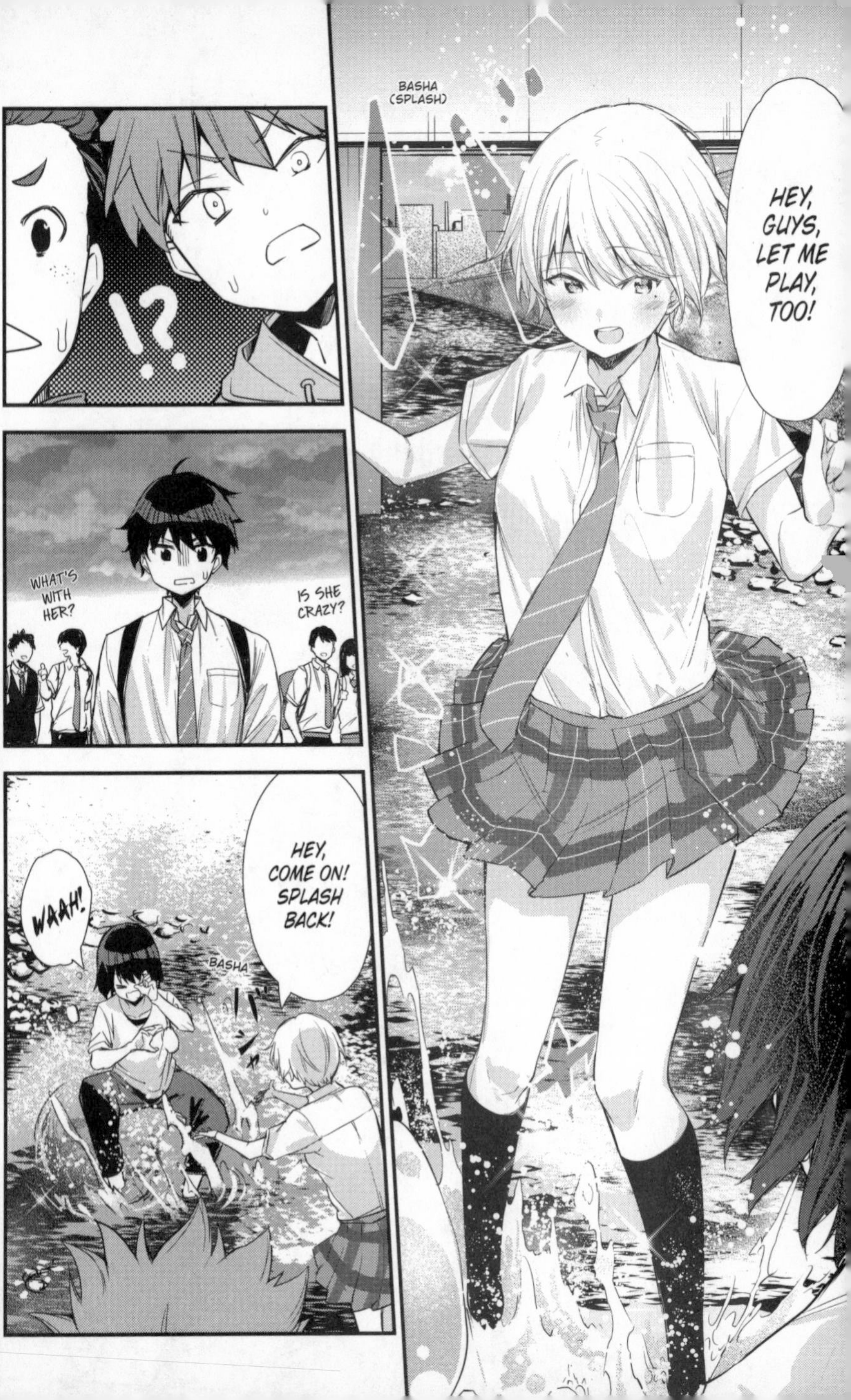
HEY, GUYS, LET ME PLAY, TOO!
BASHA (SPLASH)
!?
IS SHE CRAZY?
WHAT'S WITH HER?
HEY, COME ON! SPLASH BACK!
BASHA
WAAH!

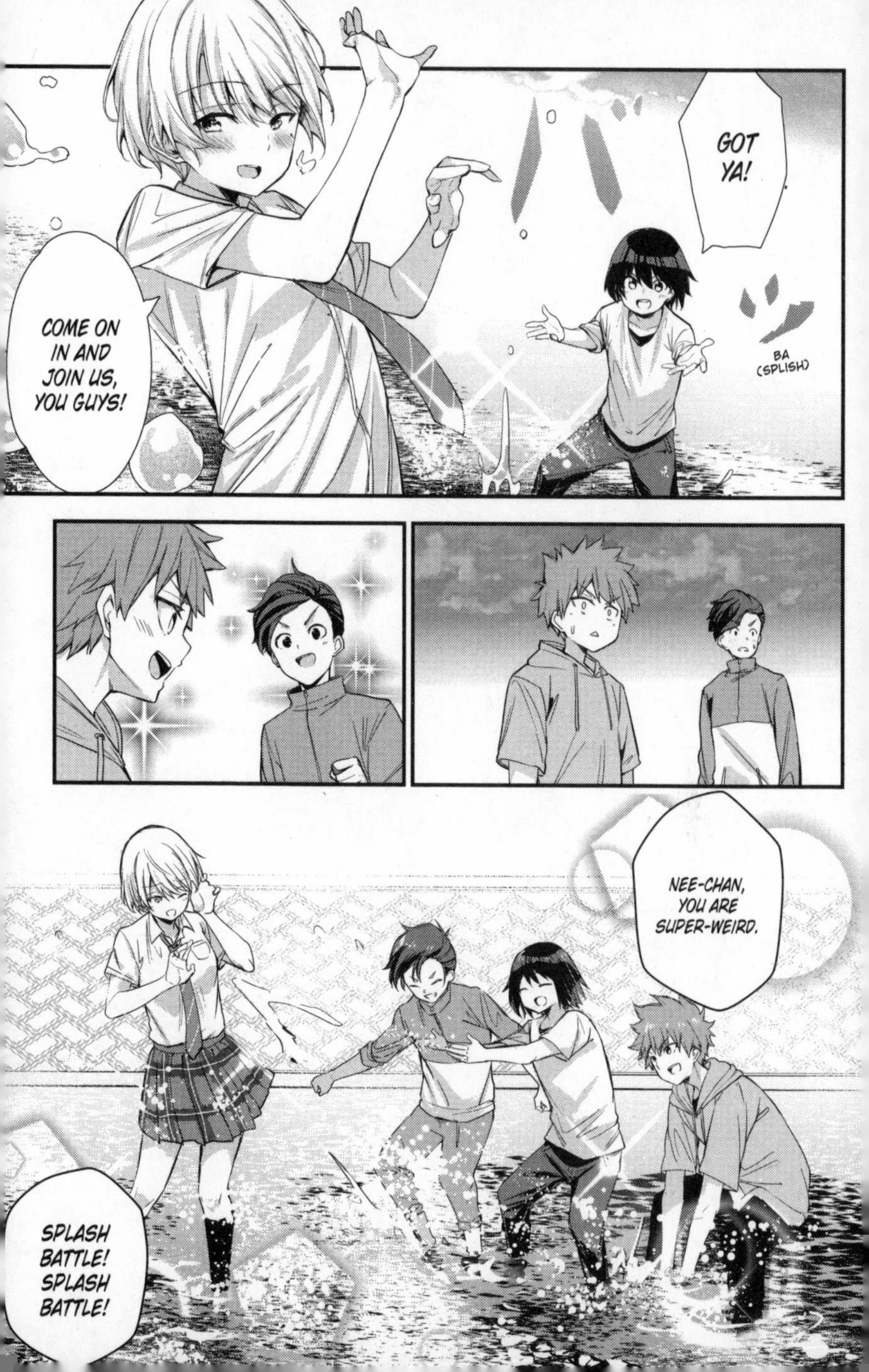
GOT YA!
BA (SPLISH)
COME ON IN AND JOIN US, YOU GUYS!
NEE-CHAN, YOU ARE SUPER-WEIRD.
SPLASH BATTLE! SPLASH BATTLE!

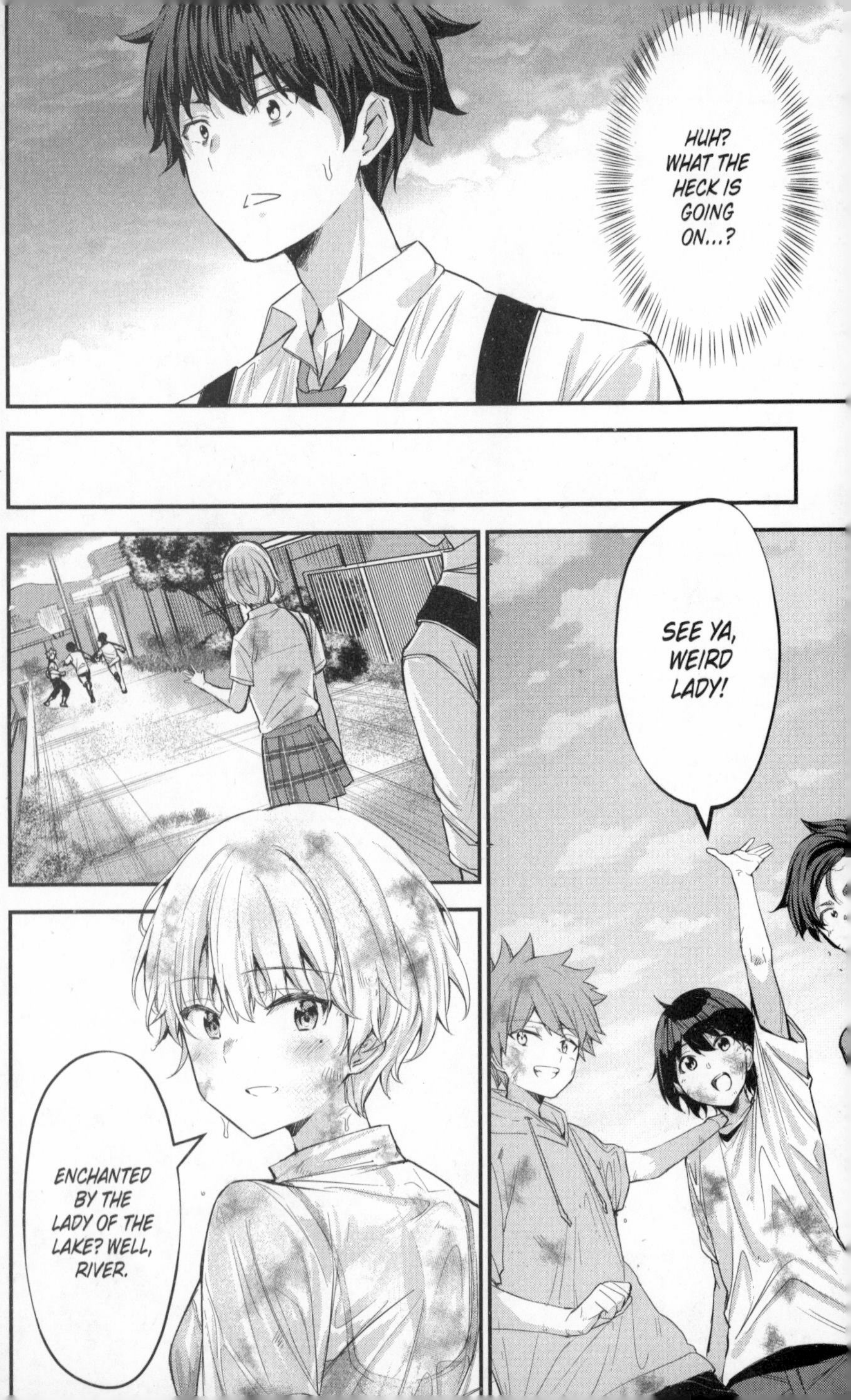
HUH? WHAT THE HECK IS GOING ON...?
SEE YA, WEIRD LADY!
ENCHANTED BY THE LADY OF THE LAKE? WELL, RIVER.

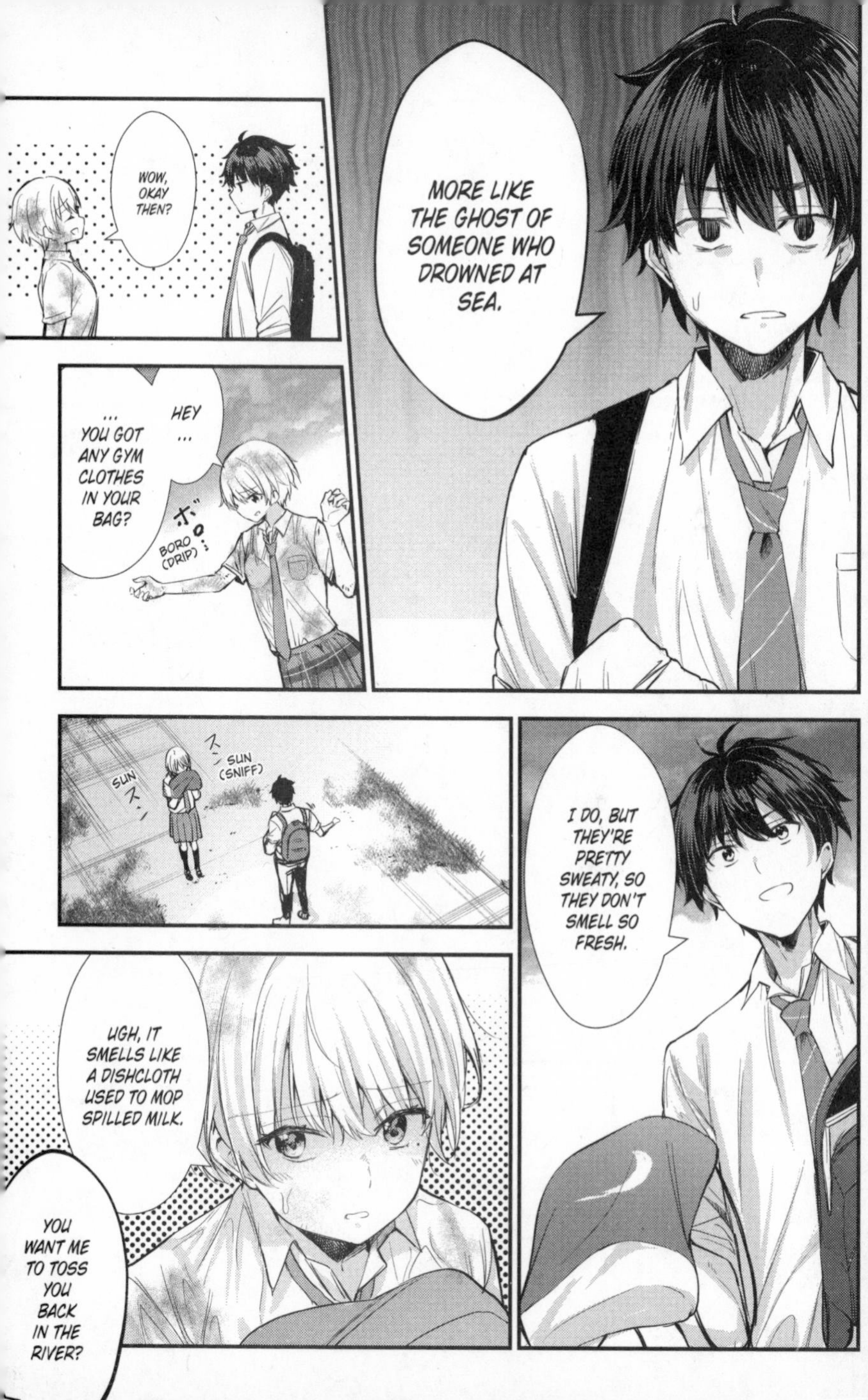
MORE LIKE THE GHOST OF SOMEONE WHO DROWNED AT SEA.
WOW, OKAY THEN?
HEY ...
... YOU GOT ANY GYM CLOTHES IN YOUR BAG?
ボロ BORO (DRIP)
I DO, BUT THEY'RE PRETTY SWEATY, SO THEY DON'T SMELL SO FRESH.
スン SUN (SNIFF)
SUN スン
UGH, IT SMELLS LIKE A DISHCLOTH USED TO MOP SPILLED MILK.
YOU WANT ME TO TOSS YOU BACK IN THE RIVER?

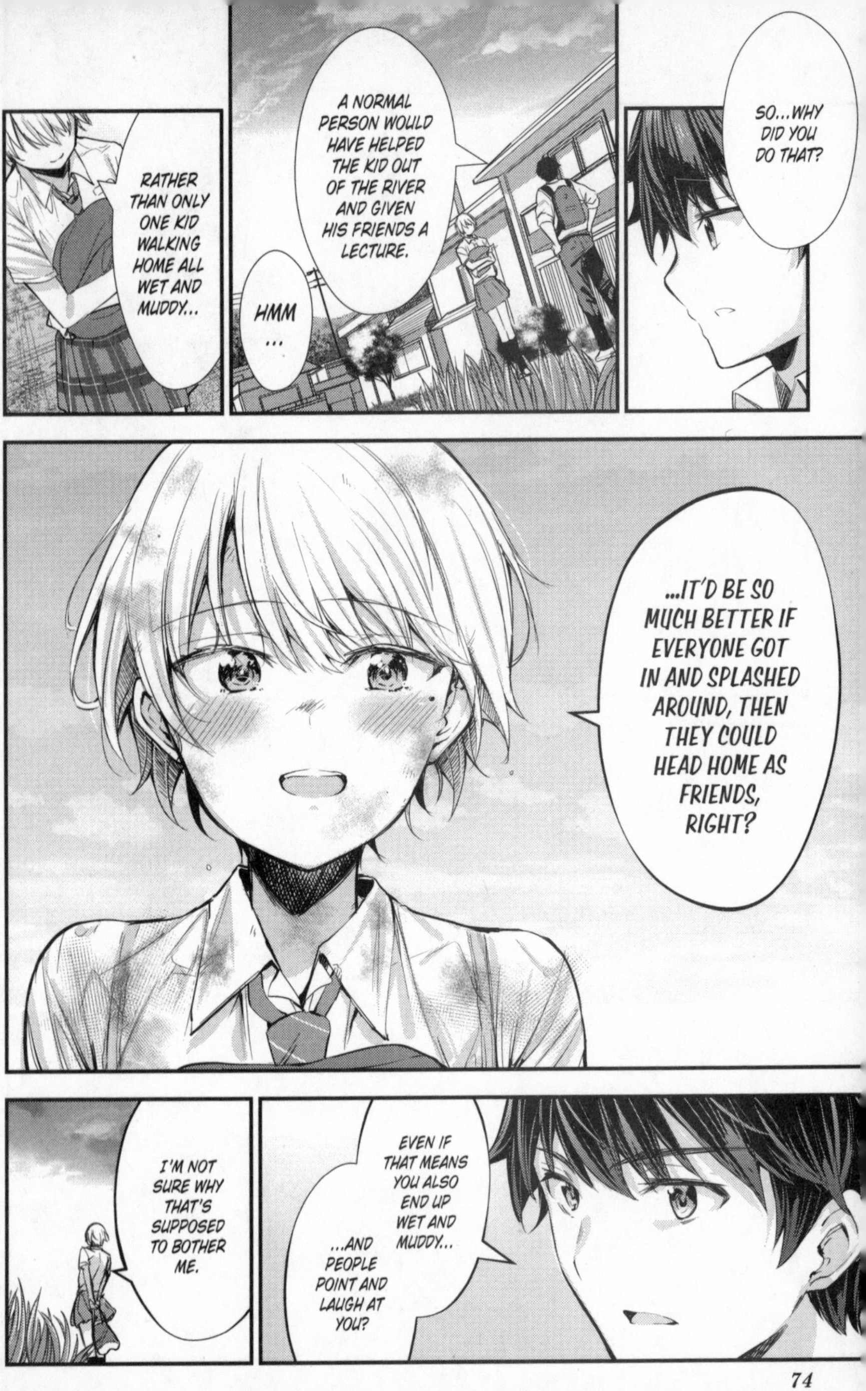
SO...WHY DID YOU DO THAT?
A NORMAL PERSON WOULD HAVE HELPED THE KID OUT OF THE RIVER AND GIVEN HIS FRIENDS A LECTURE.
HMM ...
RATHER THAN ONLY ONE KID WALKING HOME ALL WET AND MUDDY...
...IT'D BE SO MUCH BETTER IF EVERYONE GOT IN AND SPLASHED AROUND, THEN THEY COULD HEAD HOME AS FRIENDS, RIGHT?
EVEN IF THAT MEANS YOU ALSO END UP WET AND MUDDY...
...AND PEOPLE POINT AND LAUGH AT YOU?
I'M NOT SURE WHY THAT'S SUPPOSED TO BOTHER ME.

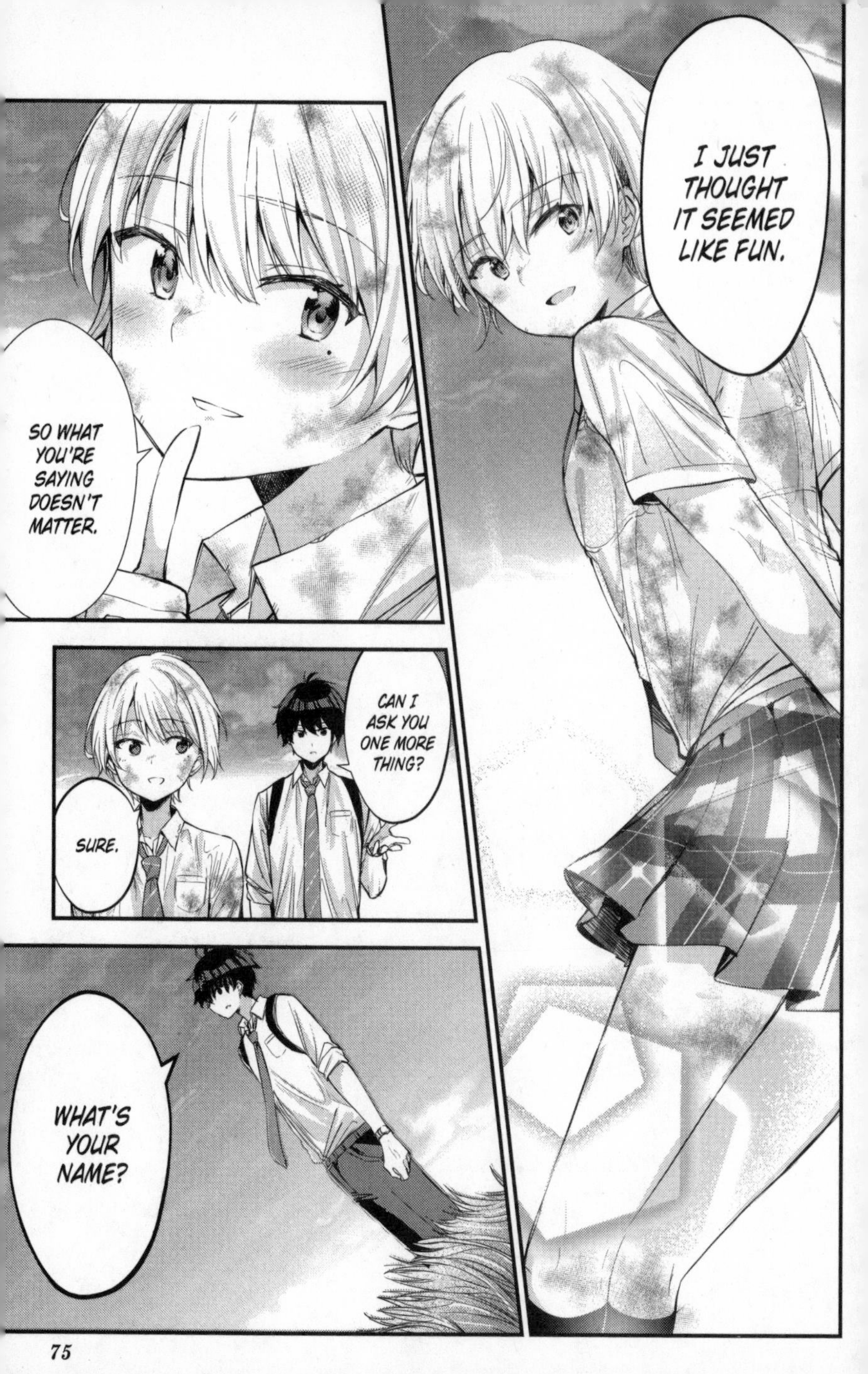
I JUST THOUGHT IT SEEMED LIKE FUN.
SO WHAT YOU'RE SAYING DOESN'T MATTER.
CAN I ASK YOU ONE MORE THING?
SURE.
WHAT'S YOUR NAME?

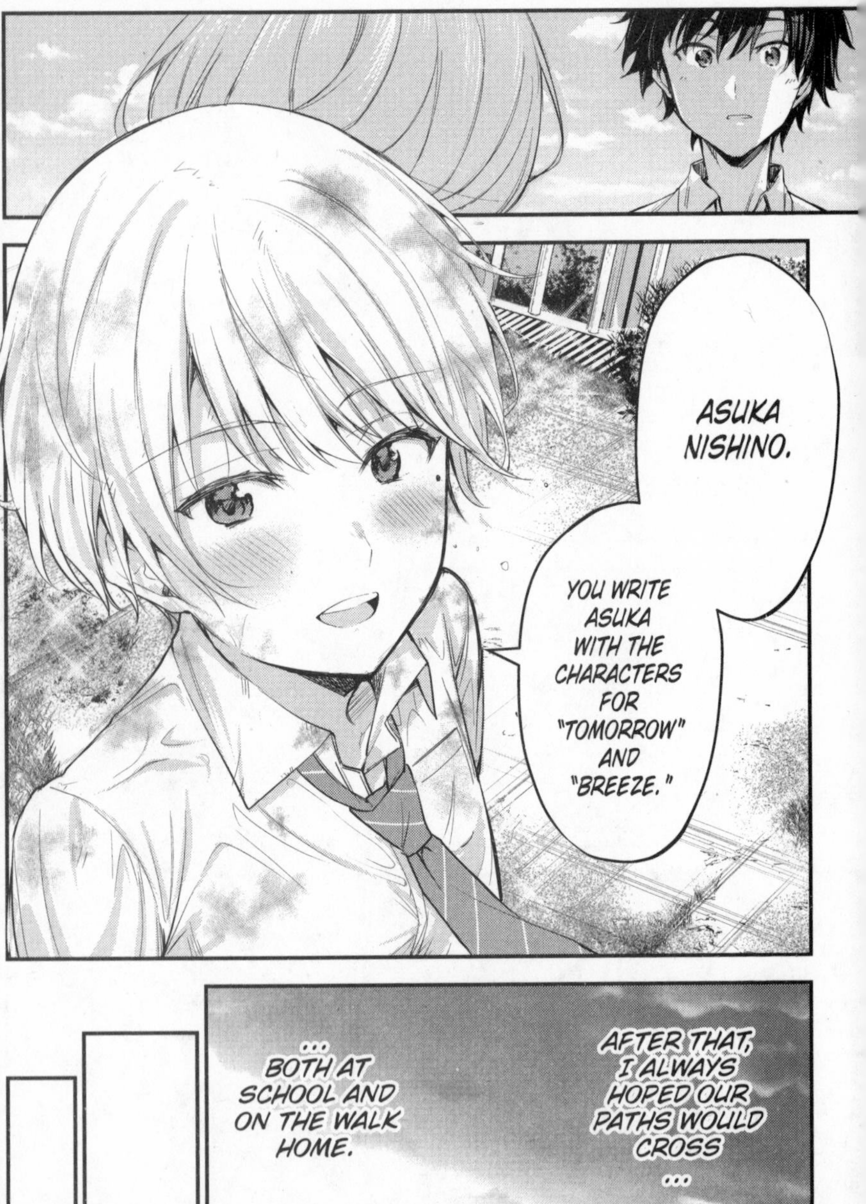
ASUKA NISHINO.
YOU WRITE ASUKA WITH THE CHARACTERS FOR "TOMORROW" AND "BREEZE."
AFTER THAT, I ALWAYS HOPED OUR PATHS WOULD CROSS ...
... BOTH AT SCHOOL AND ON THE WALK HOME.

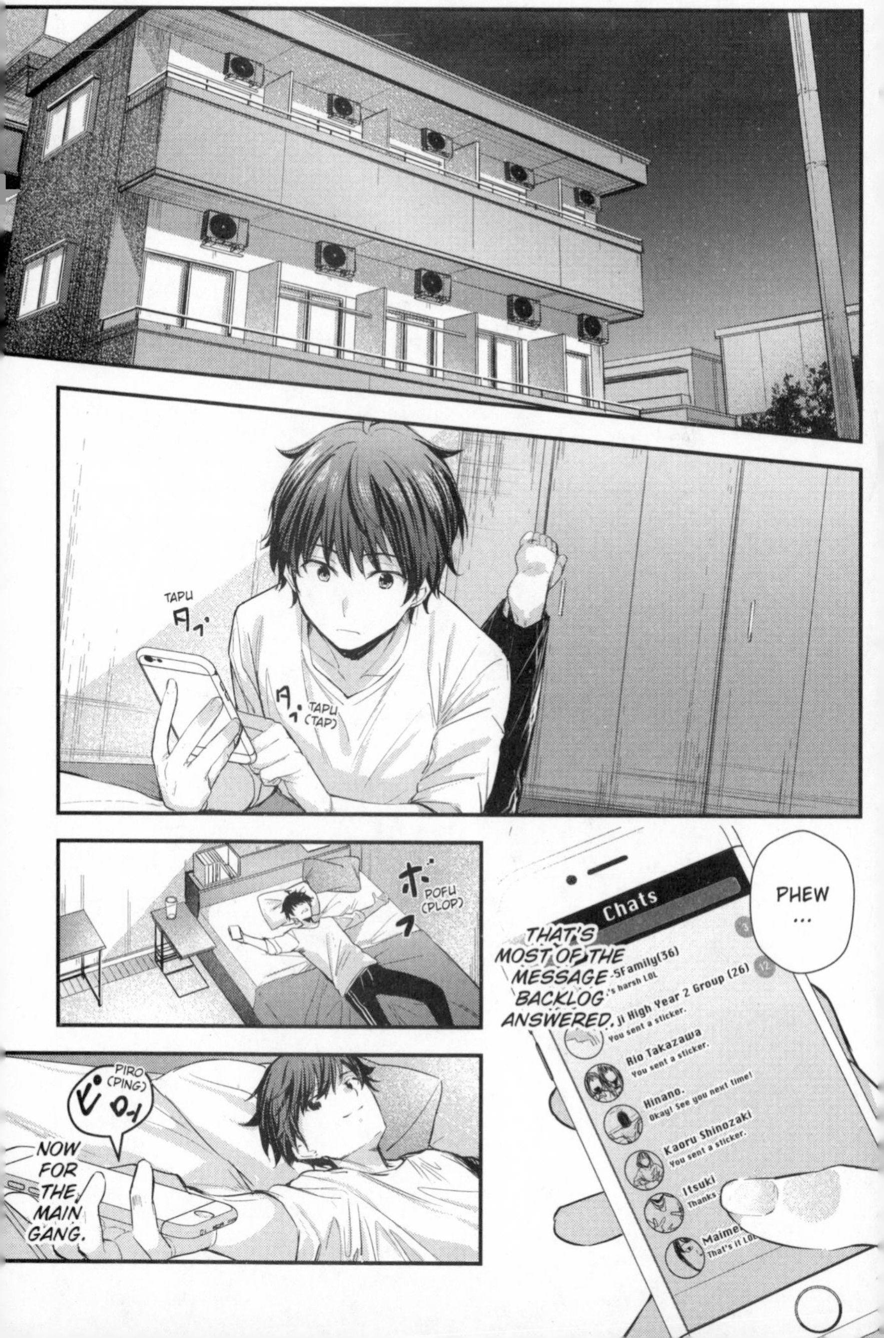

TAPU
TAPU (TAP)
PHEW...
THAT'S MOST OF THE MESSAGE BACKLOG ANSWERED.
Chats
5Family(36)
's harsh LOL
ji High Year 2 Group (26)
You sent a sticker.
Rio Takazawa
You sent a sticker.
Hinano.
Okay! See you next time!
Kaoru Shinozaki
You sent a sticker.
Itsuki
Thanks
POFU (PLOP)
PIRO (PING)
NOW FOR THE MAIN GANG.

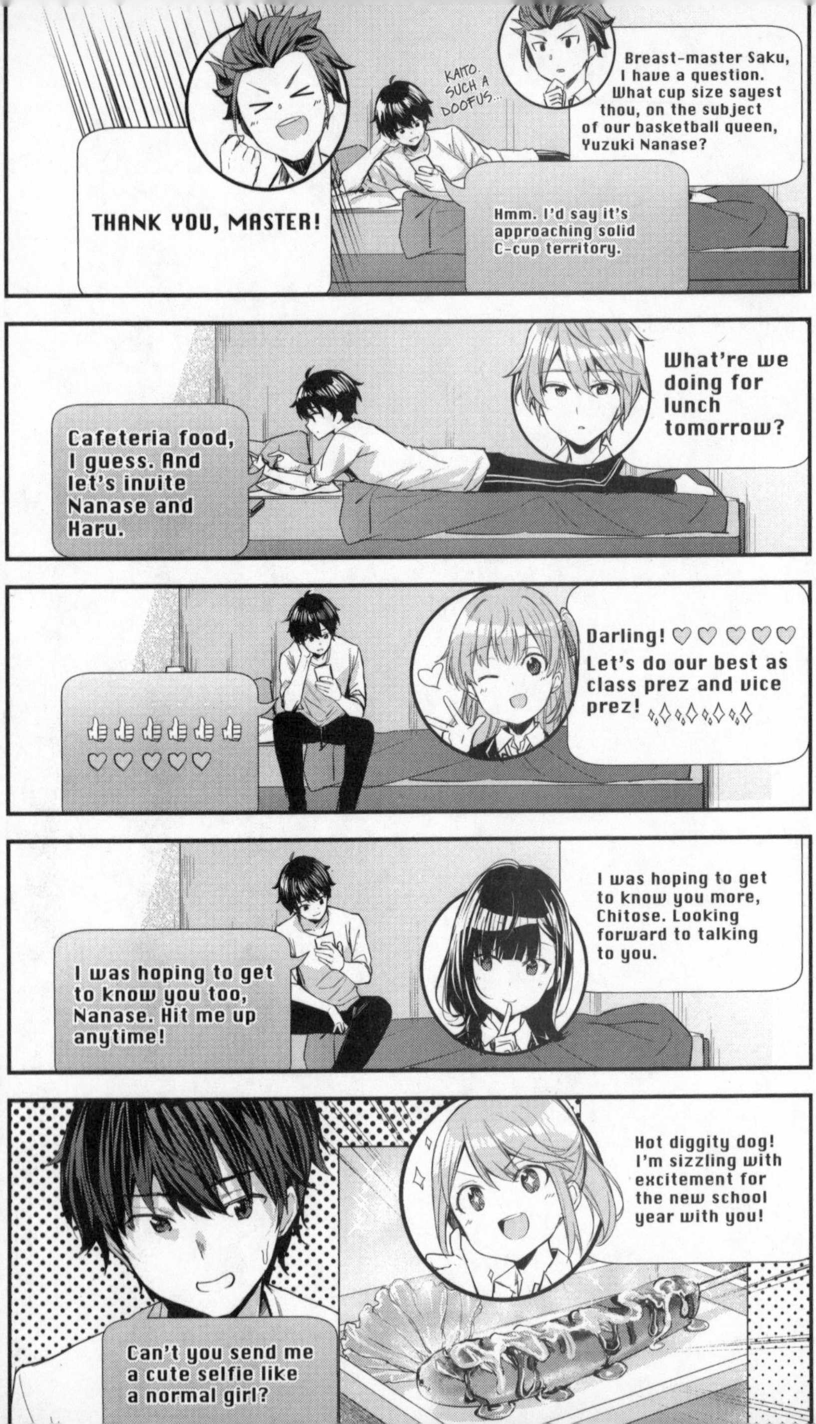
Breast-master Saku, I have a question. What cup size sayest thou, on the subject of our basketball queen, Yuzuki Nanase?
KAITO. SUCH A DOOFUS...
Hmm. I'd say it's approaching solid C-cup territory.
THANK YOU, MASTER!
What're we doing for lunch tomorrow?
Cafeteria food, I guess. And let's invite Nanase and Haru.
Darling! ♡♡♡♡♡ Let's do our best as class prez and vice prez! ✧✧✧✧✧
👍👍👍👍👍👍 ♡♡♡♡♡
I was hoping to get to know you more, Chitose. Looking forward to talking to you.
I was hoping to get to know you too, Nanase. Hit me up anytime!
Hot diggity dog! I'm sizzling with excitement for the new school year with you!
Can't you send me a cute selfie like a normal girl?

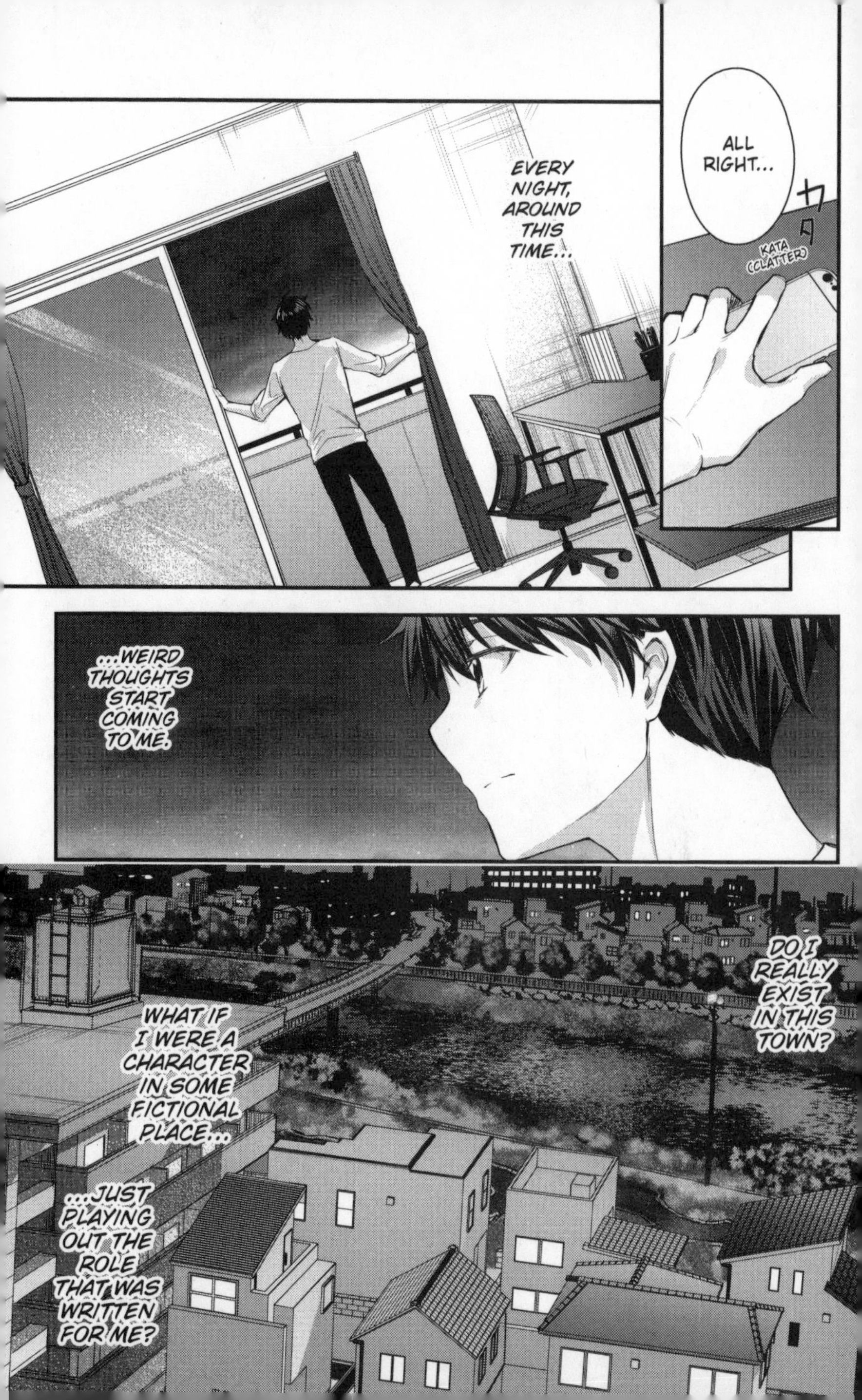
ALL RIGHT...
カタ
KATA (CLATTER)
EVERY NIGHT, AROUND THIS TIME...
...WEIRD THOUGHTS START COMING TO ME.
DO I REALLY EXIST IN THIS TOWN?
WHAT IF I WERE A CHARACTER IN SOME FICTIONAL PLACE...
...JUST PLAYING OUT THE ROLE THAT WAS WRITTEN FOR ME?

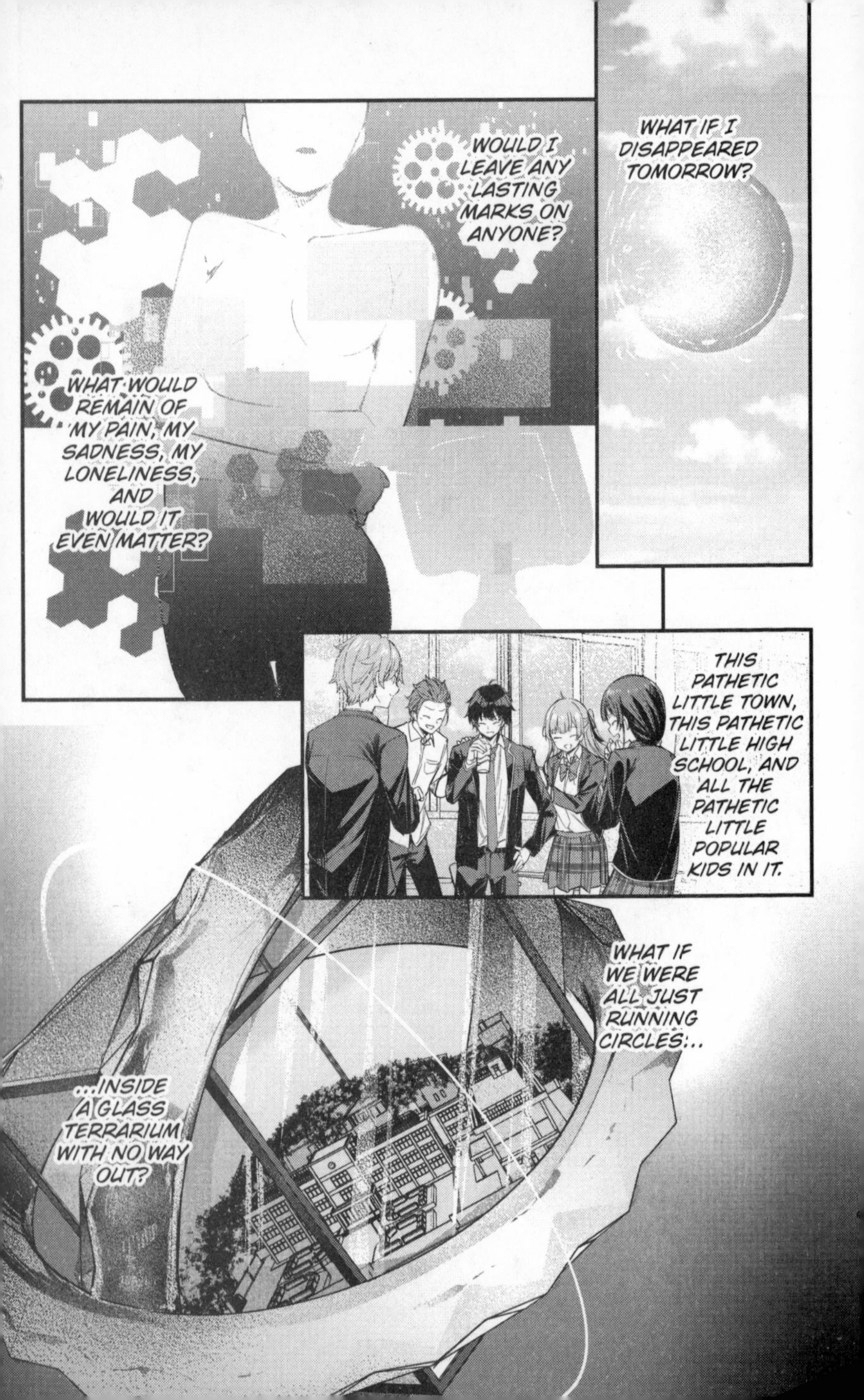
WHAT IF I DISAPPEARED TOMORROW?
WOULD I LEAVE ANY LASTING MARKS ON ANYONE?
WHAT WOULD REMAIN OF MY PAIN, MY SADNESS, MY LONELINESS, AND WOULD IT EVEN MATTER?
THIS PATHETIC LITTLE TOWN, THIS PATHETIC LITTLE HIGH SCHOOL, AND ALL THE PATHETIC LITTLE POPULAR KIDS IN IT.
WHAT IF WE WERE ALL JUST RUNNING CIRCLES...
...INSIDE A GLASS TERRARIUM WITH NO WAY OUT?

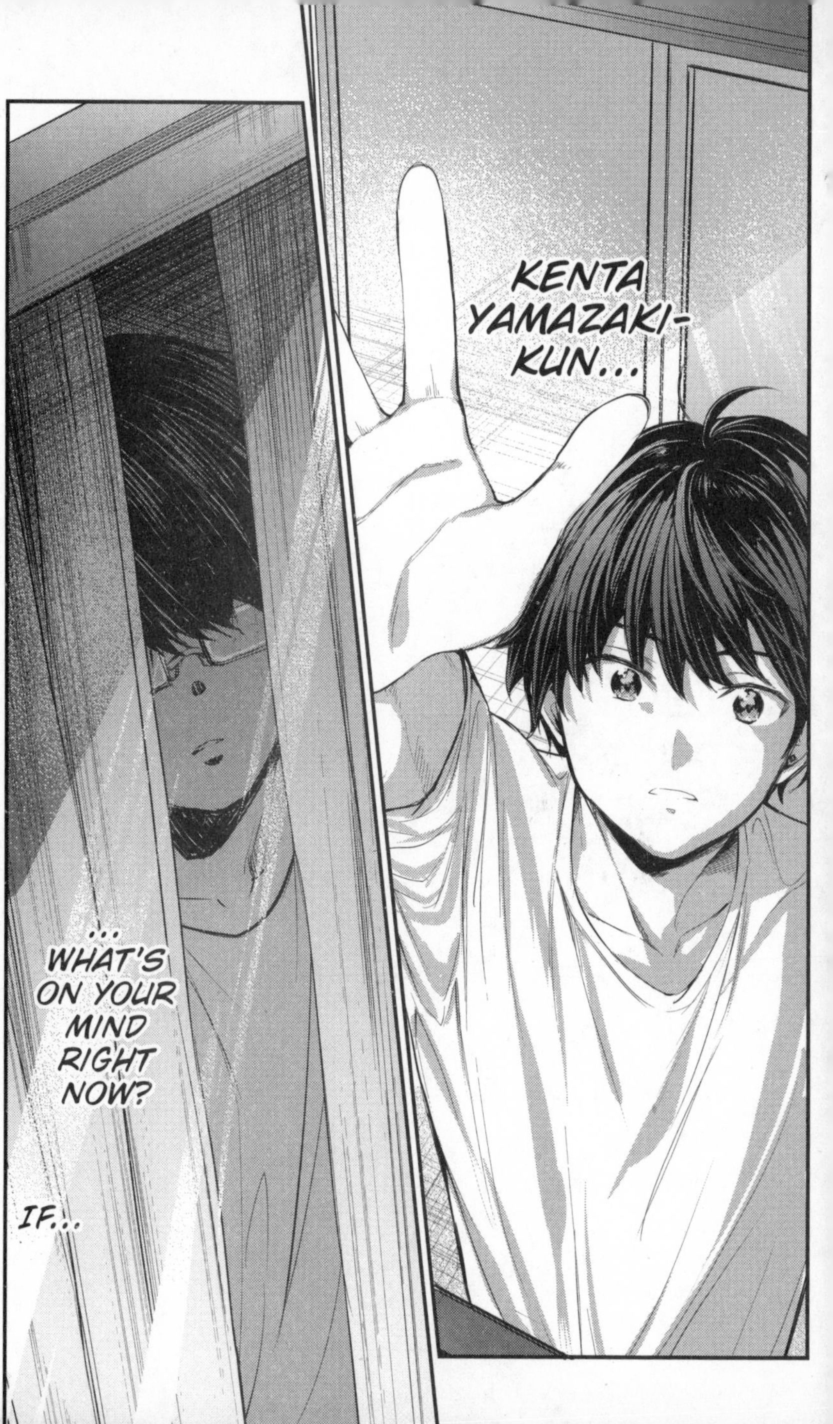
KENTA YAMAZAKI-KUN...
... WHAT'S ON YOUR MIND RIGHT NOW?
IF...

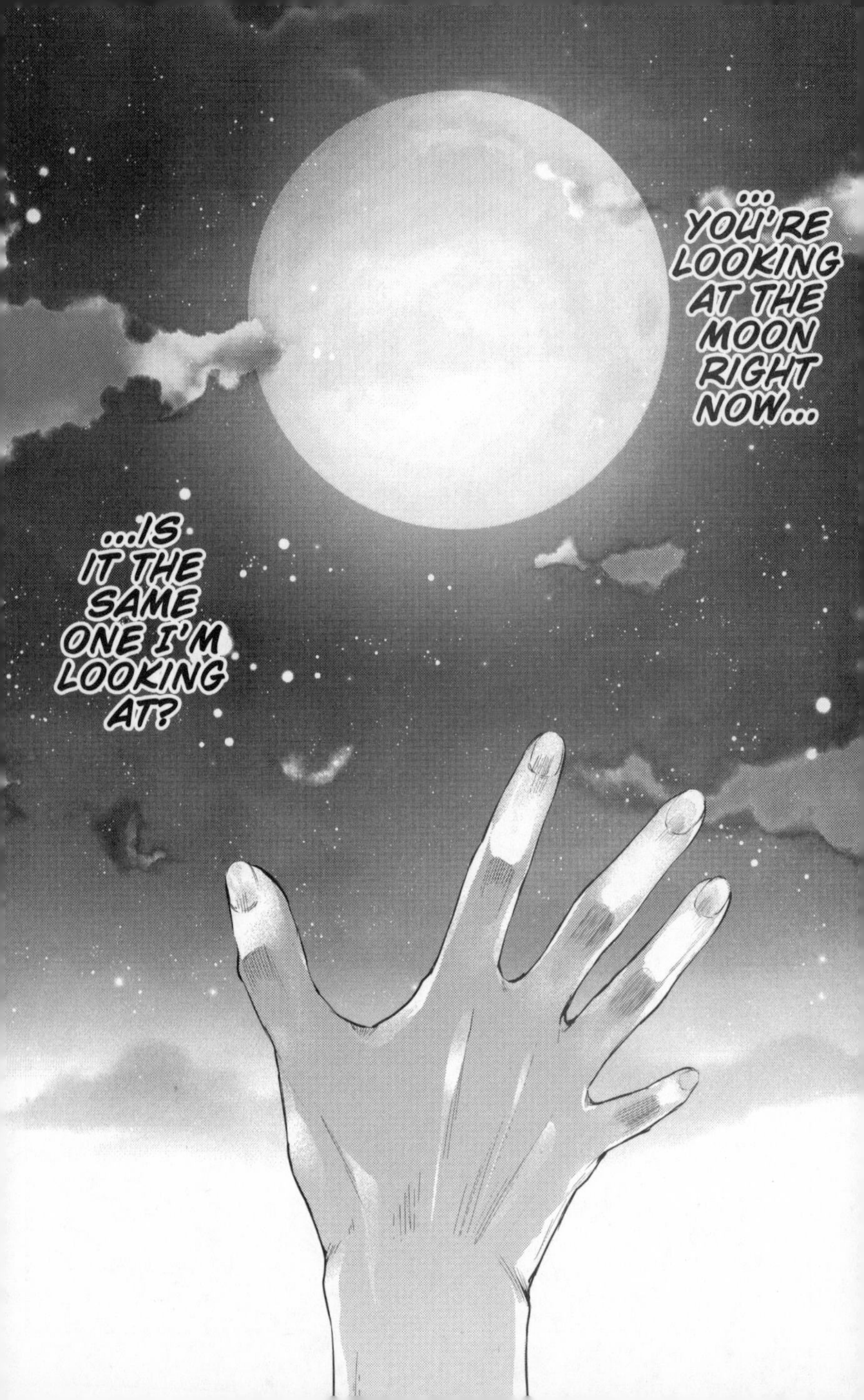
...YOU'RE LOOKING AT THE MOON RIGHT NOW...
...IS IT THE SAME ONE I'M LOOKING AT?

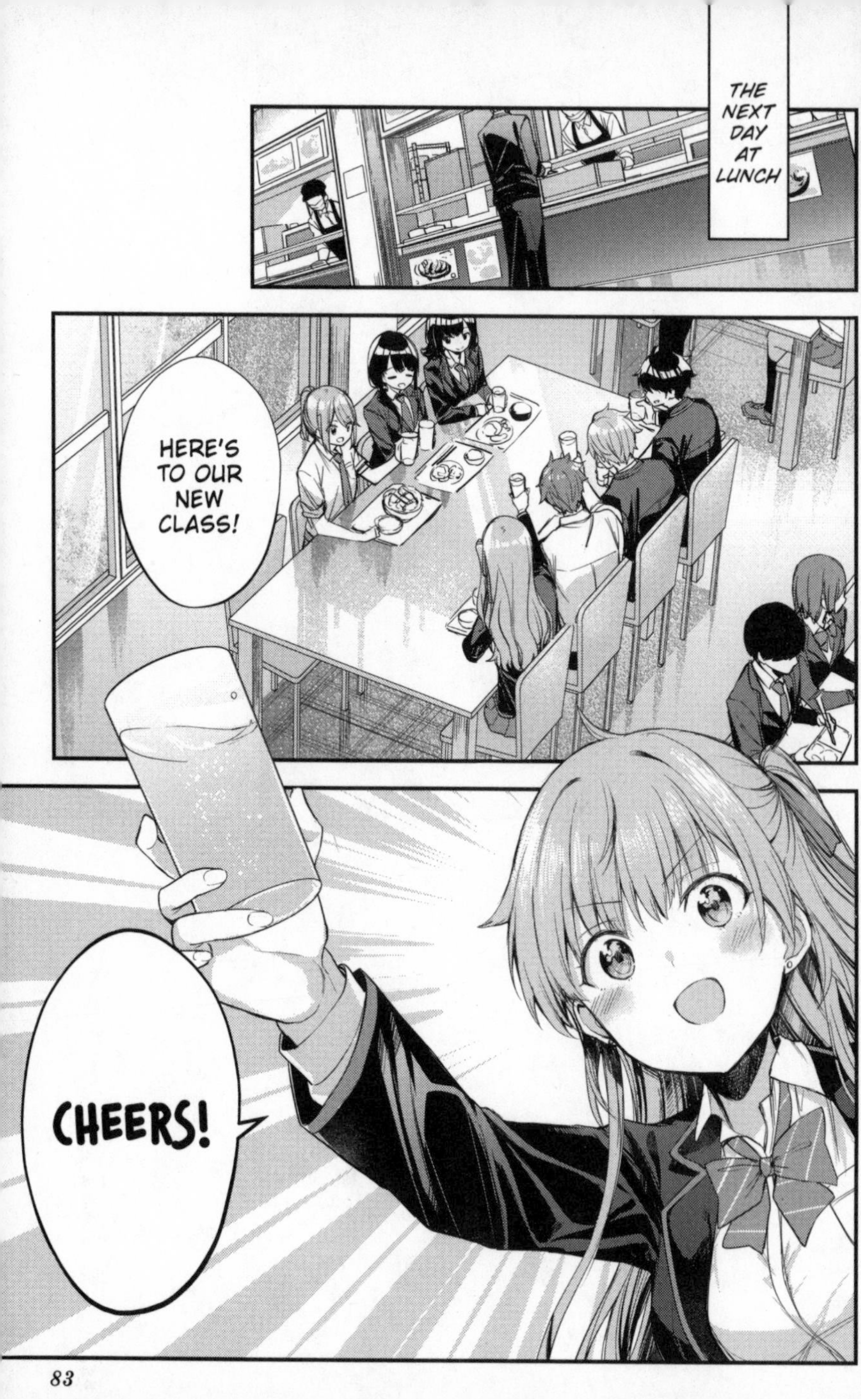
THE NEXT DAY AT LUNCH
HERE'S TO OUR NEW CLASS!
CHEERS!

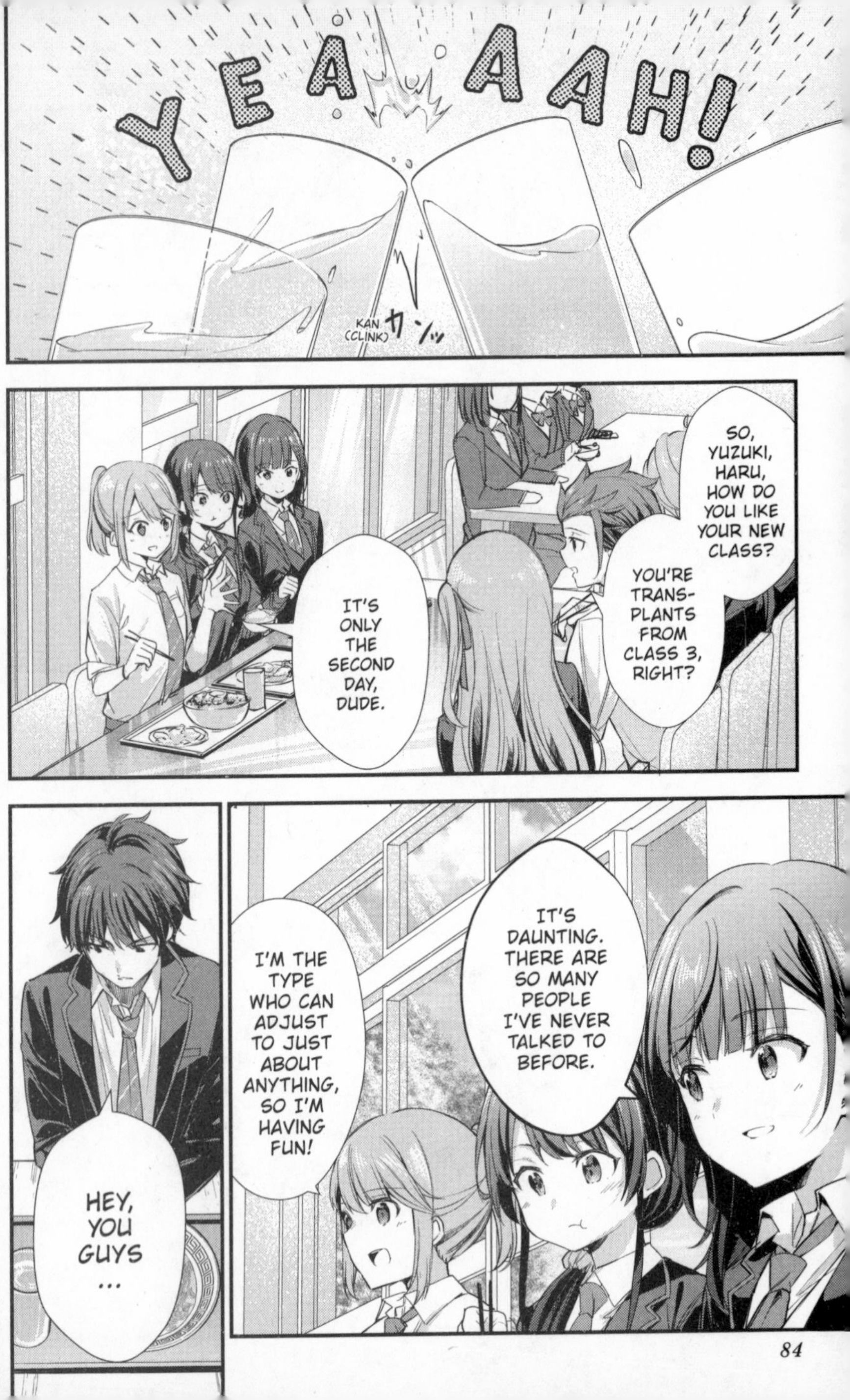

YEAAAH!
KAN (CLINK) カンッ
SO, YUZUKI, HARU, HOW DO YOU LIKE YOUR NEW CLASS?
YOU'RE TRANS-PLANTS FROM CLASS 3, RIGHT?
IT'S ONLY THE SECOND DAY, DUDE.
IT'S DAUNTING. THERE ARE SO MANY PEOPLE I'VE NEVER TALKED TO BEFORE.
I'M THE TYPE WHO CAN ADJUST TO JUST ABOUT ANYTHING, SO I'M HAVING FUN!
HEY, YOU GUYS...

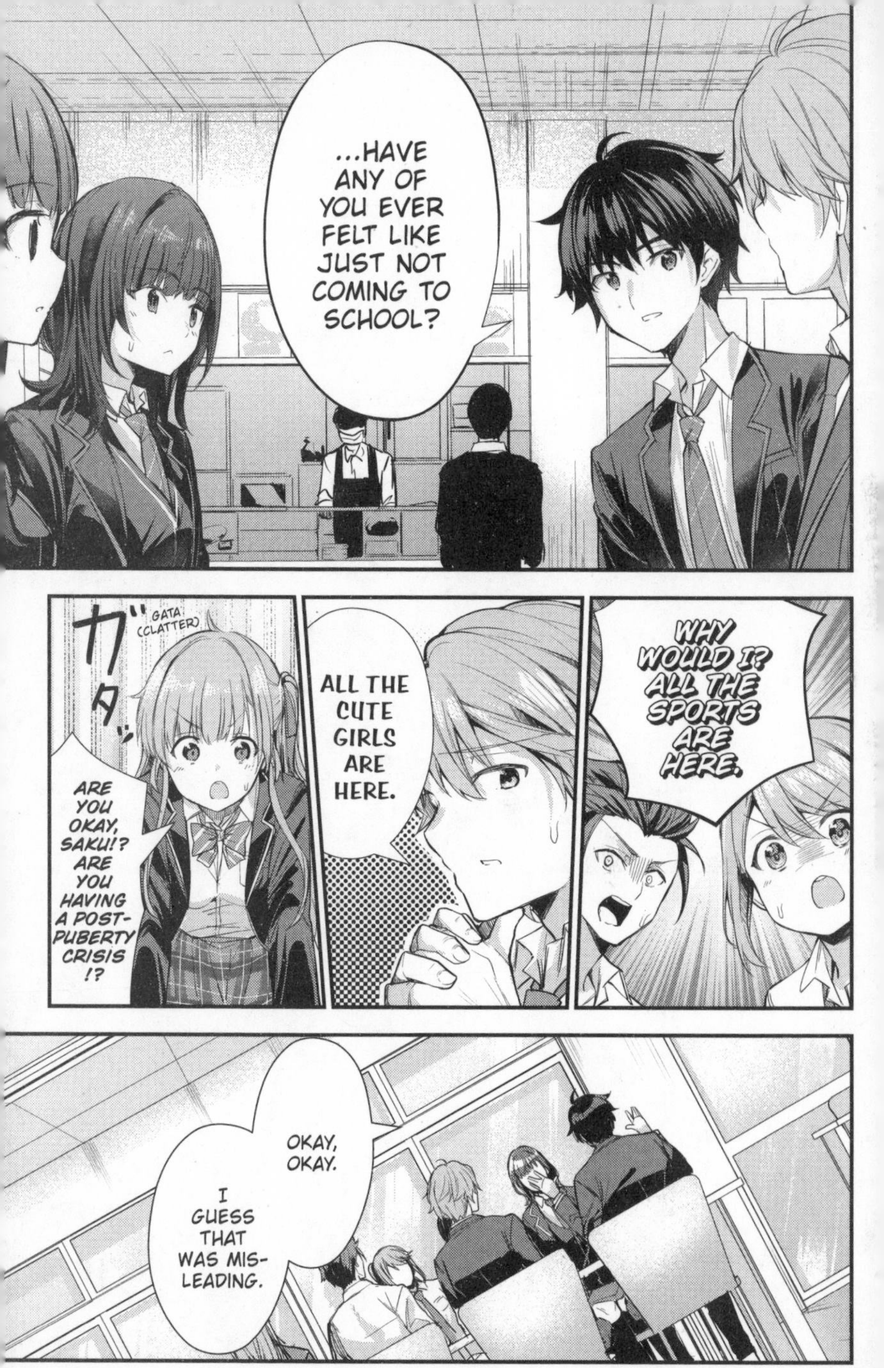
...HAVE ANY OF YOU EVER FELT LIKE JUST NOT COMING TO SCHOOL?
WHY WOULD I? ALL THE SPORTS ARE HERE.
ALL THE CUTE GIRLS ARE HERE.
ガタッ
GATA (CLATTER)
ARE YOU OKAY, SAKU!? ARE YOU HAVING A POST-PUBERTY CRISIS!?
OKAY, OKAY.
I GUESS THAT WAS MIS-LEADING.

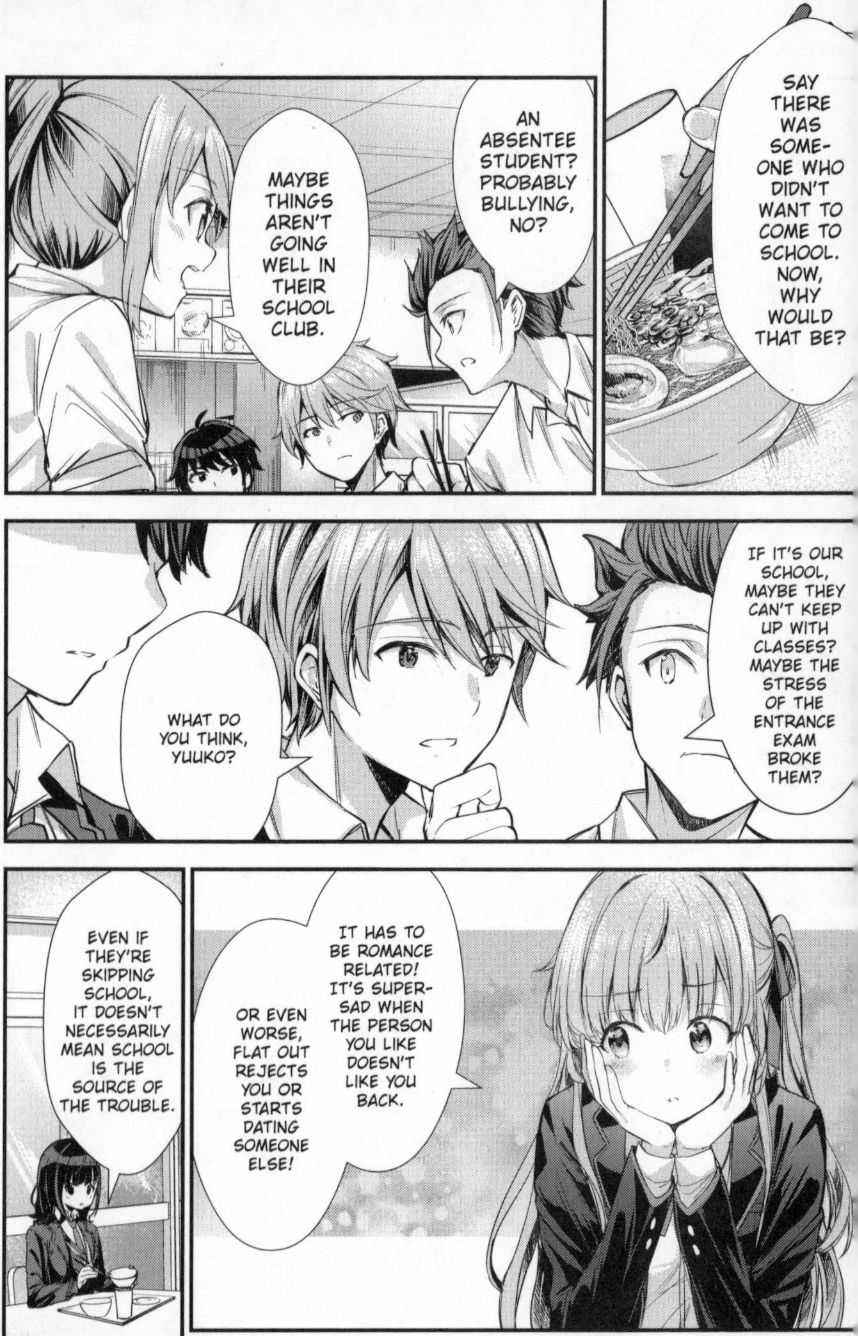
SAY THERE WAS SOME-ONE WHO DIDN'T WANT TO COME TO SCHOOL. NOW, WHY WOULD THAT BE?
AN ABSENTEE STUDENT? PROBABLY BULLYING, NO?
MAYBE THINGS AREN'T GOING WELL IN THEIR SCHOOL CLUB.
IF IT'S OUR SCHOOL, MAYBE THEY CAN'T KEEP UP WITH CLASSES? MAYBE THE STRESS OF THE ENTRANCE EXAM BROKE THEM?
WHAT DO YOU THINK, YUUKO?
IT HAS TO BE ROMANCE RELATED! IT'S SUPER-SAD WHEN THE PERSON YOU LIKE DOESN'T LIKE YOU BACK.
OR EVEN WORSE, FLAT OUT REJECTS YOU OR STARTS DATING SOMEONE ELSE!
EVEN IF THEY'RE SKIPPING SCHOOL, IT DOESN'T NECESSARILY MEAN SCHOOL IS THE SOURCE OF THE TROUBLE.

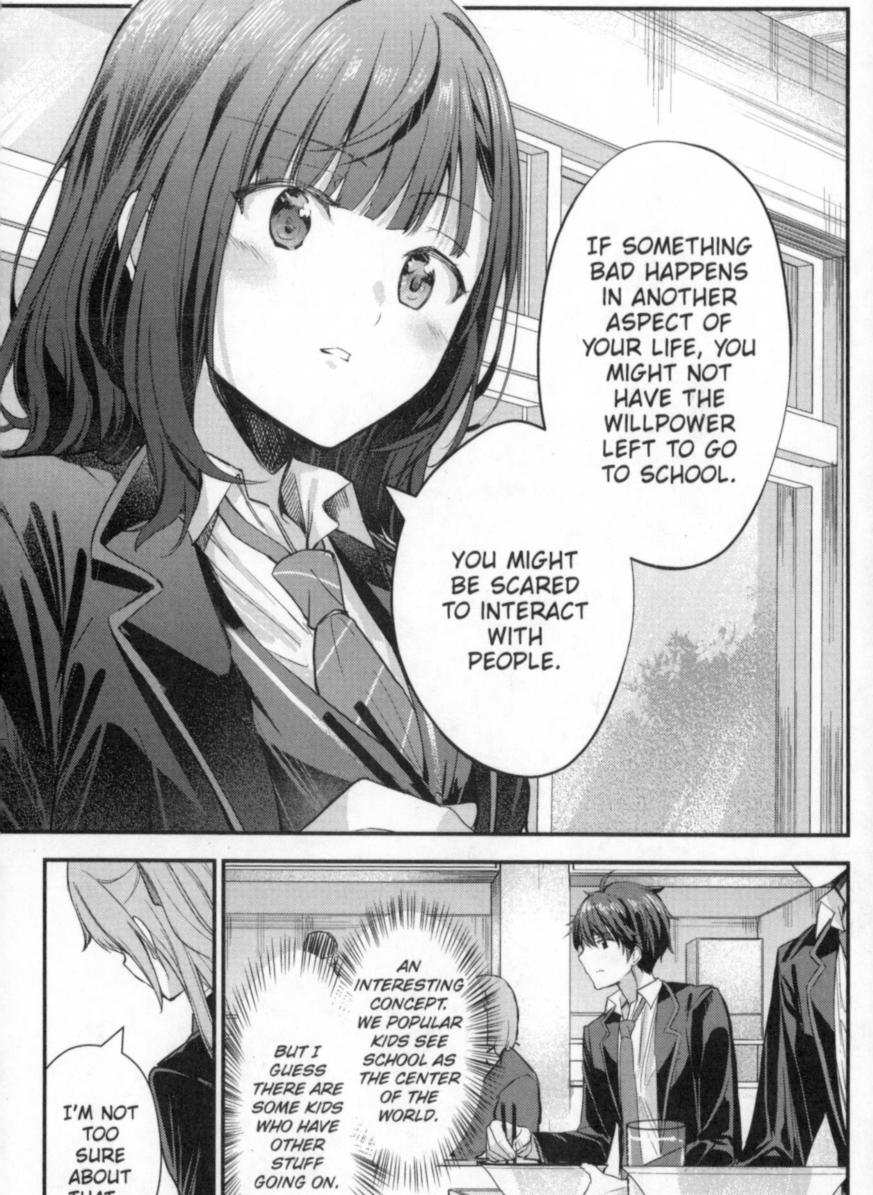
IF SOMETHING BAD HAPPENS IN ANOTHER ASPECT OF YOUR LIFE, YOU MIGHT NOT HAVE THE WILLPOWER LEFT TO GO TO SCHOOL.
YOU MIGHT BE SCARED TO INTERACT WITH PEOPLE.
AN INTERESTING CONCEPT. WE POPULAR KIDS SEE SCHOOL AS THE CENTER OF THE WORLD.
BUT I GUESS THERE ARE SOME KIDS WHO HAVE OTHER STUFF GOING ON.
I'M NOT TOO SURE ABOUT THAT...

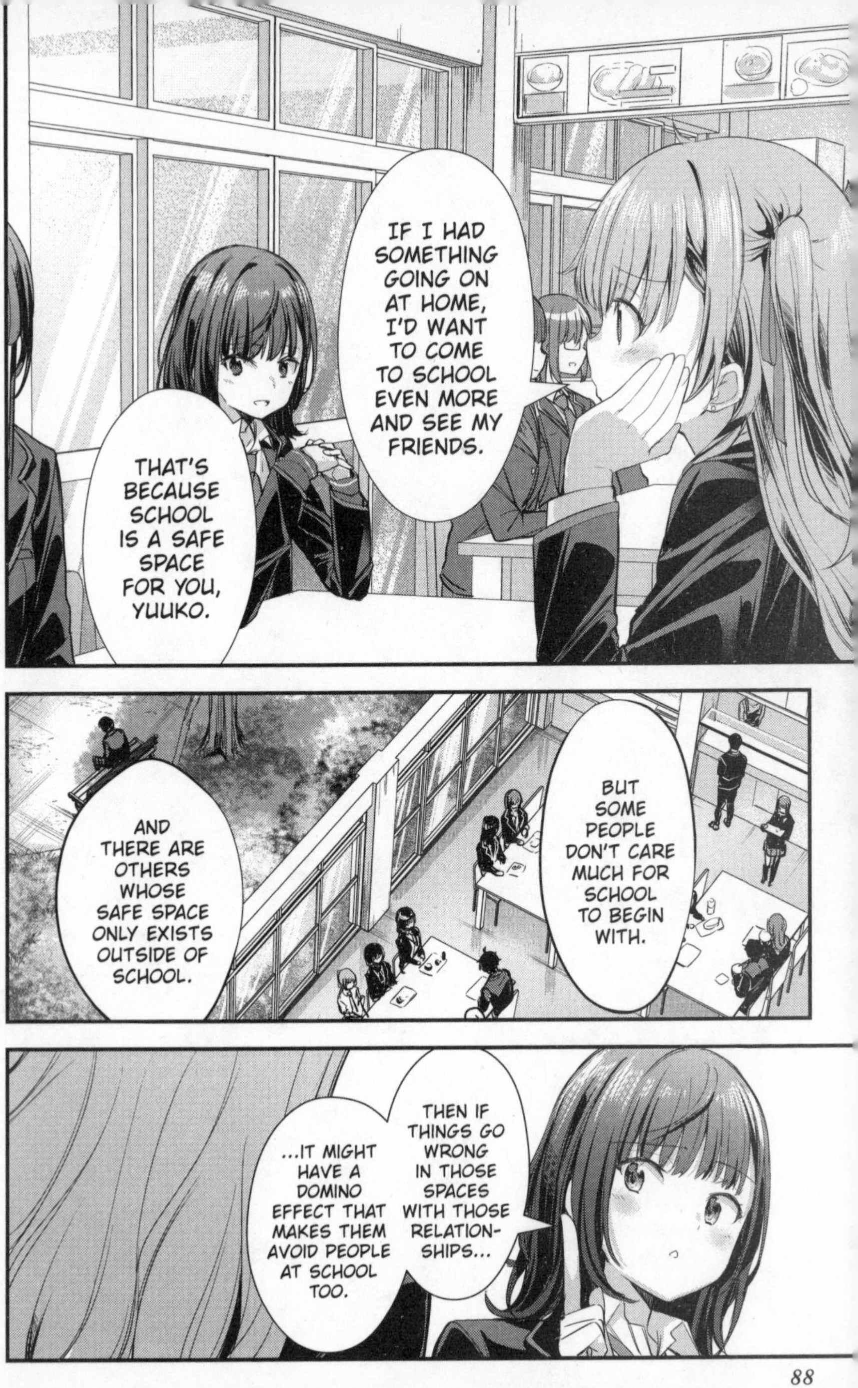
IF I HAD SOMETHING GOING ON AT HOME, I'D WANT TO COME TO SCHOOL EVEN MORE AND SEE MY FRIENDS.
THAT'S BECAUSE SCHOOL IS A SAFE SPACE FOR YOU, YUUKO.
BUT SOME PEOPLE DON'T CARE MUCH FOR SCHOOL TO BEGIN WITH.
AND THERE ARE OTHERS WHOSE SAFE SPACE ONLY EXISTS OUTSIDE OF SCHOOL.
THEN IF THINGS GO WRONG IN THOSE SPACES WITH THOSE RELATION-SHIPS...
...IT MIGHT HAVE A DOMINO EFFECT THAT MAKES THEM AVOID PEOPLE AT SCHOOL TOO.

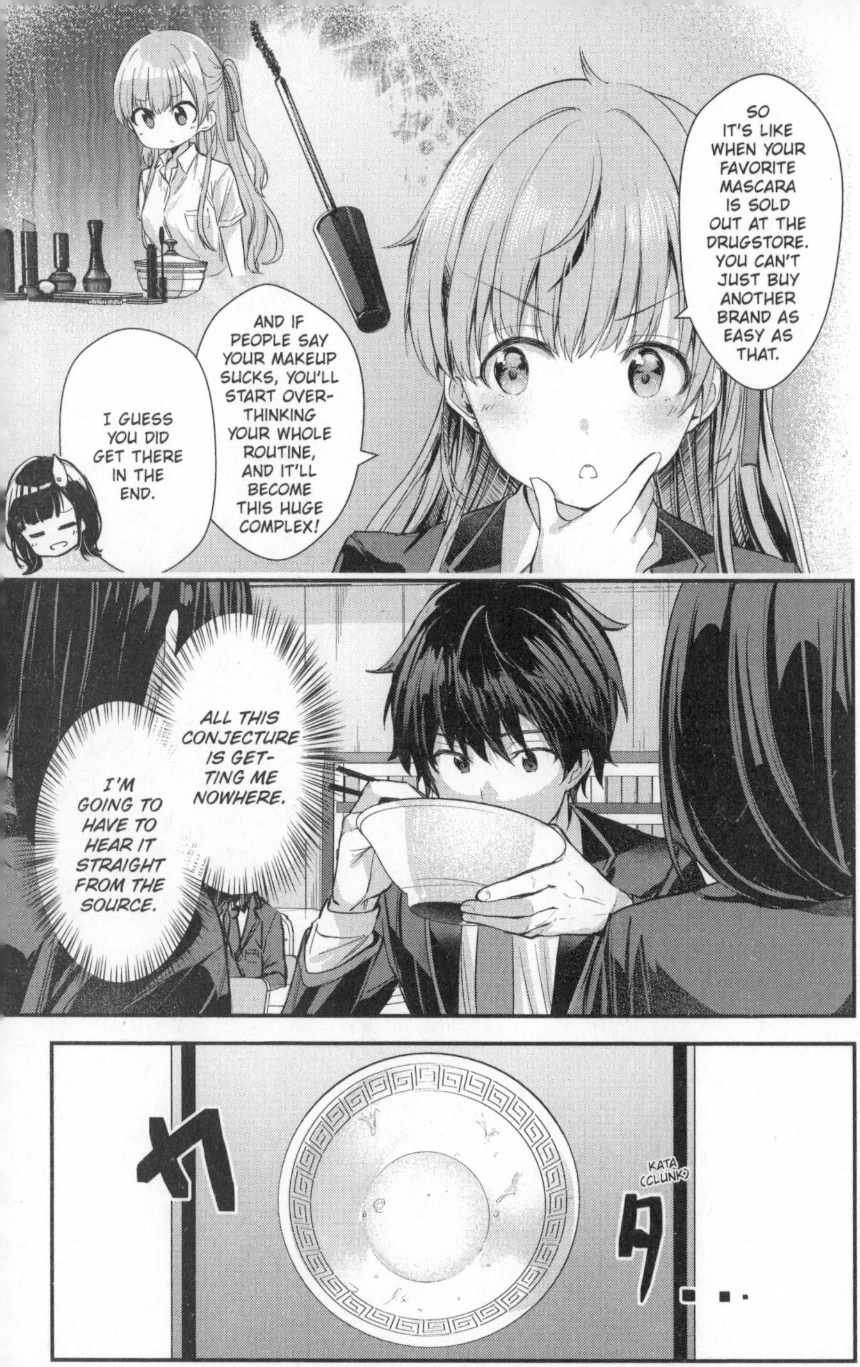
SO IT'S LIKE WHEN YOUR FAVORITE MASCARA IS SOLD OUT AT THE DRUGSTORE. YOU CAN'T JUST BUY ANOTHER BRAND AS EASY AS THAT.
AND IF PEOPLE SAY YOUR MAKEUP SUCKS, YOU'LL START OVER-THINKING YOUR WHOLE ROUTINE, AND IT'LL BECOME THIS HUGE COMPLEX!
I GUESS YOU DID GET THERE IN THE END.
ALL THIS CONJECTURE IS GET-TING ME NOWHERE.
I'M GOING TO HAVE TO HEAR IT STRAIGHT FROM THE SOURCE.
KATA (CLUNK)

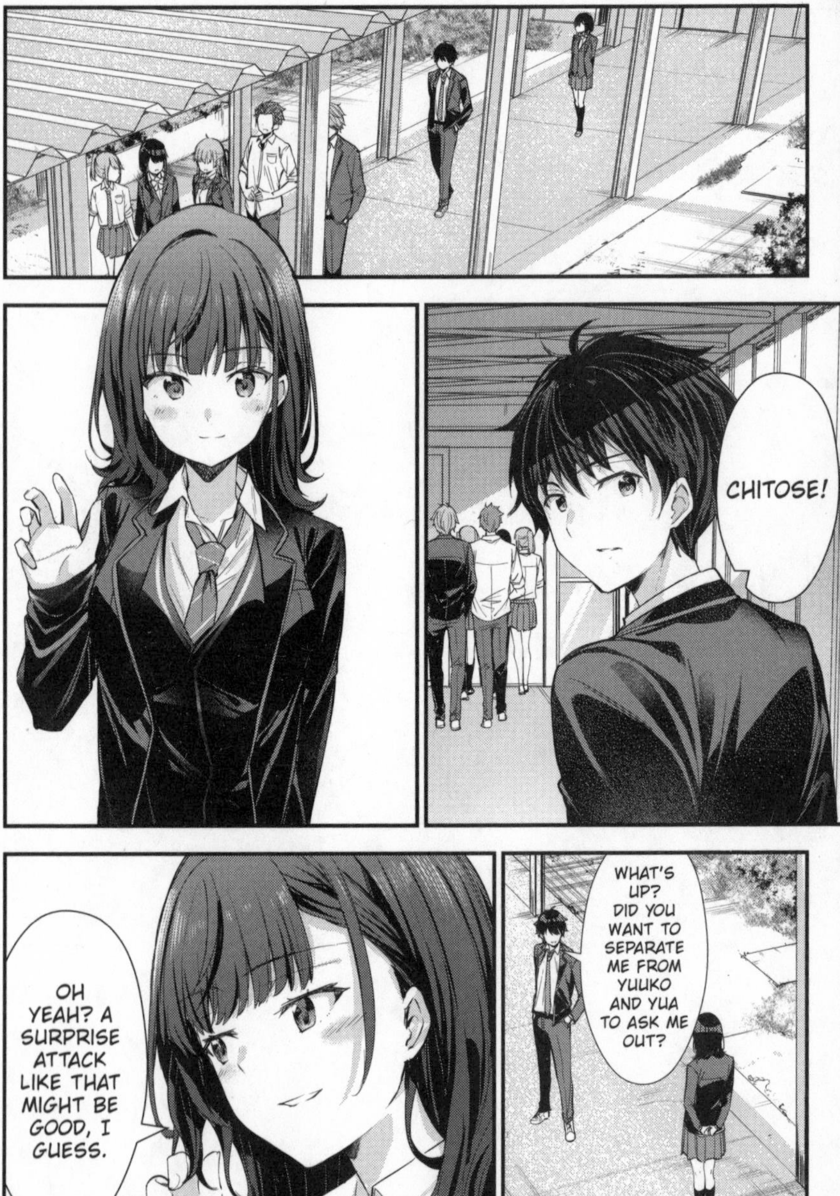
CHITOSE!
WHAT'S UP? DID YOU WANT TO SEPARATE ME FROM YUUKO AND YUA TO ASK ME OUT?
OH YEAH? A SURPRISE ATTACK LIKE THAT MIGHT BE GOOD, I GUESS.

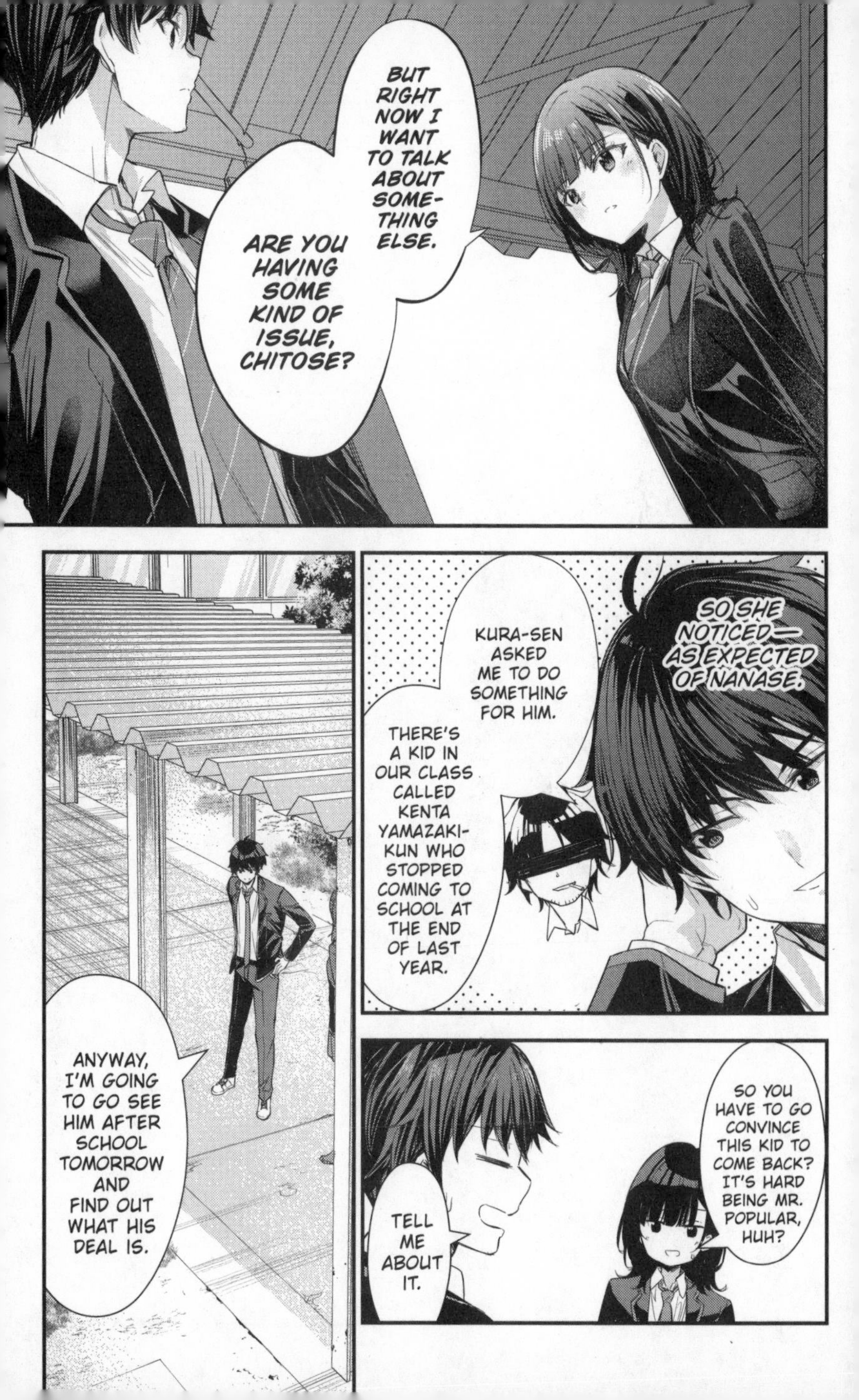
BUT RIGHT NOW I WANT TO TALK ABOUT SOMETHING ELSE.
ARE YOU HAVING SOME KIND OF ISSUE, CHITOSE?
SO SHE NOTICED—AS EXPECTED OF NANASE.
KURA-SEN ASKED ME TO DO SOMETHING FOR HIM.
THERE'S A KID IN OUR CLASS CALLED KENTA YAMAZAKI-KUN WHO STOPPED COMING TO SCHOOL AT THE END OF LAST YEAR.
SO YOU HAVE TO GO CONVINCE THIS KID TO COME BACK? IT'S HARD BEING MR. POPULAR, HUH?
TELL ME ABOUT IT.
ANYWAY, I'M GOING TO GO SEE HIM AFTER SCHOOL TOMORROW AND FIND OUT WHAT HIS DEAL IS.

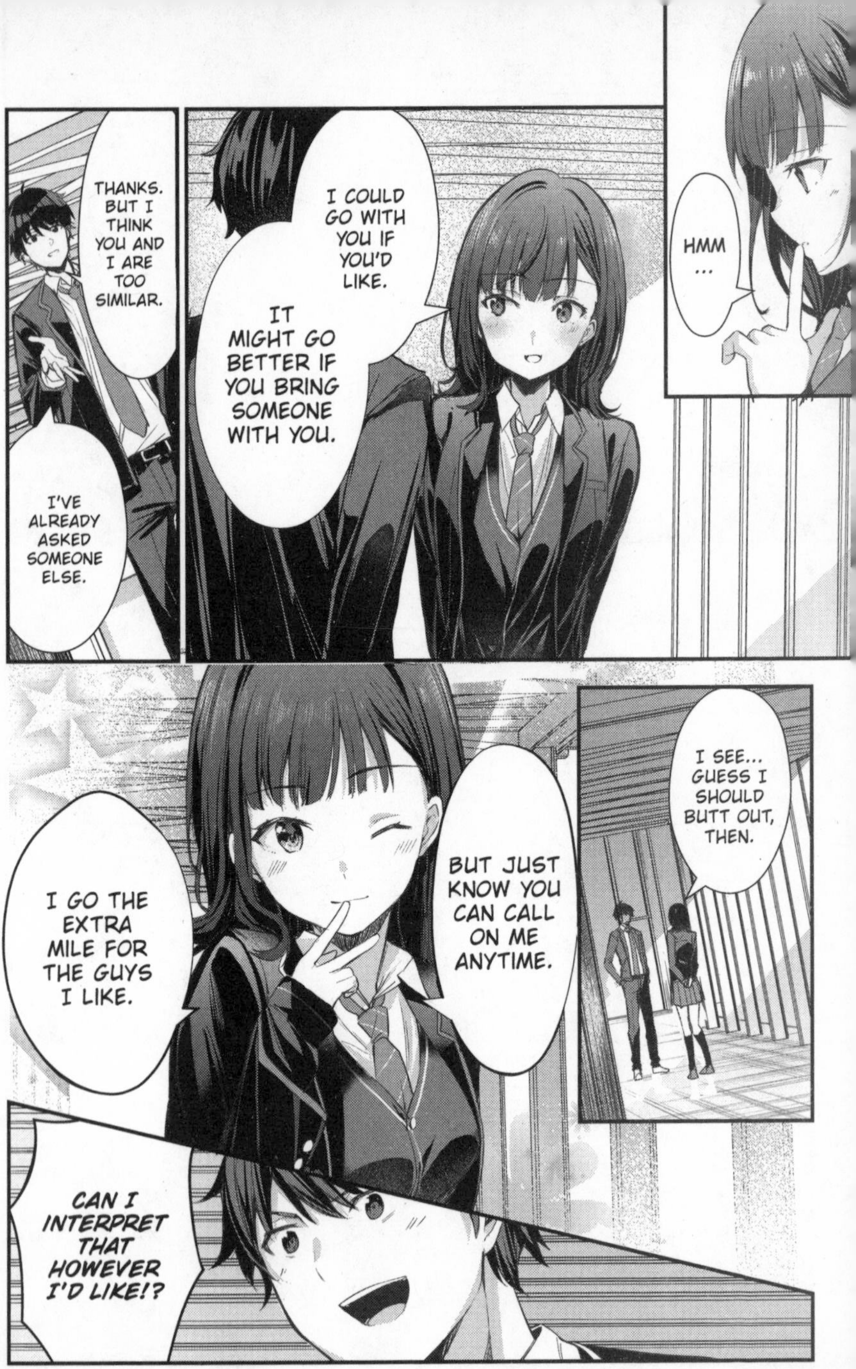
HMM ...
I COULD GO WITH YOU IF YOU'D LIKE.
IT MIGHT GO BETTER IF YOU BRING SOMEONE WITH YOU.
THANKS. BUT I THINK YOU AND I ARE TOO SIMILAR.
I'VE ALREADY ASKED SOMEONE ELSE.
I SEE... GUESS I SHOULD BUTT OUT, THEN.
BUT JUST KNOW YOU CAN CALL ON ME ANYTIME.
I GO THE EXTRA MILE FOR THE GUYS I LIKE.
CAN I INTERPRET THAT HOWEVER I'D LIKE!?

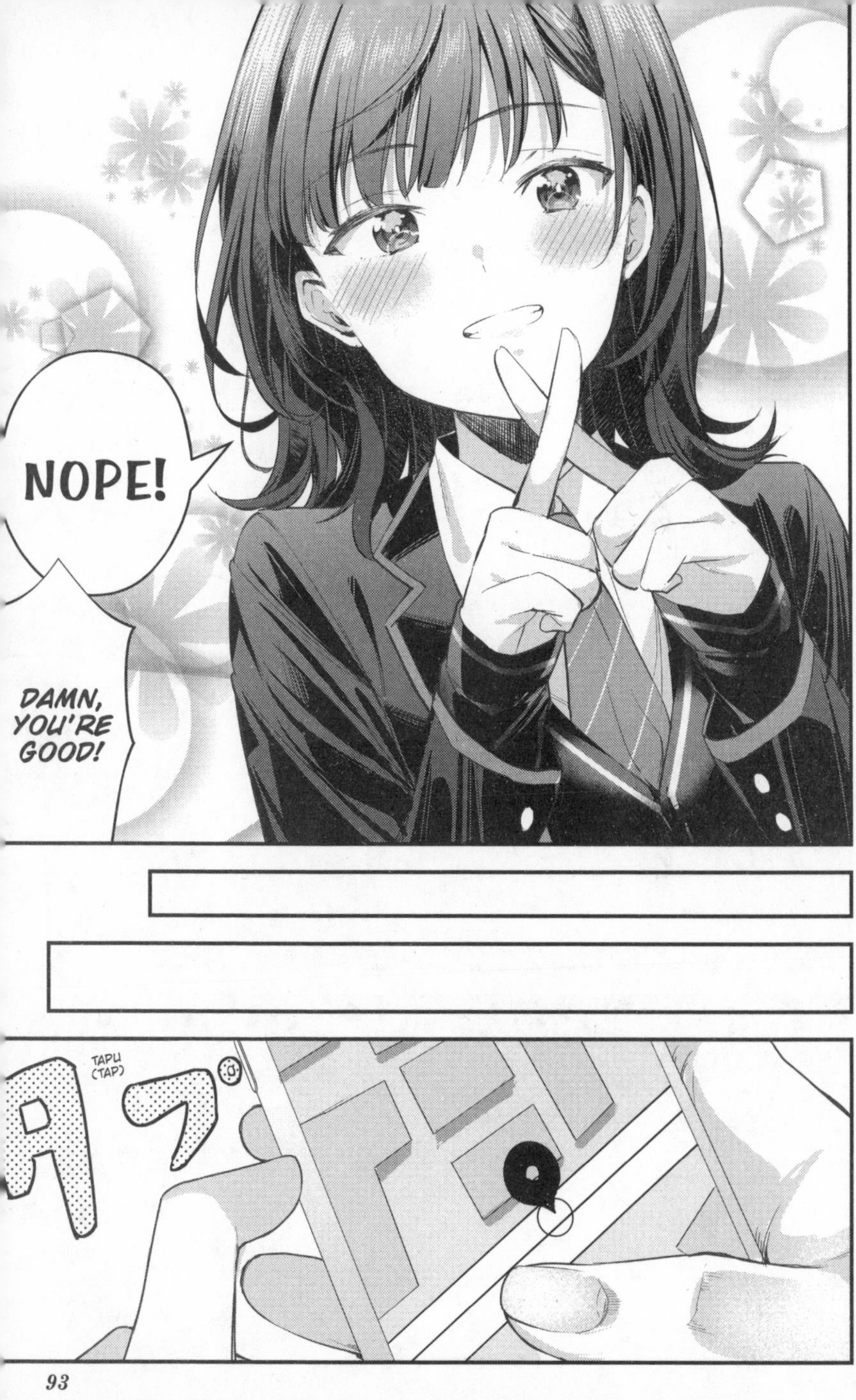
NOPE!
DAMN, YOU'RE GOOD!
TAPU (TAP)

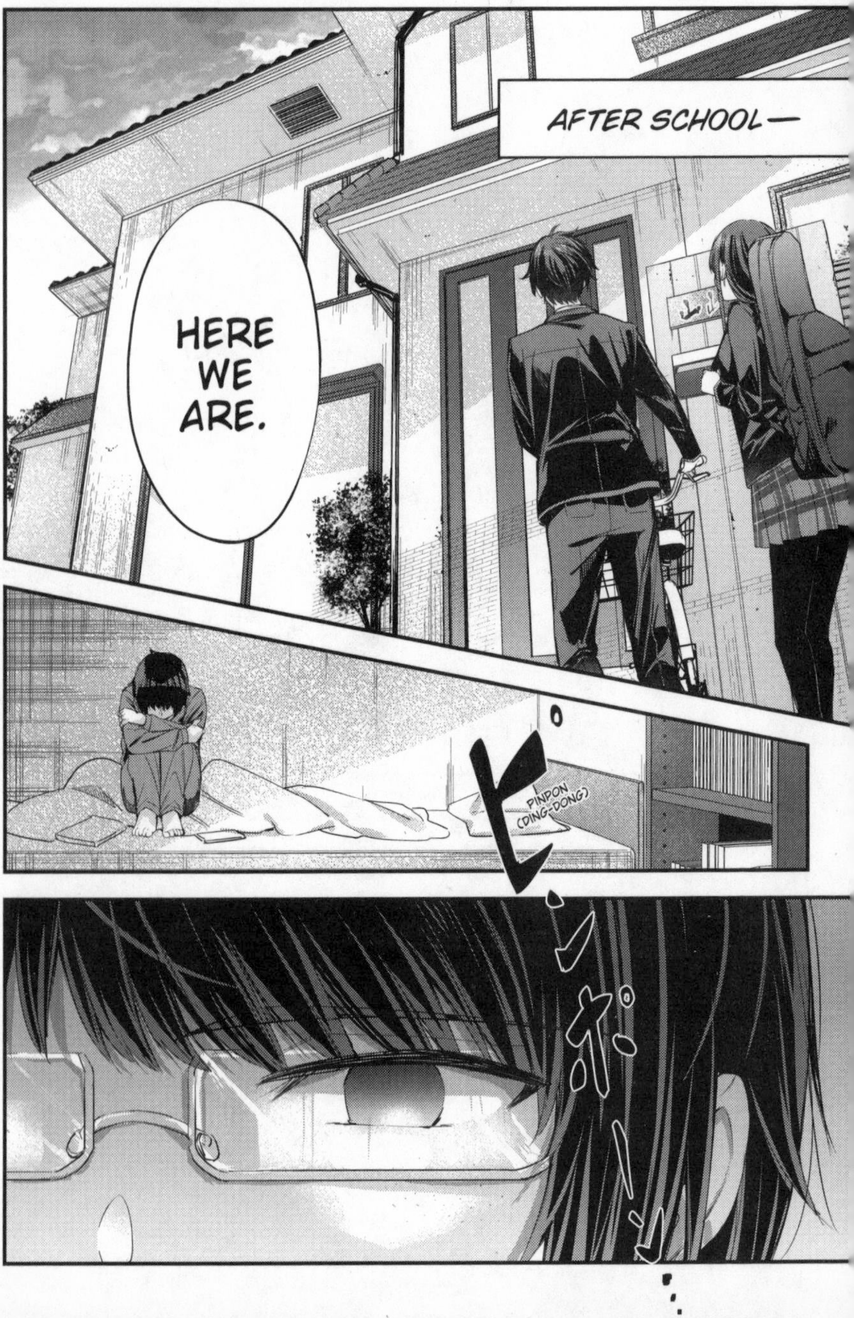
AFTER SCHOOL—
HERE WE ARE.
PINPON (DING-DONG)

CHARACTER PROFILE

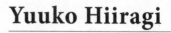

Yuuko Hiiragi

Age: 16 years old

Height: 5’2” (157 cm)

School Club: Tennis Club

Bra Size: D

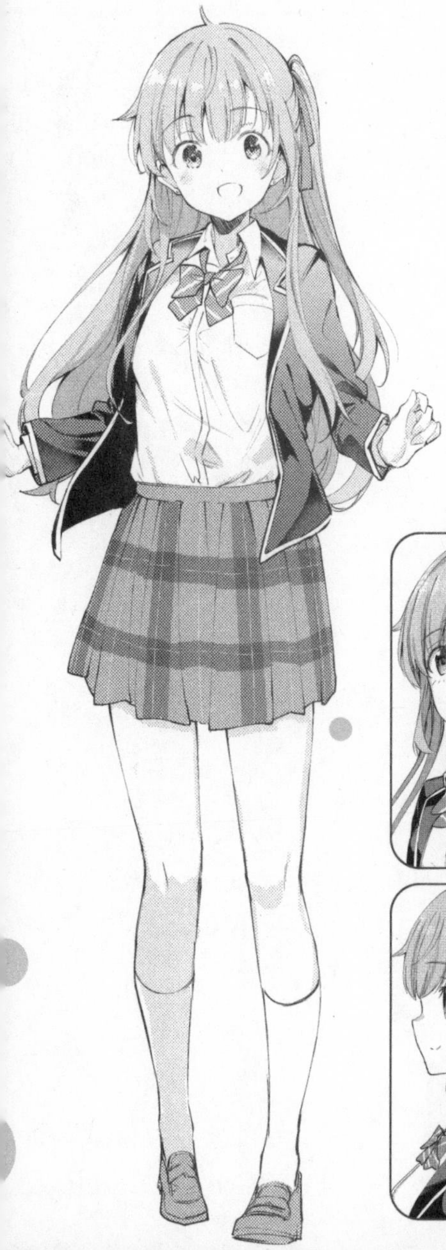

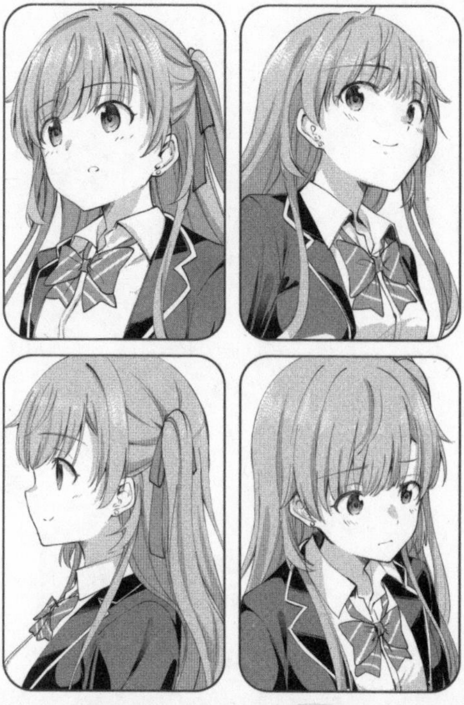

CHARACTER PROFILE

Yua Uchida

Age: 16 years old

Height: 5’1” (155 cm)

School Club: Music Club

Bra Size: C

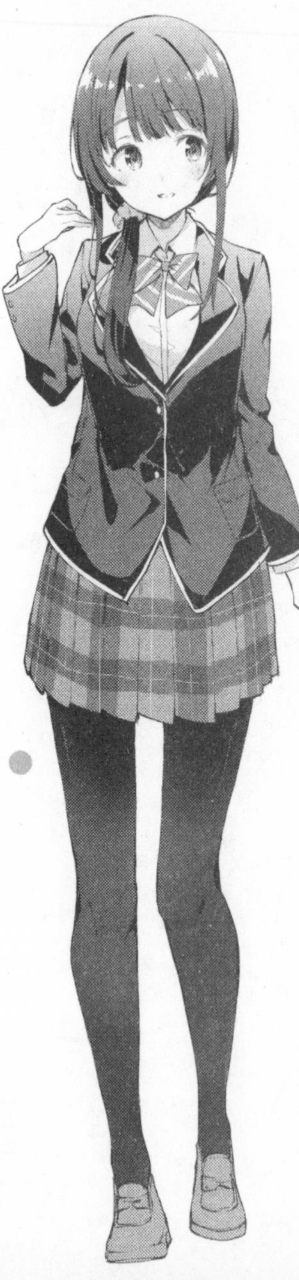

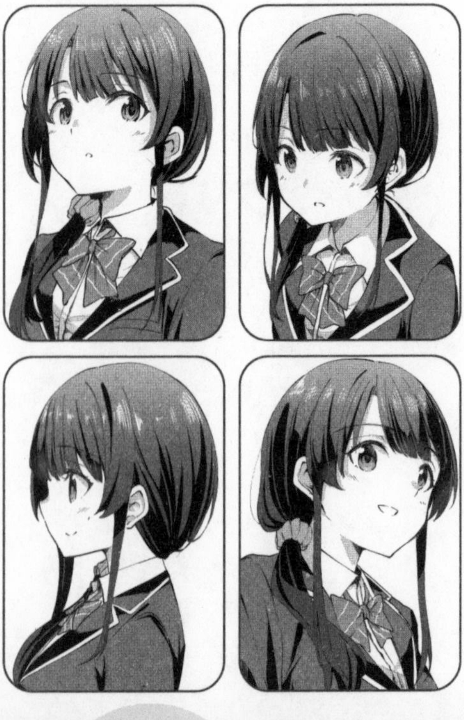

STORY 3:
A CHANCE ENCOUNTER

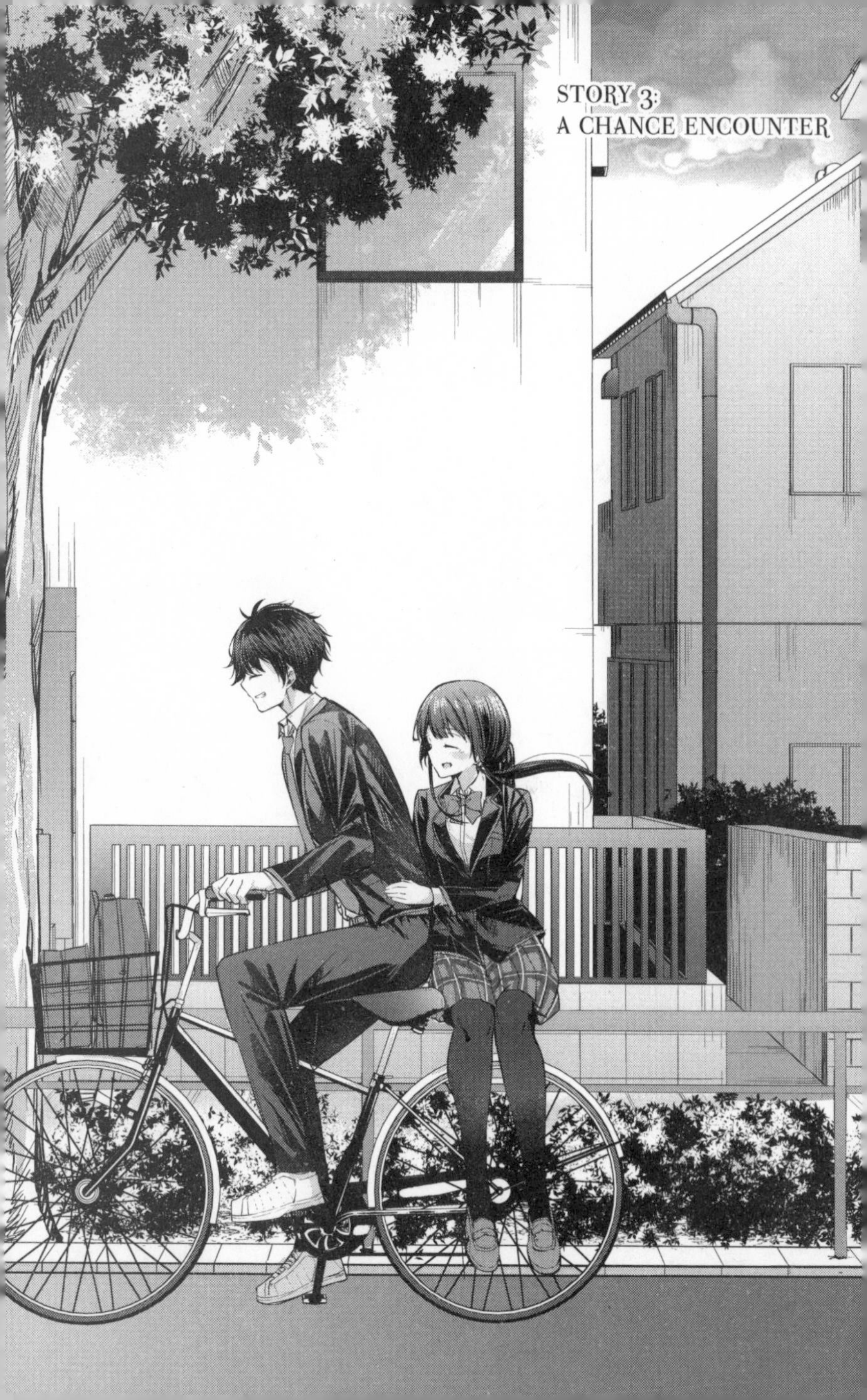

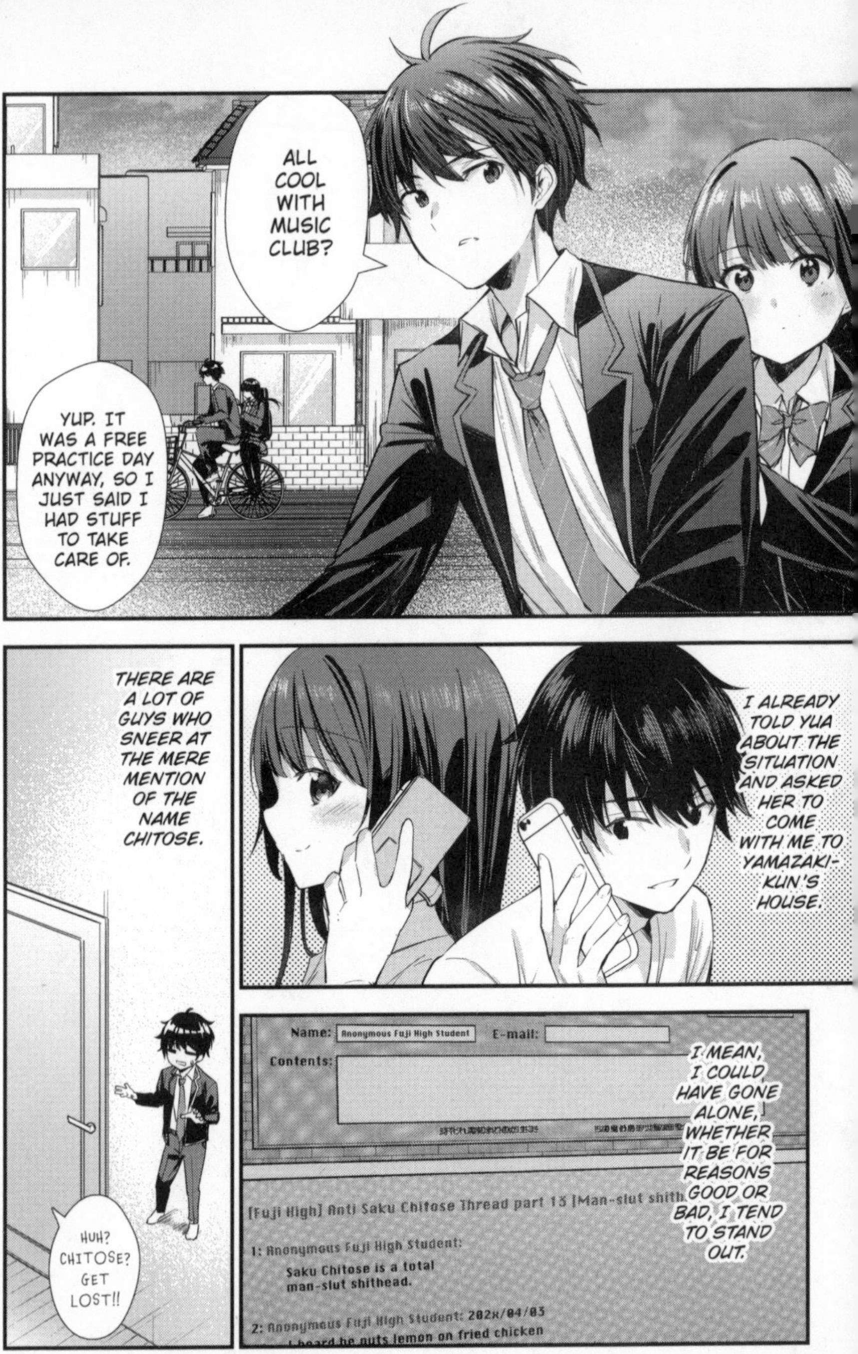
ALL COOL WITH MUSIC CLUB?
YUP. IT WAS A FREE PRACTICE DAY ANYWAY, SO I JUST SAID I HAD STUFF TO TAKE CARE OF.
I ALREADY TOLD YUA ABOUT THE SITUATION AND ASKED HER TO COME WITH ME TO YAMAZAKI-KUN'S HOUSE.
Name: Anonymous Fuji High Student
E-mail:
Contents:
I MEAN, I COULD HAVE GONE ALONE, WHETHER IT BE FOR REASONS GOOD OR BAD, I TEND TO STAND OUT.
[Fuji High] Anti Saku Chitose Thread part 15 [Man-slut shith
1: Anonymous Fuji High Student:
Saku Chitose is a total man-slut shithead.
2: Anonymous Fuji High Student: 202x/04/03
I heard he puts lemon on fried chicken
THERE ARE A LOT OF GUYS WHO SNEER AT THE MERE MENTION OF THE NAME CHITOSE.
HUH? CHITOSE? GET LOST!!

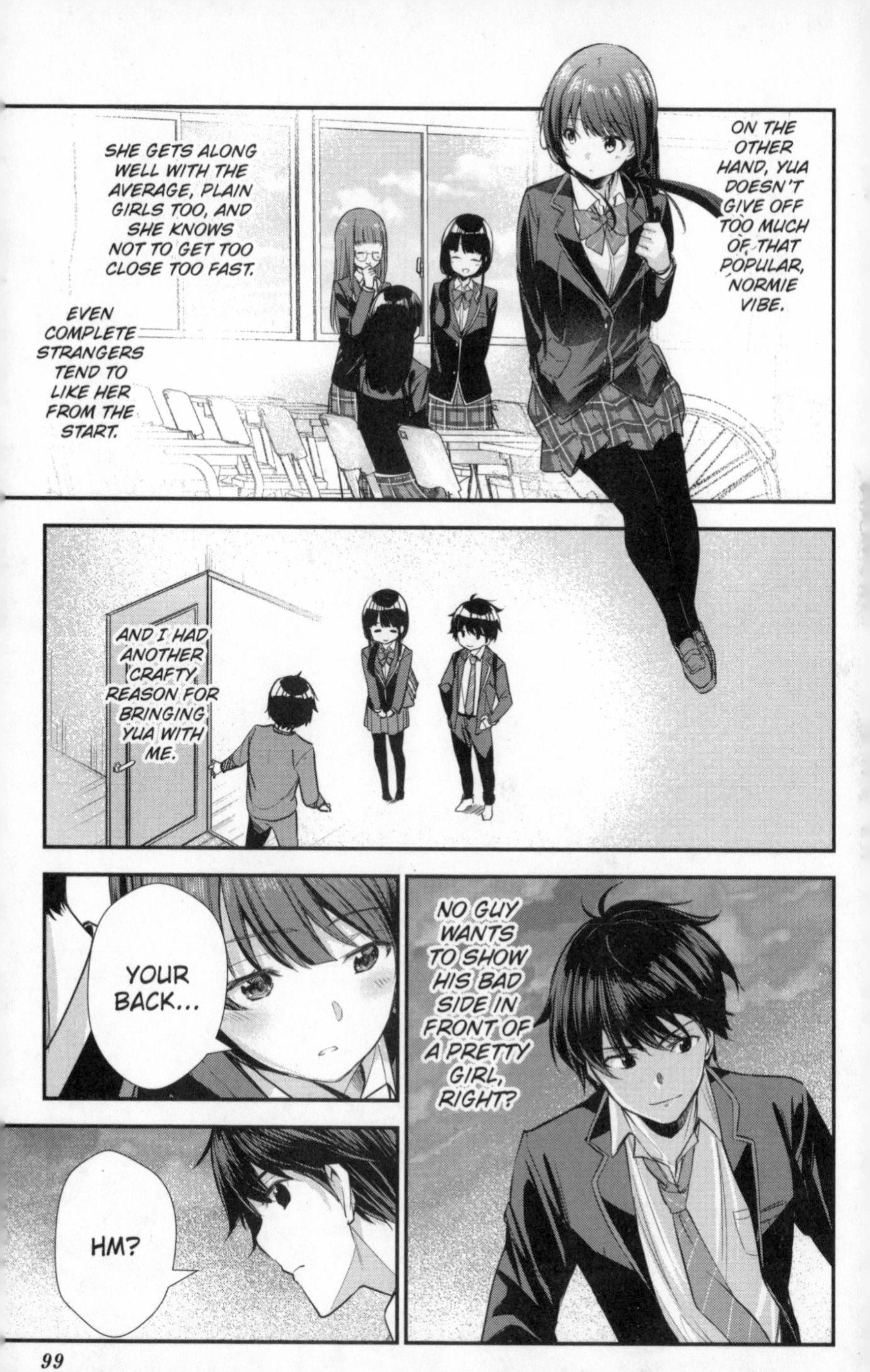
ON THE OTHER HAND, YUA DOESN'T GIVE OFF TOO MUCH OF THAT POPULAR, NORMIE VIBE.
SHE GETS ALONG WELL WITH THE AVERAGE, PLAIN GIRLS TOO, AND SHE KNOWS NOT TO GET TOO CLOSE TOO FAST.
EVEN COMPLETE STRANGERS TEND TO LIKE HER FROM THE START.
AND I HAD ANOTHER CRAFTY REASON FOR BRINGING YUA WITH ME.
NO GUY WANTS TO SHOW HIS BAD SIDE IN FRONT OF A PRETTY GIRL, RIGHT?
YOUR BACK...
HM?

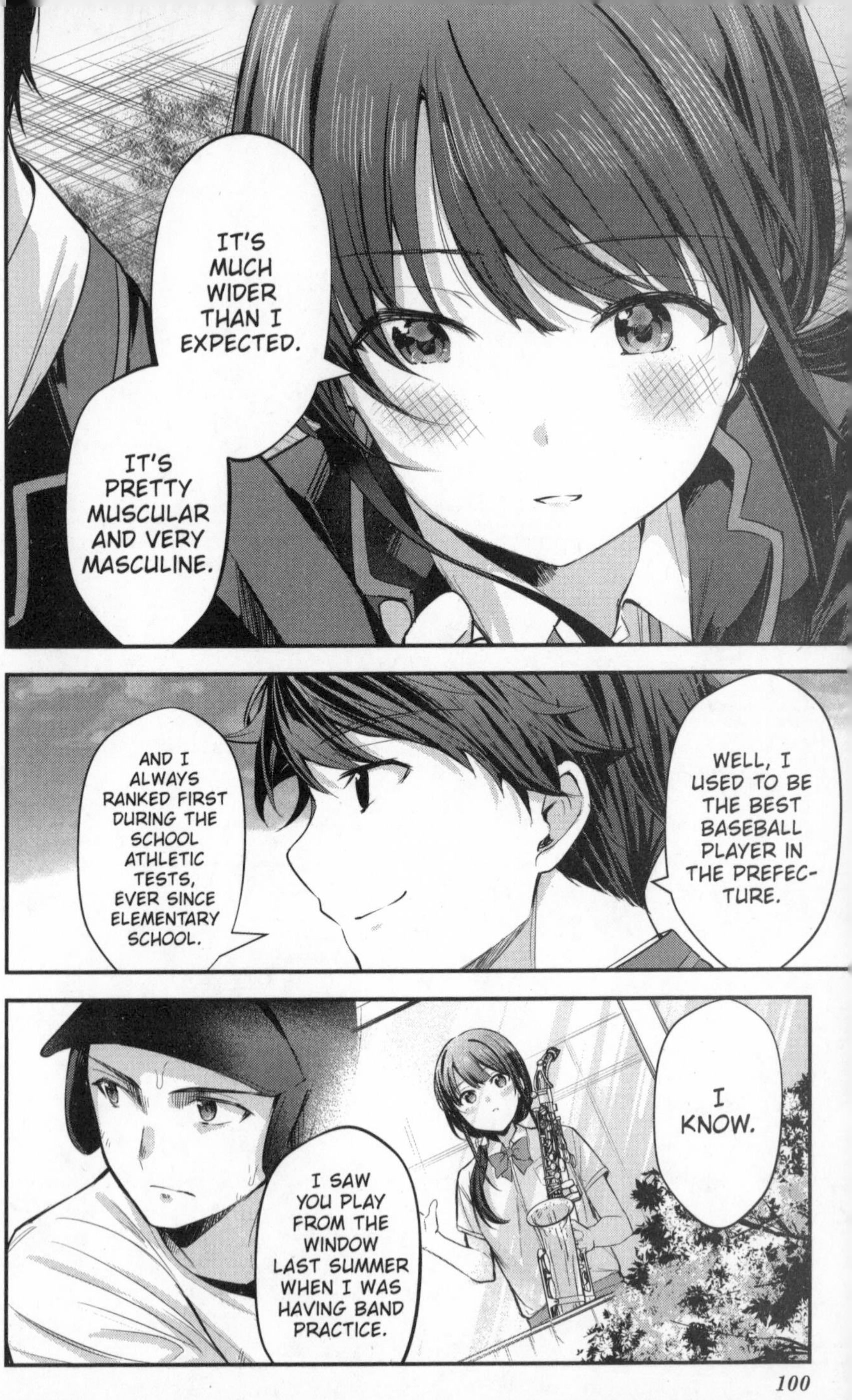
IT'S MUCH WIDER THAN I EXPECTED.
IT'S PRETTY MUSCULAR AND VERY MASCULINE.
WELL, I USED TO BE THE BEST BASEBALL PLAYER IN THE PREFEC-TURE.
AND I ALWAYS RANKED FIRST DURING THE SCHOOL ATHLETIC TESTS, EVER SINCE ELEMENTARY SCHOOL.
I KNOW.
I SAW YOU PLAY FROM THE WINDOW LAST SUMMER WHEN I WAS HAVING BAND PRACTICE.

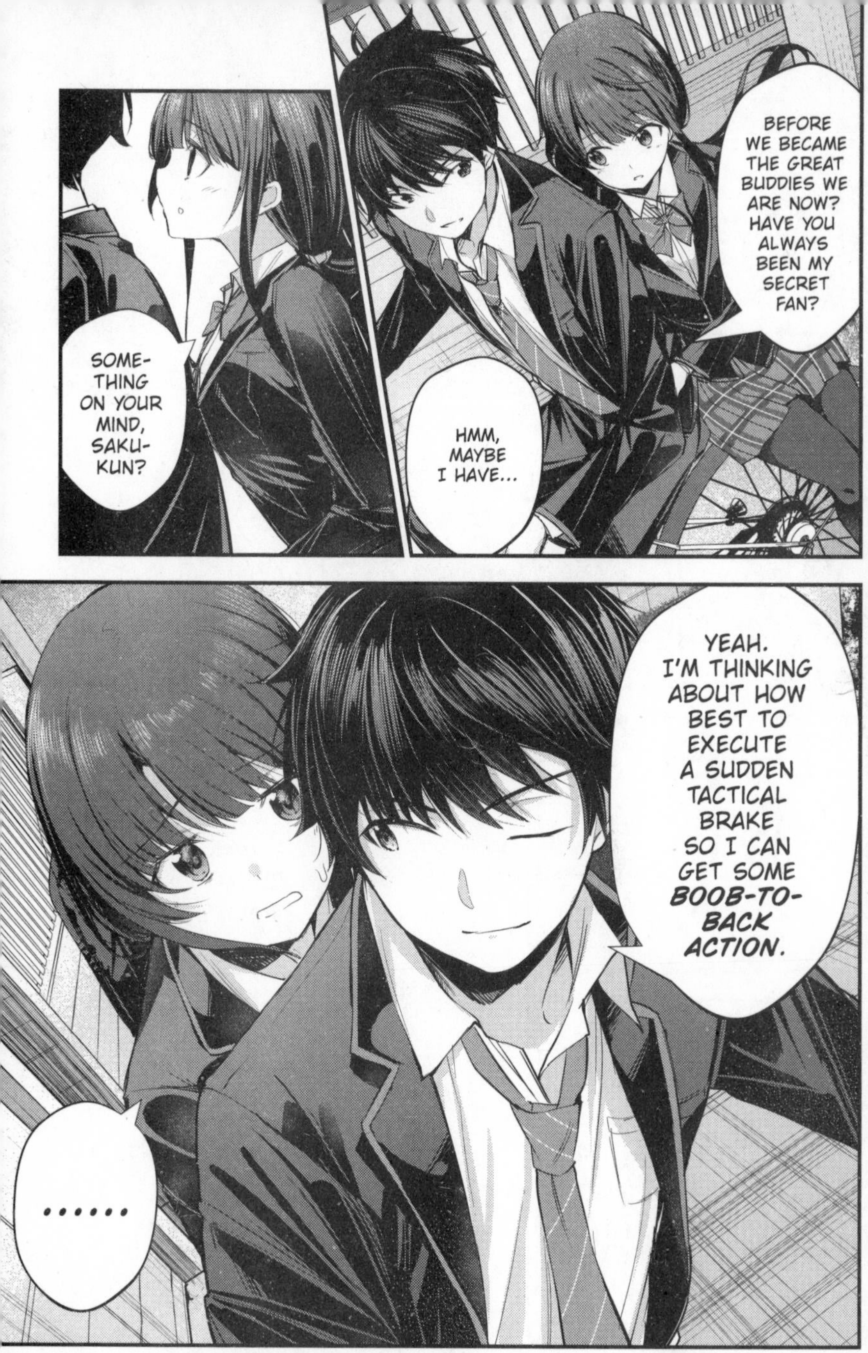
BEFORE WE BECAME THE GREAT BUDDIES WE ARE NOW? HAVE YOU ALWAYS BEEN MY SECRET FAN?
HMM, MAYBE I HAVE...
SOME-THING ON YOUR MIND, SAKU-KUN?
YEAH. I'M THINKING ABOUT HOW BEST TO EXECUTE A SUDDEN TACTICAL BRAKE SO I CAN GET SOME *BOOB-TO-BACK ACTION*.
......

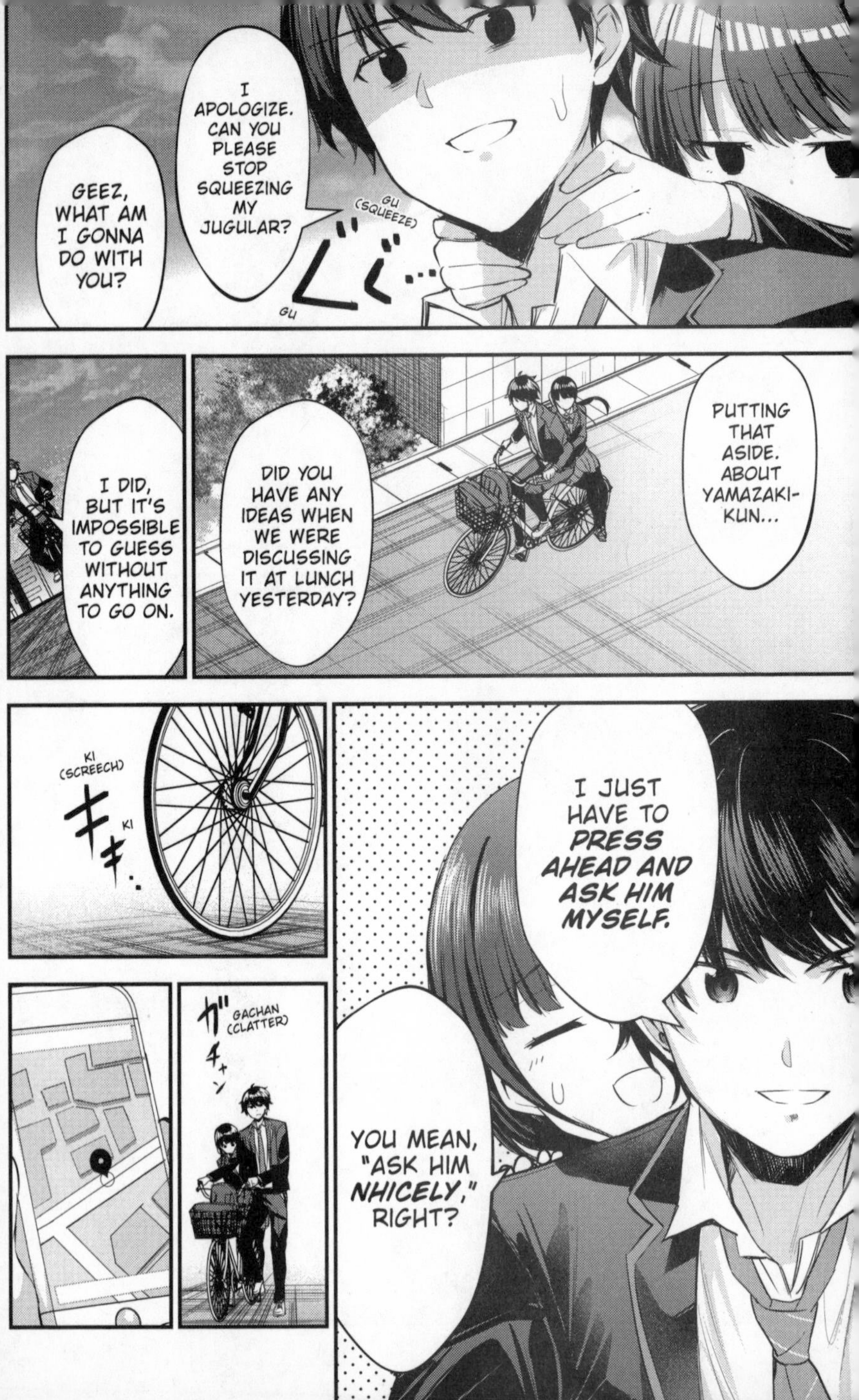
I APOLOGIZE. CAN YOU PLEASE STOP SQUEEZING MY JUGULAR?
GU (SQUEEZE)
GU
GEEZ, WHAT AM I GONNA DO WITH YOU?
PUTTING THAT ASIDE. ABOUT YAMAZAKI-KUN...
DID YOU HAVE ANY IDEAS WHEN WE WERE DISCUSSING IT AT LUNCH YESTERDAY?
I DID, BUT IT'S IMPOSSIBLE TO GUESS WITHOUT ANYTHING TO GO ON.
I JUST HAVE TO *PRESS AHEAD AND ASK HIM MYSELF.*
YOU MEAN, "ASK HIM *NHICELY*," RIGHT?
KI (SCREECH)
KI
GACHAN (CLATTER)

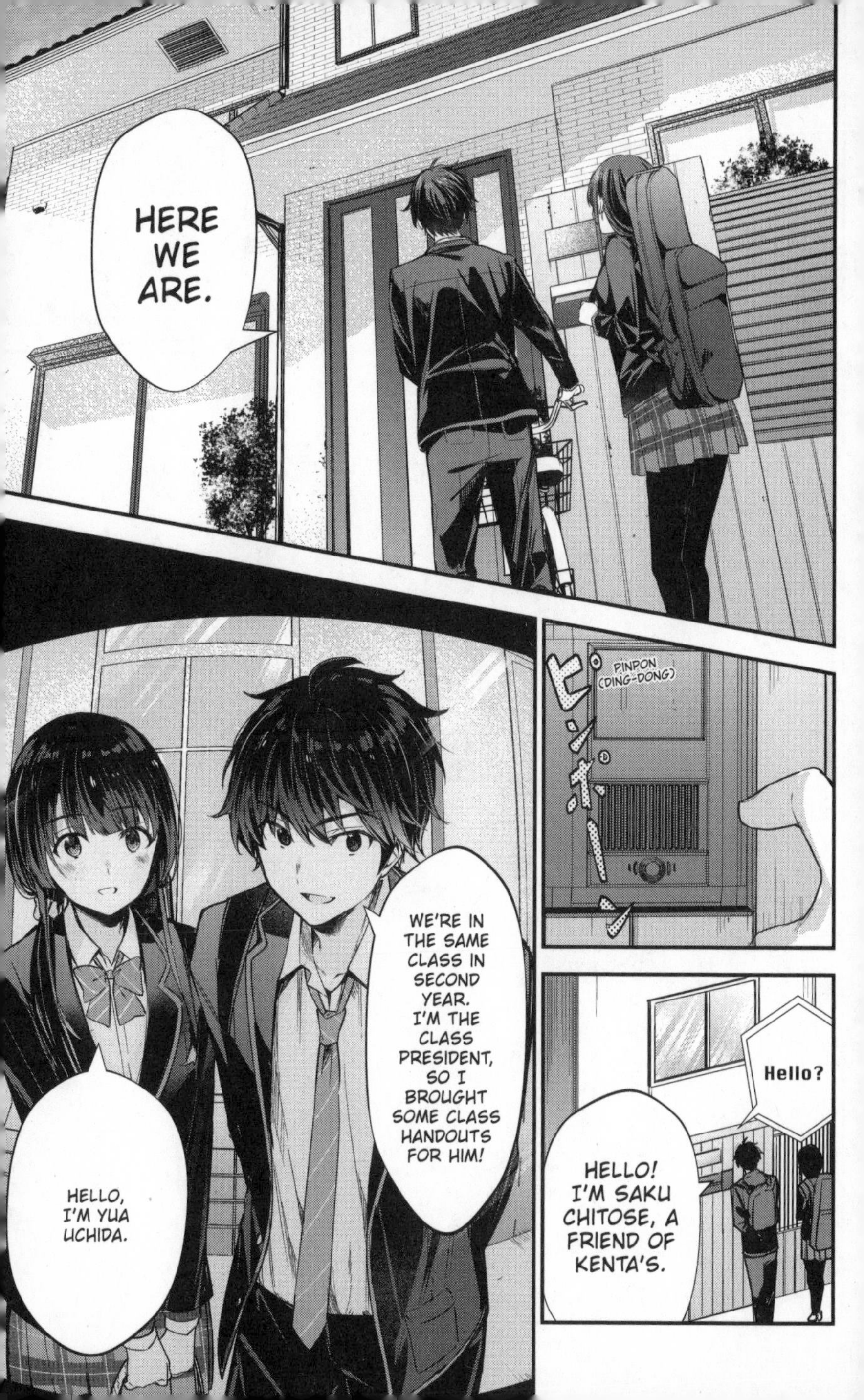
HERE WE ARE.
PINPON (DING-DONG)
Hello?
HELLO! I'M SAKU CHITOSE, A FRIEND OF KENTA'S.
WE'RE IN THE SAME CLASS IN SECOND YEAR. I'M THE CLASS PRESIDENT, SO I BROUGHT SOME CLASS HANDOUTS FOR HIM!
HELLO, I'M YUA UCHIDA.

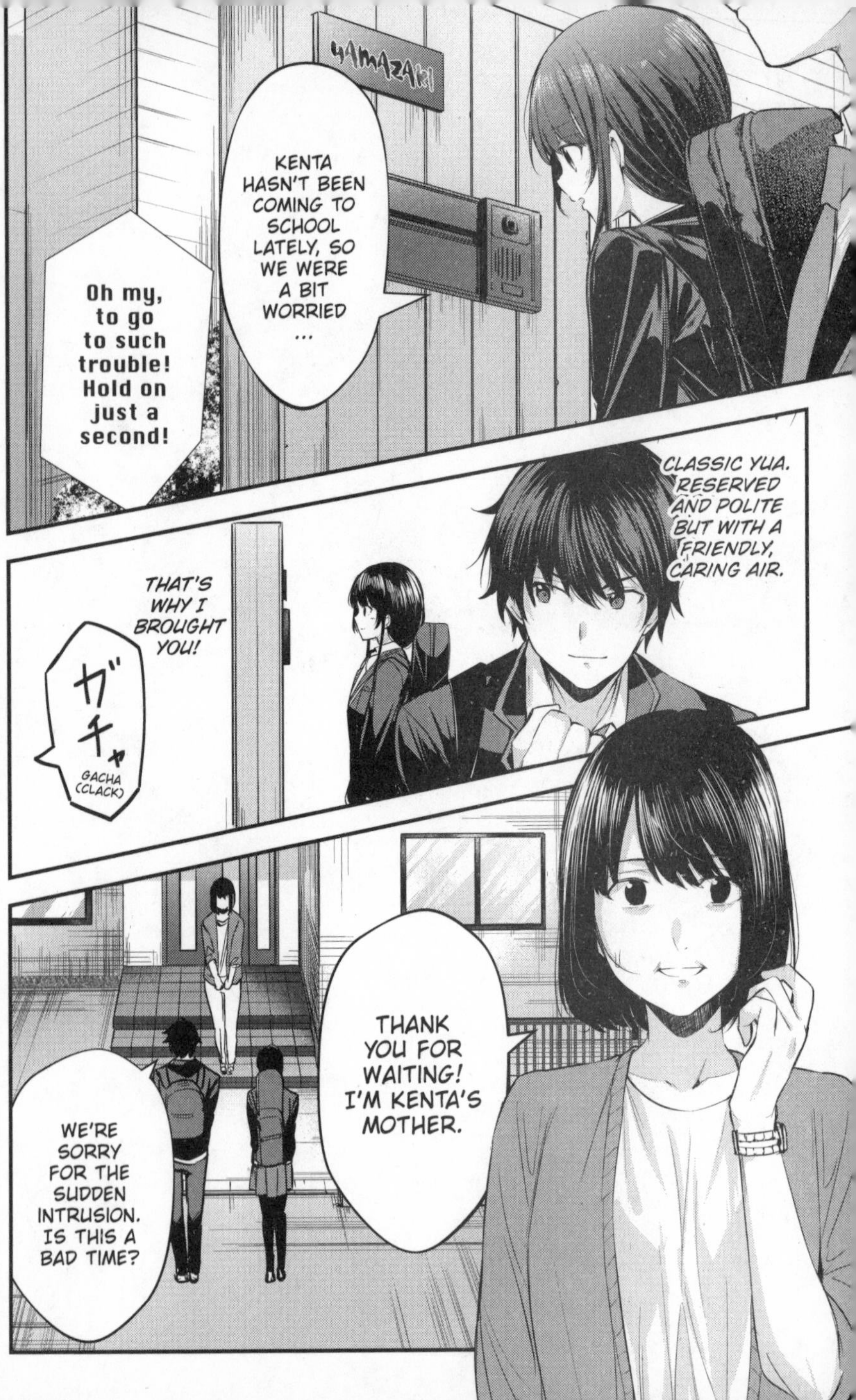
YAMAZAKI
KENTA HASN'T BEEN COMING TO SCHOOL LATELY, SO WE WERE A BIT WORRIED ...
Oh my, to go to such trouble! Hold on just a second!
CLASSIC YUA. RESERVED AND POLITE BUT WITH A FRIENDLY, CARING AIR.
THAT'S WHY I BROUGHT YOU!
ガチャ
GACHA (CLACK)
THANK YOU FOR WAITING! I'M KENTA'S MOTHER.
WE'RE SORRY FOR THE SUDDEN INTRUSION. IS THIS A BAD TIME?

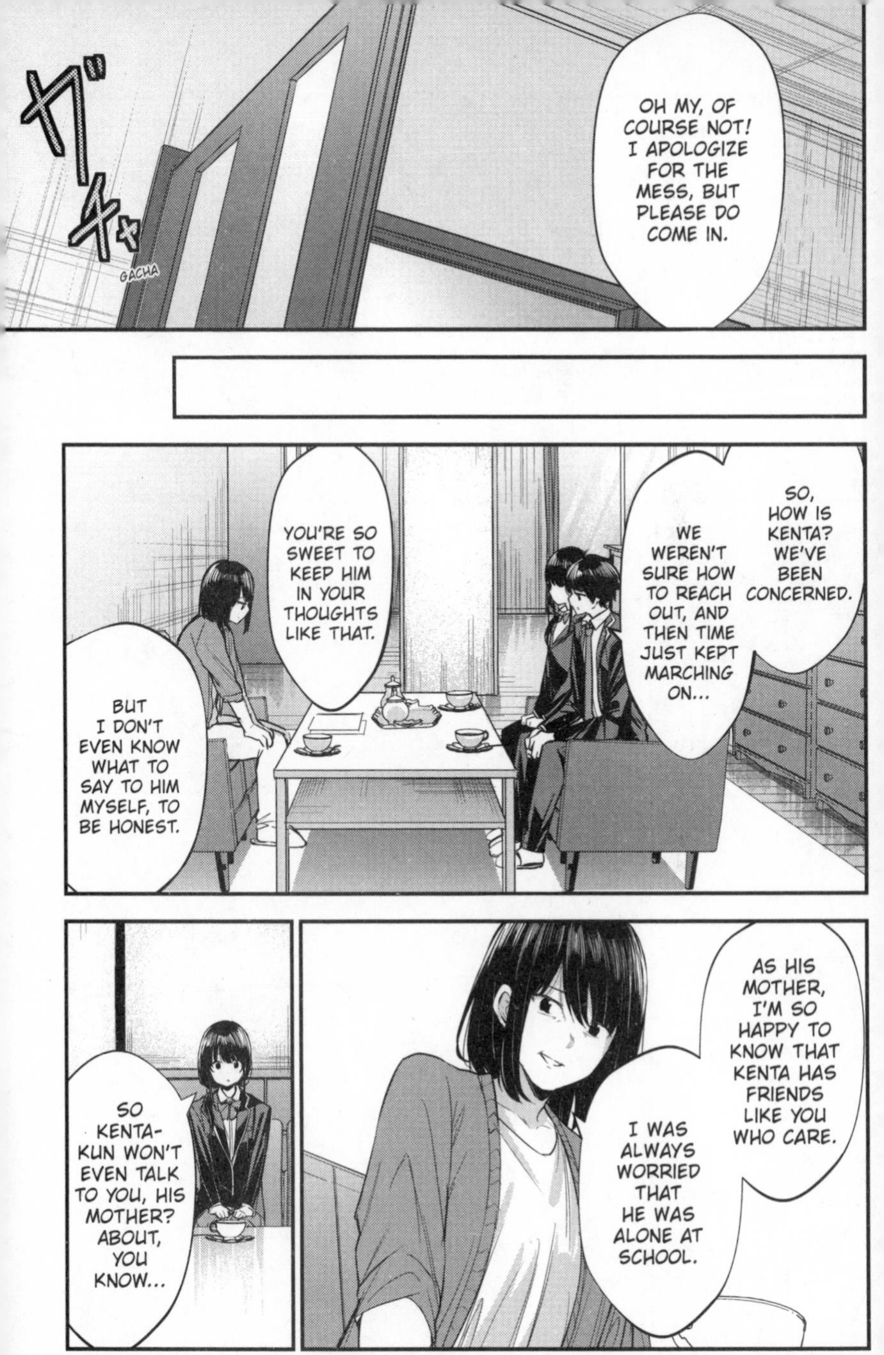
OH MY, OF COURSE NOT! I APOLOGIZE FOR THE MESS, BUT PLEASE DO COME IN.
ガチャ
GACHA
SO, HOW IS KENTA? WE'VE BEEN CONCERNED.
WE WEREN'T SURE HOW TO REACH OUT, AND THEN TIME JUST KEPT MARCHING ON...
YOU'RE SO SWEET TO KEEP HIM IN YOUR THOUGHTS LIKE THAT.
BUT I DON'T EVEN KNOW WHAT TO SAY TO HIM MYSELF, TO BE HONEST.
AS HIS MOTHER, I'M SO HAPPY TO KNOW THAT KENTA HAS FRIENDS LIKE YOU WHO CARE.
I WAS ALWAYS WORRIED THAT HE WAS ALONE AT SCHOOL.
SO KENTA-KUN WON'T EVEN TALK TO YOU, HIS MOTHER? ABOUT, YOU KNOW...

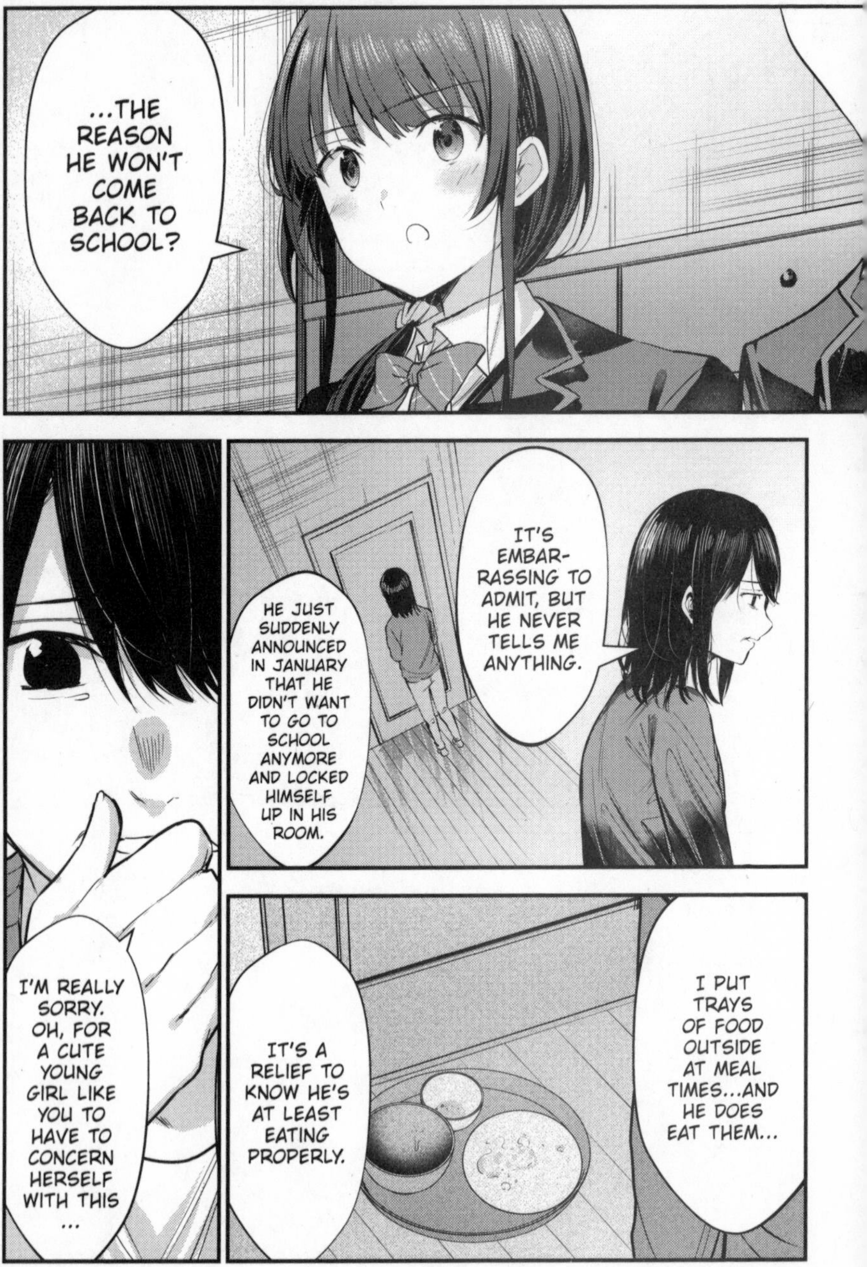
...THE REASON HE WON'T COME BACK TO SCHOOL?
IT'S EMBARRASSING TO ADMIT, BUT HE NEVER TELLS ME ANYTHING.
HE JUST SUDDENLY ANNOUNCED IN JANUARY THAT HE DIDN'T WANT TO GO TO SCHOOL ANYMORE AND LOCKED HIMSELF UP IN HIS ROOM.
I PUT TRAYS OF FOOD OUTSIDE AT MEAL TIMES...AND HE DOES EAT THEM...
IT'S A RELIEF TO KNOW HE'S AT LEAST EATING PROPERLY.
I'M REALLY SORRY. OH, FOR A CUTE YOUNG GIRL LIKE YOU TO HAVE TO CONCERN HERSELF WITH THIS ...

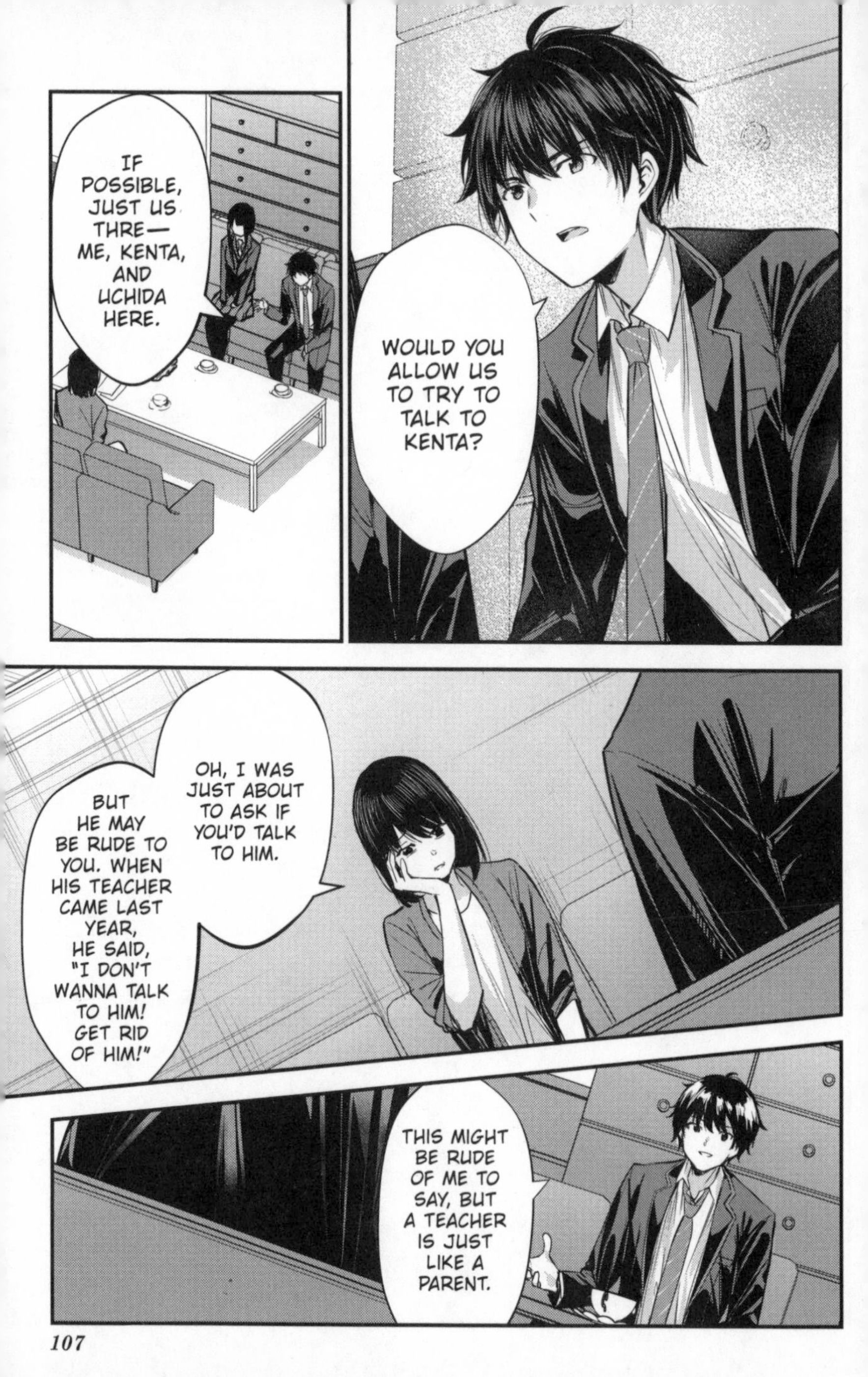
WOULD YOU ALLOW US TO TRY TO TALK TO KENTA?
IF POSSIBLE, JUST US THRE— ME, KENTA, AND UCHIDA HERE.
OH, I WAS JUST ABOUT TO ASK IF YOU'D TALK TO HIM.
BUT HE MAY BE RUDE TO YOU. WHEN HIS TEACHER CAME LAST YEAR, HE SAID, "I DON'T WANNA TALK TO HIM! GET RID OF HIM!"
THIS MIGHT BE RUDE OF ME TO SAY, BUT A TEACHER IS JUST LIKE A PARENT.

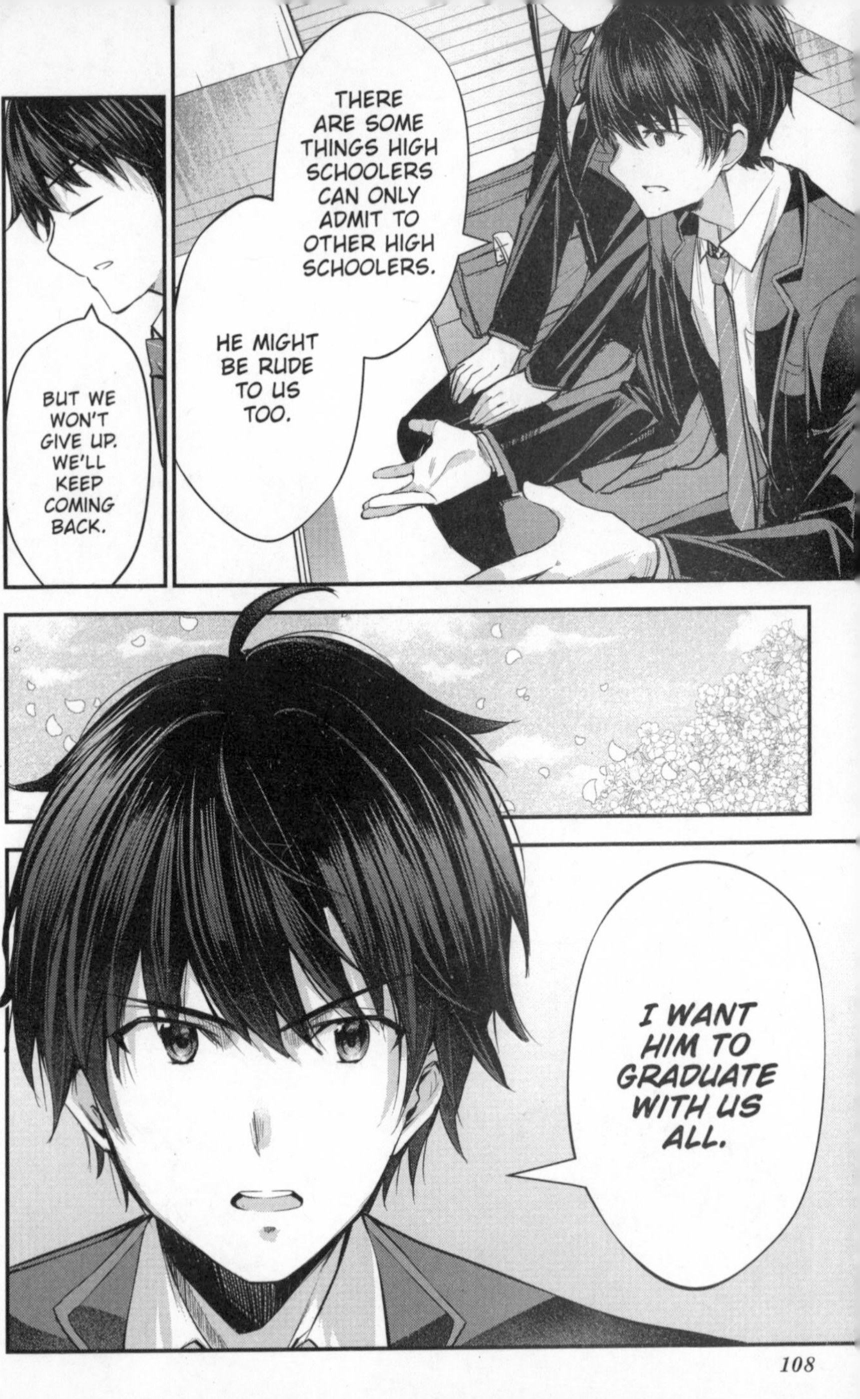
THERE ARE SOME THINGS HIGH SCHOOLERS CAN ONLY ADMIT TO OTHER HIGH SCHOOLERS.
HE MIGHT BE RUDE TO US TOO.
BUT WE WON'T GIVE UP. WE'LL KEEP COMING BACK.
I WANT HIM TO GRADUATE WITH US ALL.

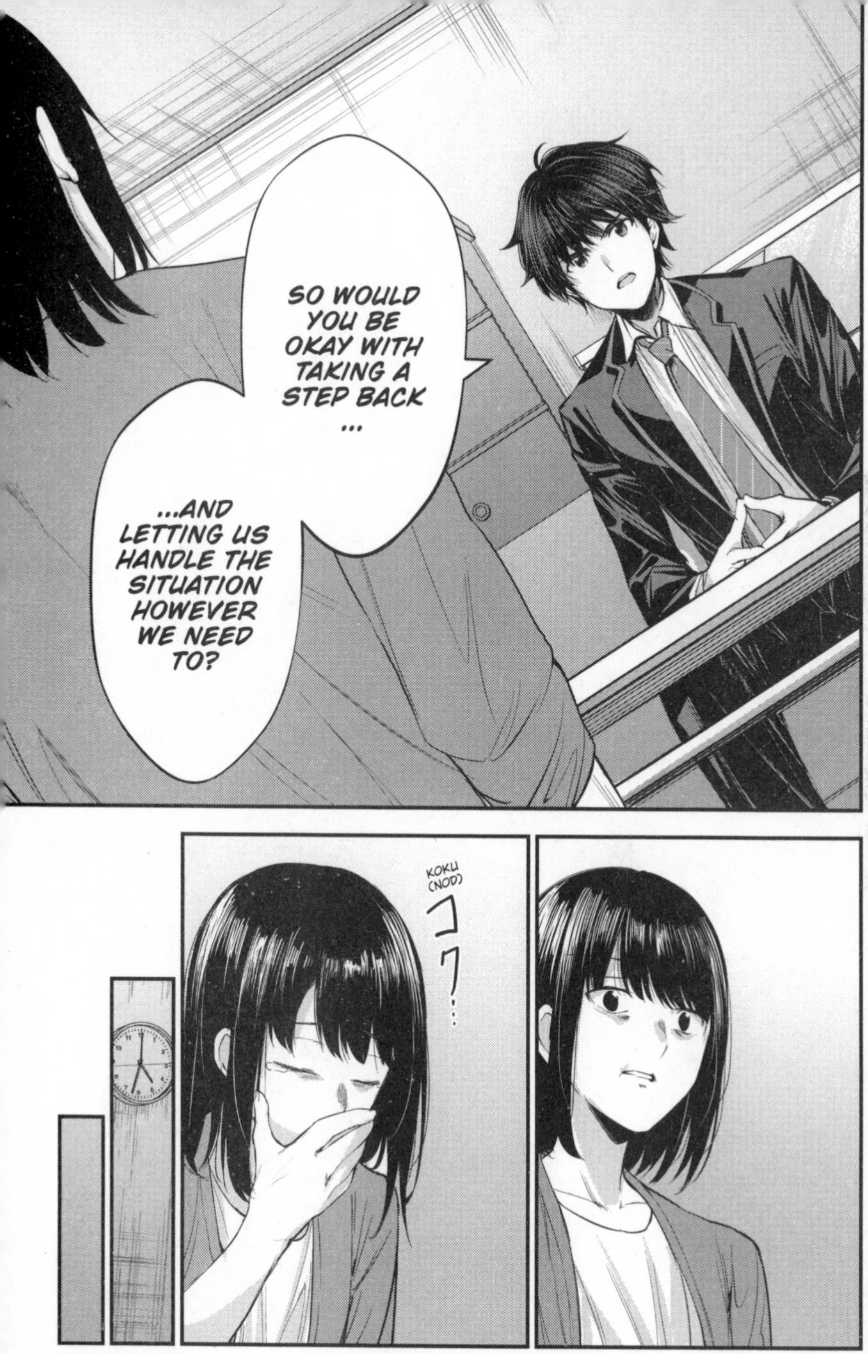
SO WOULD YOU BE OKAY WITH TAKING A STEP BACK ...
...AND LETTING US HANDLE THE SITUATION HOWEVER WE NEED TO?
KOKU (NOD)
コク...

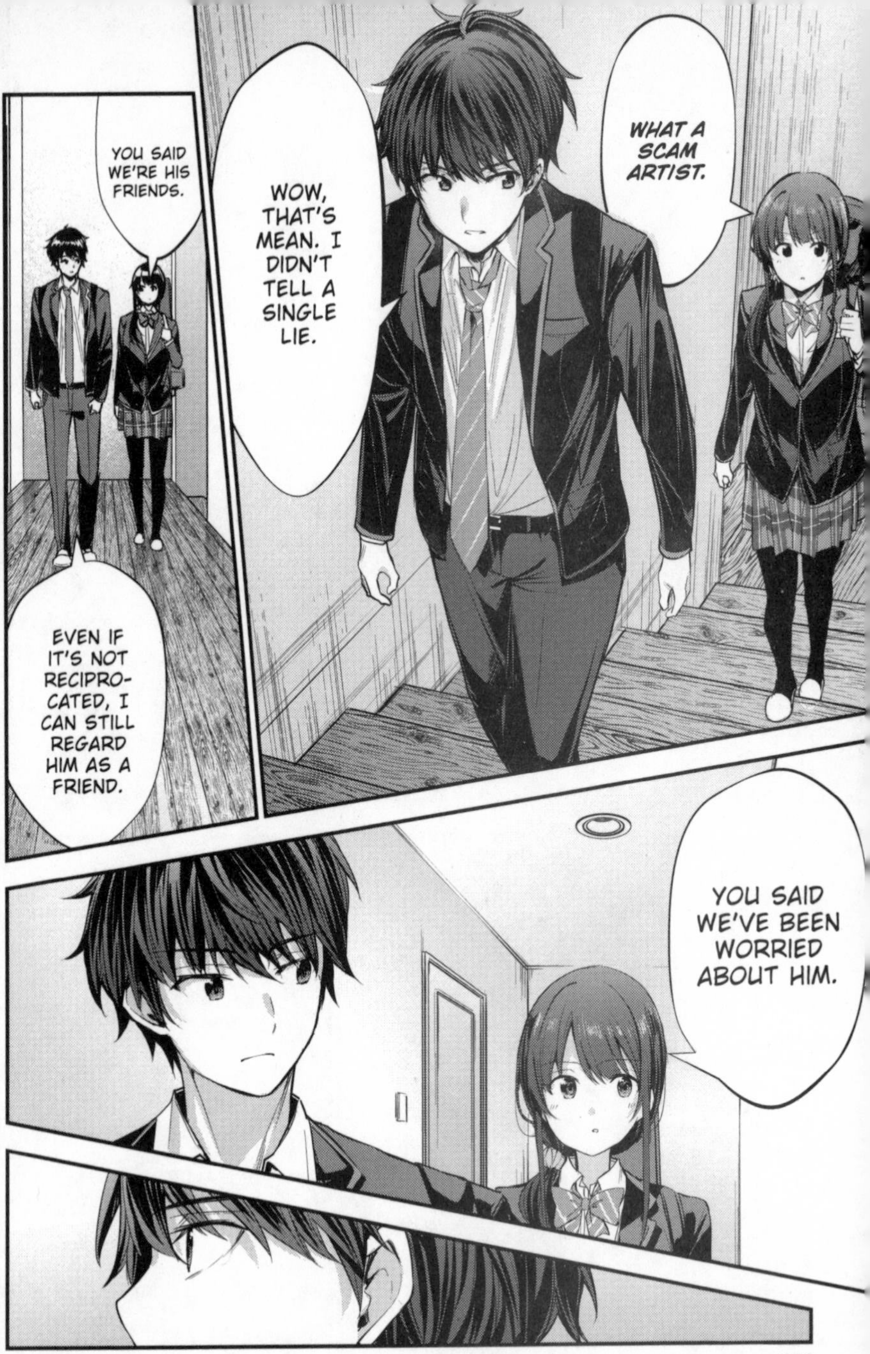
WHAT A SCAM ARTIST.
WOW, THAT'S MEAN. I DIDN'T TELL A SINGLE LIE.
YOU SAID WE'RE HIS FRIENDS.
EVEN IF IT'S NOT RECIPRO-CATED, I CAN STILL REGARD HIM AS A FRIEND.
YOU SAID WE'VE BEEN WORRIED ABOUT HIM.

SU
(LIFT)

AND WE HAVE BEEN WORRIED SINCE LUNCH YESTER-DAY.

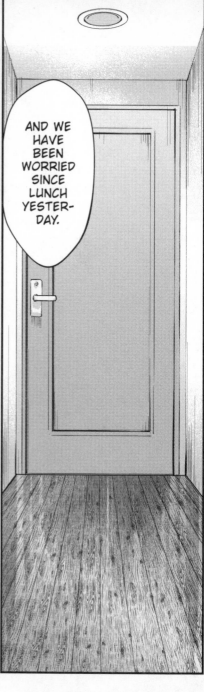

KON
(KNOCK)

KON

KON

...

SHIN
(SILENCE)

KNOCK

KNOCK

KNOCK

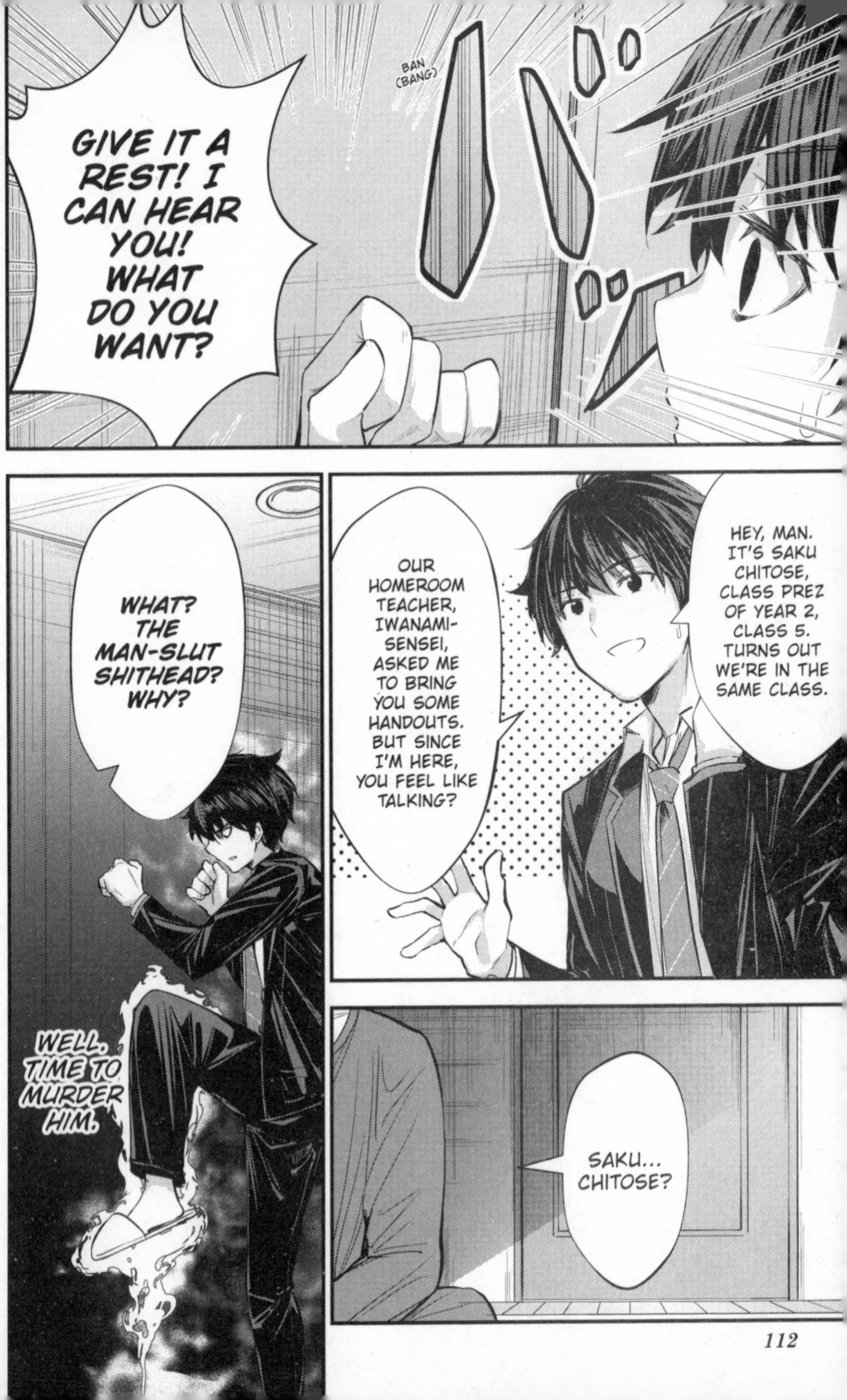
BAN (BANG)
GIVE IT A REST! I CAN HEAR YOU! WHAT DO YOU WANT?
HEY, MAN. IT'S SAKU CHITOSE, CLASS PREZ OF YEAR 2, CLASS 5. TURNS OUT WE'RE IN THE SAME CLASS.
OUR HOMEROOM TEACHER, IWANAMI-SENSEI, ASKED ME TO BRING YOU SOME HANDOUTS. BUT SINCE I'M HERE, YOU FEEL LIKE TALKING?
SAKU... CHITOSE?
WHAT? THE MAN-SLUT SHITHEAD? WHY?
WELL. TIME TO MURDER HIM.

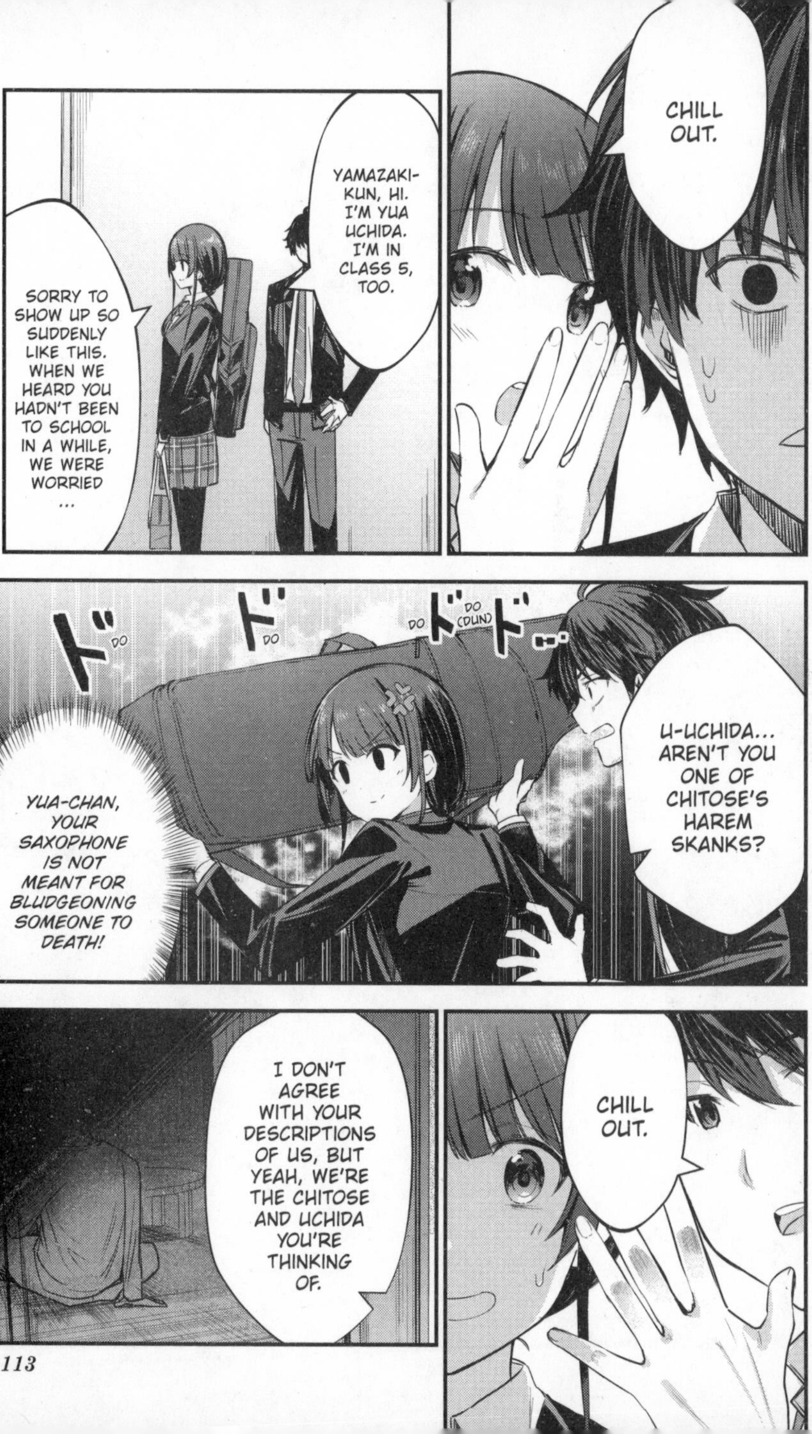
CHILL OUT.
YAMAZAKI-KUN, HI. I'M YUA UCHIDA. I'M IN CLASS 5, TOO.
SORRY TO SHOW UP SO SUDDENLY LIKE THIS. WHEN WE HEARD YOU HADN'T BEEN TO SCHOOL IN A WHILE, WE WERE WORRIED ...
DO DO (DUN) DO DO DO
U-UCHIDA... AREN'T YOU ONE OF CHITOSE'S HAREM SKANKS?
YUA-CHAN, YOUR SAXOPHONE IS NOT MEANT FOR BLUDGEONING SOMEONE TO DEATH!
CHILL OUT.
I DON'T AGREE WITH YOUR DESCRIPTIONS OF US, BUT YEAH, WE'RE THE CHITOSE AND UCHIDA YOU'RE THINKING OF.

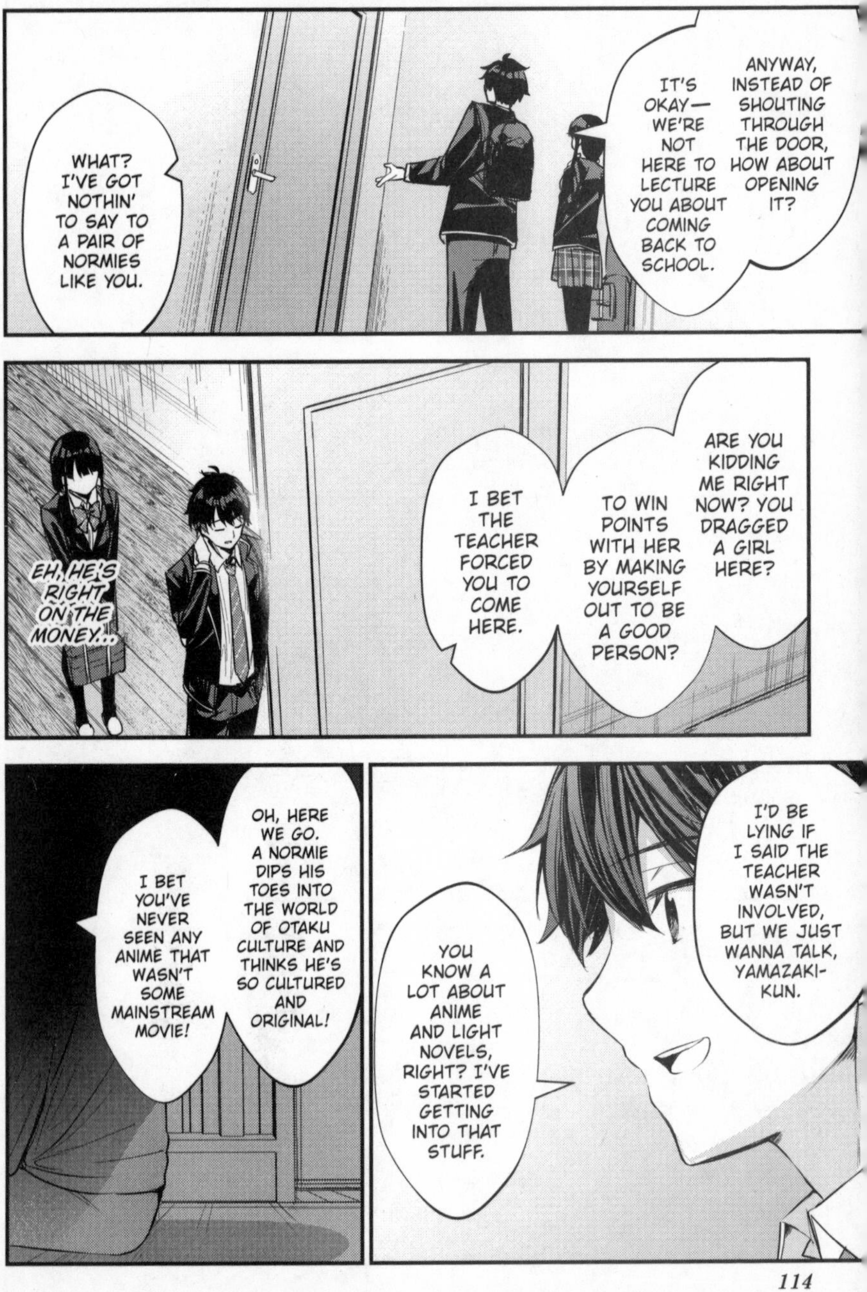
ANYWAY, INSTEAD OF SHOUTING THROUGH THE DOOR, HOW ABOUT OPENING IT?
IT'S OKAY— WE'RE NOT HERE TO LECTURE YOU ABOUT COMING BACK TO SCHOOL.
WHAT? I'VE GOT NOTHIN' TO SAY TO A PAIR OF NORMIES LIKE YOU.
ARE YOU KIDDING ME RIGHT NOW? YOU DRAGGED A GIRL HERE?
TO WIN POINTS WITH HER BY MAKING YOURSELF OUT TO BE A GOOD PERSON?
I BET THE TEACHER FORCED YOU TO COME HERE.
EH, HE'S RIGHT ON THE MONEY...
I'D BE LYING IF I SAID THE TEACHER WASN'T INVOLVED, BUT WE JUST WANNA TALK, YAMAZAKI-KUN.
YOU KNOW A LOT ABOUT ANIME AND LIGHT NOVELS, RIGHT? I'VE STARTED GETTING INTO THAT STUFF.
OH, HERE WE GO. A NORMIE DIPS HIS TOES INTO THE WORLD OF OTAKU CULTURE AND THINKS HE'S SO CULTURED AND ORIGINAL!
I BET YOU'VE NEVER SEEN ANY ANIME THAT WASN'T SOME MAINSTREAM MOVIE!

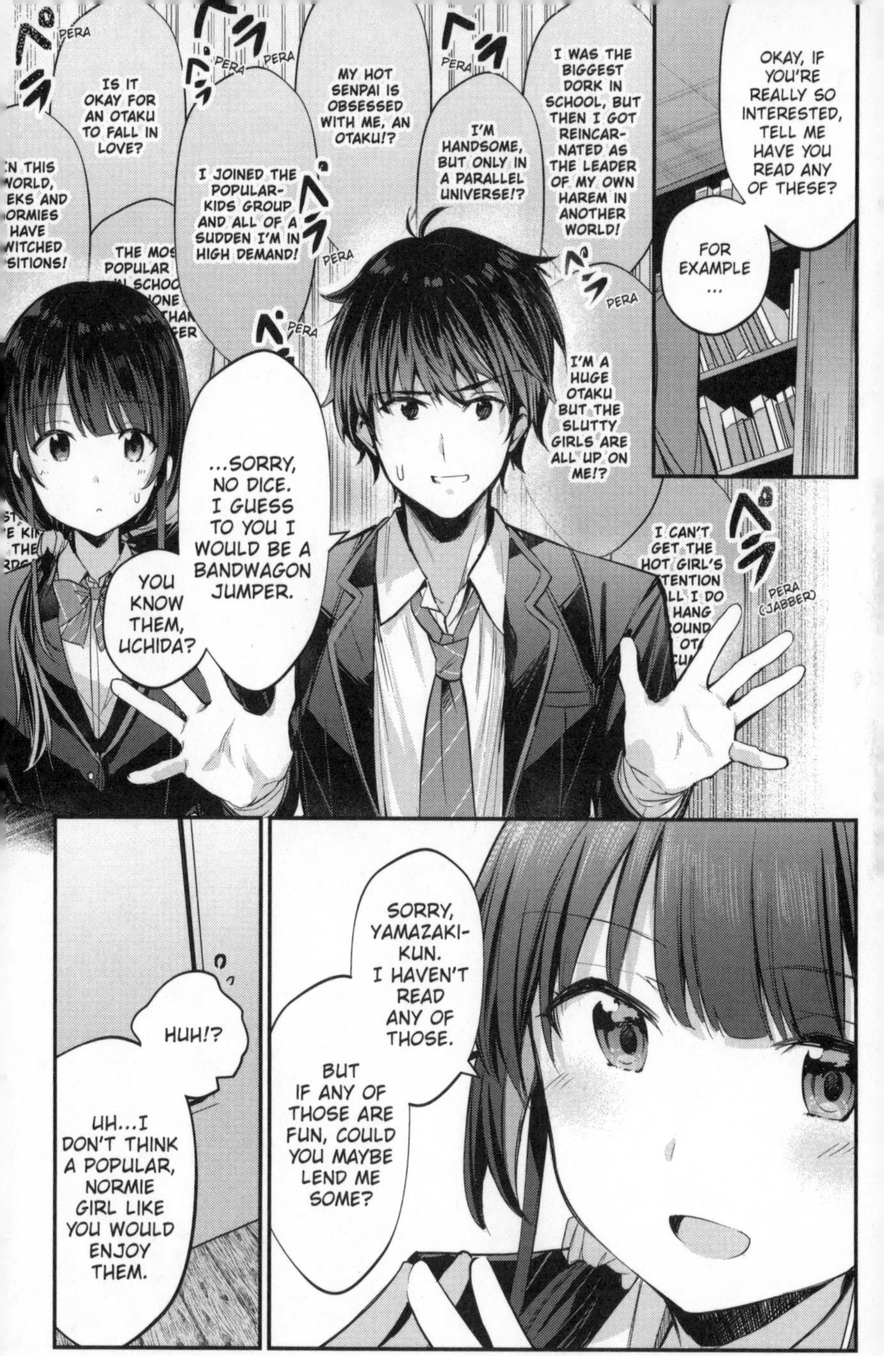
OKAY, IF YOU'RE REALLY SO INTERESTED, TELL ME HAVE YOU READ ANY OF THESE?
FOR EXAMPLE ...
I WAS THE BIGGEST DORK IN SCHOOL, BUT THEN I GOT REINCARNATED AS THE LEADER OF MY OWN HAREM IN ANOTHER WORLD!
PERA
I'M HANDSOME, BUT ONLY IN A PARALLEL UNIVERSE!?
MY HOT SENPAI IS OBSESSED WITH ME, AN OTAKU!?
PERA
PERA
I JOINED THE POPULAR-KIDS GROUP AND ALL OF A SUDDEN I'M IN HIGH DEMAND!
PERA
IS IT OKAY FOR AN OTAKU TO FALL IN LOVE?
PERA
PERA
PERA
I'M A HUGE OTAKU BUT THE SLUTTY GIRLS ARE ALL UP ON ME!?
PERA (JABBER)
...SORRY, NO DICE. I GUESS TO YOU I WOULD BE A BANDWAGON JUMPER.
YOU KNOW THEM, UCHIDA?
SORRY, YAMAZAKI-KUN. I HAVEN'T READ ANY OF THOSE.
BUT IF ANY OF THOSE ARE FUN, COULD YOU MAYBE LEND ME SOME?
HUH!?
UH...I DON'T THINK A POPULAR, NORMIE GIRL LIKE YOU WOULD ENJOY THEM.

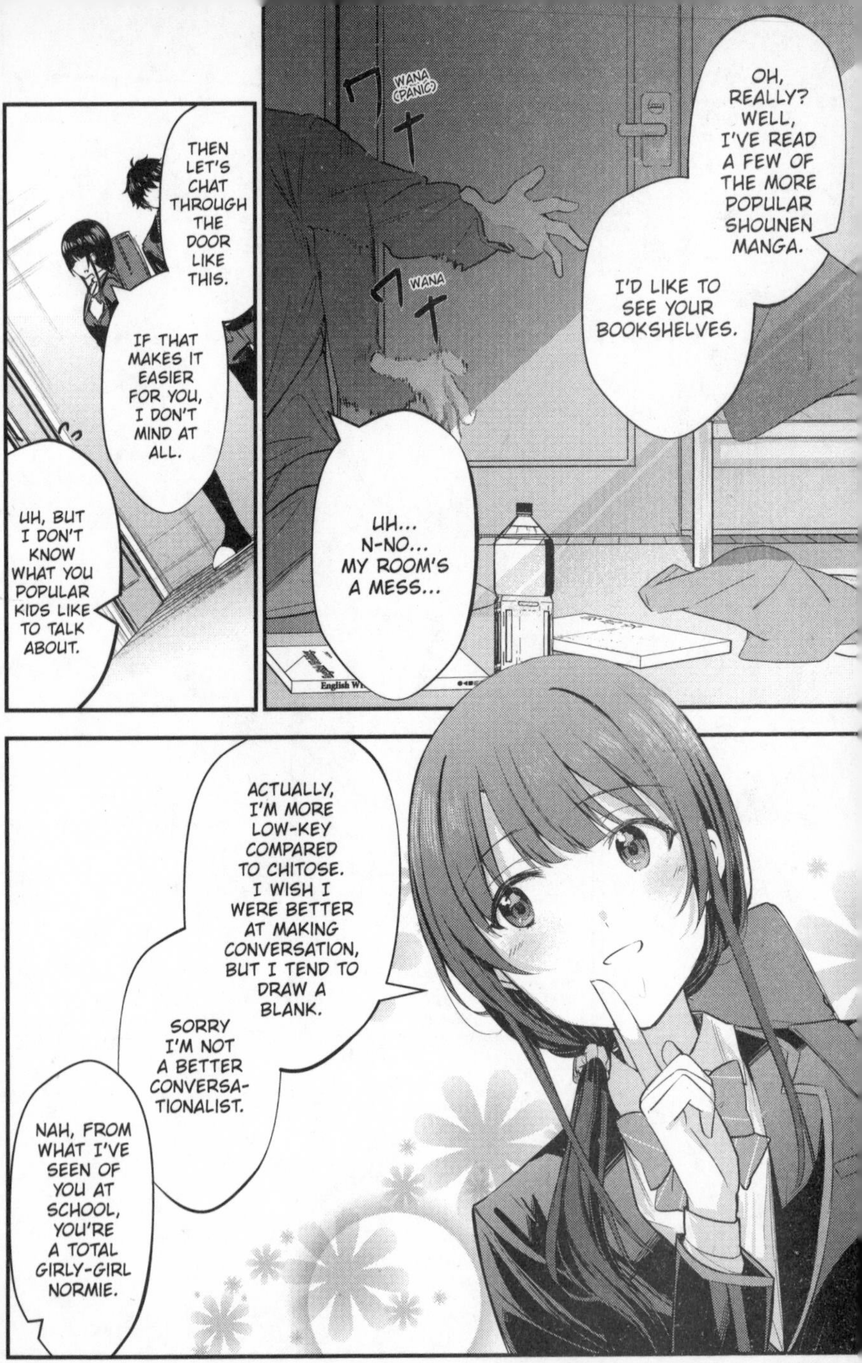
OH, REALLY? WELL, I'VE READ A FEW OF THE MORE POPULAR SHOUNEN MANGA.
I'D LIKE TO SEE YOUR BOOKSHELVES.
WANA (PANIC)
WANA
UH... N-NO... MY ROOM'S A MESS...
THEN LET'S CHAT THROUGH THE DOOR LIKE THIS.
IF THAT MAKES IT EASIER FOR YOU, I DON'T MIND AT ALL.
UH, BUT I DON'T KNOW WHAT YOU POPULAR KIDS LIKE TO TALK ABOUT.
ACTUALLY, I'M MORE LOW-KEY COMPARED TO CHITOSE. I WISH I WERE BETTER AT MAKING CONVERSATION, BUT I TEND TO DRAW A BLANK.
SORRY I'M NOT A BETTER CONVERSA-TIONALIST.
NAH, FROM WHAT I'VE SEEN OF YOU AT SCHOOL, YOU'RE A TOTAL GIRLY-GIRL NORMIE.

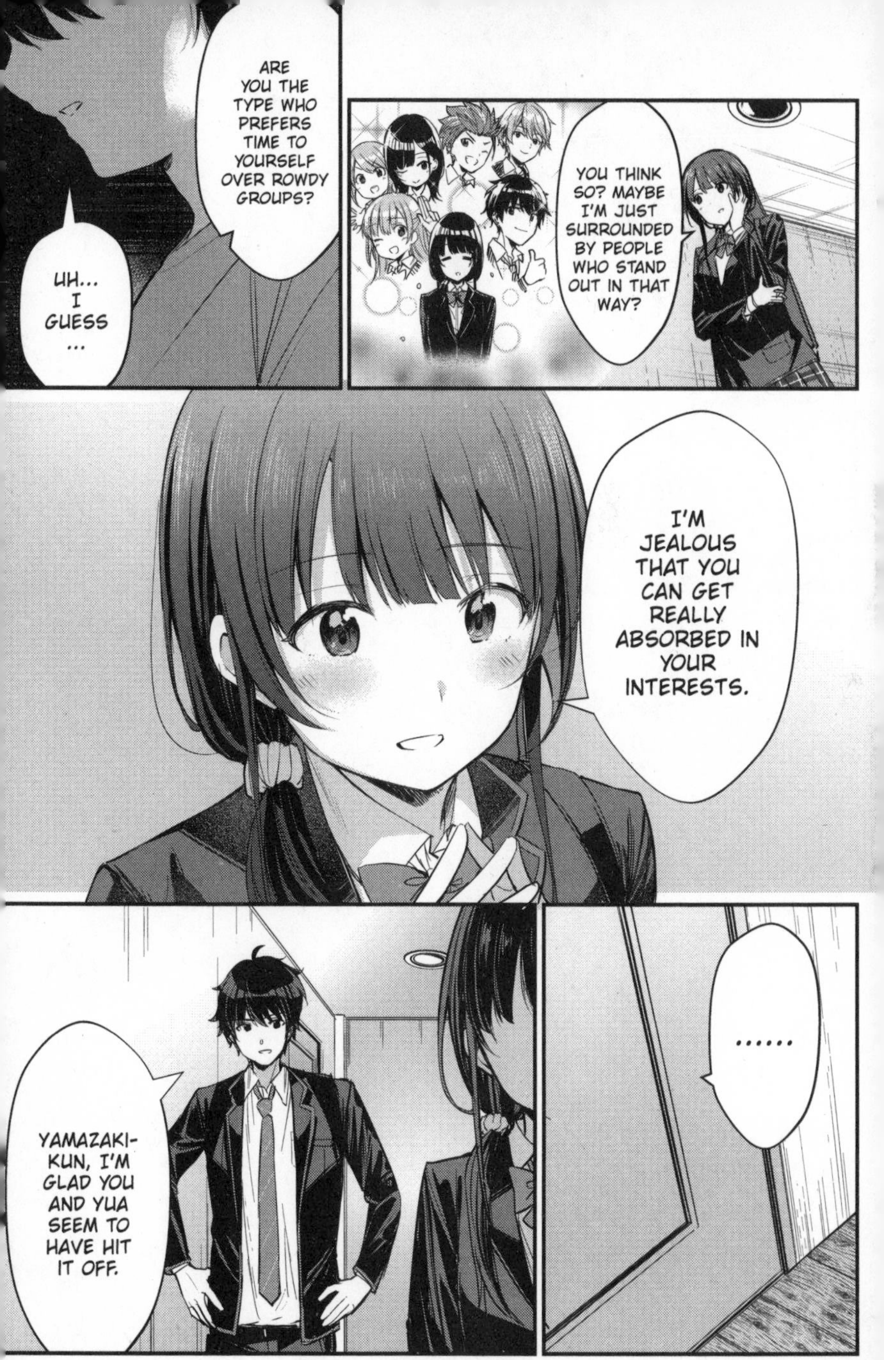
YOU THINK SO? MAYBE I'M JUST SURROUNDED BY PEOPLE WHO STAND OUT IN THAT WAY?
ARE YOU THE TYPE WHO PREFERS TIME TO YOURSELF OVER ROWDY GROUPS?
UH... I GUESS ...
I'M JEALOUS THAT YOU CAN GET REALLY ABSORBED IN YOUR INTERESTS.
......
YAMAZAKI-KUN, I'M GLAD YOU AND YUA SEEM TO HAVE HIT IT OFF.

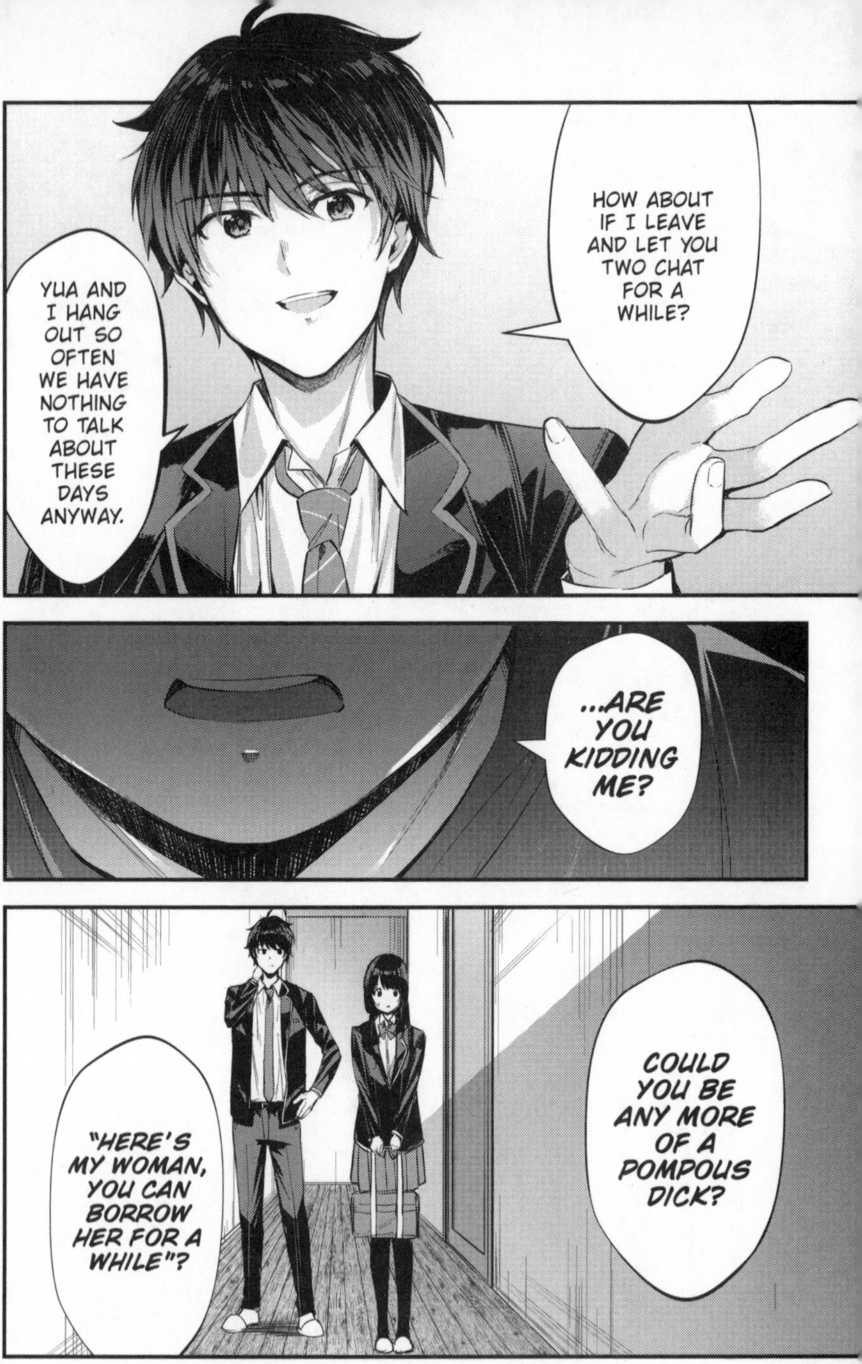
HOW ABOUT IF I LEAVE AND LET YOU TWO CHAT FOR A WHILE?
YUA AND I HANG OUT SO OFTEN WE HAVE NOTHING TO TALK ABOUT THESE DAYS ANYWAY.
...ARE YOU KIDDING ME?
COULD YOU BE ANY MORE OF A POMPOUS DICK?
"HERE'S MY WOMAN, YOU CAN BORROW HER FOR A WHILE"?

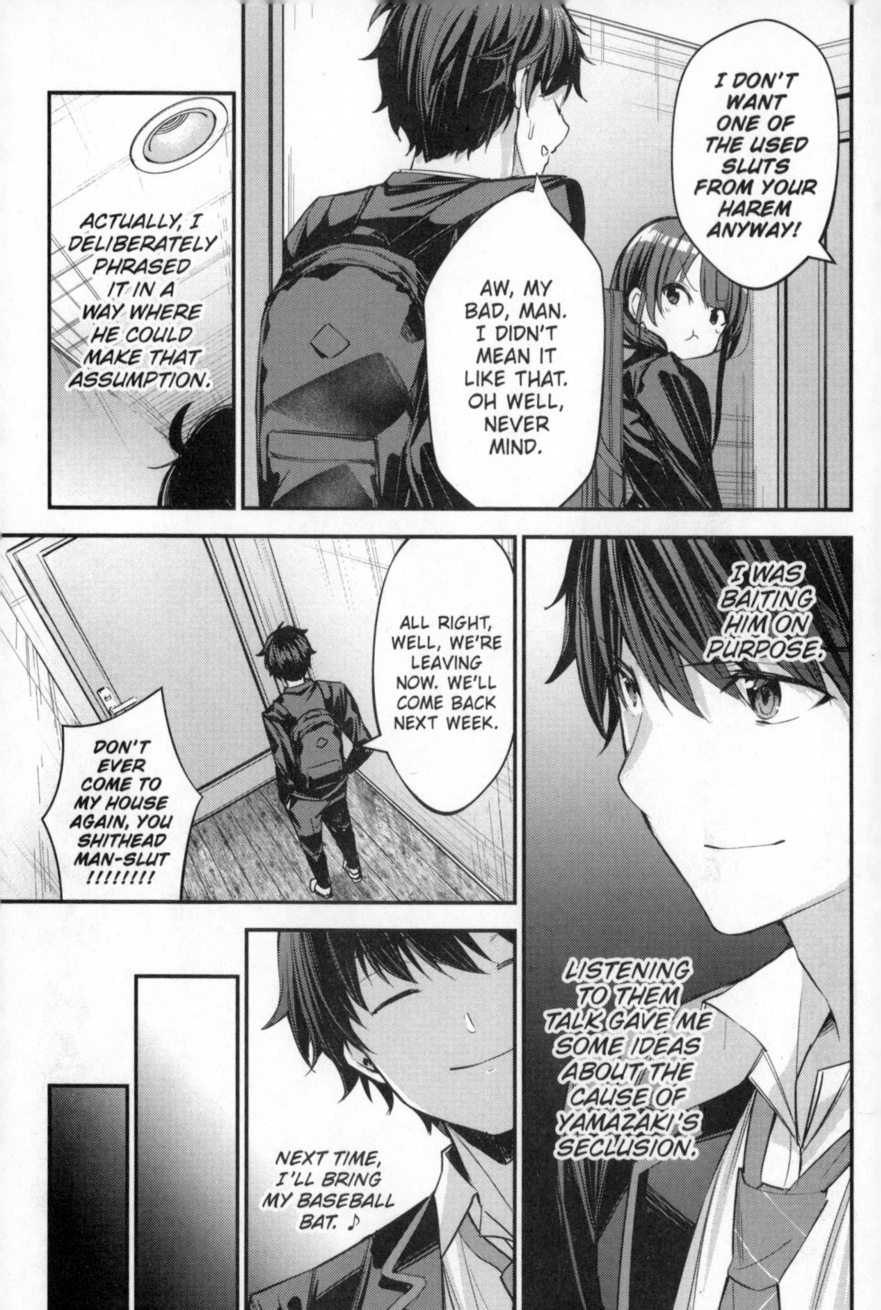
I DON'T WANT ONE OF THE USED SLUTS FROM YOUR HAREM ANYWAY!
AW, MY BAD, MAN. I DIDN'T MEAN IT LIKE THAT. OH WELL, NEVER MIND.
ACTUALLY, I DELIBERATELY PHRASED IT IN A WAY WHERE HE COULD MAKE THAT ASSUMPTION.
I WAS BAITING HIM ON PURPOSE.
LISTENING TO THEM TALK GAVE ME SOME IDEAS ABOUT THE CAUSE OF YAMAZAKI'S SECLUSION.
ALL RIGHT, WELL, WE'RE LEAVING NOW. WE'LL COME BACK NEXT WEEK.
DON'T EVER COME TO MY HOUSE AGAIN, YOU SHITHEAD MAN-SLUT !!!!!!!!
NEXT TIME, I'LL BRING MY BASEBALL BAT. ♪

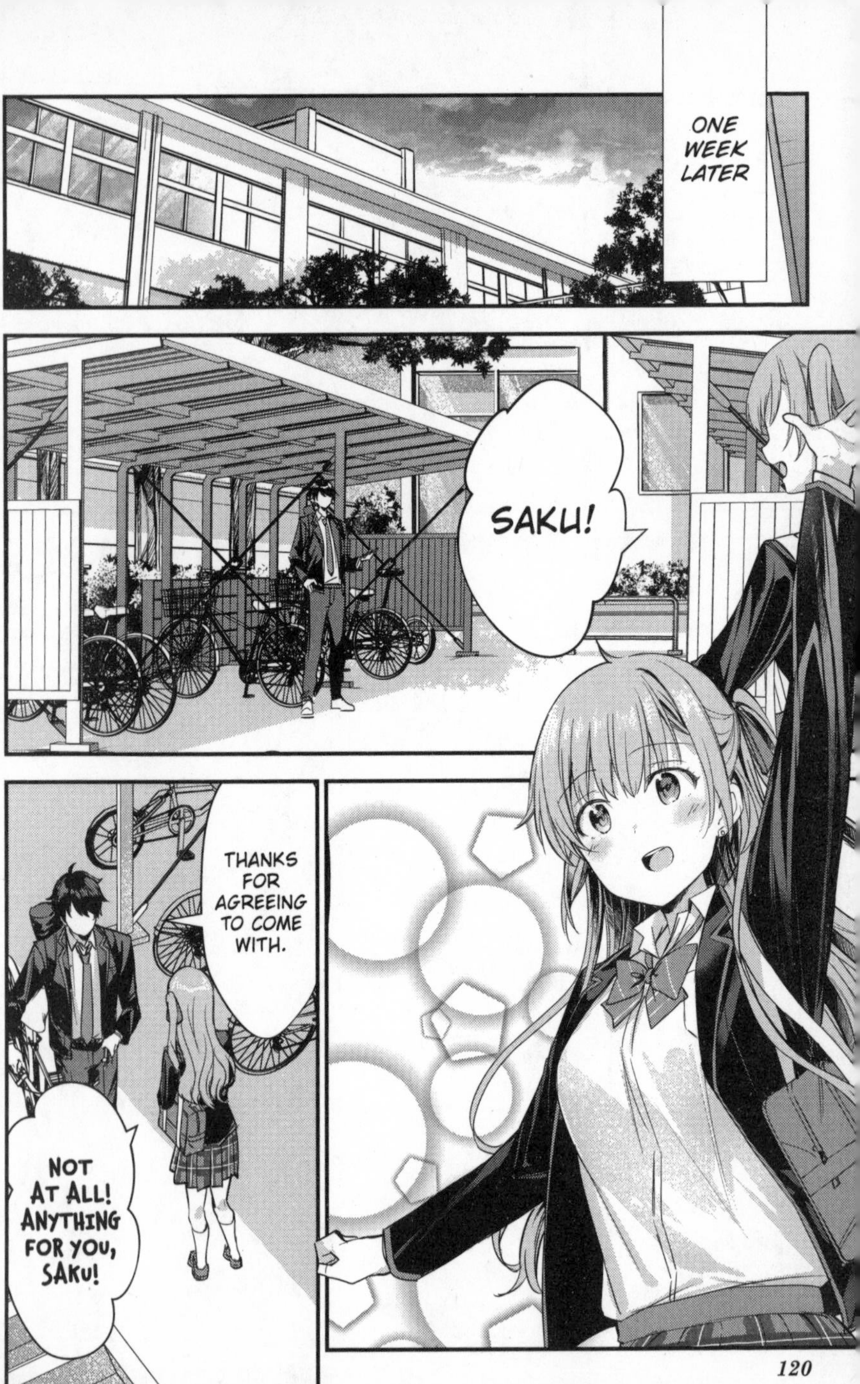

ONE WEEK LATER
SAKU!
THANKS FOR AGREEING TO COME WITH.
NOT AT ALL! ANYTHING FOR YOU, SAKU!

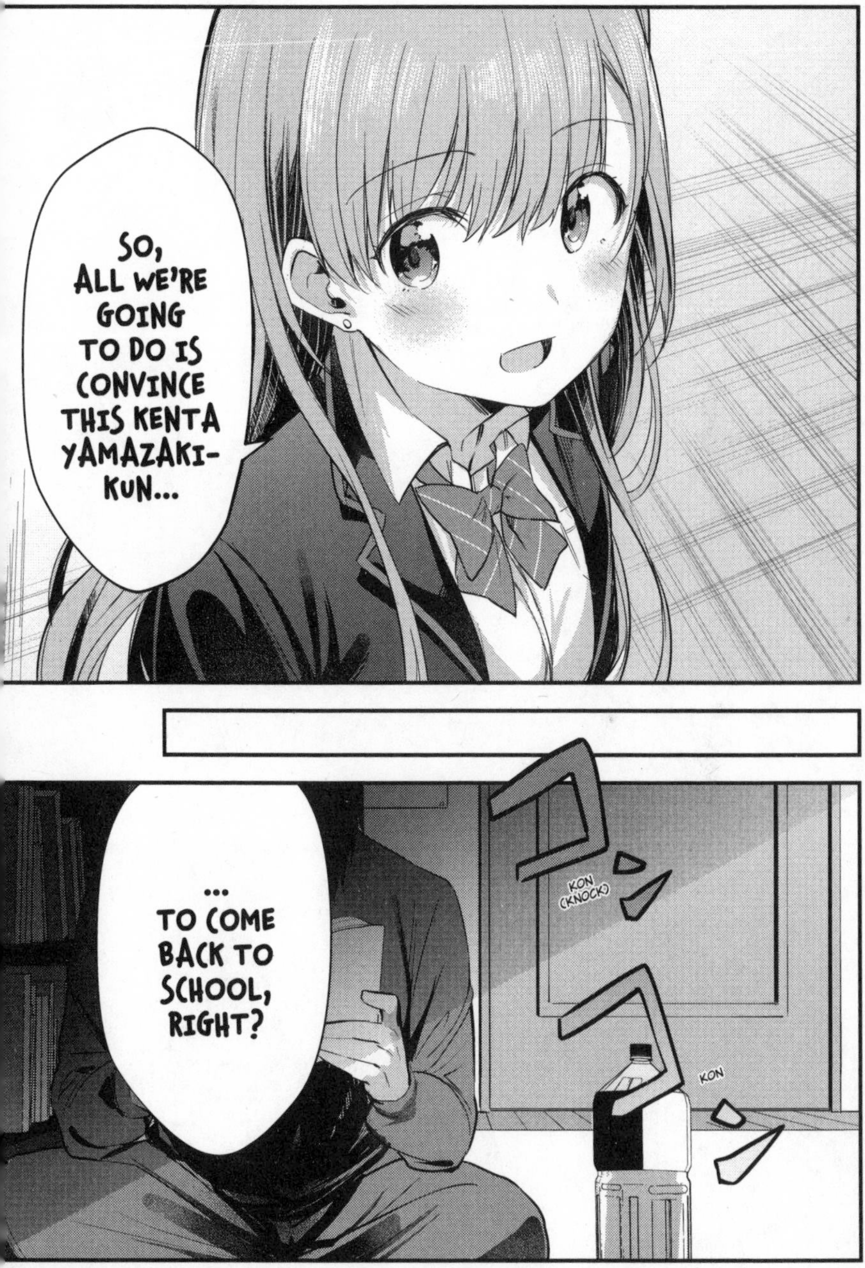
SO, ALL WE'RE GOING TO DO IS CONVINCE THIS KENTA YAMAZAKI-KUN...
KON (KNOCK)
KON
... TO COME BACK TO SCHOOL, RIGHT?

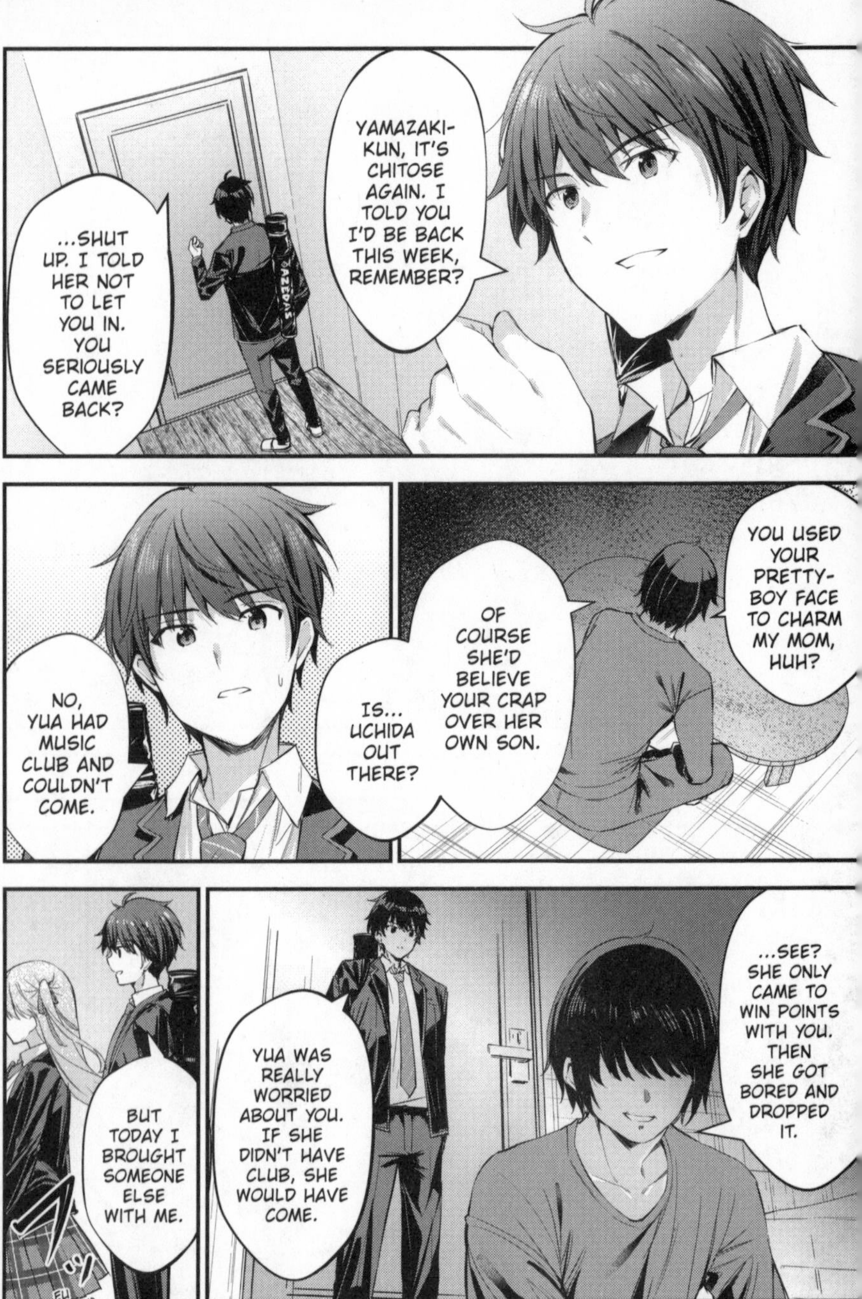
YAMAZAKI-KUN, IT'S CHITOSE AGAIN. I TOLD YOU I'D BE BACK THIS WEEK, REMEMBER?
...SHUT UP. I TOLD HER NOT TO LET YOU IN. YOU SERIOUSLY CAME BACK?
YOU USED YOUR PRETTY-BOY FACE TO CHARM MY MOM, HUH?
OF COURSE SHE'D BELIEVE YOUR CRAP OVER HER OWN SON.
IS... UCHIDA OUT THERE?
NO, YUA HAD MUSIC CLUB AND COULDN'T COME.
...SEE? SHE ONLY CAME TO WIN POINTS WITH YOU. THEN SHE GOT BORED AND DROPPED IT.
YUA WAS REALLY WORRIED ABOUT YOU. IF SHE DIDN'T HAVE CLUB, SHE WOULD HAVE COME.
BUT TODAY I BROUGHT SOMEONE ELSE WITH ME.
FU (SWOOSH)

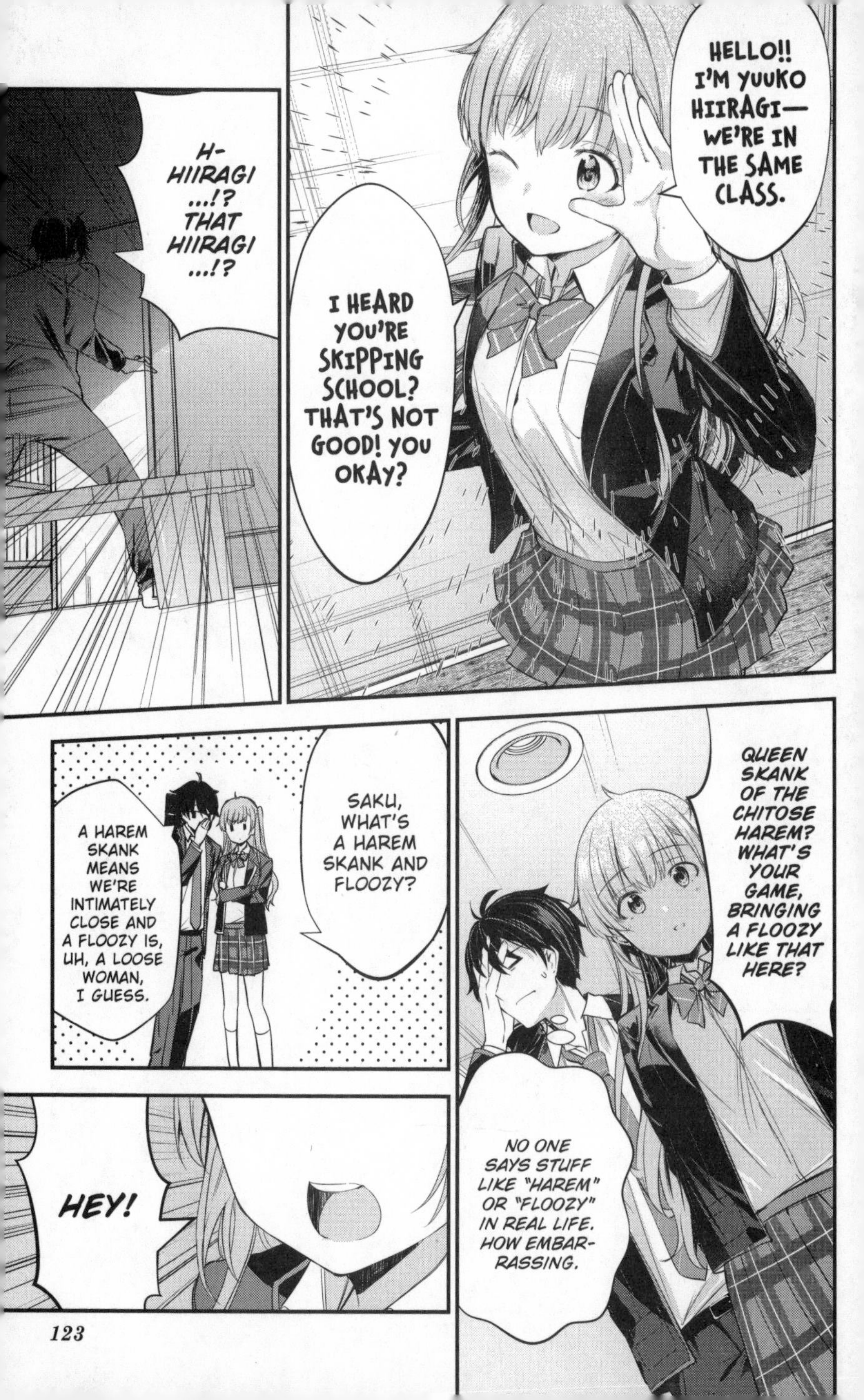
HELLO!! I'M YUUKO HIIRAGI—WE'RE IN THE SAME CLASS.
I HEARD YOU'RE SKIPPING SCHOOL? THAT'S NOT GOOD! YOU OKAY?
H-HIIRAGI ...!? THAT HIIRAGI ...!?
QUEEN SKANK OF THE CHITOSE HAREM? WHAT'S YOUR GAME, BRINGING A FLOOZY LIKE THAT HERE?
NO ONE SAYS STUFF LIKE "HAREM" OR "FLOOZY" IN REAL LIFE. HOW EMBAR-RASSING.
SAKU, WHAT'S A HAREM SKANK AND FLOOZY?
A HAREM SKANK MEANS WE'RE INTIMATELY CLOSE AND A FLOOZY IS, UH, A LOOSE WOMAN, I GUESS.
HEY!

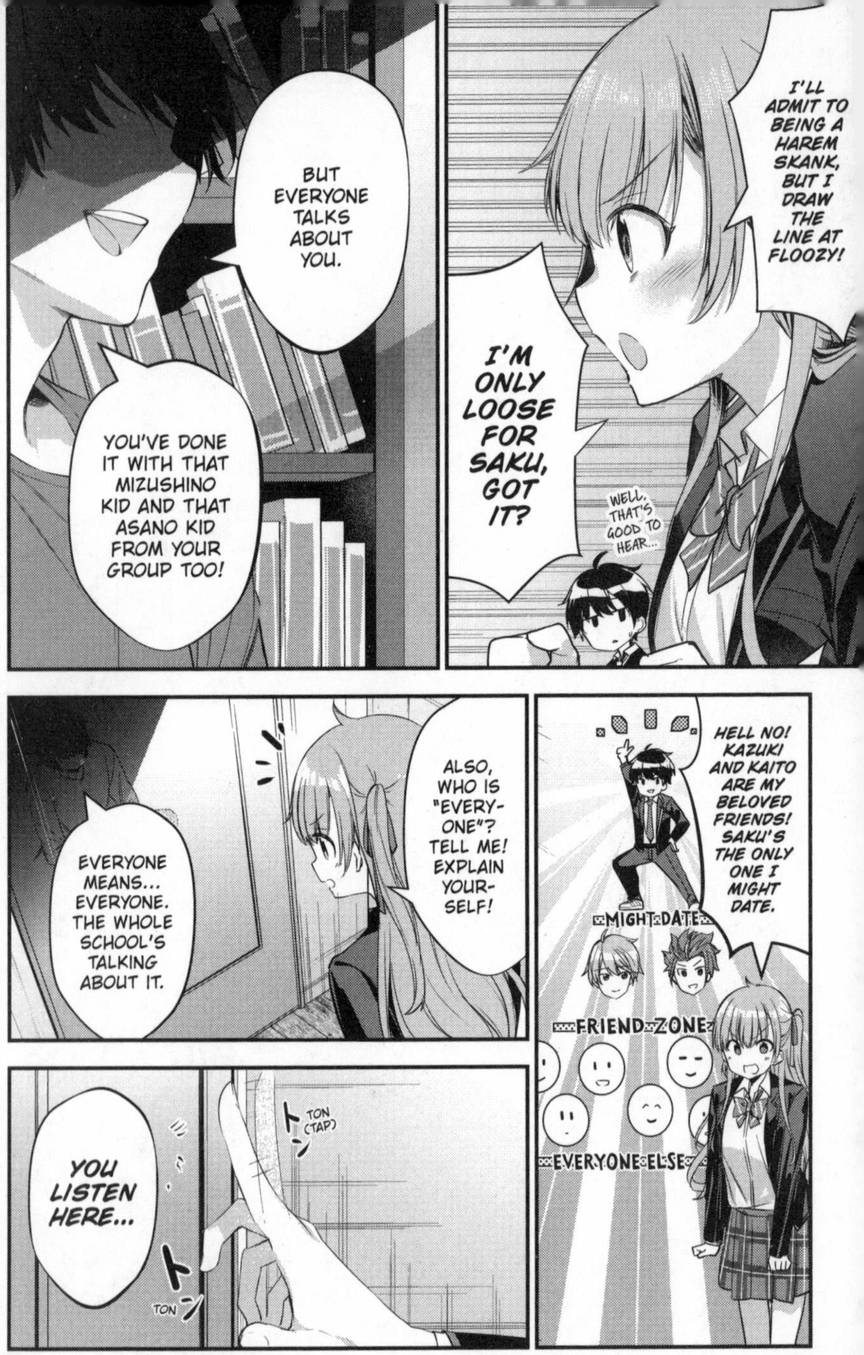

I'LL ADMIT TO BEING A HAREM SKANK, BUT I DRAW THE LINE AT FLOOZY!
I'M ONLY LOOSE FOR SAKU, GOT IT?
WELL, THAT'S GOOD TO HEAR...
BUT EVERYONE TALKS ABOUT YOU.
YOU'VE DONE IT WITH THAT MIZUSHINO KID AND THAT ASANO KID FROM YOUR GROUP TOO!
HELL NO! KAZUKI AND KAITO ARE MY BELOVED FRIENDS! SAKU'S THE ONLY ONE I MIGHT DATE.
MIGHT DATE
FRIEND ZONE
EVERYONE ELSE
ALSO, WHO IS "EVERY-ONE"? TELL ME! EXPLAIN YOUR-SELF!
EVERYONE MEANS... EVERYONE. THE WHOLE SCHOOL'S TALKING ABOUT IT.
TON (TAP)
YOU LISTEN HERE...
TON

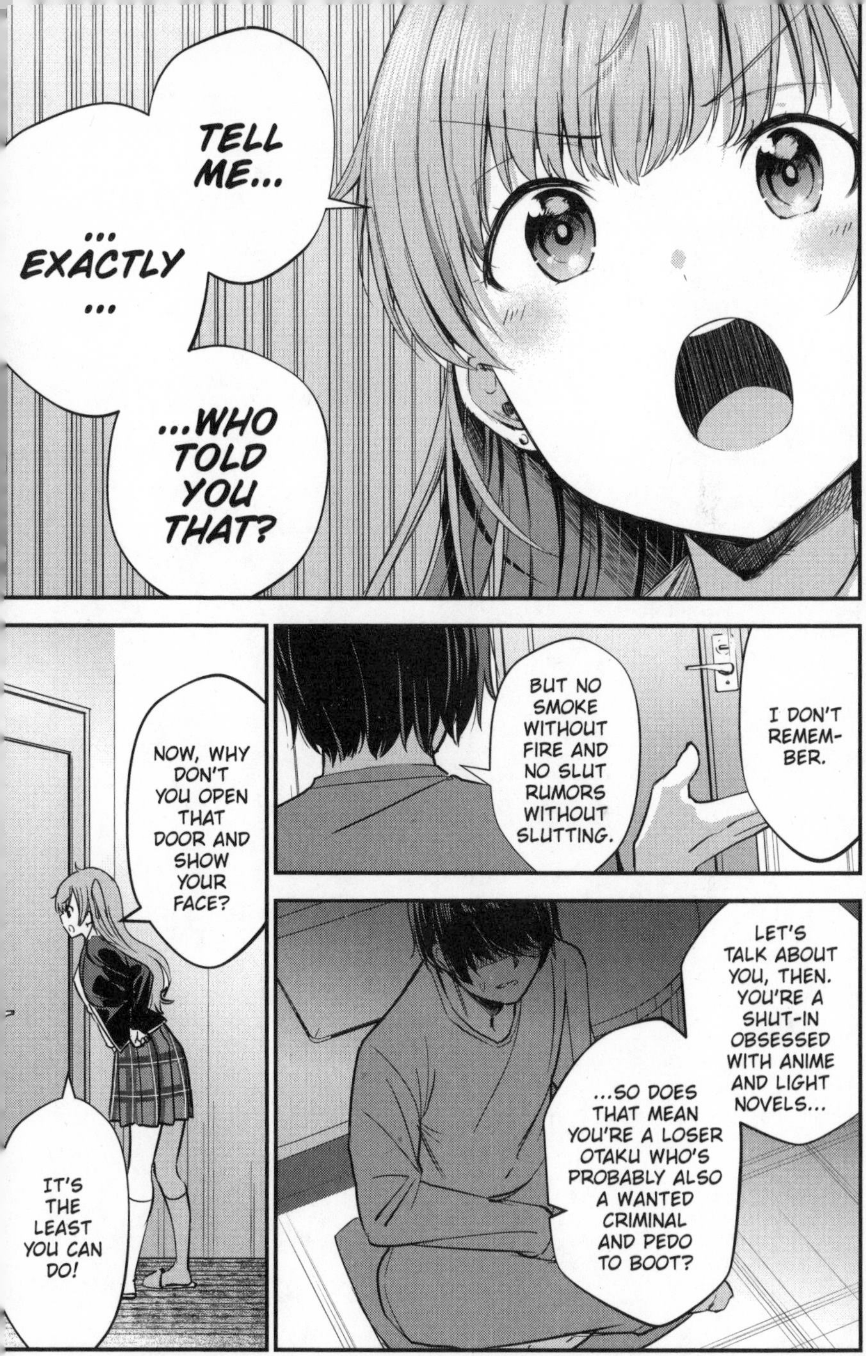
TELL ME...
...EXACTLY...
...WHO TOLD YOU THAT?
I DON'T REMEMBER.
BUT NO SMOKE WITHOUT FIRE AND NO SLUT RUMORS WITHOUT SLUTTING.
LET'S TALK ABOUT YOU, THEN. YOU'RE A SHUT-IN OBSESSED WITH ANIME AND LIGHT NOVELS...
...SO DOES THAT MEAN YOU'RE A LOSER OTAKU WHO'S PROBABLY ALSO A WANTED CRIMINAL AND PEDO TO BOOT?
NOW, WHY DON'T YOU OPEN THAT DOOR AND SHOW YOUR FACE?
IT'S THE LEAST YOU CAN DO!

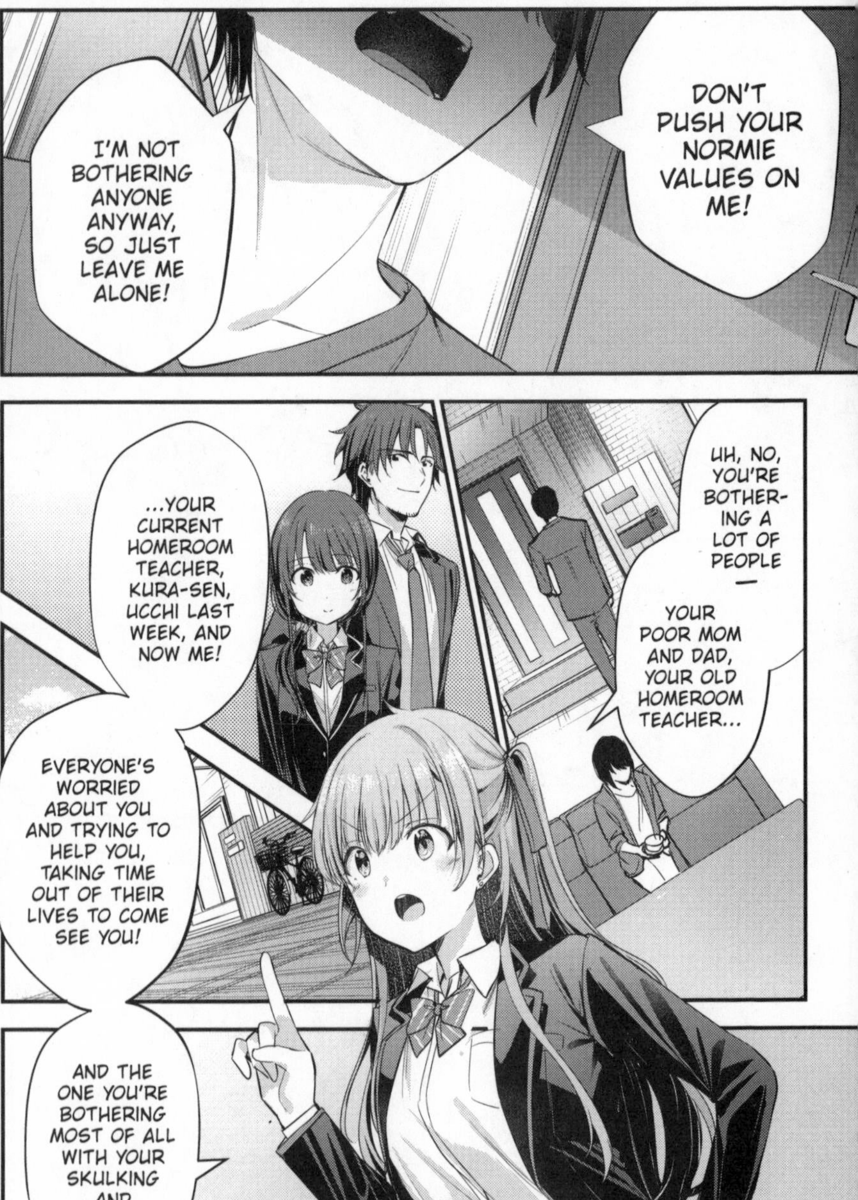
DON'T PUSH YOUR NORMIE VALUES ON ME!
I'M NOT BOTHERING ANYONE ANYWAY, SO JUST LEAVE ME ALONE!
UH, NO, YOU'RE BOTHER-ING A LOT OF PEOPLE—
YOUR POOR MOM AND DAD, YOUR OLD HOMEROOM TEACHER...
...YOUR CURRENT HOMEROOM TEACHER, KURA-SEN, UCCHI LAST WEEK, AND NOW ME!
EVERYONE'S WORRIED ABOUT YOU AND TRYING TO HELP YOU, TAKING TIME OUT OF THEIR LIVES TO COME SEE YOU!
AND THE ONE YOU'RE BOTHERING MOST OF ALL WITH YOUR SKULKING AND SULKING...

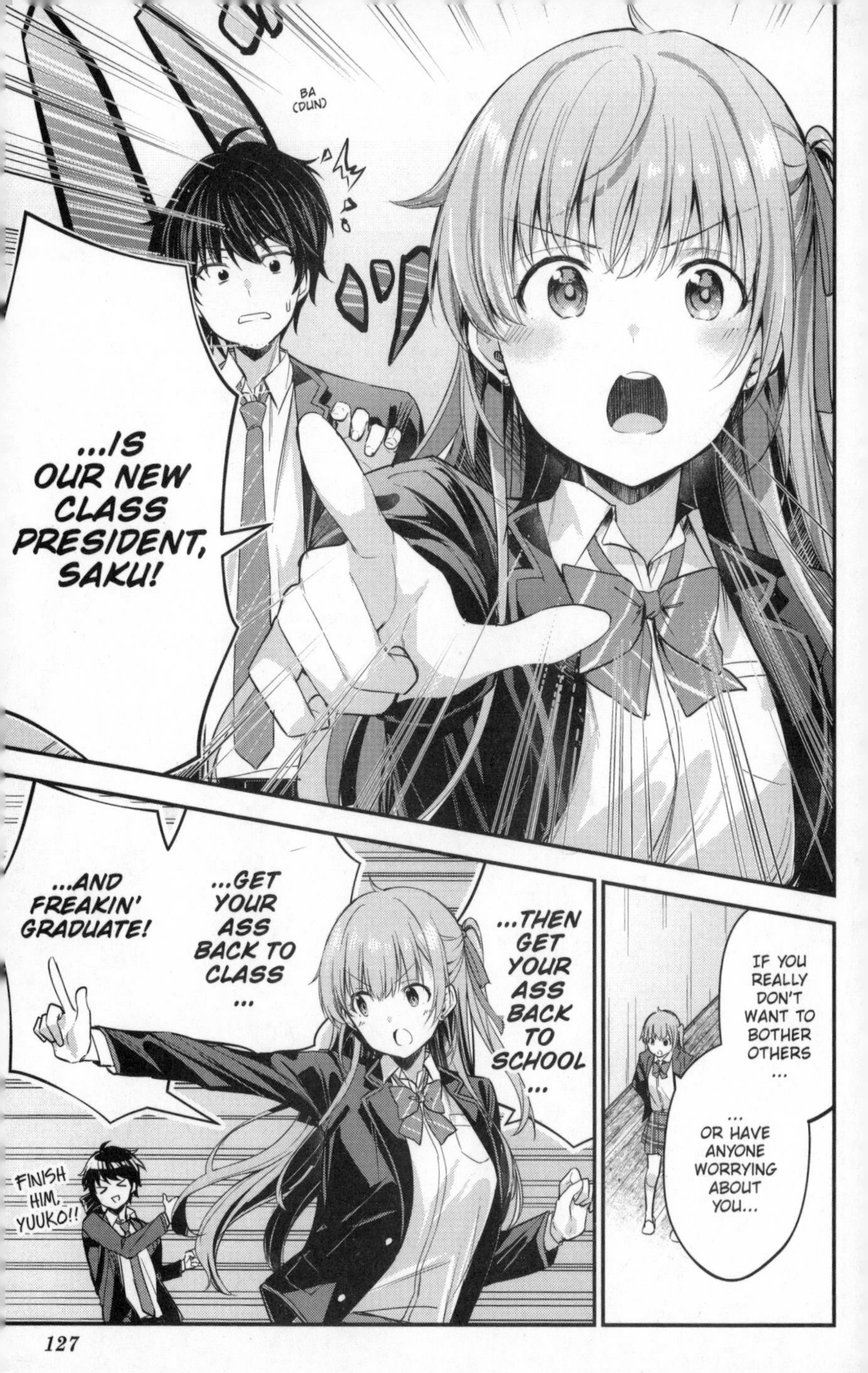
BA (DUN)
...IS OUR NEW CLASS PRESIDENT, SAKU!
IF YOU REALLY DON'T WANT TO BOTHER OTHERS...
...OR HAVE ANYONE WORRYING ABOUT YOU...
...THEN GET YOUR ASS BACK TO SCHOOL...
...GET YOUR ASS BACK TO CLASS...
...AND FREAKIN' GRADUATE!
FINISH HIM, YUUKO!!

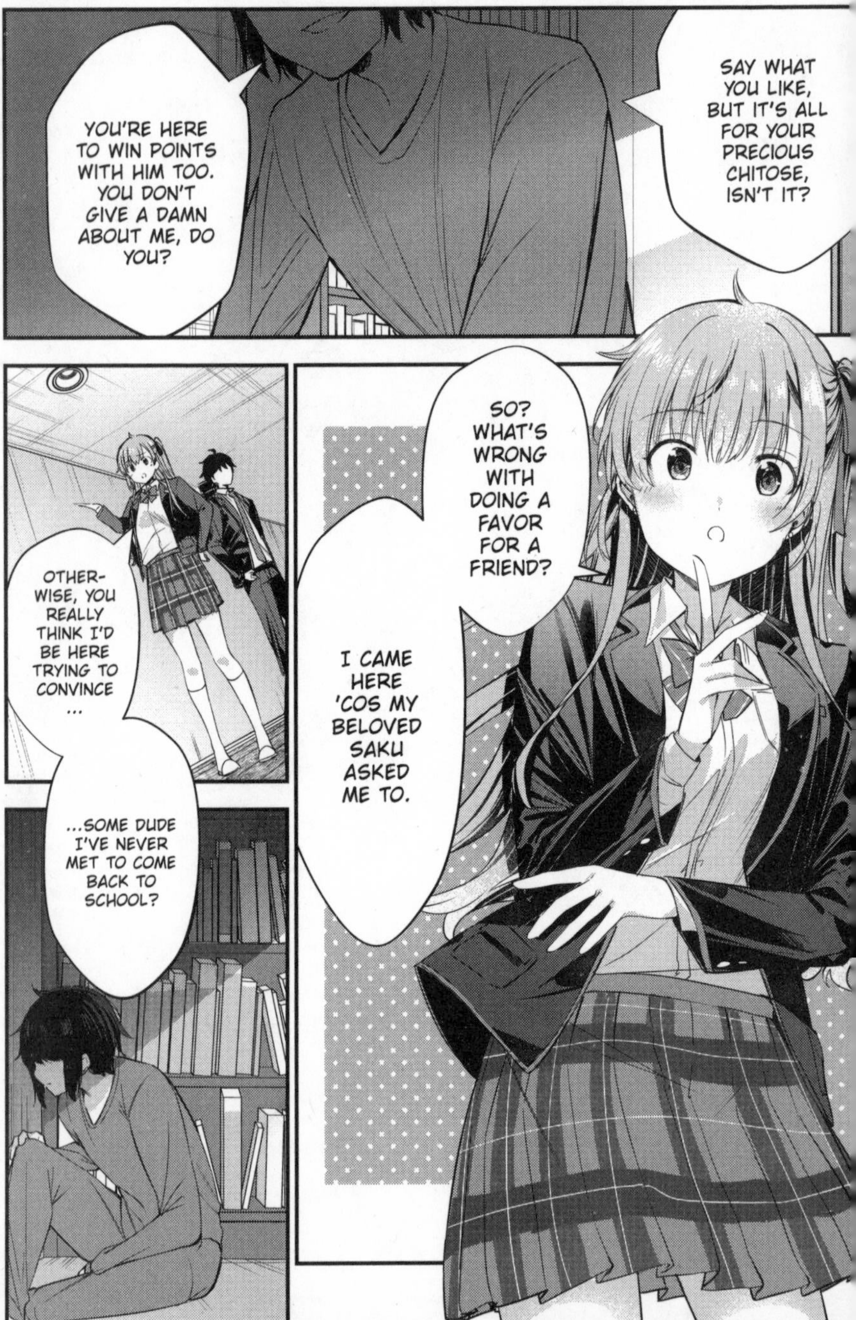
SAY WHAT YOU LIKE, BUT IT'S ALL FOR YOUR PRECIOUS CHITOSE, ISN'T IT?
YOU'RE HERE TO WIN POINTS WITH HIM TOO. YOU DON'T GIVE A DAMN ABOUT ME, DO YOU?
SO? WHAT'S WRONG WITH DOING A FAVOR FOR A FRIEND?
I CAME HERE 'COS MY BELOVED SAKU ASKED ME TO.
OTHER-WISE, YOU REALLY THINK I'D BE HERE TRYING TO CONVINCE ...
...SOME DUDE I'VE NEVER MET TO COME BACK TO SCHOOL?

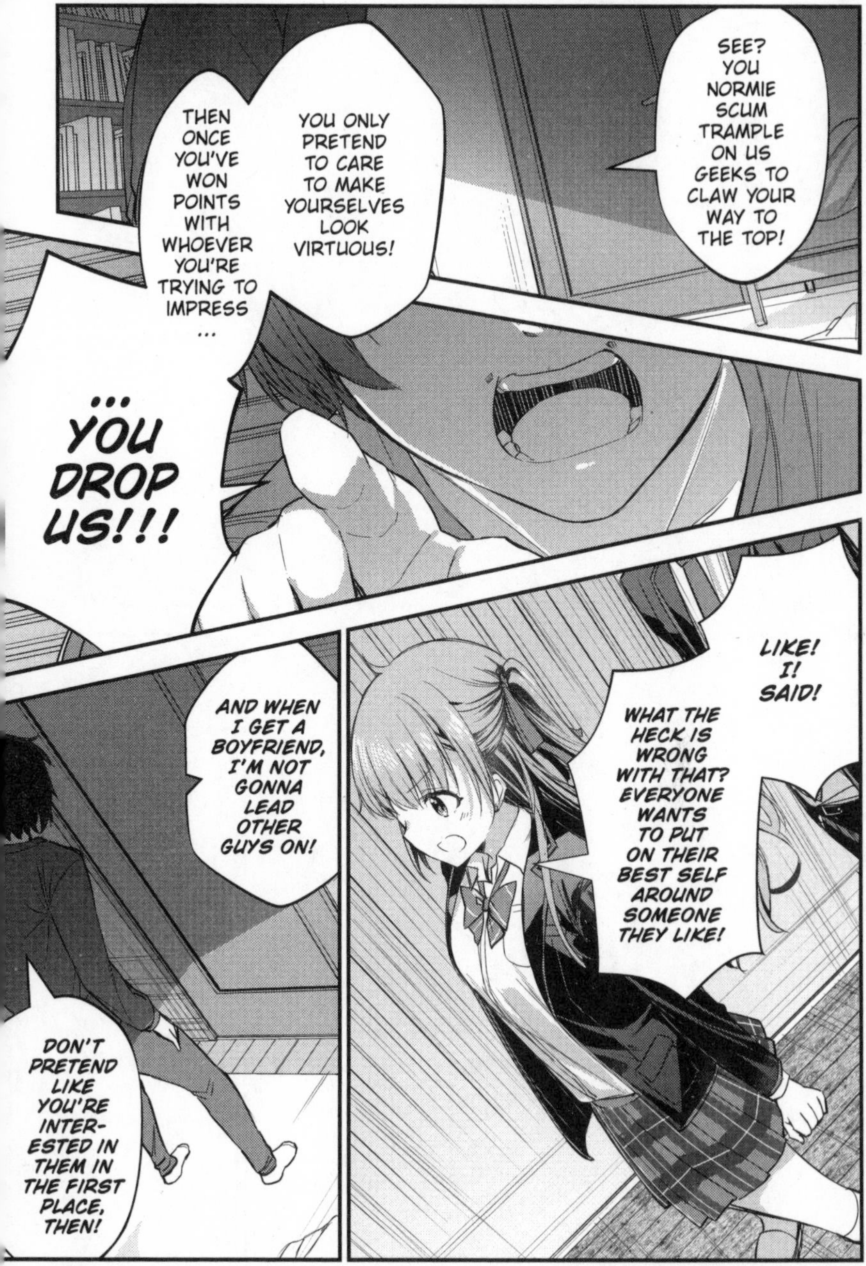
SEE? YOU NORMIE SCUM TRAMPLE ON US GEEKS TO CLAW YOUR WAY TO THE TOP!
YOU ONLY PRETEND TO CARE TO MAKE YOURSELVES LOOK VIRTUOUS!
THEN ONCE YOU'VE WON POINTS WITH WHOEVER YOU'RE TRYING TO IMPRESS ...
... YOU DROP US!!!
LIKE! I! SAID!
WHAT THE HECK IS WRONG WITH THAT? EVERYONE WANTS TO PUT ON THEIR BEST SELF AROUND SOMEONE THEY LIKE!
AND WHEN I GET A BOYFRIEND, I'M NOT GONNA LEAD OTHER GUYS ON!
DON'T PRETEND LIKE YOU'RE INTER-ESTED IN THEM IN THE FIRST PLACE, THEN!

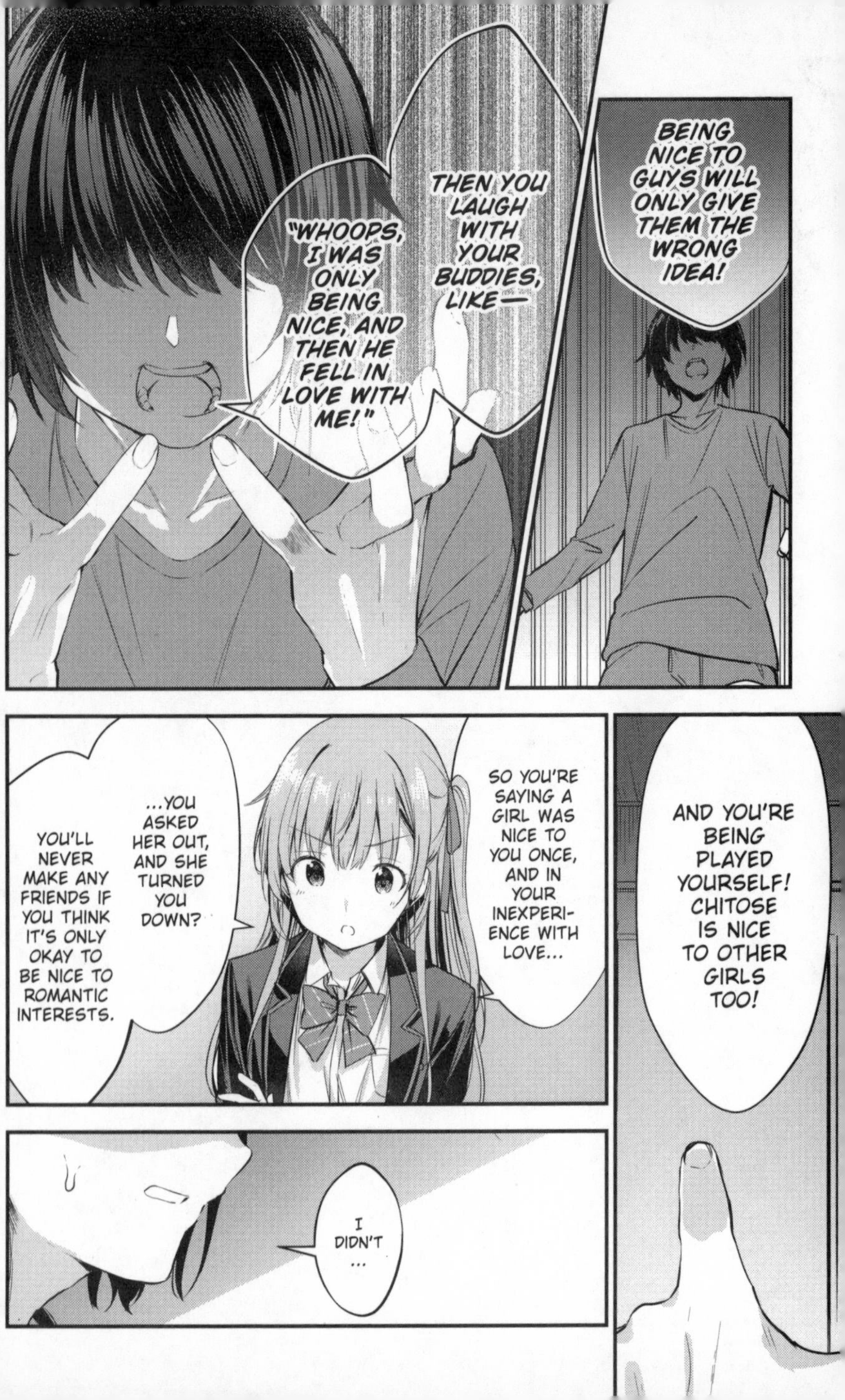
BEING NICE TO GUYS WILL ONLY GIVE THEM THE WRONG IDEA!
THEN YOU LAUGH WITH YOUR BUDDIES, LIKE—
"WHOOPS, I WAS ONLY BEING NICE, AND THEN HE FELL IN LOVE WITH ME!"
AND YOU'RE BEING PLAYED YOURSELF! CHITOSE IS NICE TO OTHER GIRLS TOO!
SO YOU'RE SAYING A GIRL WAS NICE TO YOU ONCE, AND IN YOUR INEXPERIENCE WITH LOVE...
...YOU ASKED HER OUT, AND SHE TURNED YOU DOWN?
YOU'LL NEVER MAKE ANY FRIENDS IF YOU THINK IT'S ONLY OKAY TO BE NICE TO ROMANTIC INTERESTS.
I DIDN'T ...

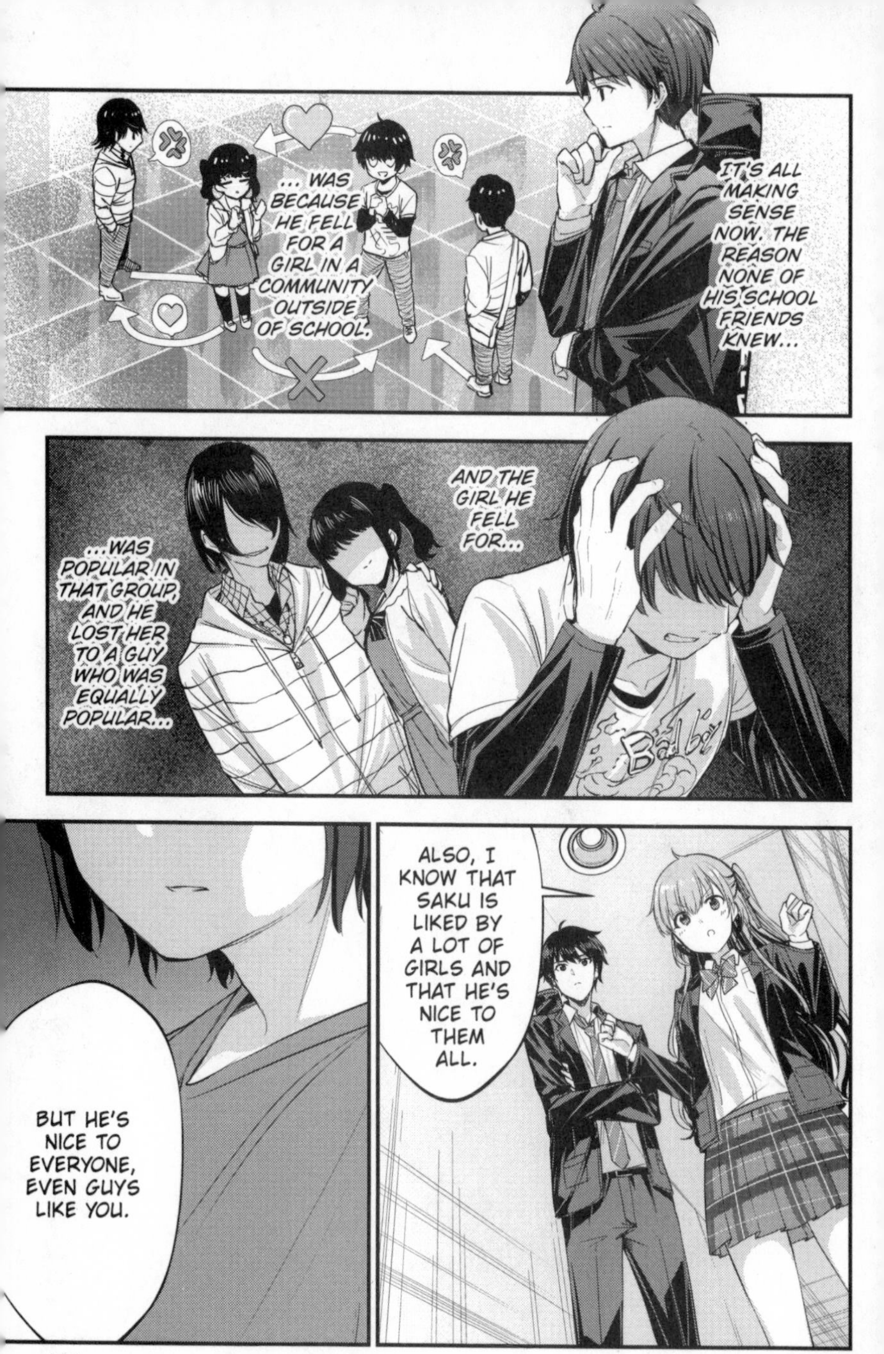
IT'S ALL MAKING SENSE NOW. THE REASON NONE OF HIS SCHOOL FRIENDS KNEW...
... WAS BECAUSE HE FELL FOR A GIRL IN A COMMUNITY OUTSIDE OF SCHOOL.
AND THE GIRL HE FELL FOR...
...WAS POPULAR IN THAT GROUP, AND HE LOST HER TO A GUY WHO WAS EQUALLY POPULAR...
ALSO, I KNOW THAT SAKU IS LIKED BY A LOT OF GIRLS AND THAT HE'S NICE TO THEM ALL.
BUT HE'S NICE TO EVERYONE, EVEN GUYS LIKE YOU.

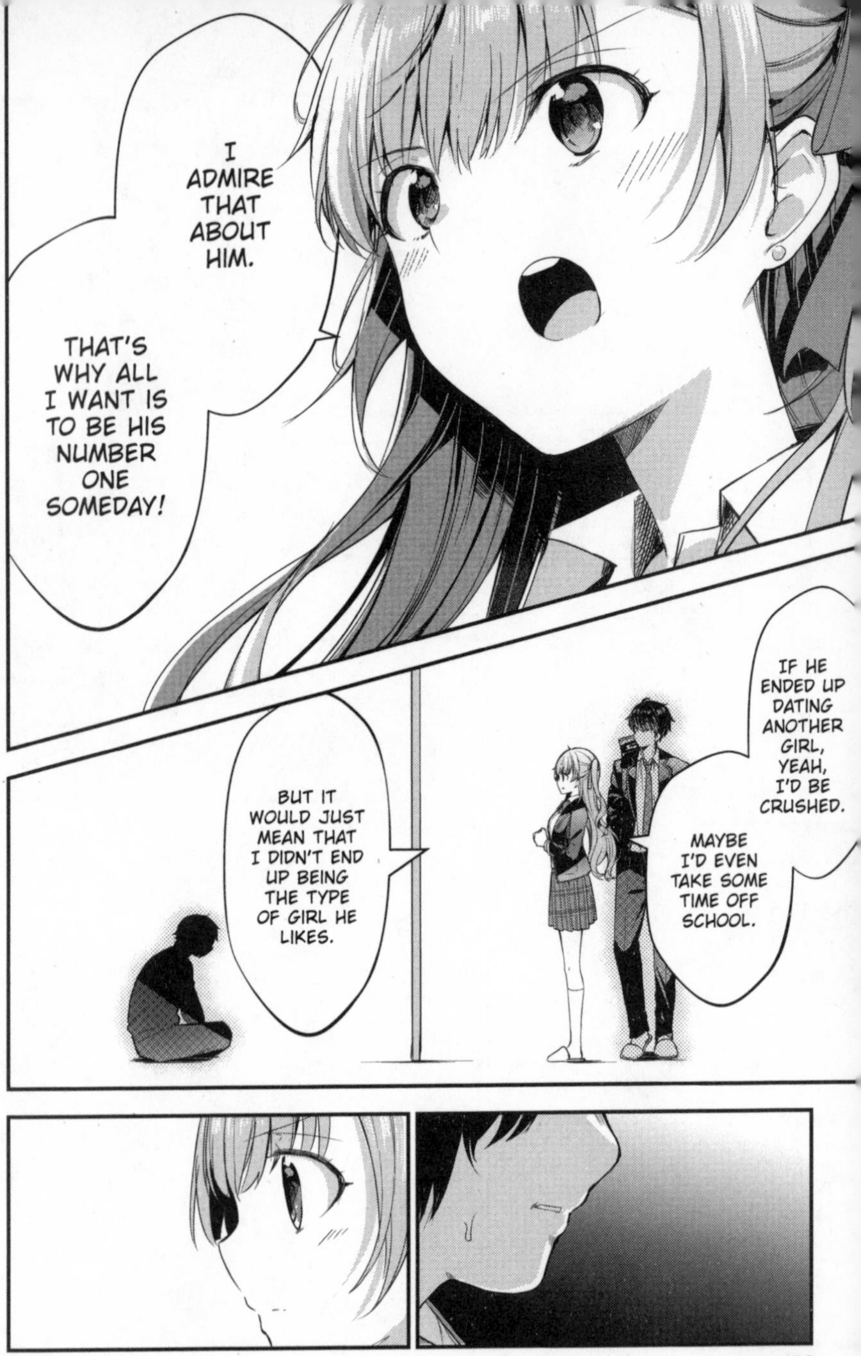
I ADMIRE THAT ABOUT HIM.
THAT'S WHY ALL I WANT IS TO BE HIS NUMBER ONE SOMEDAY!
IF HE ENDED UP DATING ANOTHER GIRL, YEAH, I'D BE CRUSHED.
MAYBE I'D EVEN TAKE SOME TIME OFF SCHOOL.
BUT IT WOULD JUST MEAN THAT I DIDN'T END UP BEING THE TYPE OF GIRL HE LIKES.

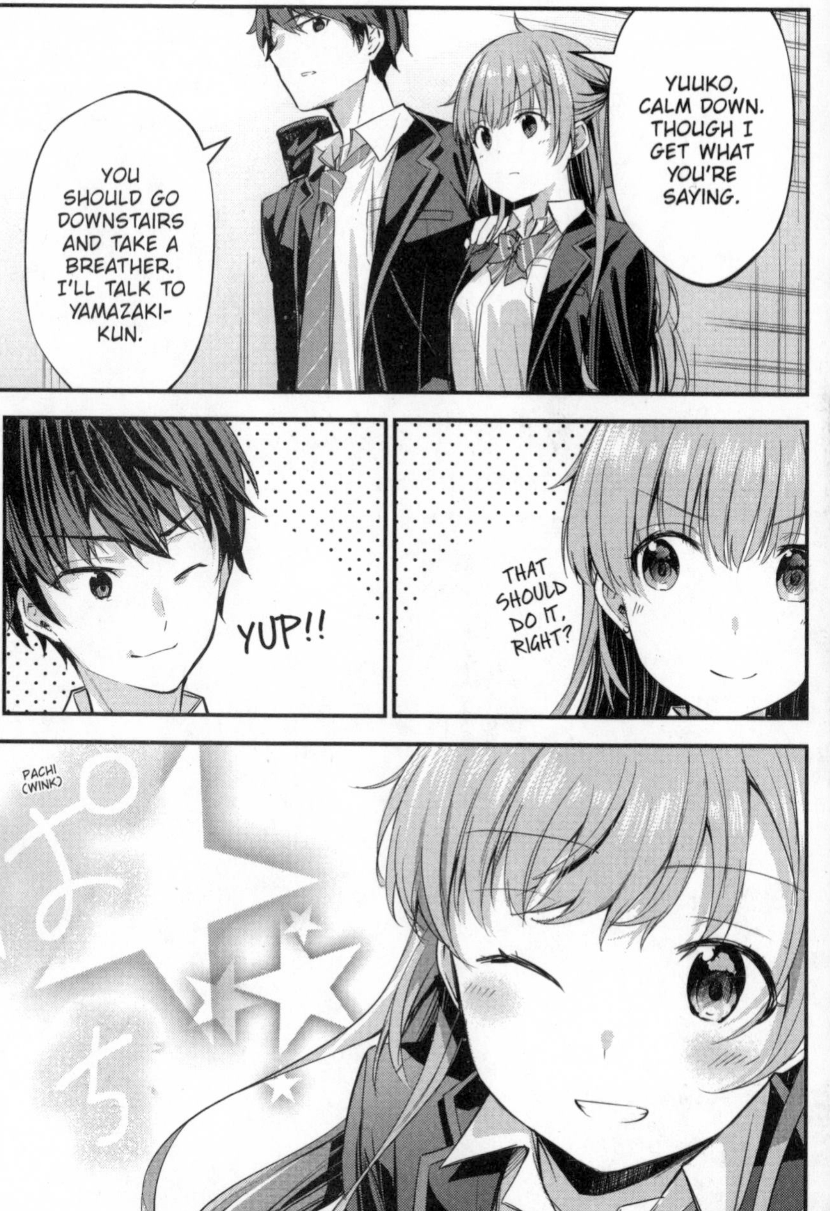
YUUKO, CALM DOWN. THOUGH I GET WHAT YOU'RE SAYING.
YOU SHOULD GO DOWNSTAIRS AND TAKE A BREATHER. I'LL TALK TO YAMAZAKI-KUN.
THAT SHOULD DO IT, RIGHT?
YUP!!
ぱち
PACHI (WINK)

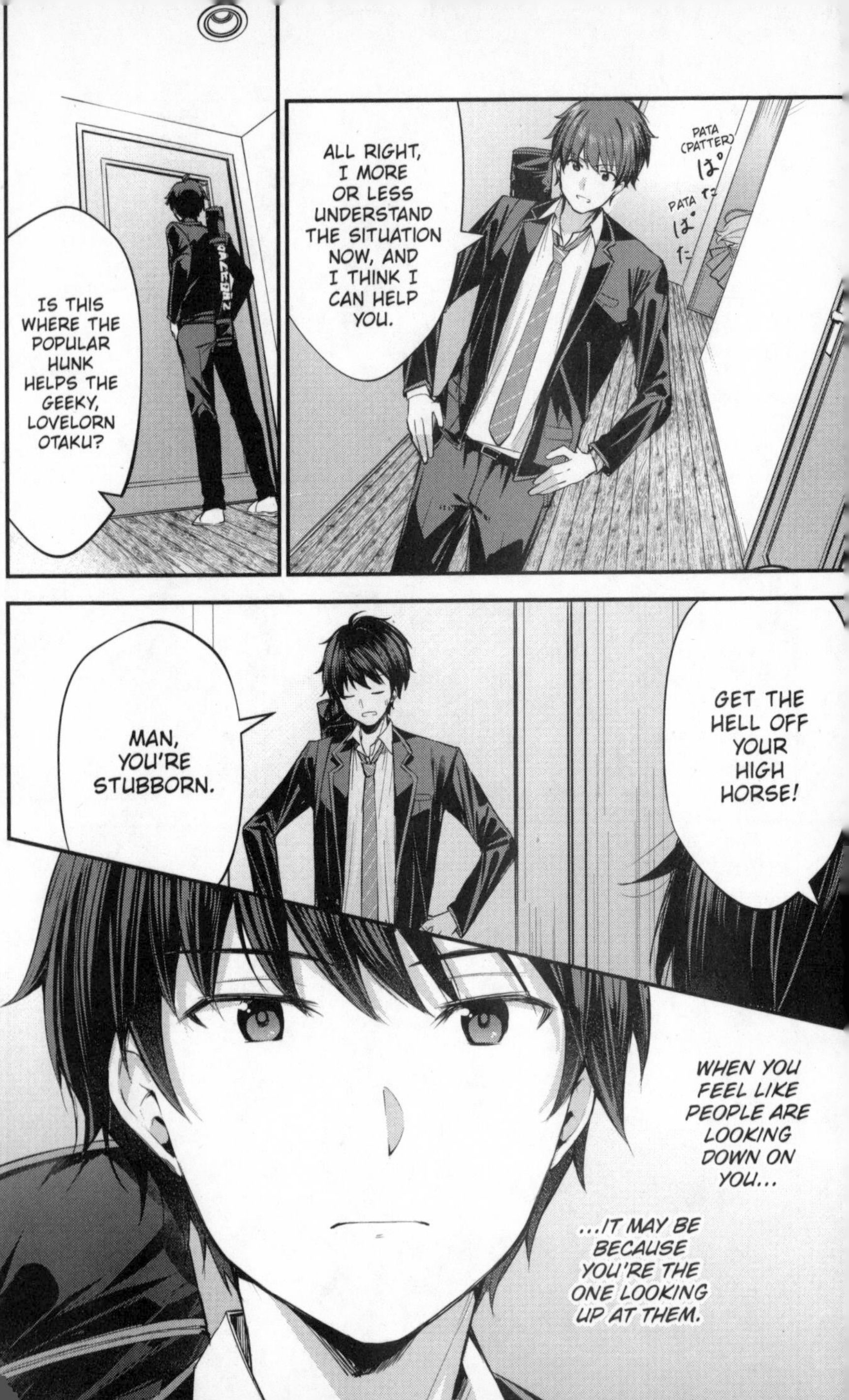
ALL RIGHT, I MORE OR LESS UNDERSTAND THE SITUATION NOW, AND I THINK I CAN HELP YOU.
PATA (PATTER) ぱた
PATA ぱた
IS THIS WHERE THE POPULAR HUNK HELPS THE GEEKY, LOVELORN OTAKU?
GET THE HELL OFF YOUR HIGH HORSE!
MAN, YOU'RE STUBBORN.
WHEN YOU FEEL LIKE PEOPLE ARE LOOKING DOWN ON YOU...
...IT MAY BE BECAUSE YOU'RE THE ONE LOOKING UP AT THEM.

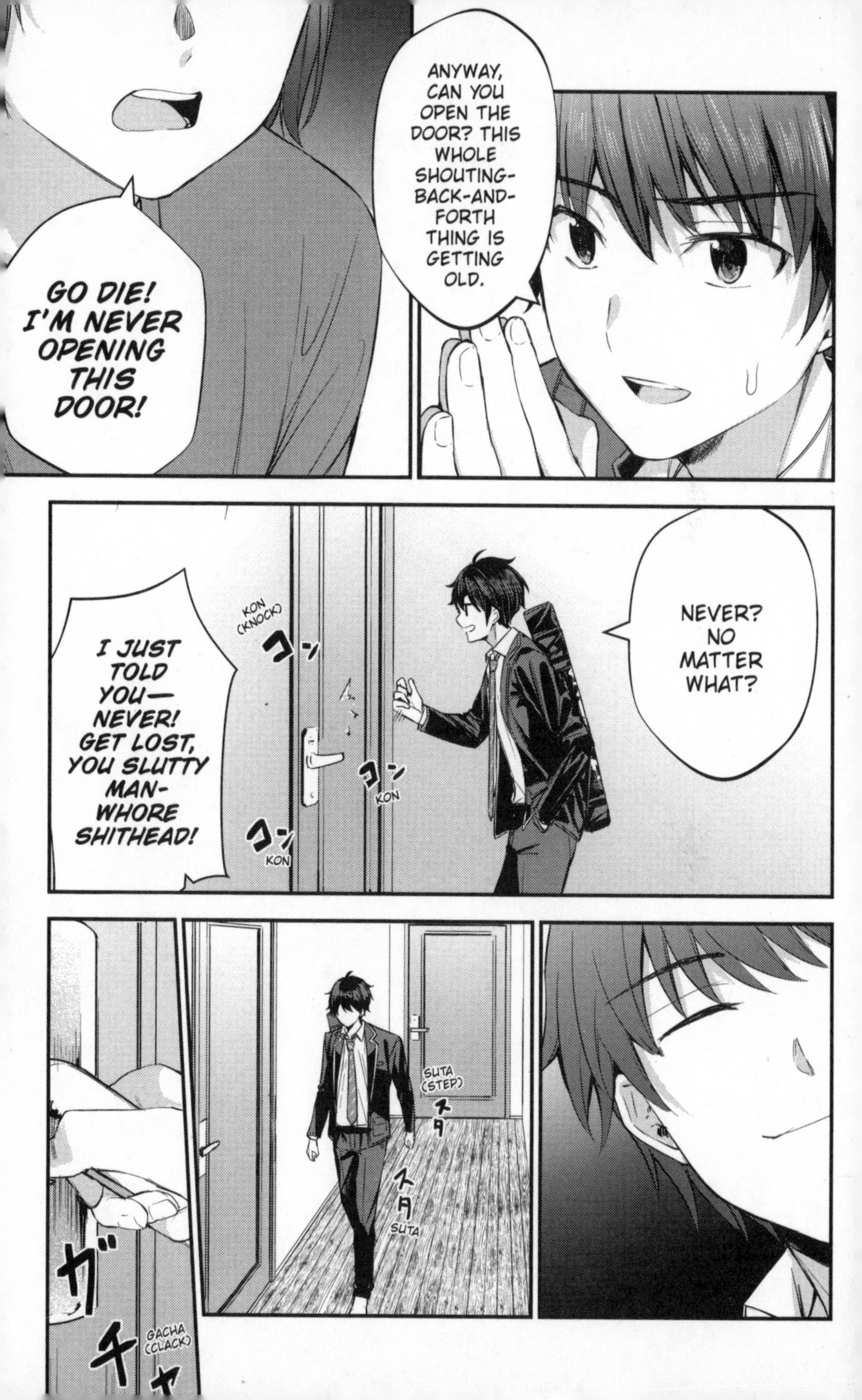
ANYWAY, CAN YOU OPEN THE DOOR? THIS WHOLE SHOUTING-BACK-AND-FORTH THING IS GETTING OLD.
GO DIE! I'M NEVER OPENING THIS DOOR!
NEVER? NO MATTER WHAT?
KON (KNOCK)
KON
KON
I JUST TOLD YOU—NEVER! GET LOST, YOU SLUTTY MAN-WHORE SHITHEAD!
SUTA (STEP)
SUTA
GACHA (CLACK)

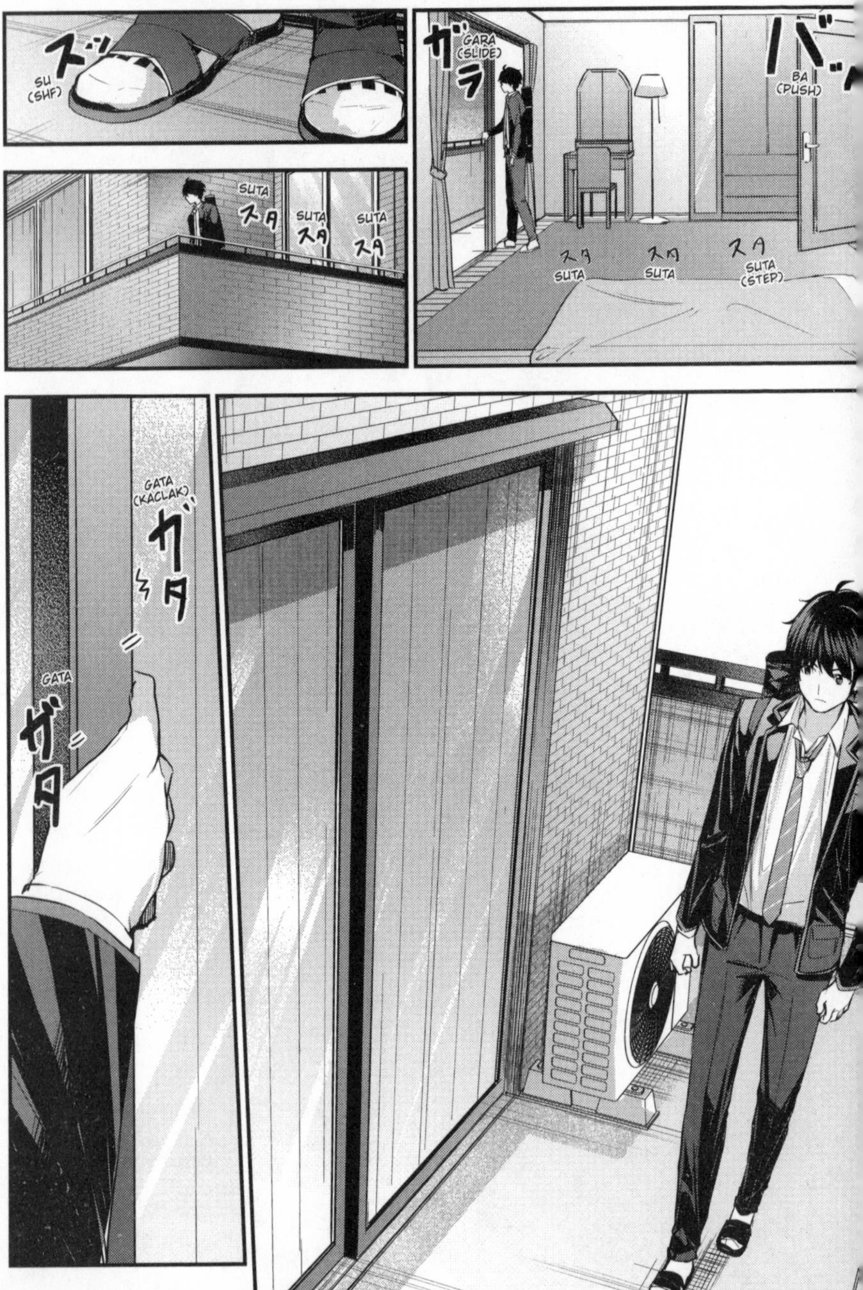
バッ
BA (PUSH)
ガラ
GARA (SLIDE)
スタ
SUTA (STEP)
スタ
SUTA
スタ
SUTA
スッ
SU (SHF)
スタ
SUTA
スタ
SUTA
スタ
SUTA
ガタ
GATA (KACLAK)
ガタ
GATA

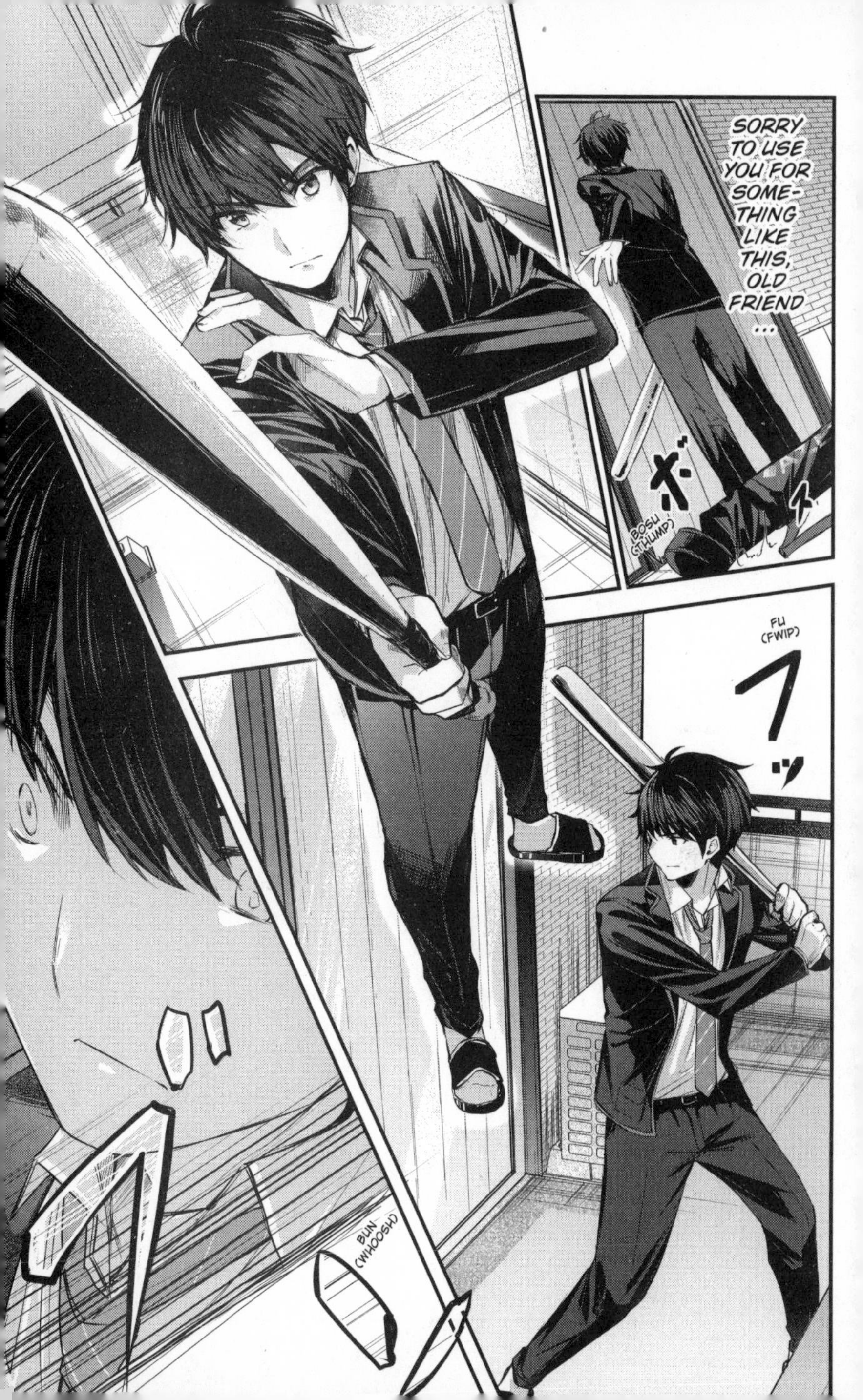
SORRY TO USE YOU FOR SOMETHING LIKE THIS, OLD FRIEND...
BOSU (THUMP)
FU (FWIP)
BUN (WHOOSH)

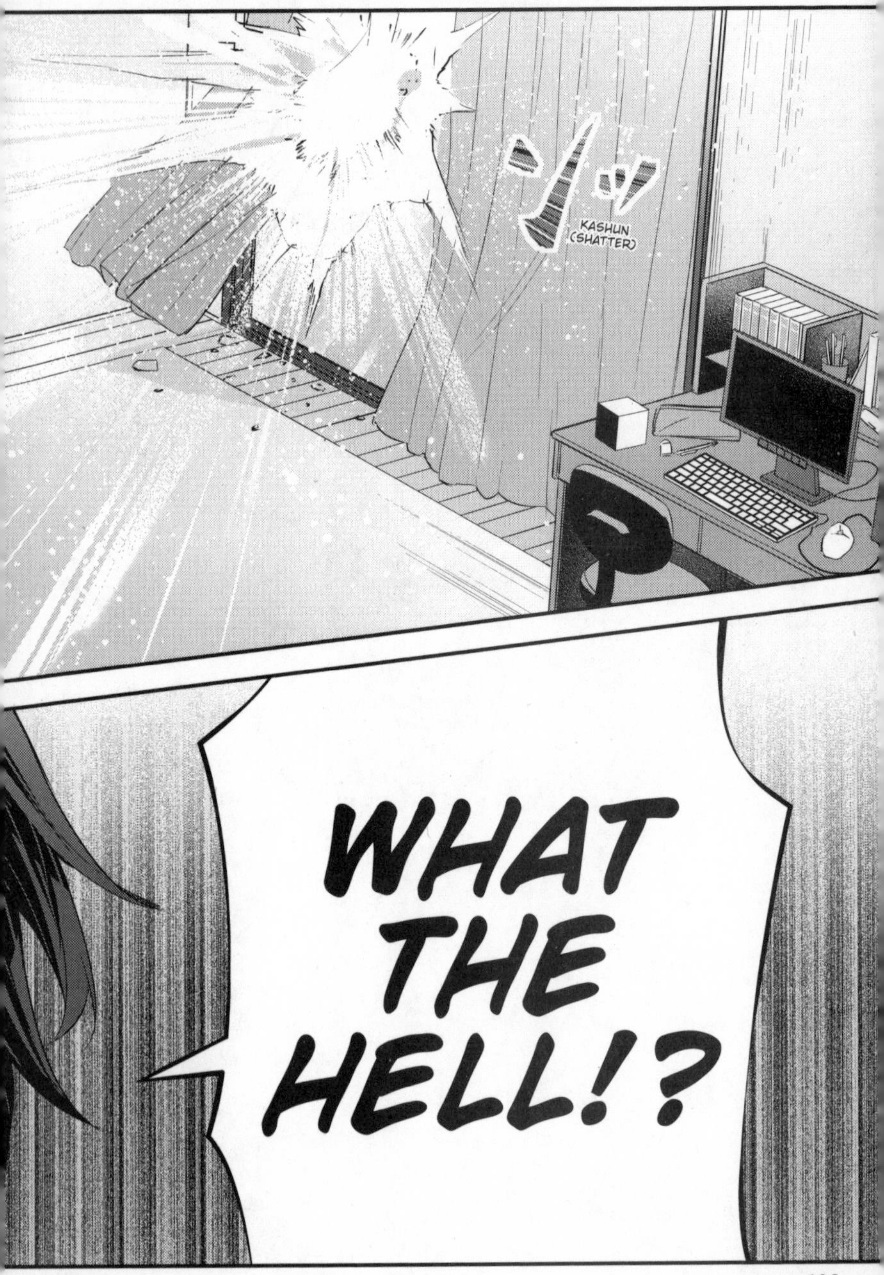
KASHUN (SHATTER)
WHAT THE HELL!?

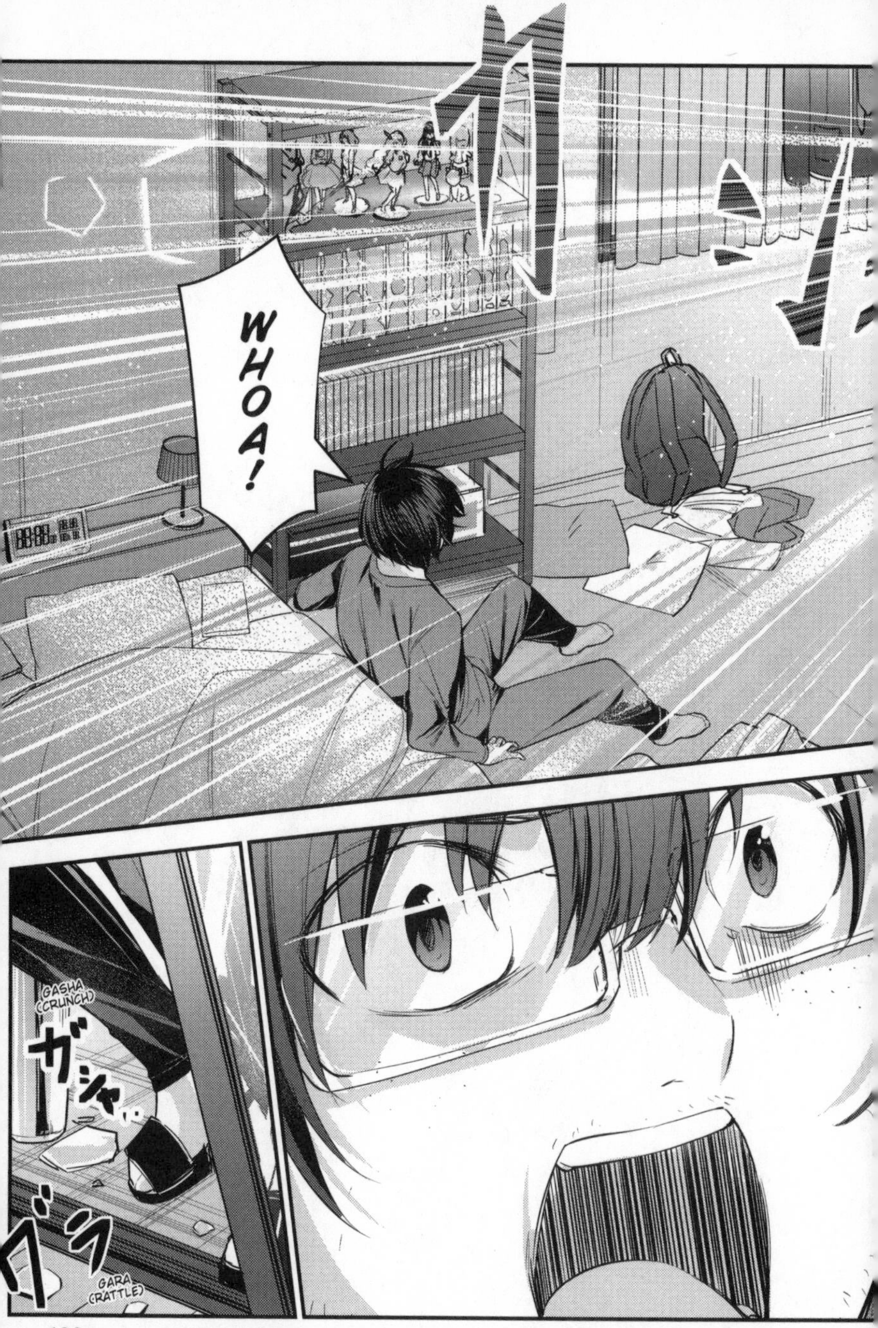
WHOA!
GASHA (CRUNCH)
ガシャ
GARA (RATTLE)
ガラ

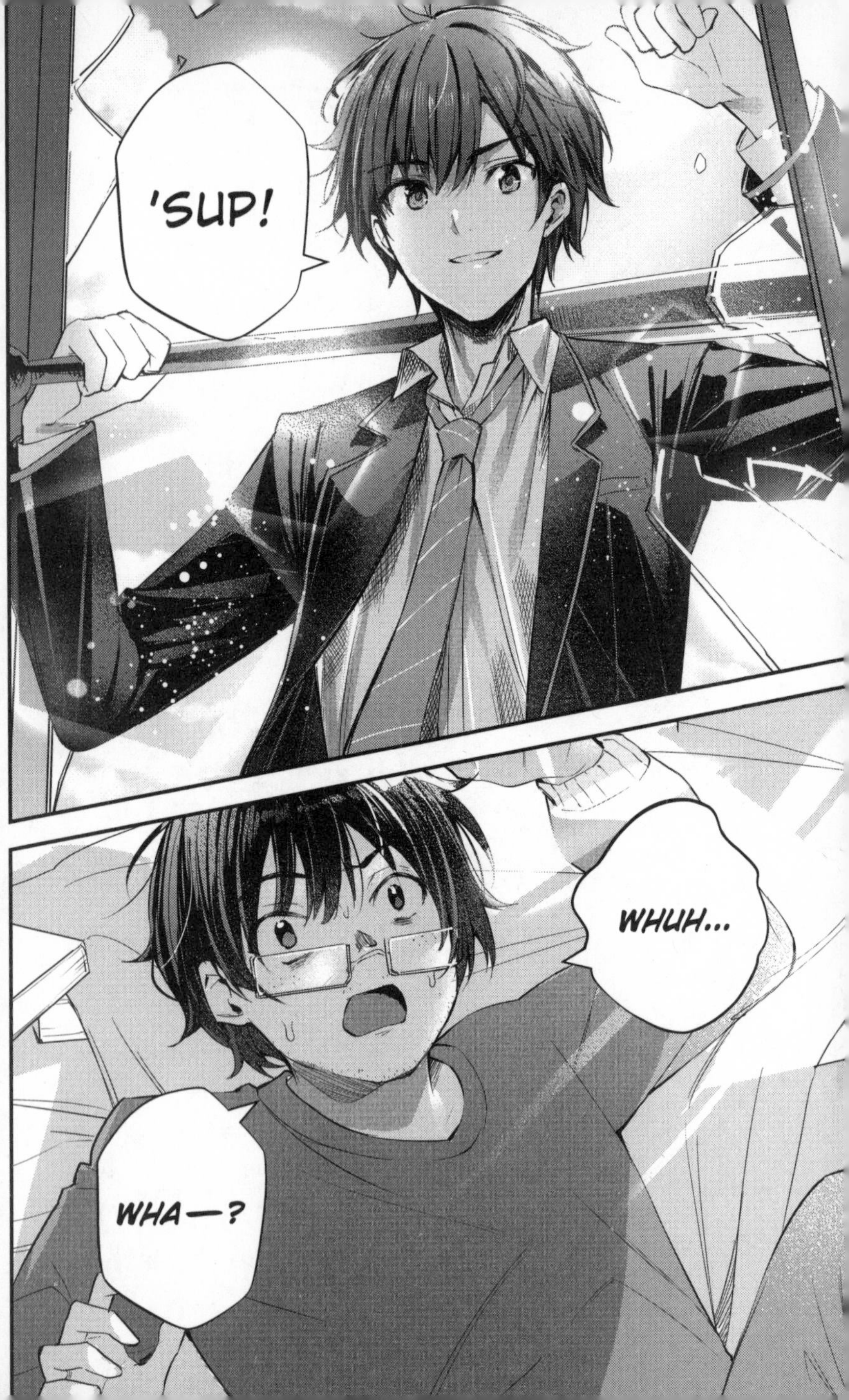
'SUP!
WHUH...
WHA—?

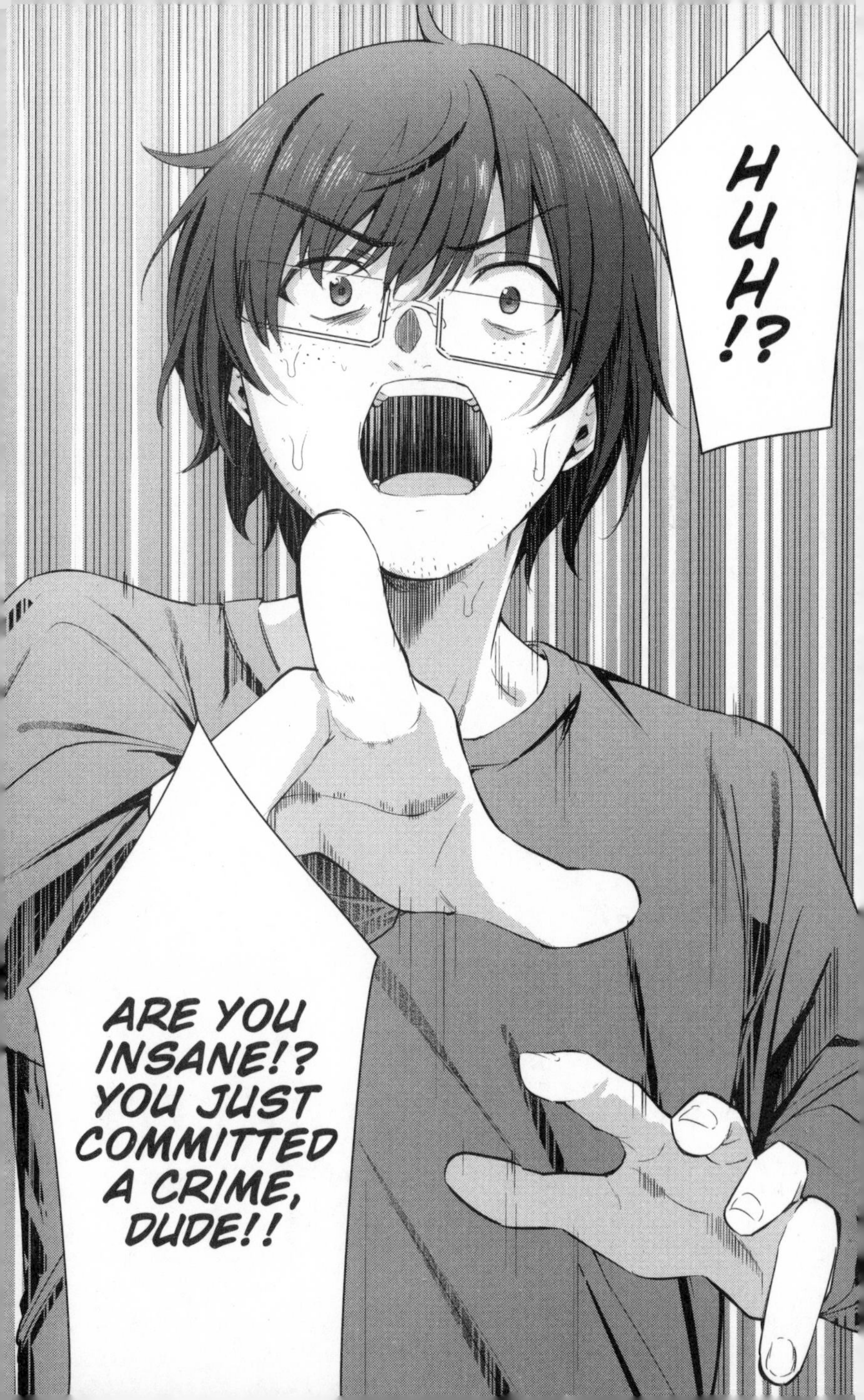
HUH!?
ARE YOU INSANE!? YOU JUST COMMITTED A CRIME, DUDE!!

Chitose Is in the Ramune Bottle

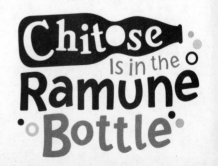

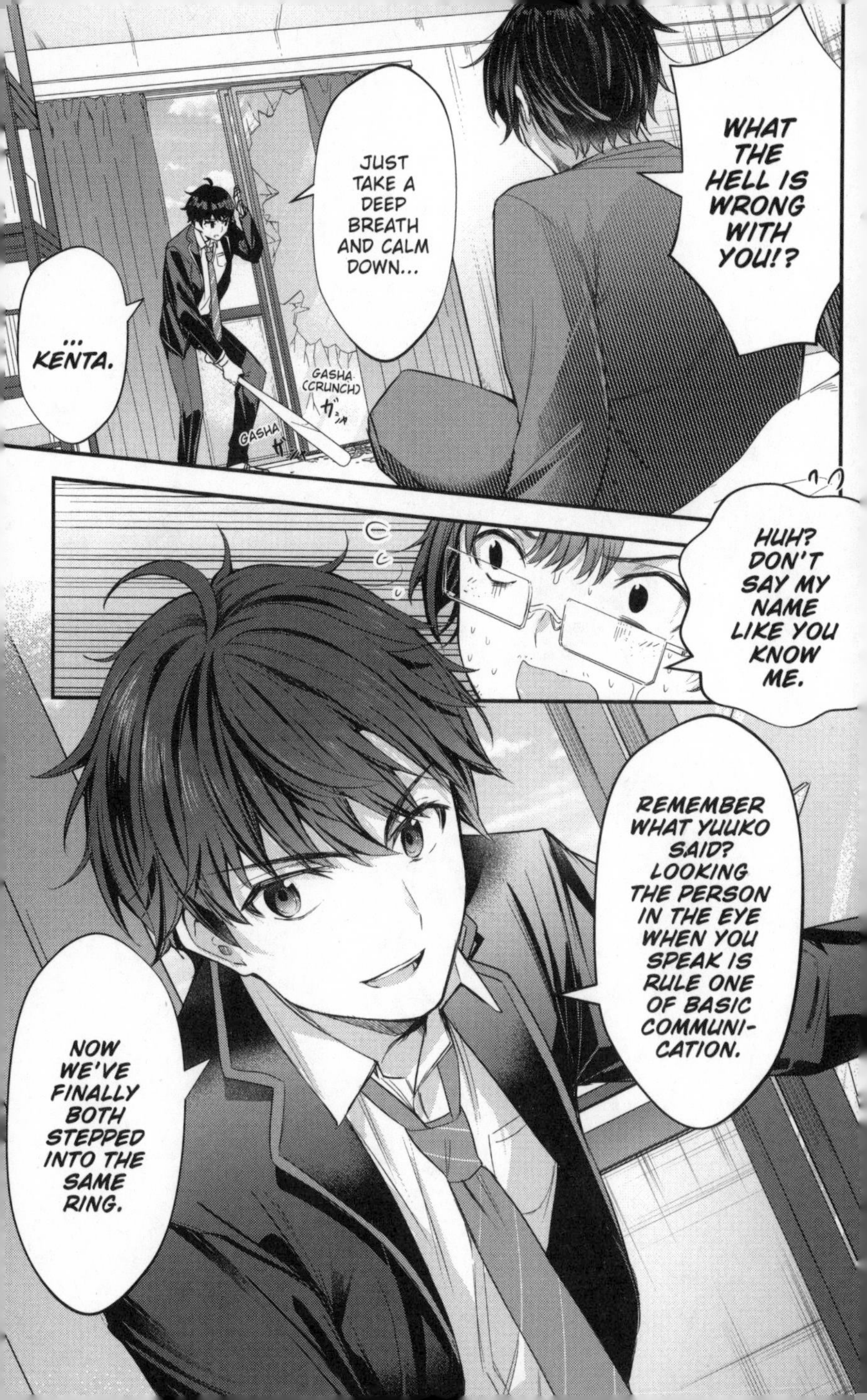
WHAT THE HELL IS WRONG WITH YOU!?
JUST TAKE A DEEP BREATH AND CALM DOWN...
GASHA (CRUNCH)
GASHA
...KENTA.
HUH? DON'T SAY MY NAME LIKE YOU KNOW ME.
REMEMBER WHAT YUUKO SAID? LOOKING THE PERSON IN THE EYE WHEN YOU SPEAK IS RULE ONE OF BASIC COMMUNI-CATION.
NOW WE'VE FINALLY BOTH STEPPED INTO THE SAME RING.

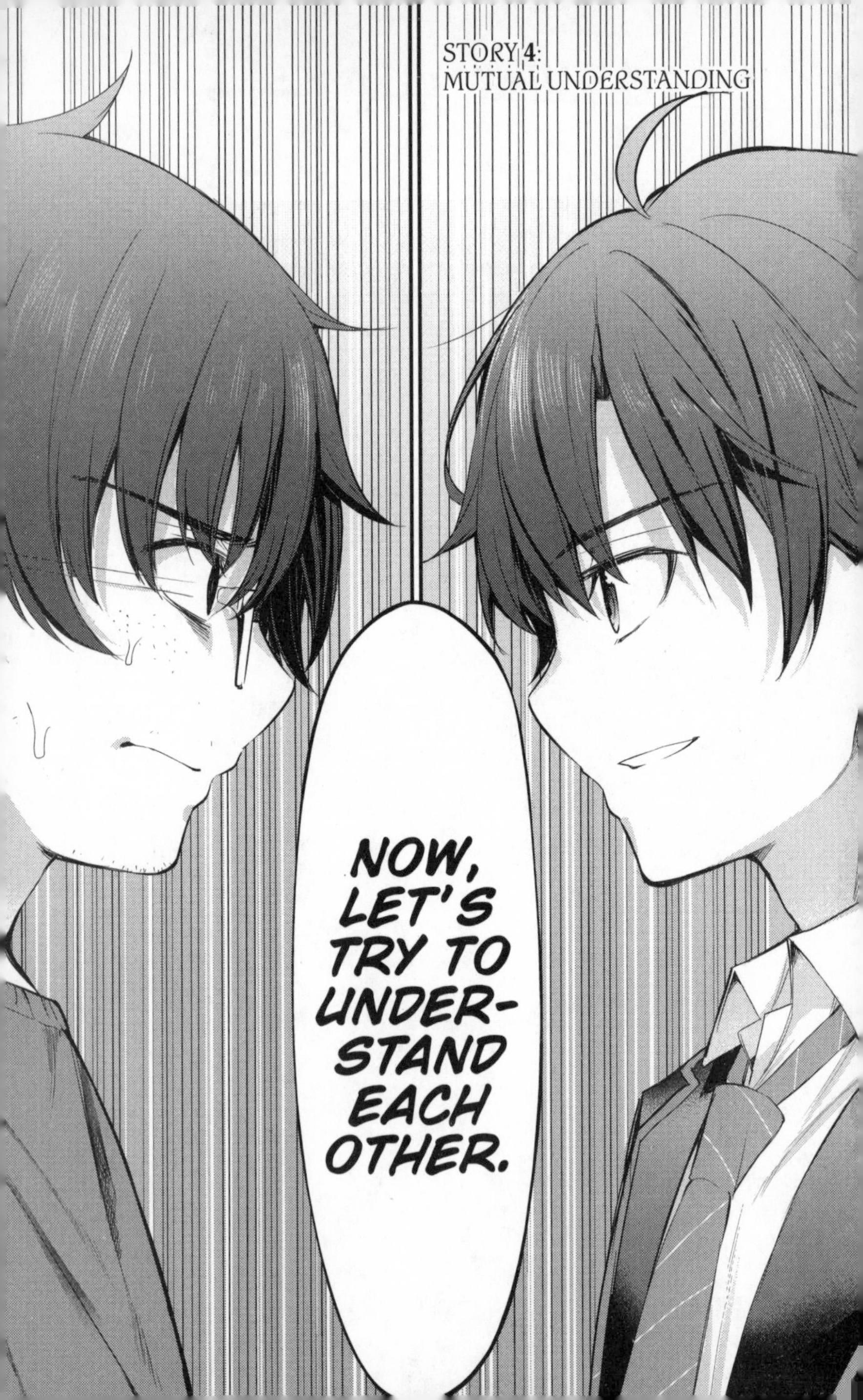
STORY 4: MUTUAL UNDERSTANDING
NOW, LET'S TRY TO UNDER-STAND EACH OTHER.

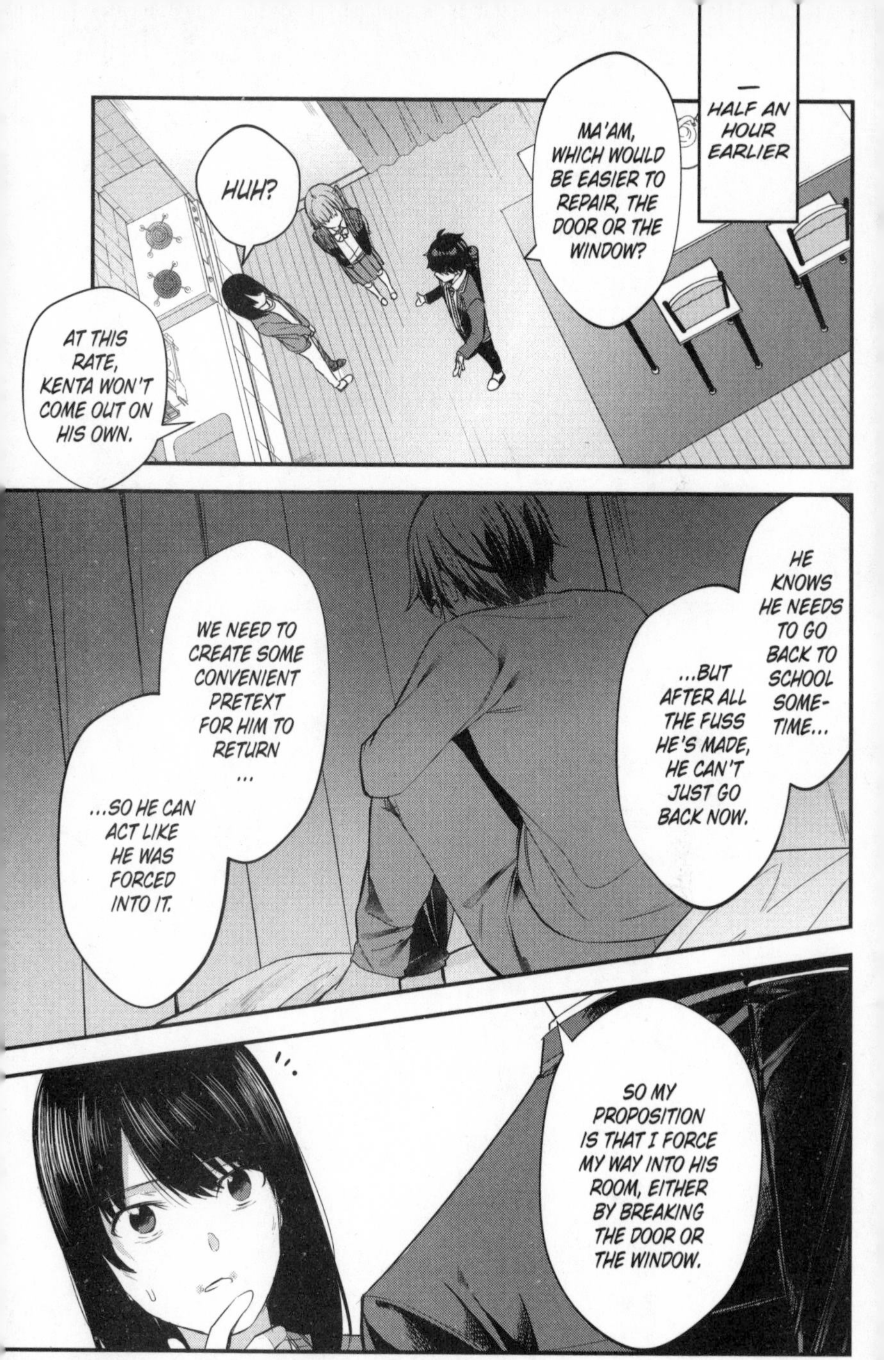
—HALF AN HOUR EARLIER
MA'AM, WHICH WOULD BE EASIER TO REPAIR, THE DOOR OR THE WINDOW?
HUH?
AT THIS RATE, KENTA WON'T COME OUT ON HIS OWN.
HE KNOWS HE NEEDS TO GO BACK TO SCHOOL SOME-TIME...
...BUT AFTER ALL THE FUSS HE'S MADE, HE CAN'T JUST GO BACK NOW.
WE NEED TO CREATE SOME CONVENIENT PRETEXT FOR HIM TO RETURN...
...SO HE CAN ACT LIKE HE WAS FORCED INTO IT.
SO MY PROPOSITION IS THAT I FORCE MY WAY INTO HIS ROOM, EITHER BY BREAKING THE DOOR OR THE WINDOW.

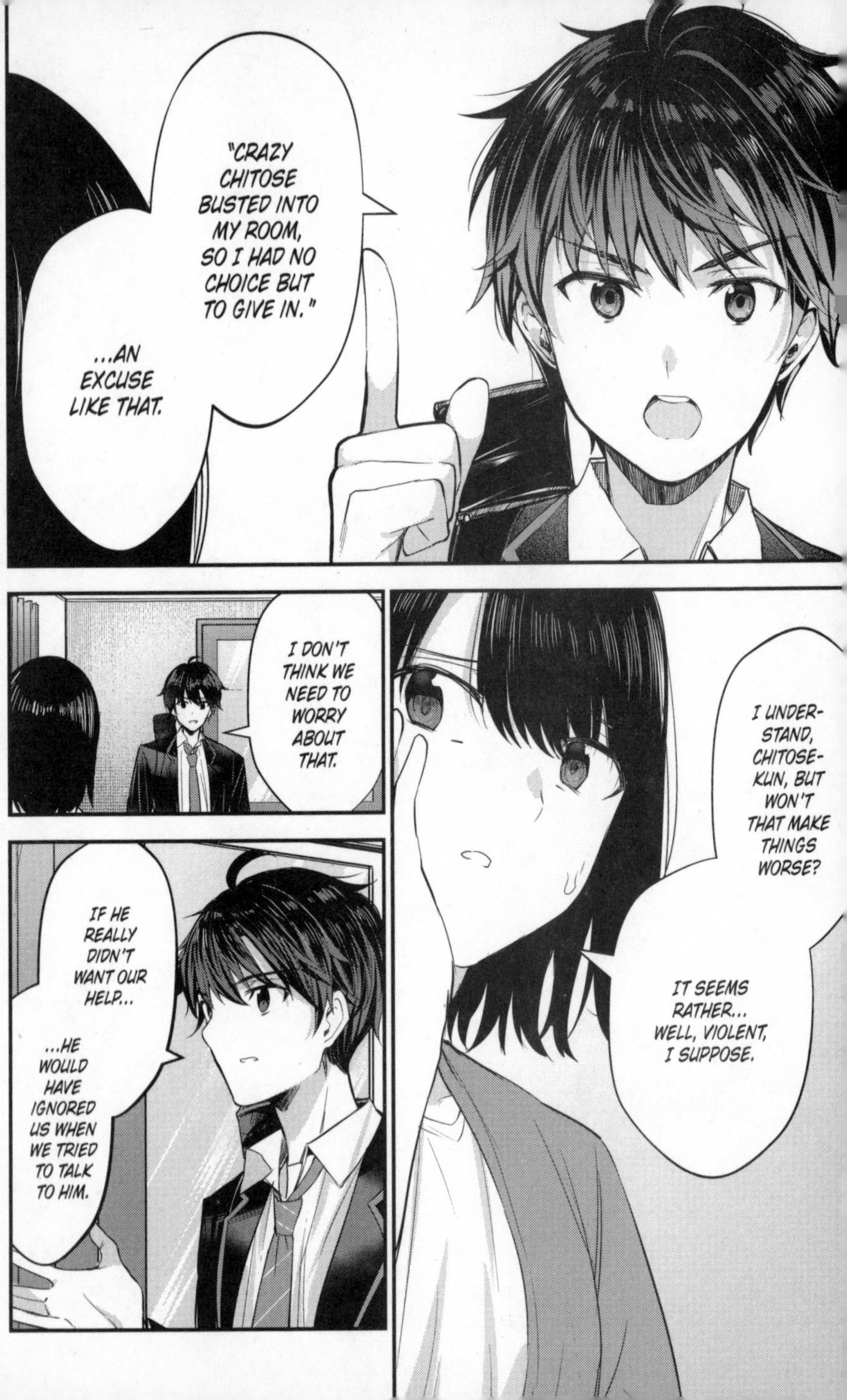
"CRAZY CHITOSE BUSTED INTO MY ROOM, SO I HAD NO CHOICE BUT TO GIVE IN."
...AN EXCUSE LIKE THAT.
I UNDER-STAND, CHITOSE-KUN, BUT WON'T THAT MAKE THINGS WORSE?
IT SEEMS RATHER... WELL, VIOLENT, I SUPPOSE.
I DON'T THINK WE NEED TO WORRY ABOUT THAT.
IF HE REALLY DIDN'T WANT OUR HELP...
...HE WOULD HAVE IGNORED US WHEN WE TRIED TO TALK TO HIM.

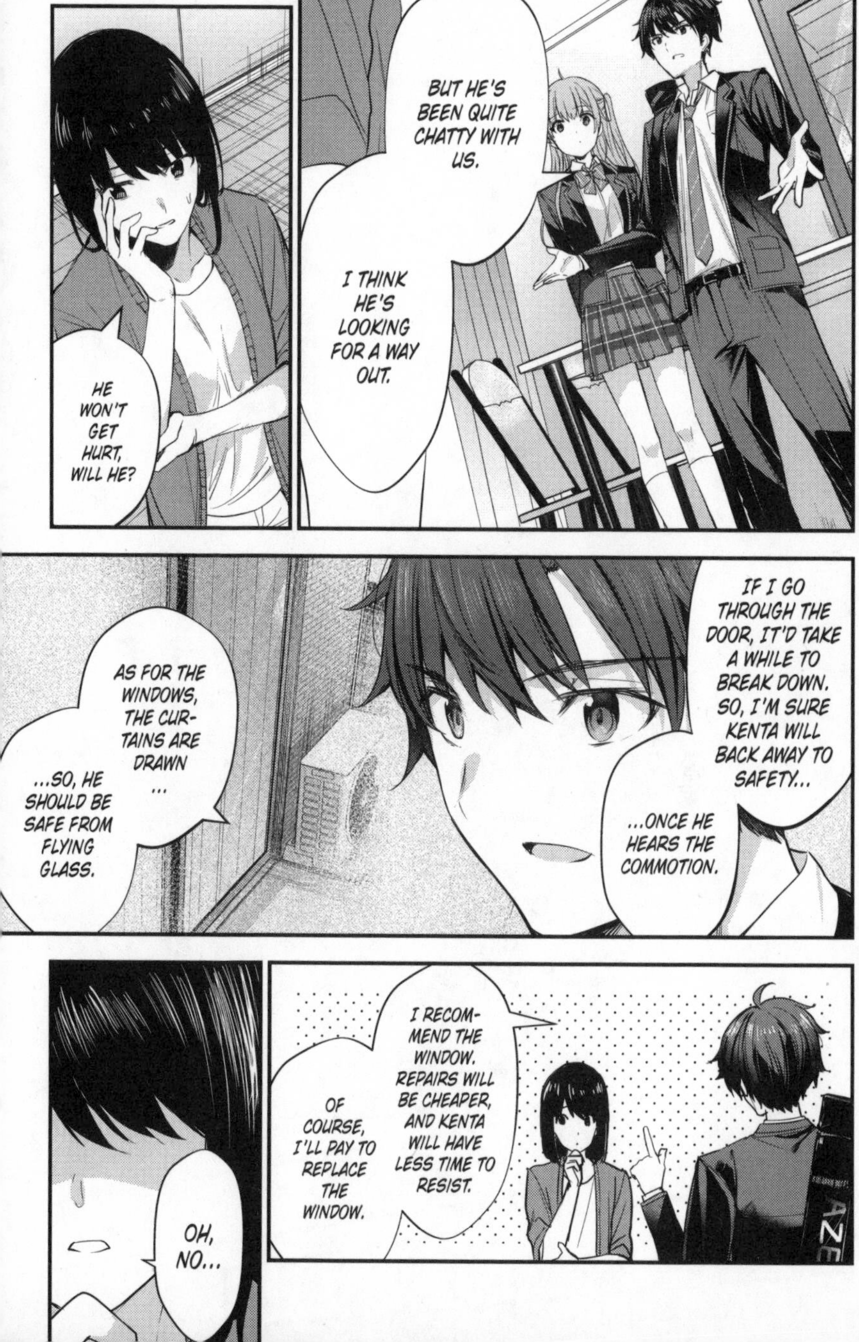
BUT HE'S BEEN QUITE CHATTY WITH US.
I THINK HE'S LOOKING FOR A WAY OUT.
HE WON'T GET HURT, WILL HE?
IF I GO THROUGH THE DOOR, IT'D TAKE A WHILE TO BREAK DOWN. SO, I'M SURE KENTA WILL BACK AWAY TO SAFETY...
...ONCE HE HEARS THE COMMOTION.
AS FOR THE WINDOWS, THE CUR-TAINS ARE DRAWN ...
...SO, HE SHOULD BE SAFE FROM FLYING GLASS.
I RECOM-MEND THE WINDOW. REPAIRS WILL BE CHEAPER, AND KENTA WILL HAVE LESS TIME TO RESIST.
OF COURSE, I'LL PAY TO REPLACE THE WINDOW.
OH, NO...

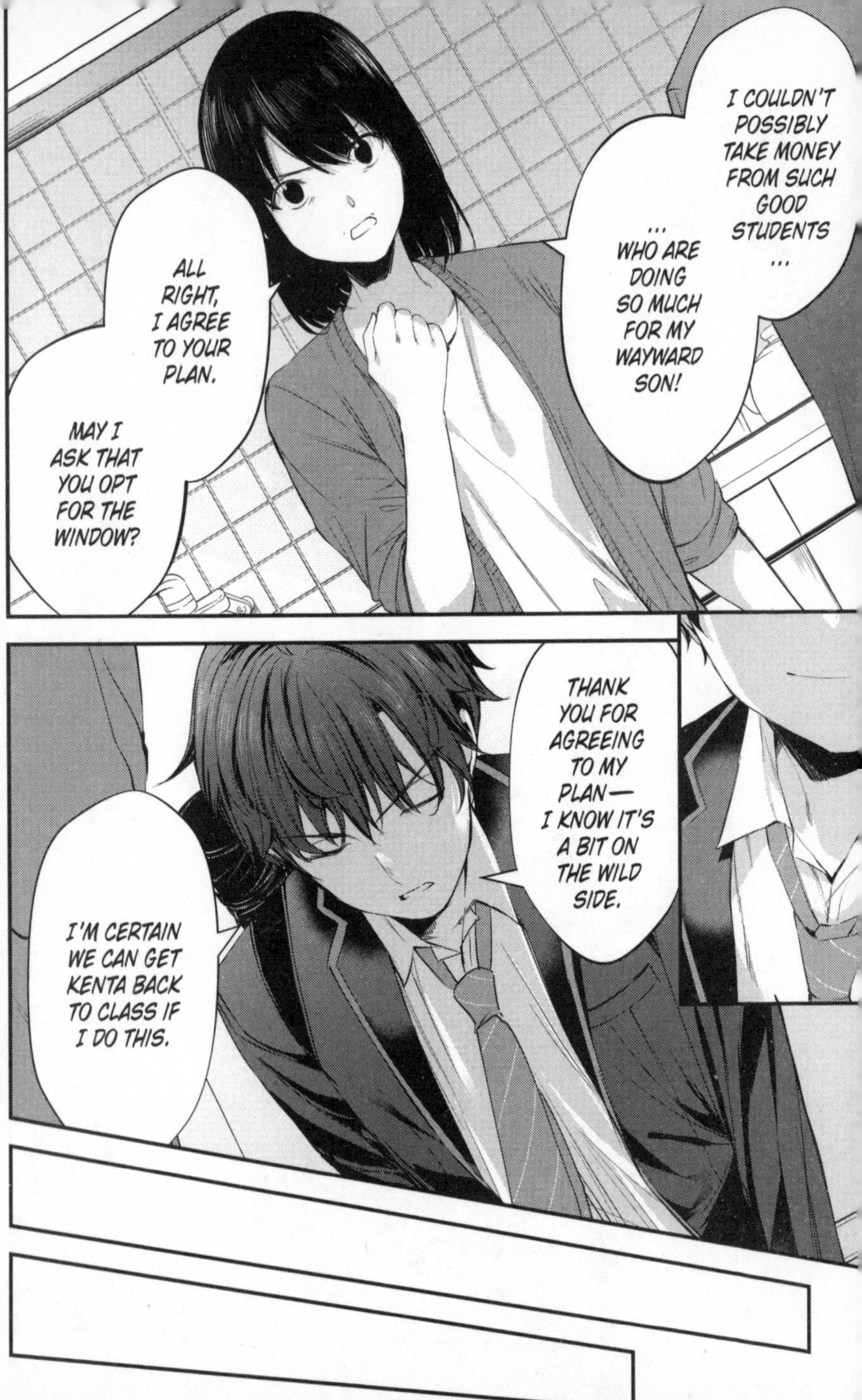
I COULDN'T POSSIBLY TAKE MONEY FROM SUCH GOOD STUDENTS ...
... WHO ARE DOING SO MUCH FOR MY WAYWARD SON!
ALL RIGHT, I AGREE TO YOUR PLAN.
MAY I ASK THAT YOU OPT FOR THE WINDOW?
THANK YOU FOR AGREEING TO MY PLAN— I KNOW IT'S A BIT ON THE WILD SIDE.
I'M CERTAIN WE CAN GET KENTA BACK TO CLASS IF I DO THIS.

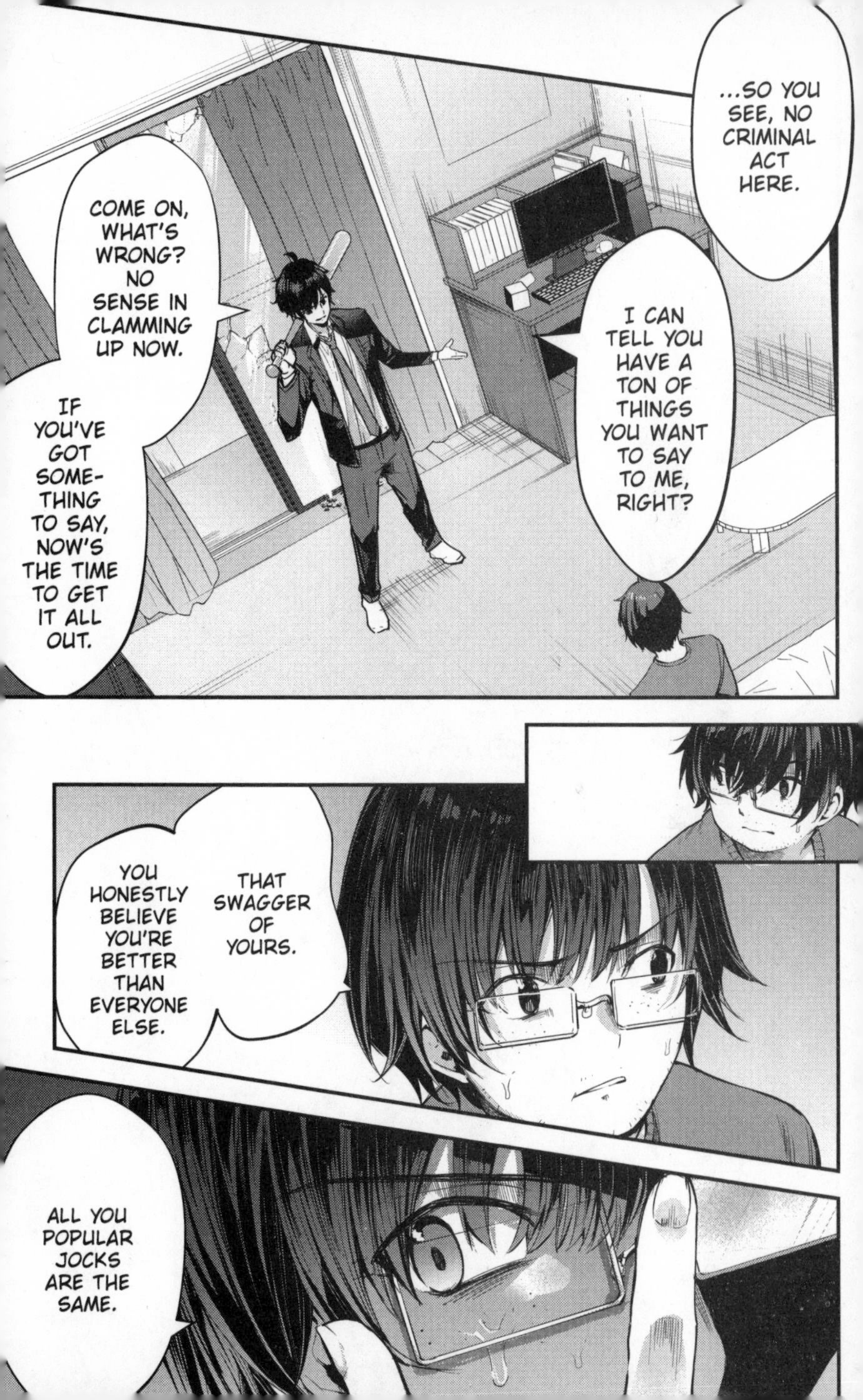
...SO YOU SEE, NO CRIMINAL ACT HERE.
I CAN TELL YOU HAVE A TON OF THINGS YOU WANT TO SAY TO ME, RIGHT?
COME ON, WHAT'S WRONG? NO SENSE IN CLAMMING UP NOW.
IF YOU'VE GOT SOME-THING TO SAY, NOW'S THE TIME TO GET IT ALL OUT.
THAT SWAGGER OF YOURS.
YOU HONESTLY BELIEVE YOU'RE BETTER THAN EVERYONE ELSE.
ALL YOU POPULAR JOCKS ARE THE SAME.

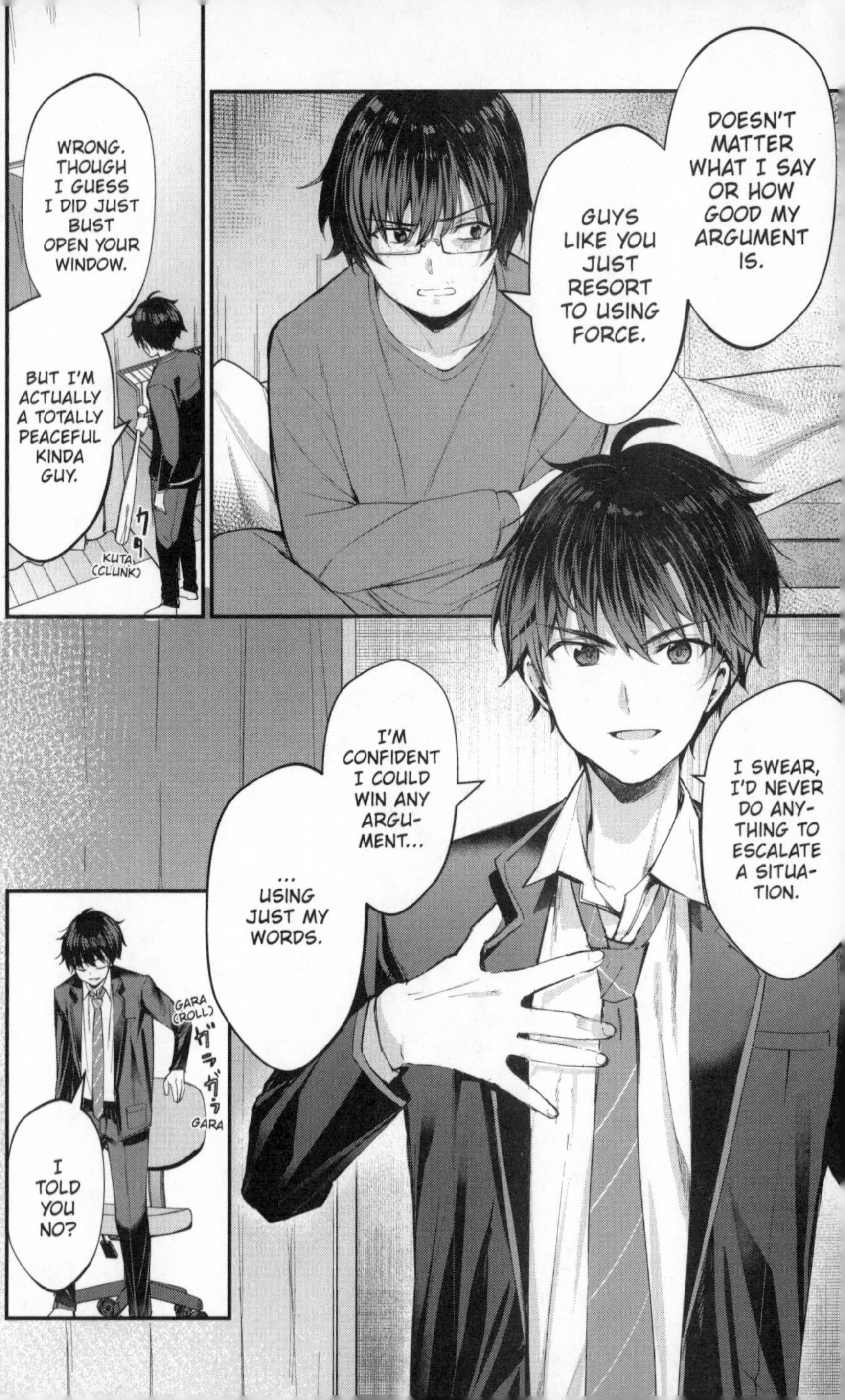
DOESN'T MATTER WHAT I SAY OR HOW GOOD MY ARGUMENT IS.
GUYS LIKE YOU JUST RESORT TO USING FORCE.
WRONG. THOUGH I GUESS I DID JUST BUST OPEN YOUR WINDOW.
BUT I'M ACTUALLY A TOTALLY PEACEFUL KINDA GUY.
KUTA (CLUNK)
I SWEAR, I'D NEVER DO ANY-THING TO ESCALATE A SITUA-TION.
I'M CONFIDENT I COULD WIN ANY ARGU-MENT...
... USING JUST MY WORDS.
GARA (ROLL)
GARA
I TOLD YOU NO?

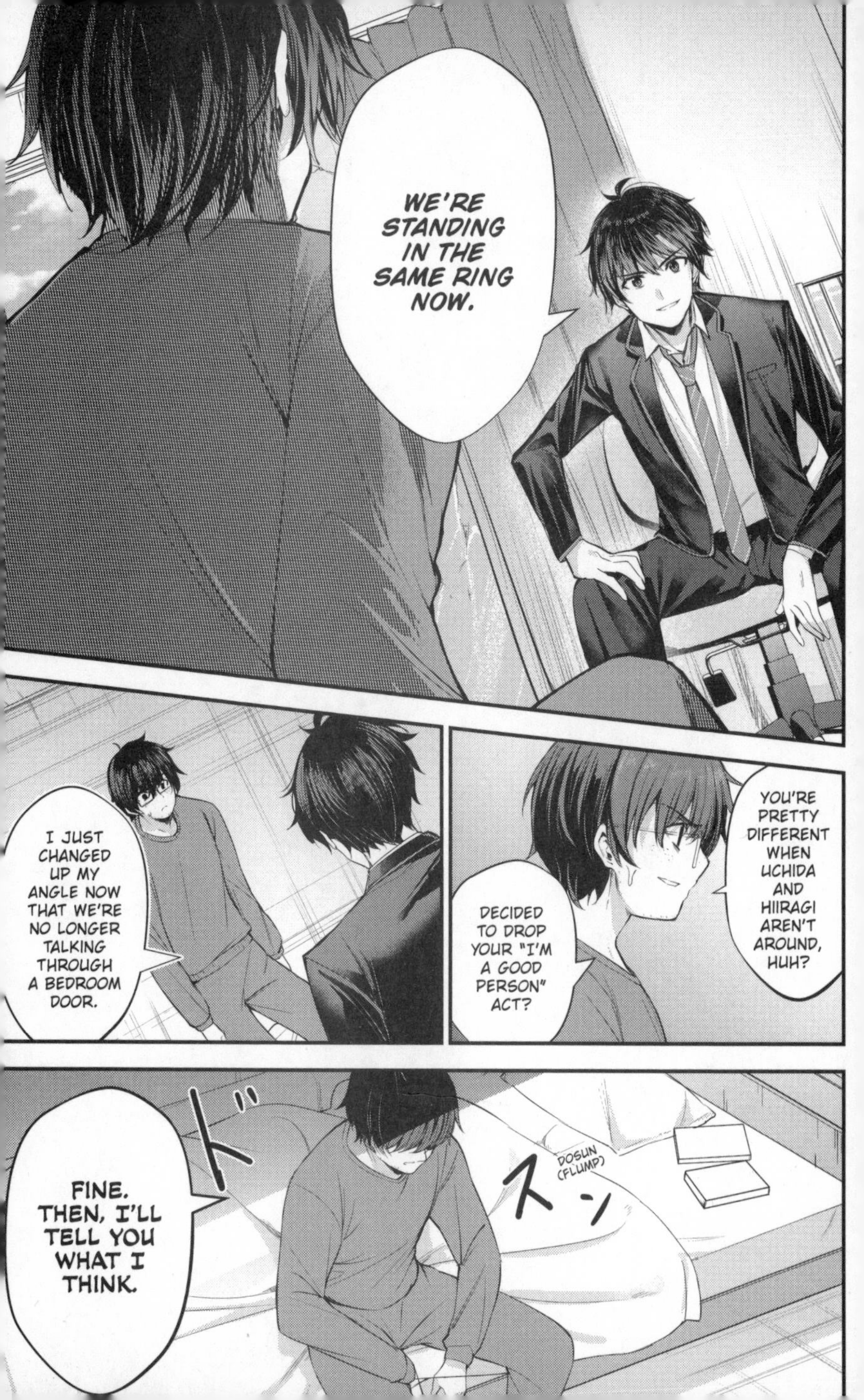
WE'RE STANDING IN THE SAME RING NOW.
YOU'RE PRETTY DIFFERENT WHEN UCHIDA AND HIIRAGI AREN'T AROUND, HUH?
DECIDED TO DROP YOUR "I'M A GOOD PERSON" ACT?
I JUST CHANGED UP MY ANGLE NOW THAT WE'RE NO LONGER TALKING THROUGH A BEDROOM DOOR.
ドスン
DOSUN (FLUMP)
FINE. THEN, I'LL TELL YOU WHAT I THINK.

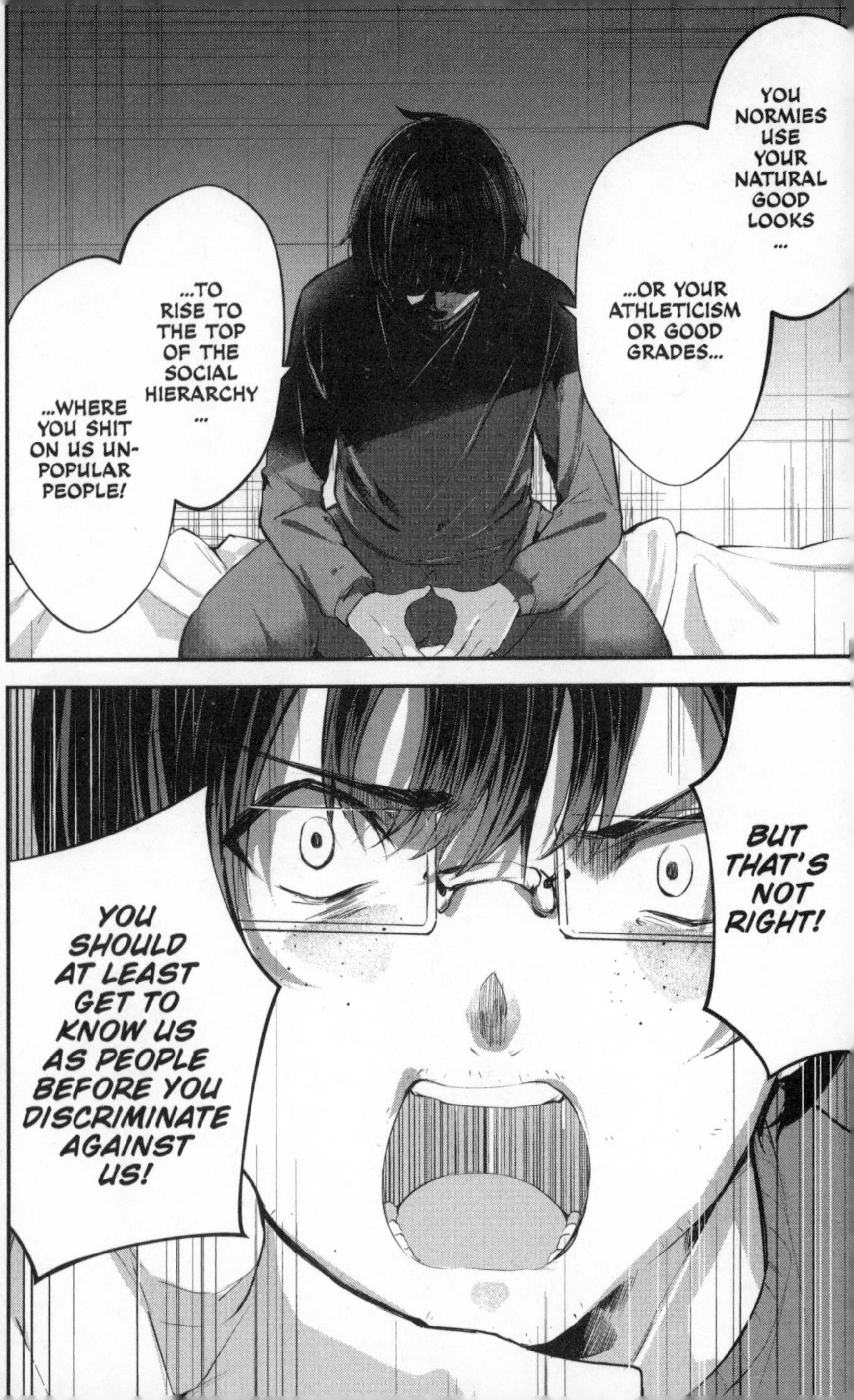
YOU NORMIES USE YOUR NATURAL GOOD LOOKS ...
...OR YOUR ATHLETICISM OR GOOD GRADES...
...TO RISE TO THE TOP OF THE SOCIAL HIERARCHY ...
...WHERE YOU SHIT ON US UN-POPULAR PEOPLE!
BUT THAT'S NOT RIGHT!
YOU SHOULD AT LEAST GET TO KNOW US AS PEOPLE BEFORE YOU DISCRIMINATE AGAINST US!

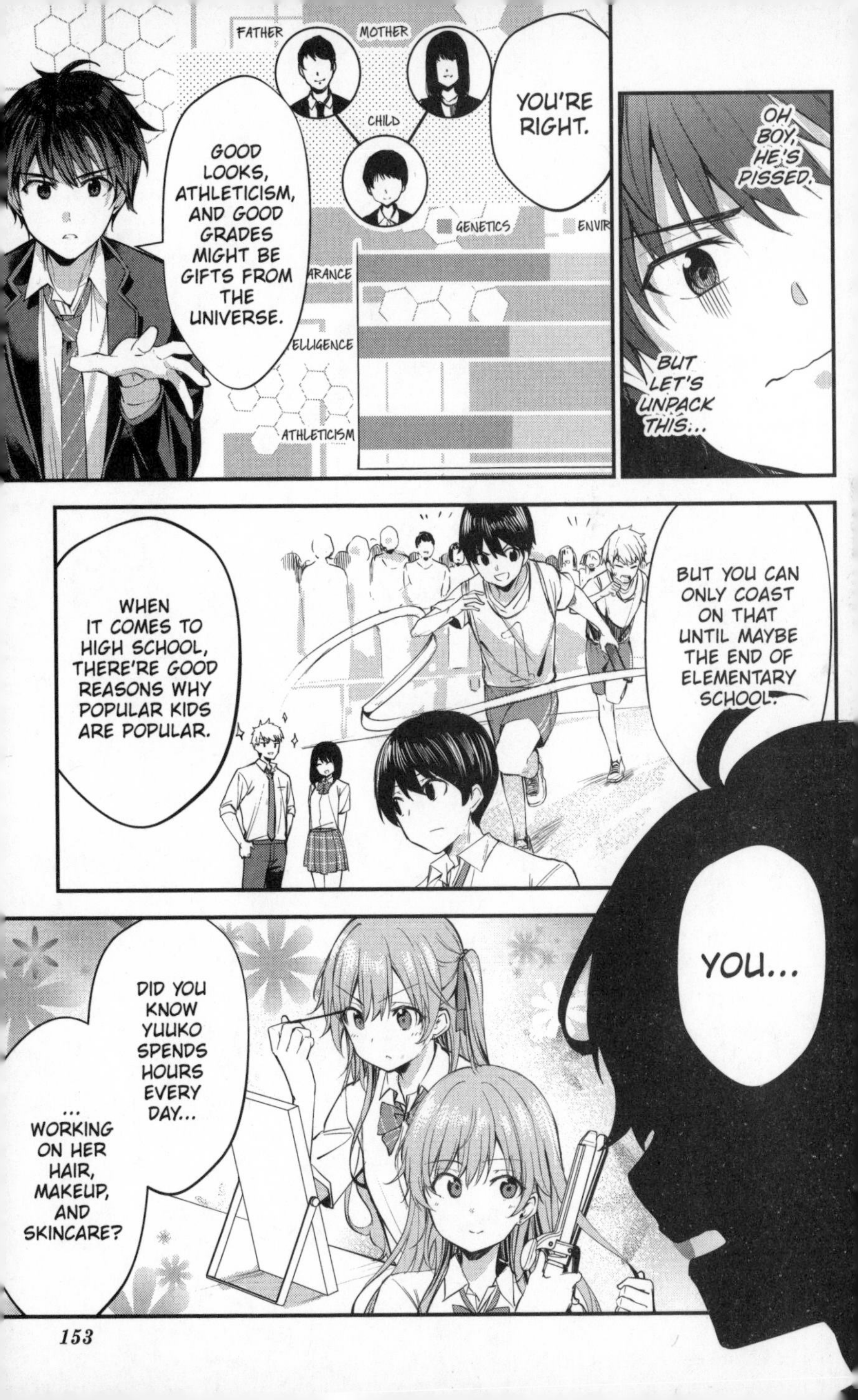
OH BOY, HE'S PISSED.
BUT LET'S UNPACK THIS...
FATHER
MOTHER
CHILD
GENETICS
ENVIR
ARANCE
ELLIGENCE
ATHLETICISM
YOU'RE RIGHT.
GOOD LOOKS, ATHLETICISM, AND GOOD GRADES MIGHT BE GIFTS FROM THE UNIVERSE.
BUT YOU CAN ONLY COAST ON THAT UNTIL MAYBE THE END OF ELEMENTARY SCHOOL.
WHEN IT COMES TO HIGH SCHOOL, THERE'RE GOOD REASONS WHY POPULAR KIDS ARE POPULAR.
YOU...
DID YOU KNOW YUUKO SPENDS HOURS EVERY DAY...
...WORKING ON HER HAIR, MAKEUP, AND SKINCARE?

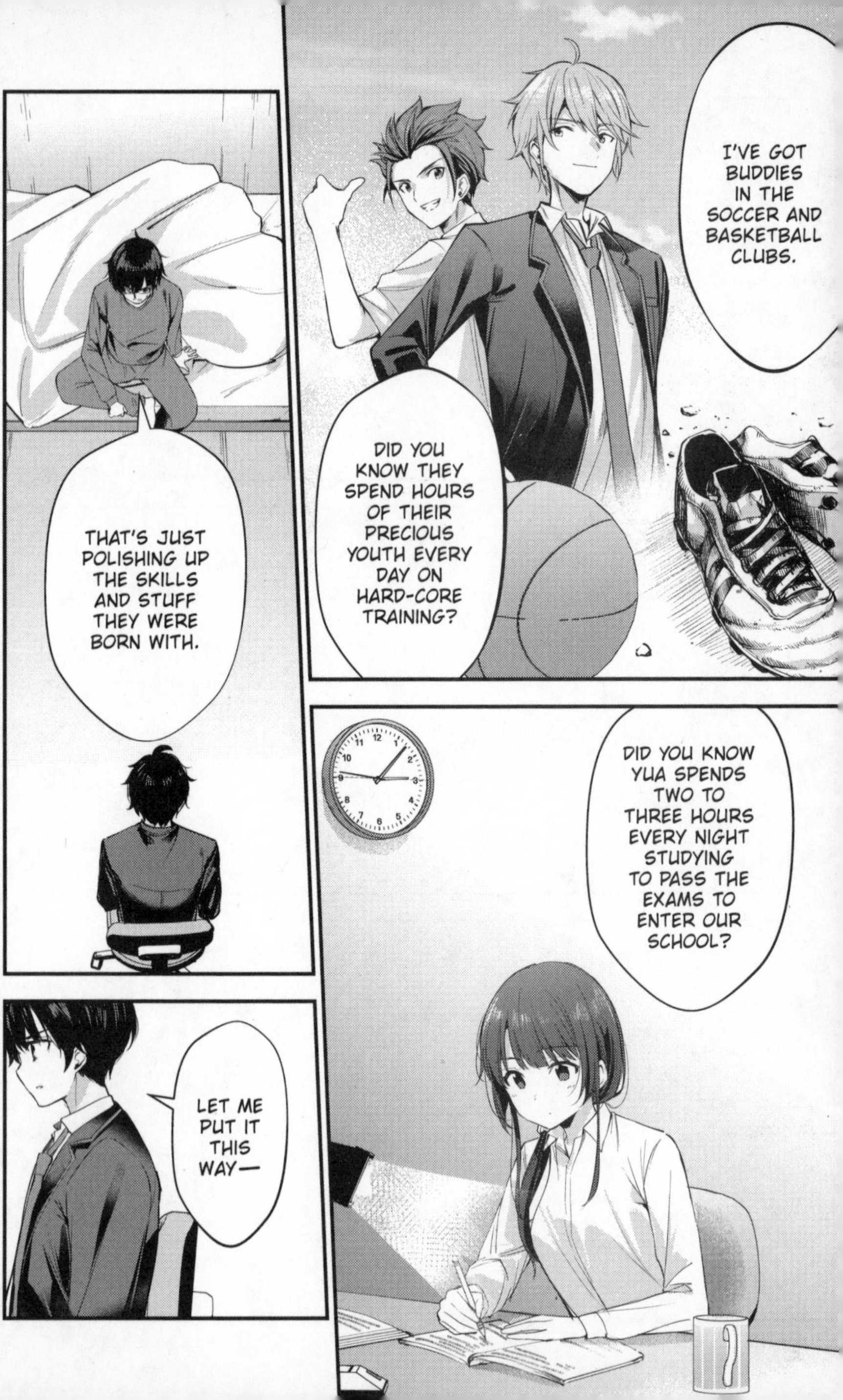
I'VE GOT BUDDIES IN THE SOCCER AND BASKETBALL CLUBS.
DID YOU KNOW THEY SPEND HOURS OF THEIR PRECIOUS YOUTH EVERY DAY ON HARD-CORE TRAINING?
THAT'S JUST POLISHING UP THE SKILLS AND STUFF THEY WERE BORN WITH.
DID YOU KNOW YUA SPENDS TWO TO THREE HOURS EVERY NIGHT STUDYING TO PASS THE EXAMS TO ENTER OUR SCHOOL?
LET ME PUT IT THIS WAY—

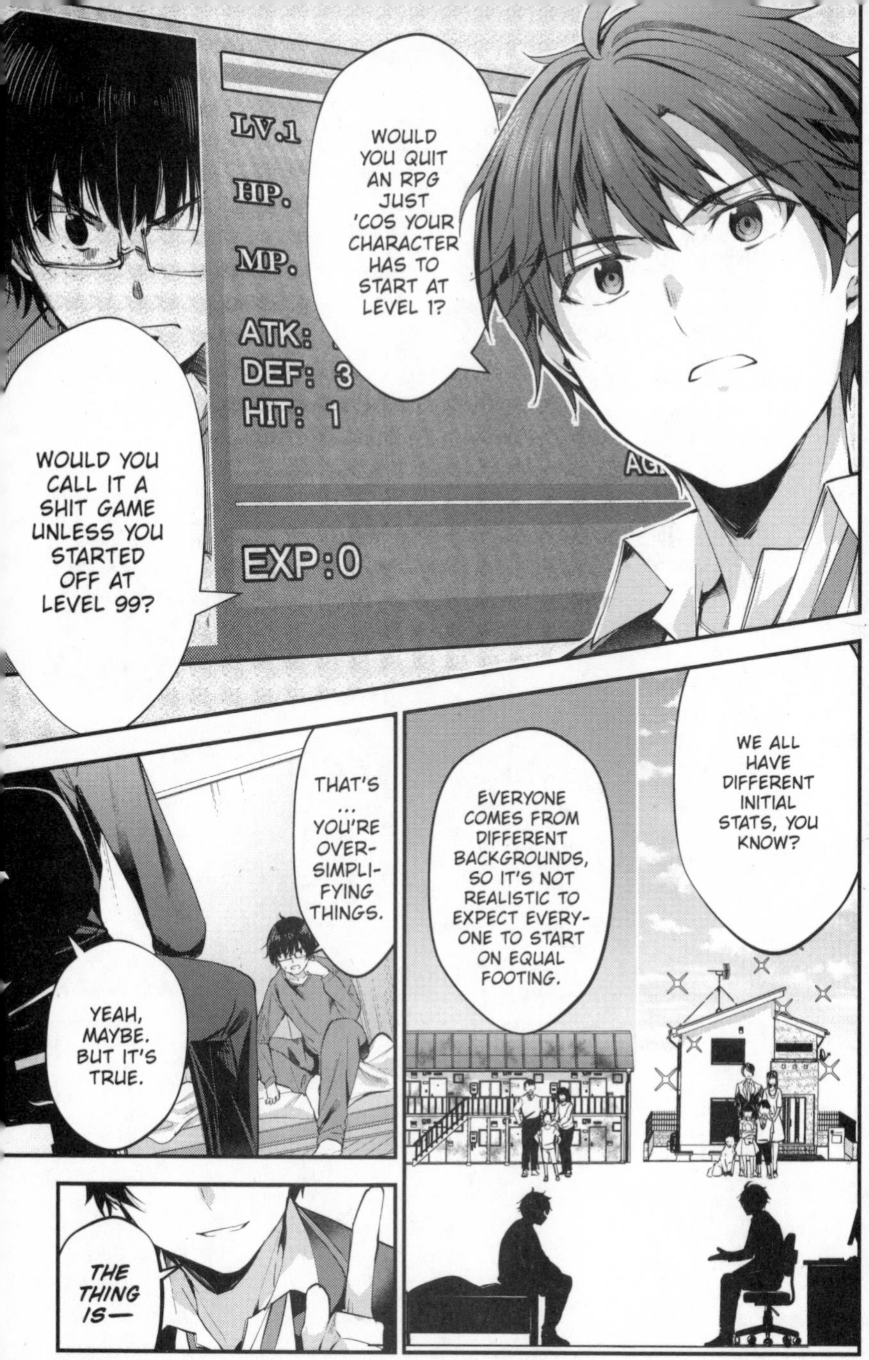
LV.1
HP.
MP.
ATK:
DEF: 3
HIT: 1
EXP:0
WOULD YOU QUIT AN RPG JUST 'COS YOUR CHARACTER HAS TO START AT LEVEL 1?
WOULD YOU CALL IT A SHIT GAME UNLESS YOU STARTED OFF AT LEVEL 99?
WE ALL HAVE DIFFERENT INITIAL STATS, YOU KNOW?
EVERYONE COMES FROM DIFFERENT BACKGROUNDS, SO IT'S NOT REALISTIC TO EXPECT EVERY-ONE TO START ON EQUAL FOOTING.
THAT'S ... YOU'RE OVER-SIMPLI-FYING THINGS.
YEAH, MAYBE. BUT IT'S TRUE.
THE THING IS—

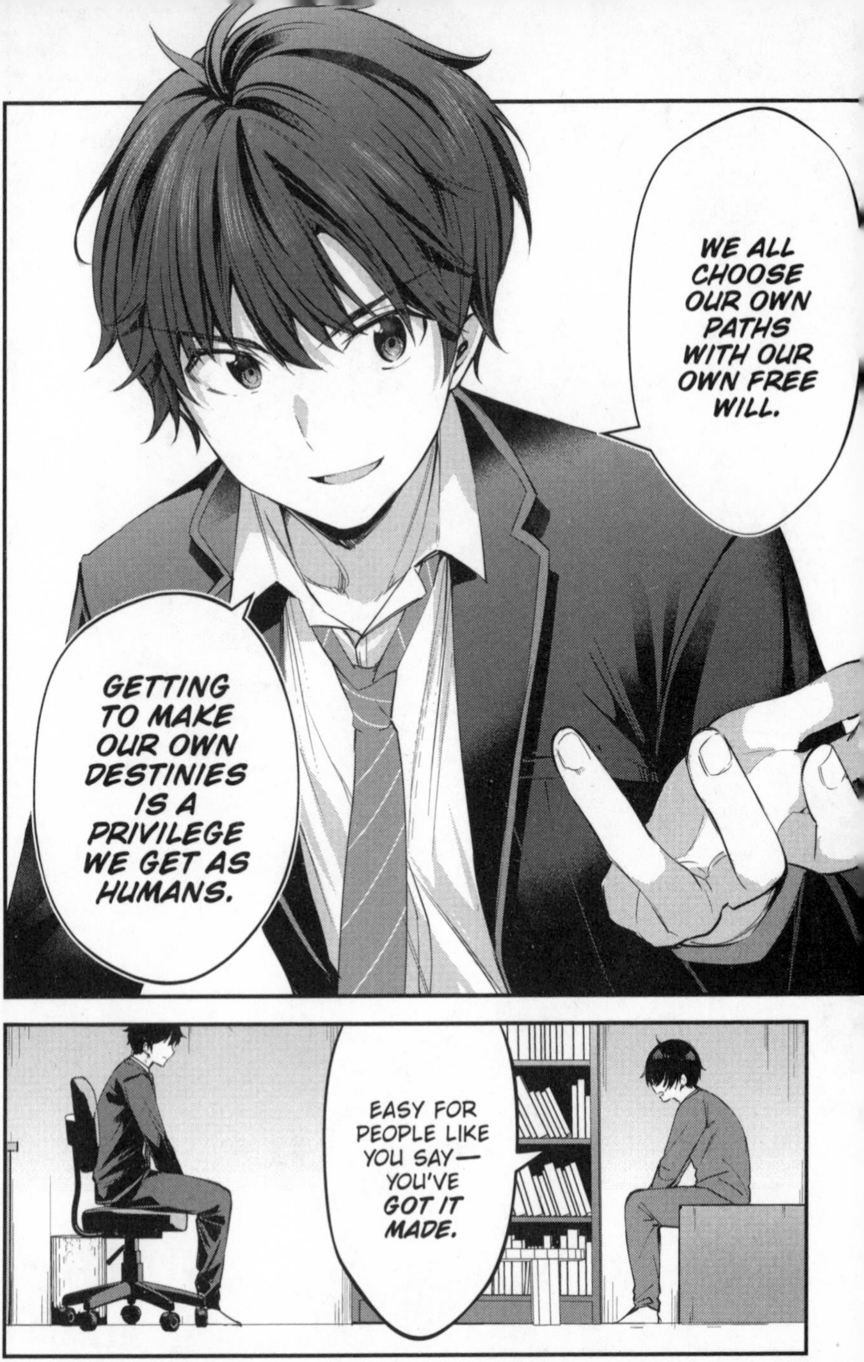
WE ALL CHOOSE OUR OWN PATHS WITH OUR OWN FREE WILL.
GETTING TO MAKE OUR OWN DESTINIES IS A PRIVILEGE WE GET AS HUMANS.
EASY FOR PEOPLE LIKE YOU SAY—YOU'VE *GOT IT MADE.*

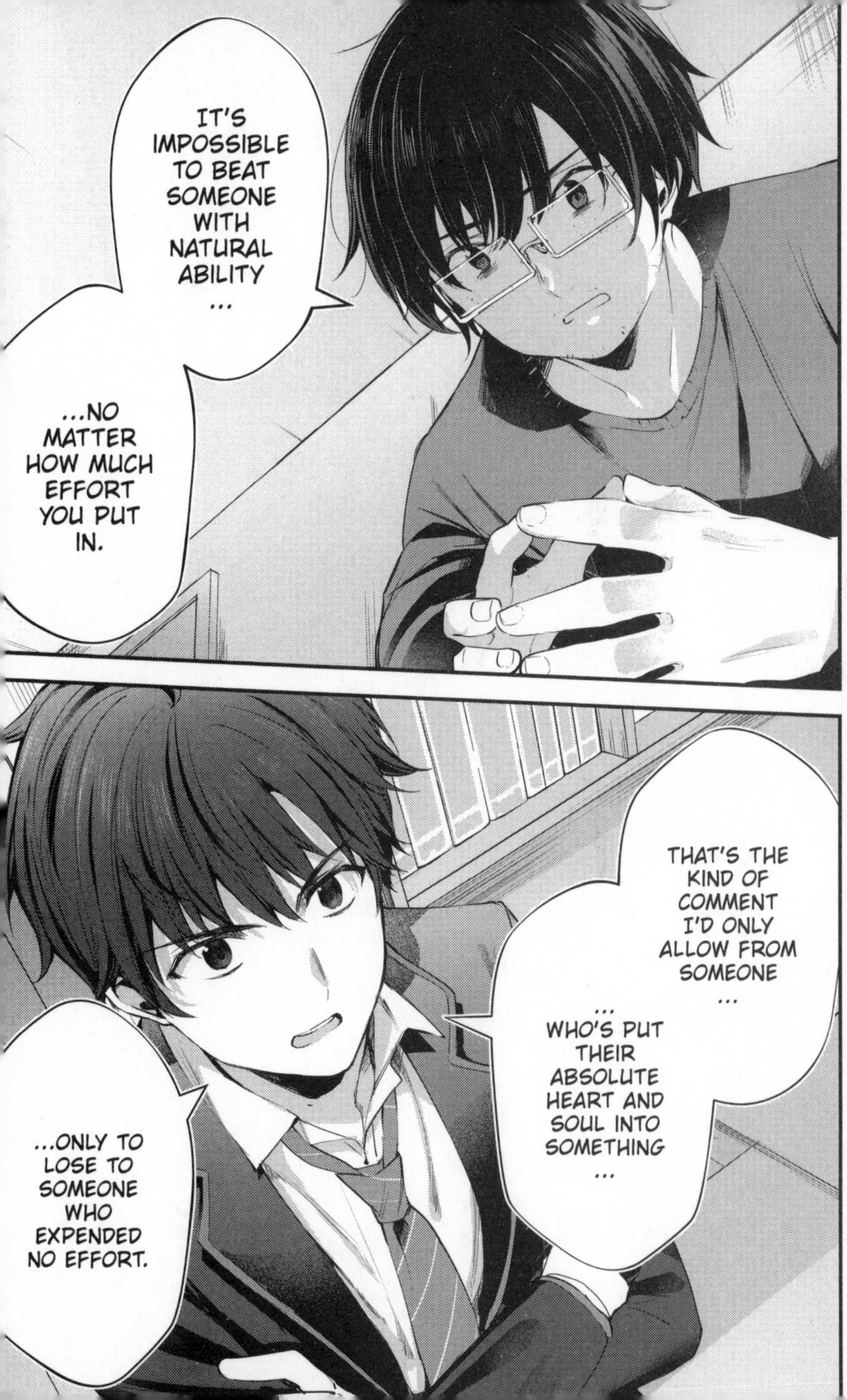
IT'S IMPOSSIBLE TO BEAT SOMEONE WITH NATURAL ABILITY ...
...NO MATTER HOW MUCH EFFORT YOU PUT IN.
THAT'S THE KIND OF COMMENT I'D ONLY ALLOW FROM SOMEONE ...
... WHO'S PUT THEIR ABSOLUTE HEART AND SOUL INTO SOMETHING ...
...ONLY TO LOSE TO SOMEONE WHO EXPENDED NO EFFORT.

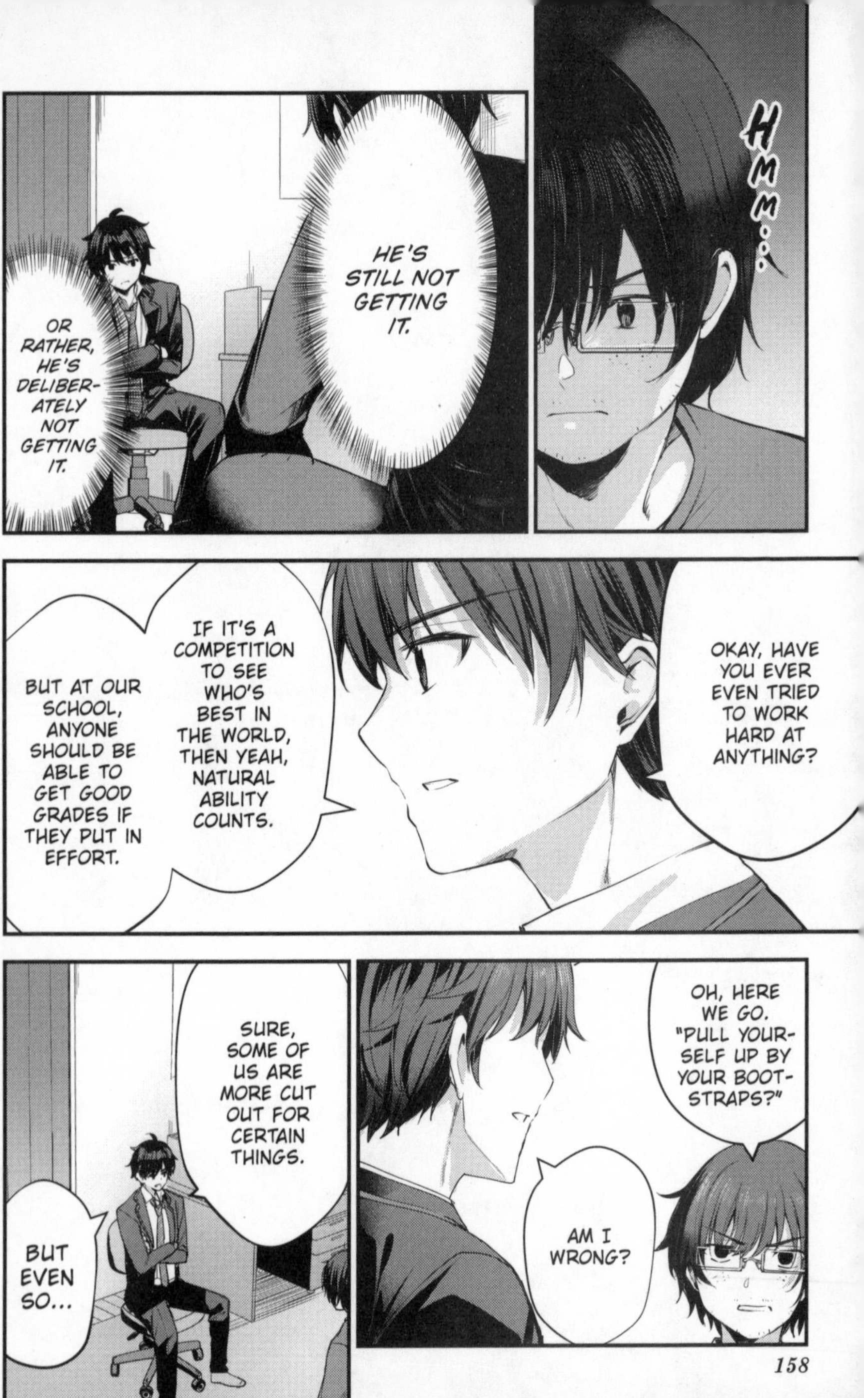
HMMM...
HE'S STILL NOT GETTING IT.
OR RATHER, HE'S DELIBERATELY NOT GETTING IT.
OKAY, HAVE YOU EVER EVEN TRIED TO WORK HARD AT ANYTHING?
IF IT'S A COMPETITION TO SEE WHO'S BEST IN THE WORLD, THEN YEAH, NATURAL ABILITY COUNTS.
BUT AT OUR SCHOOL, ANYONE SHOULD BE ABLE TO GET GOOD GRADES IF THEY PUT IN EFFORT.
OH, HERE WE GO. "PULL YOURSELF UP BY YOUR BOOTSTRAPS?"
AM I WRONG?
SURE, SOME OF US ARE MORE CUT OUT FOR CERTAIN THINGS.
BUT EVEN SO...

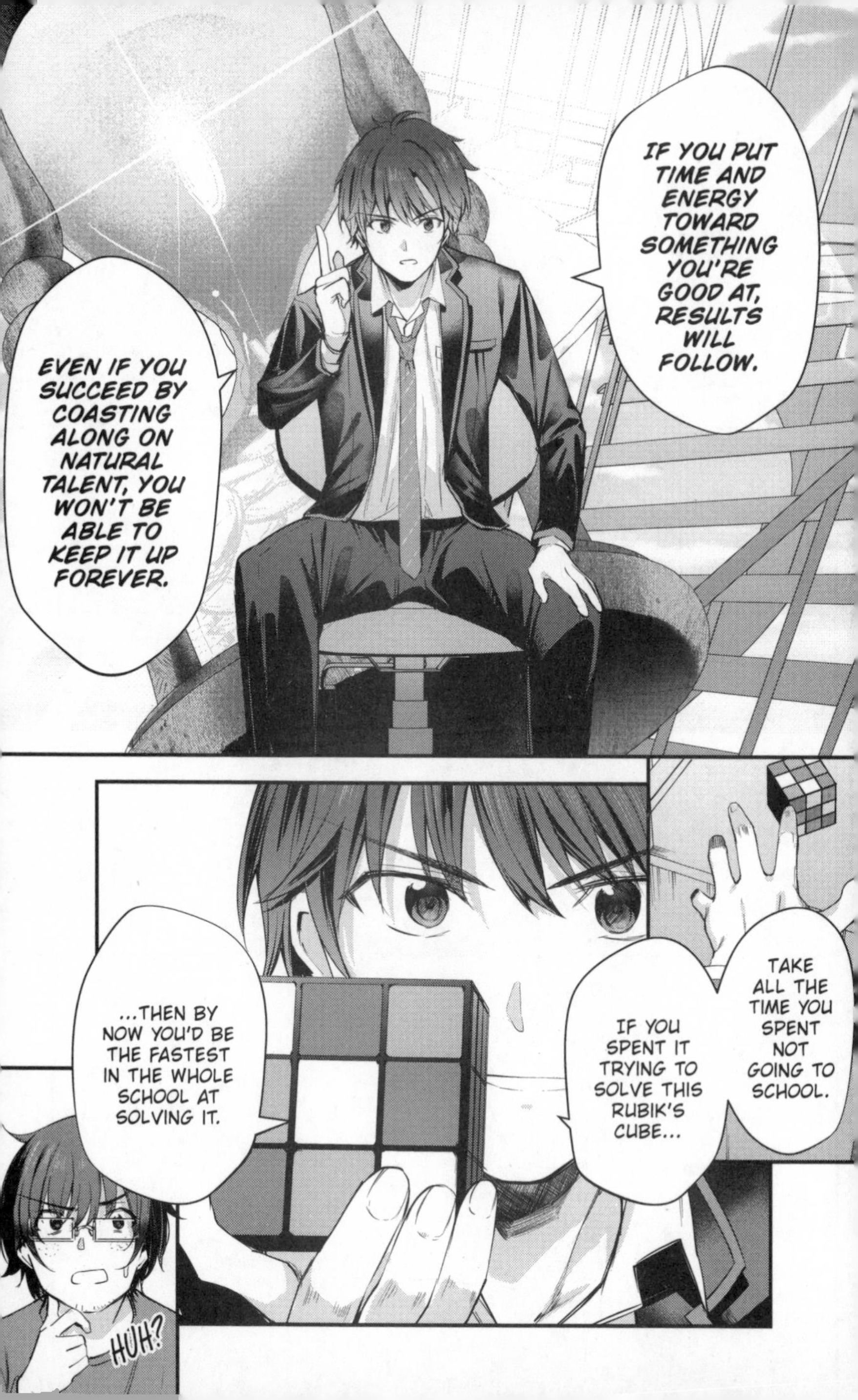
IF YOU PUT TIME AND ENERGY TOWARD SOMETHING YOU'RE GOOD AT, RESULTS WILL FOLLOW.
EVEN IF YOU SUCCEED BY COASTING ALONG ON NATURAL TALENT, YOU WON'T BE ABLE TO KEEP IT UP FOREVER.
TAKE ALL THE TIME YOU SPENT NOT GOING TO SCHOOL.
IF YOU SPENT IT TRYING TO SOLVE THIS RUBIK'S CUBE...
...THEN BY NOW YOU'D BE THE FASTEST IN THE WHOLE SCHOOL AT SOLVING IT.
HUH?

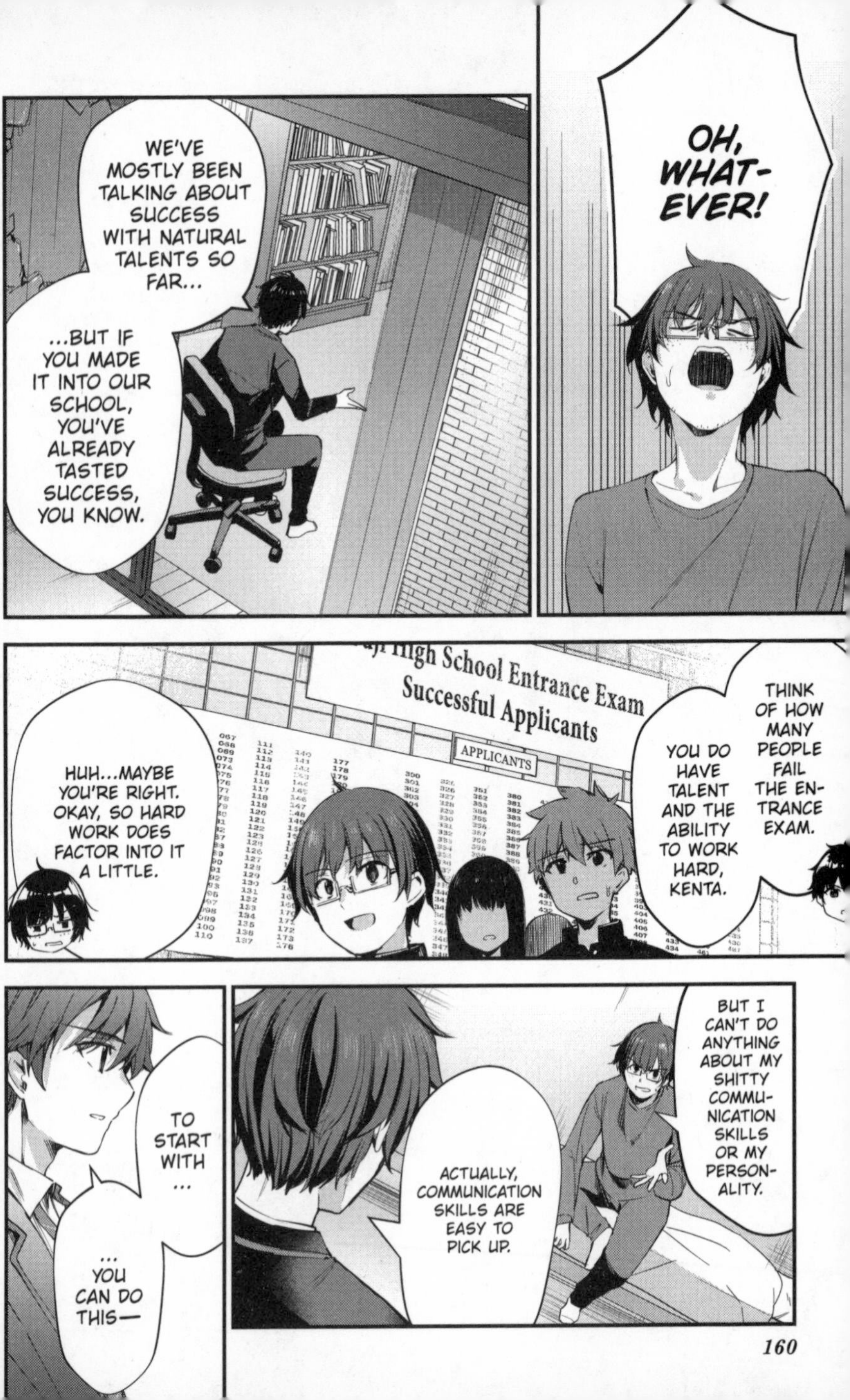

OH, WHAT-EVER!
WE'VE MOSTLY BEEN TALKING ABOUT SUCCESS WITH NATURAL TALENTS SO FAR...
...BUT IF YOU MADE IT INTO OUR SCHOOL, YOU'VE ALREADY TASTED SUCCESS, YOU KNOW.
High School Entrance Exam
Successful Applicants
APPLICANTS
THINK OF HOW MANY PEOPLE FAIL THE EN-TRANCE EXAM.
YOU DO HAVE TALENT AND THE ABILITY TO WORK HARD, KENTA.
HUH...MAYBE YOU'RE RIGHT. OKAY, SO HARD WORK DOES FACTOR INTO IT A LITTLE.
BUT I CAN'T DO ANYTHING ABOUT MY SHITTY COMMU-NICATION SKILLS OR MY PERSON-ALITY.
ACTUALLY, COMMUNICATION SKILLS ARE EASY TO PICK UP.
TO START WITH ...
... YOU CAN DO THIS—

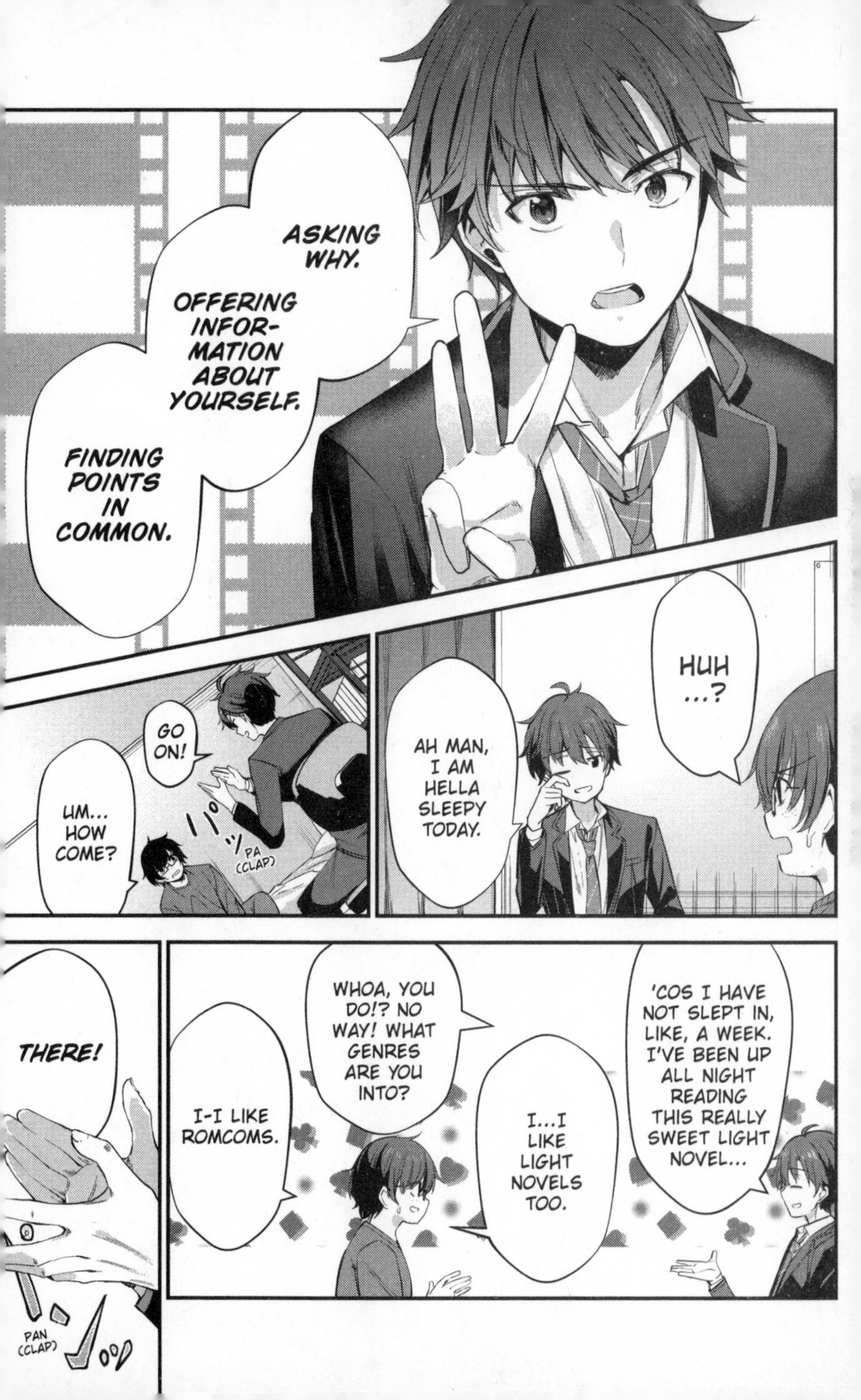
ASKING WHY.
OFFERING INFORMATION ABOUT YOURSELF.
FINDING POINTS IN COMMON.
HUH ...?
AH MAN, I AM HELLA SLEEPY TODAY.
GO ON!
PA (CLAP)
UM... HOW COME?
'COS I HAVE NOT SLEPT IN, LIKE, A WEEK. I'VE BEEN UP ALL NIGHT READING THIS REALLY SWEET LIGHT NOVEL...
I...I LIKE LIGHT NOVELS TOO.
WHOA, YOU DO!? NO WAY! WHAT GENRES ARE YOU INTO?
I-I LIKE ROMCOMS.
THERE!
PAN (CLAP)

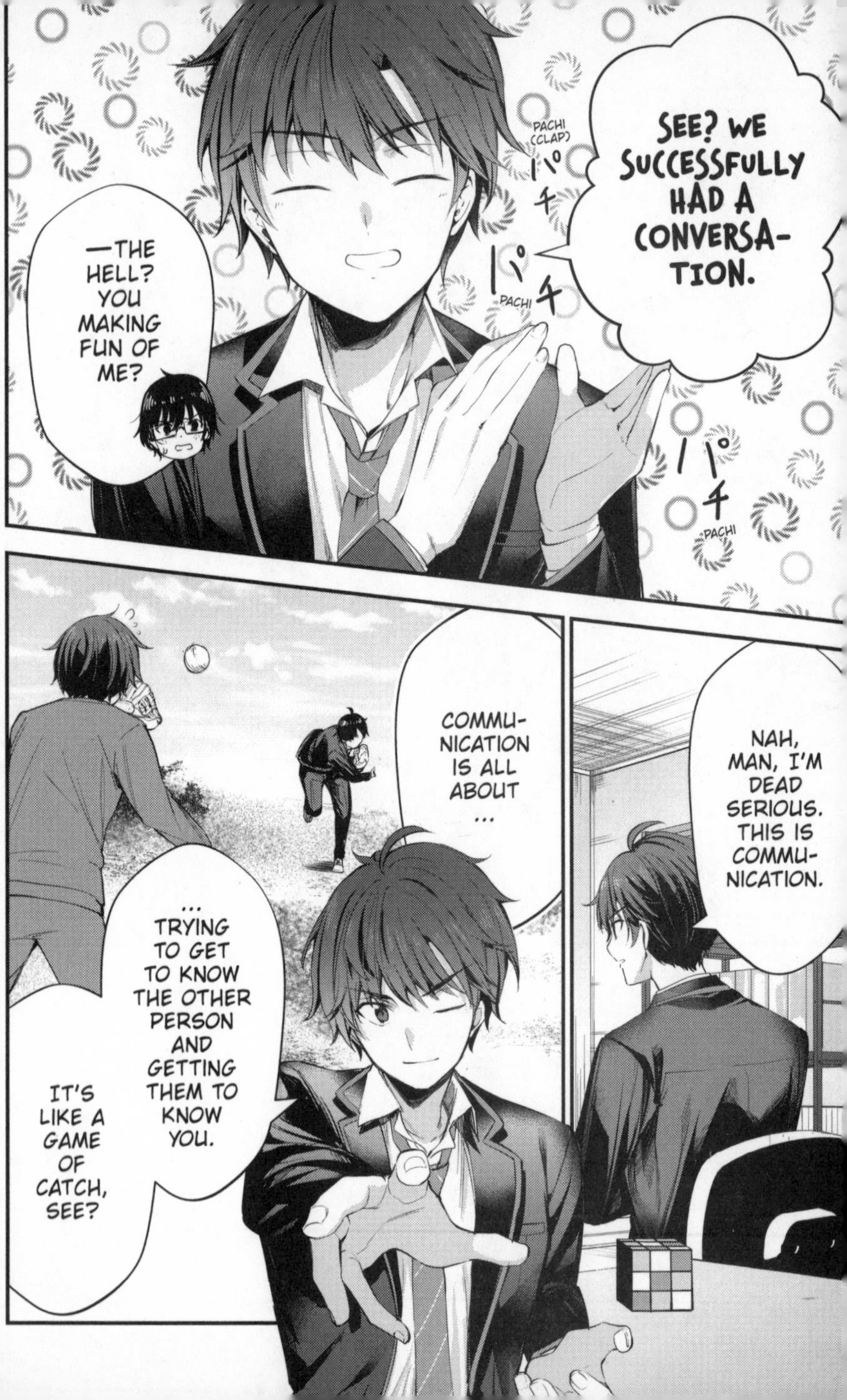
SEE? WE SUCCESSFULLY HAD A CONVERSA-TION.
パチ PACHI (CLAP)
パチ PACHI
パチ PACHI
—THE HELL? YOU MAKING FUN OF ME?
NAH, MAN, I'M DEAD SERIOUS. THIS IS COMMU-NICATION.
COMMU-NICATION IS ALL ABOUT...
...TRYING TO GET TO KNOW THE OTHER PERSON AND GETTING THEM TO KNOW YOU.
IT'S LIKE A GAME OF CATCH, SEE?

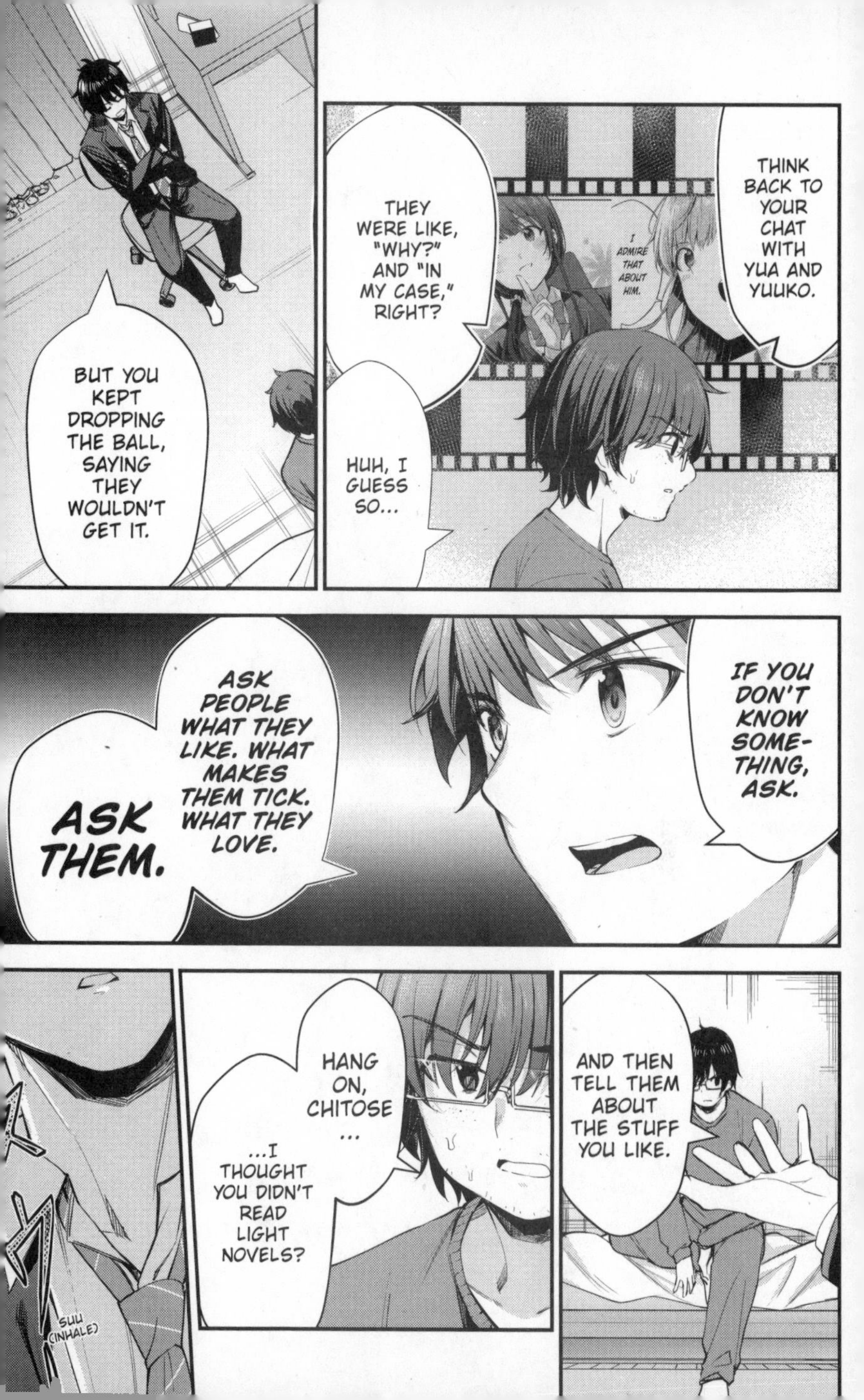
THINK BACK TO YOUR CHAT WITH YUA AND YUUKO.
I ADMIRE THAT ABOUT HIM.
THEY WERE LIKE, "WHY?" AND "IN MY CASE," RIGHT?
HUH, I GUESS SO...
BUT YOU KEPT DROPPING THE BALL, SAYING THEY WOULDN'T GET IT.
IF YOU DON'T KNOW SOME-THING, ASK.
ASK PEOPLE WHAT THEY LIKE. WHAT MAKES THEM TICK. WHAT THEY LOVE.
ASK THEM.
AND THEN TELL THEM ABOUT THE STUFF YOU LIKE.
HANG ON, CHITOSE...
...I THOUGHT YOU DIDN'T READ LIGHT NOVELS?
SUU (INHALE)

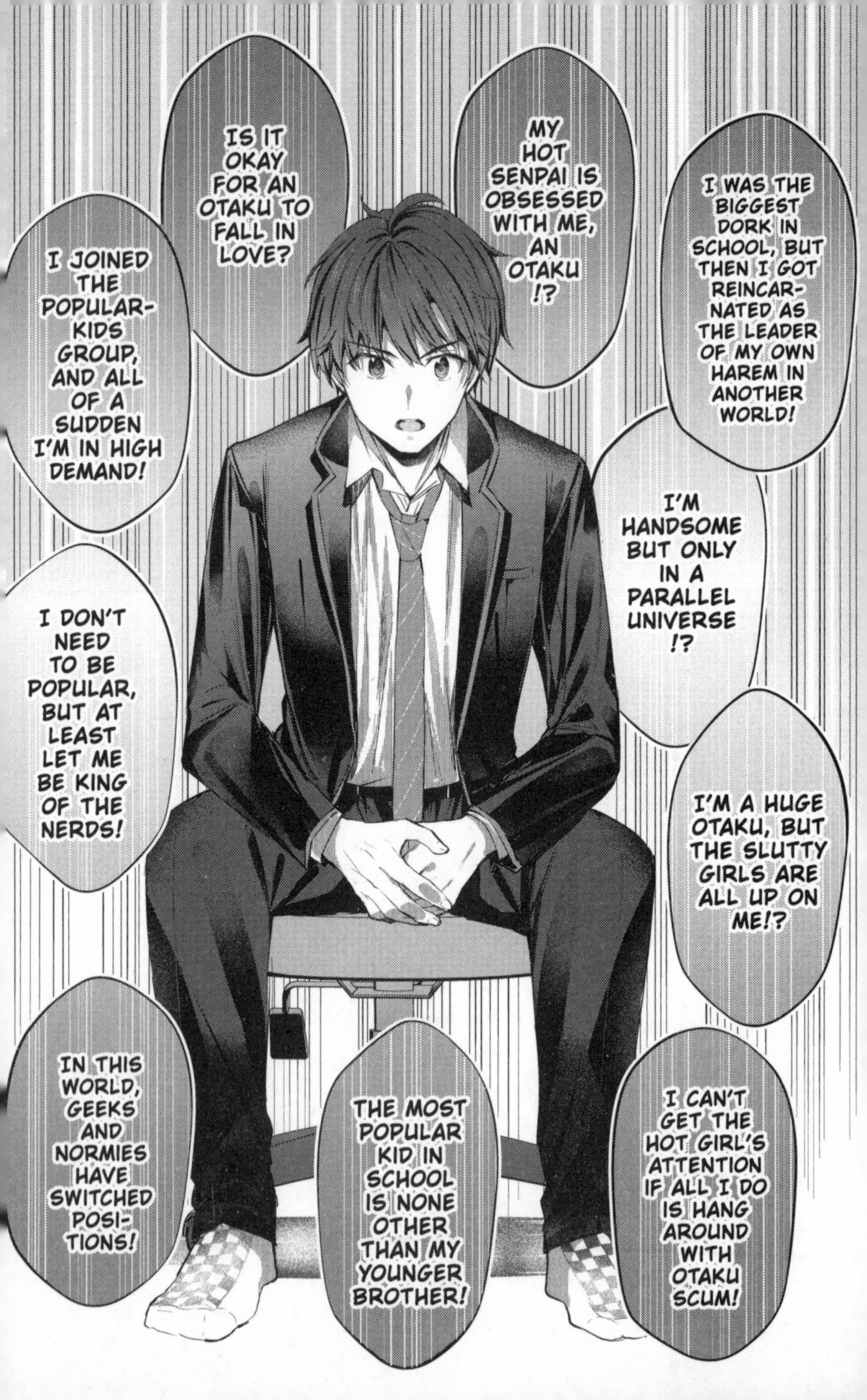
I WAS THE BIGGEST DORK IN SCHOOL, BUT THEN I GOT REINCAR-NATED AS THE LEADER OF MY OWN HAREM IN ANOTHER WORLD!
MY HOT SENPAI IS OBSESSED WITH ME, AN OTAKU !?
IS IT OKAY FOR AN OTAKU TO FALL IN LOVE?
I JOINED THE POPULAR-KIDS GROUP, AND ALL OF A SUDDEN I'M IN HIGH DEMAND!
I'M HANDSOME BUT ONLY IN A PARALLEL UNIVERSE !?
I DON'T NEED TO BE POPULAR, BUT AT LEAST LET ME BE KING OF THE NERDS!
I'M A HUGE OTAKU, BUT THE SLUTTY GIRLS ARE ALL UP ON ME!?
I CAN'T GET THE HOT GIRL'S ATTENTION IF ALL I DO IS HANG AROUND WITH OTAKU SCUM!
THE MOST POPULAR KID IN SCHOOL IS NONE OTHER THAN MY YOUNGER BROTHER!
IN THIS WORLD, GEEKS AND NORMIES HAVE SWITCHED POSI-TIONS!

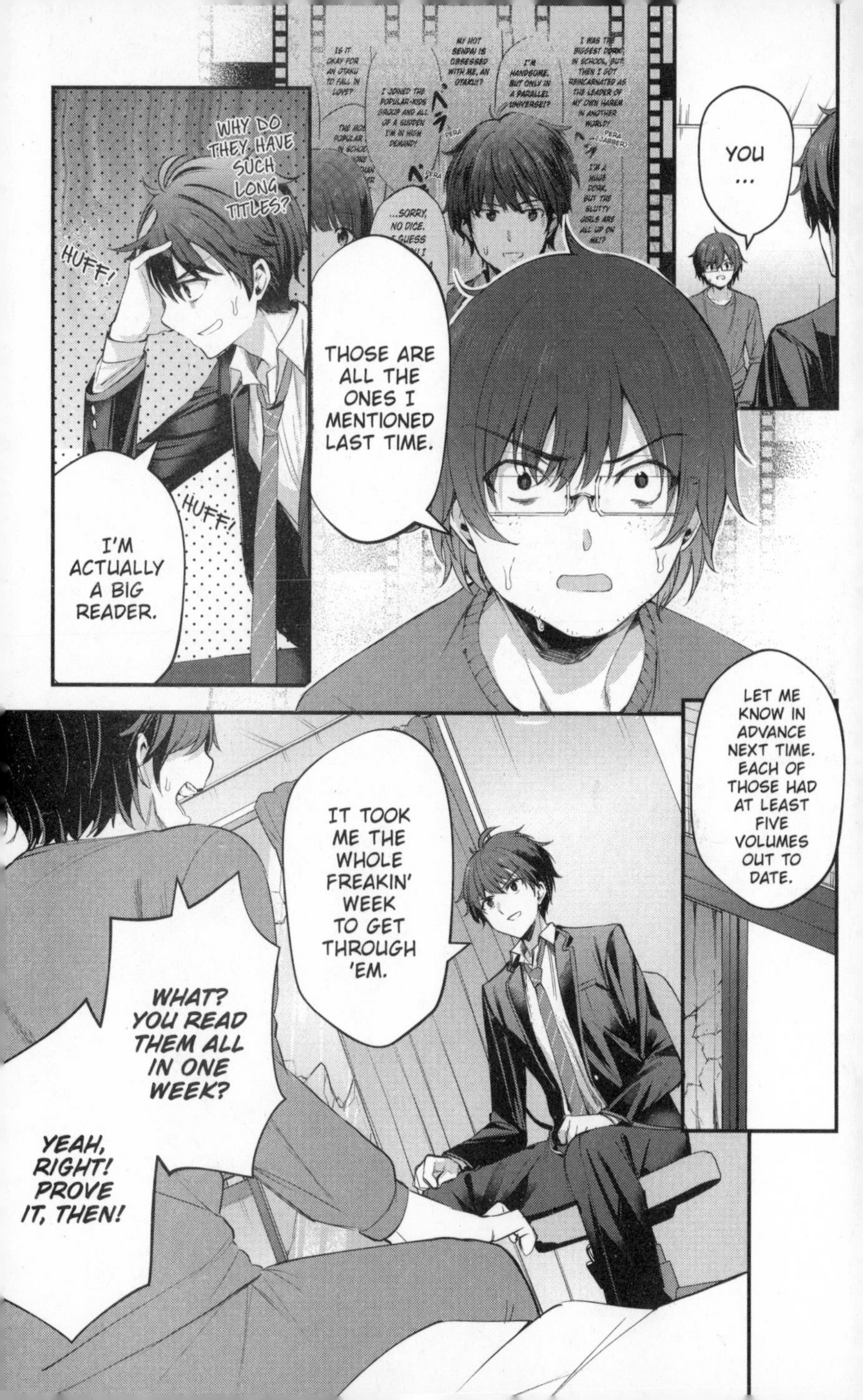
YOU ...
I WAS THE BIGGEST DORK IN SCHOOL, BUT THEN I GOT REINCARNATED AS THE LEADER OF MY OWN HAREM IN ANOTHER WORLD!
PERA (JABBER)
I'M A HUGE DORK, BUT THE SLUTTY GIRLS ARE ALL UP ON ME!?
I'M HANDSOME, BUT ONLY IN A PARALLEL UNIVERSE!?
MY HOT SENPAI IS OBSESSED WITH ME, AN OTAKU!!?
PERA
I JOINED THE POPULAR-KIDS GROUP AND ALL OF A SUDDEN I'M IN HIGH DEMAND!
IS IT OKAY FOR AN OTAKU TO FALL IN LOVE?
PERA
...SORRY, NO DICE.
THOSE ARE ALL THE ONES I MENTIONED LAST TIME.
WHY DO THEY HAVE SUCH LONG TITLES?
HUFF!
HUFF!
I'M ACTUALLY A BIG READER.
LET ME KNOW IN ADVANCE NEXT TIME. EACH OF THOSE HAD AT LEAST FIVE VOLUMES OUT TO DATE.
IT TOOK ME THE WHOLE FREAKIN' WEEK TO GET THROUGH 'EM.
WHAT? YOU READ THEM ALL IN ONE WEEK?
YEAH, RIGHT! PROVE IT, THEN!

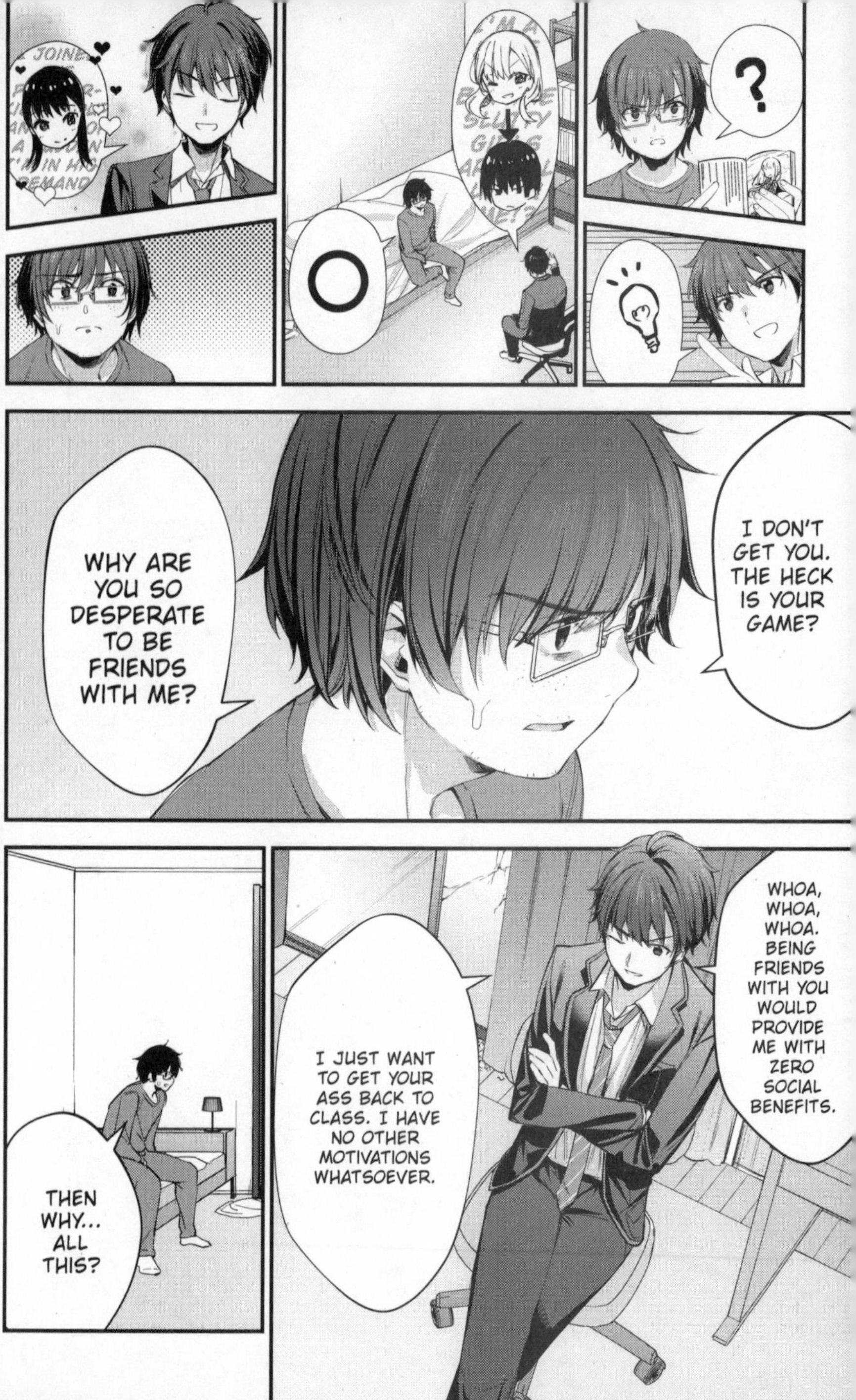
?
I DON'T GET YOU. THE HECK IS YOUR GAME?
WHY ARE YOU SO DESPERATE TO BE FRIENDS WITH ME?
WHOA, WHOA, WHOA. BEING FRIENDS WITH YOU WOULD PROVIDE ME WITH ZERO SOCIAL BENEFITS.
I JUST WANT TO GET YOUR ASS BACK TO CLASS. I HAVE NO OTHER MOTIVATIONS WHATSOEVER.
THEN WHY... ALL THIS?

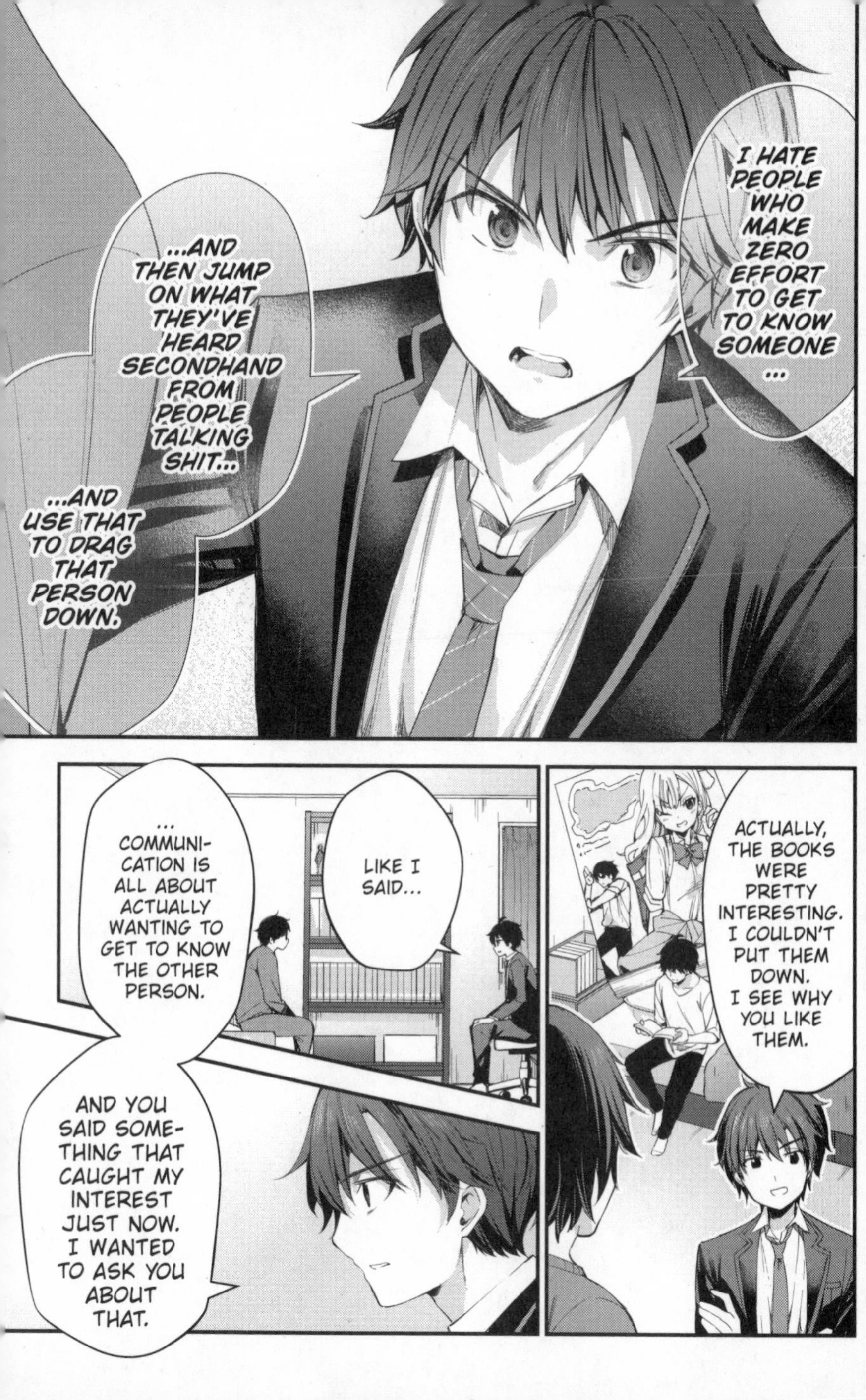
I HATE PEOPLE WHO MAKE ZERO EFFORT TO GET TO KNOW SOMEONE...
...AND THEN JUMP ON WHAT THEY'VE HEARD SECONDHAND FROM PEOPLE TALKING SHIT...
...AND USE THAT TO DRAG THAT PERSON DOWN.
ACTUALLY, THE BOOKS WERE PRETTY INTERESTING. I COULDN'T PUT THEM DOWN. I SEE WHY YOU LIKE THEM.
LIKE I SAID...
...COMMUNICATION IS ALL ABOUT ACTUALLY WANTING TO GET TO KNOW THE OTHER PERSON.
AND YOU SAID SOMETHING THAT CAUGHT MY INTEREST JUST NOW. I WANTED TO ASK YOU ABOUT THAT.

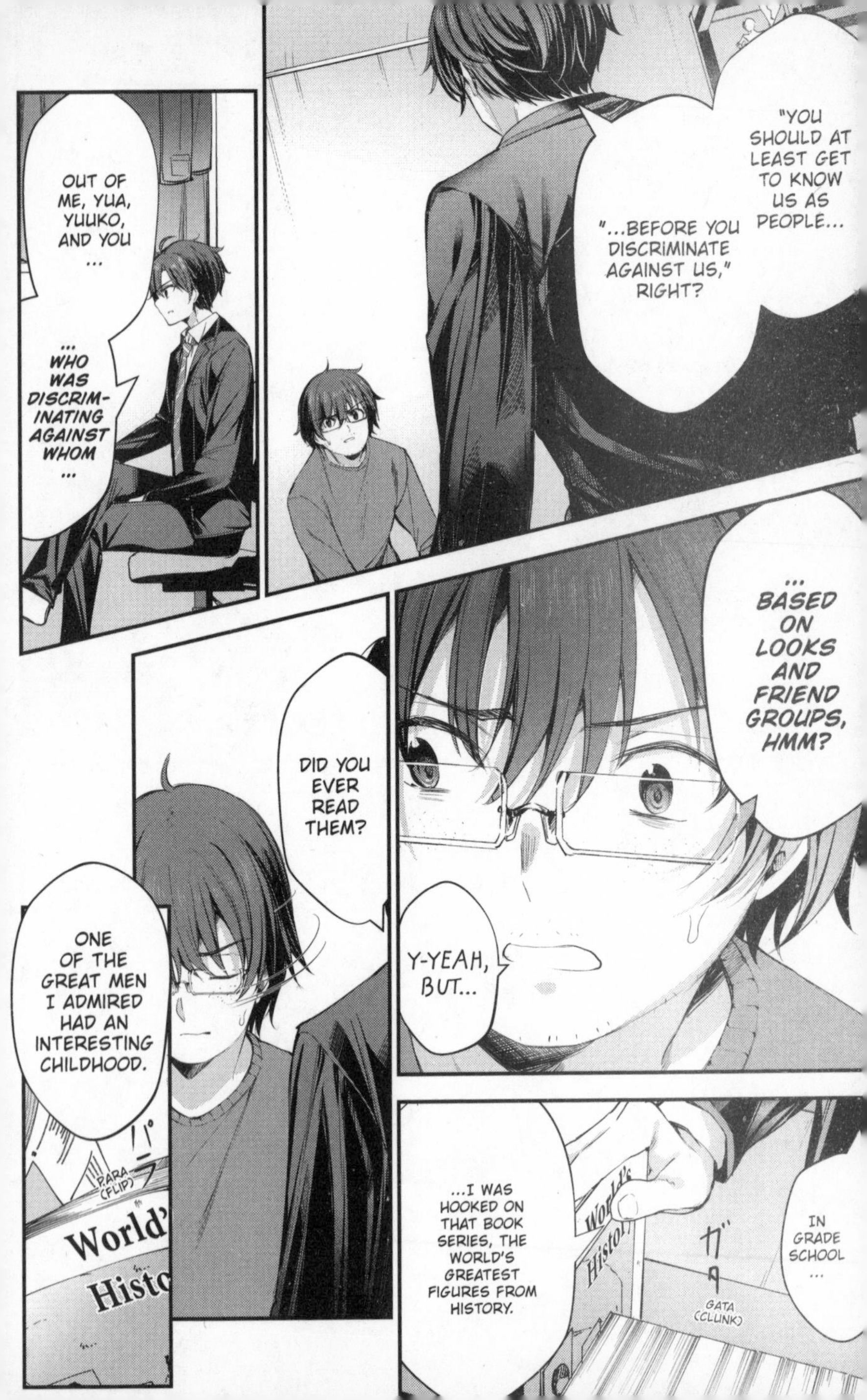
"YOU SHOULD AT LEAST GET TO KNOW US AS PEOPLE...
"...BEFORE YOU DISCRIMINATE AGAINST US," RIGHT?
OUT OF ME, YUA, YUUKO, AND YOU ...
... *WHO WAS DISCRIMINATING AGAINST WHOM* ...
... *BASED ON LOOKS AND FRIEND GROUPS, HMM?*
Y-YEAH, BUT...
IN GRADE SCHOOL ...
...I WAS HOOKED ON THAT BOOK SERIES, THE WORLD'S GREATEST FIGURES FROM HISTORY.
GATA (CLUNK)
World's Histo
DID YOU EVER READ THEM?
ONE OF THE GREAT MEN I ADMIRED HAD AN INTERESTING CHILDHOOD.
PARA (FLIP)
World' Histo

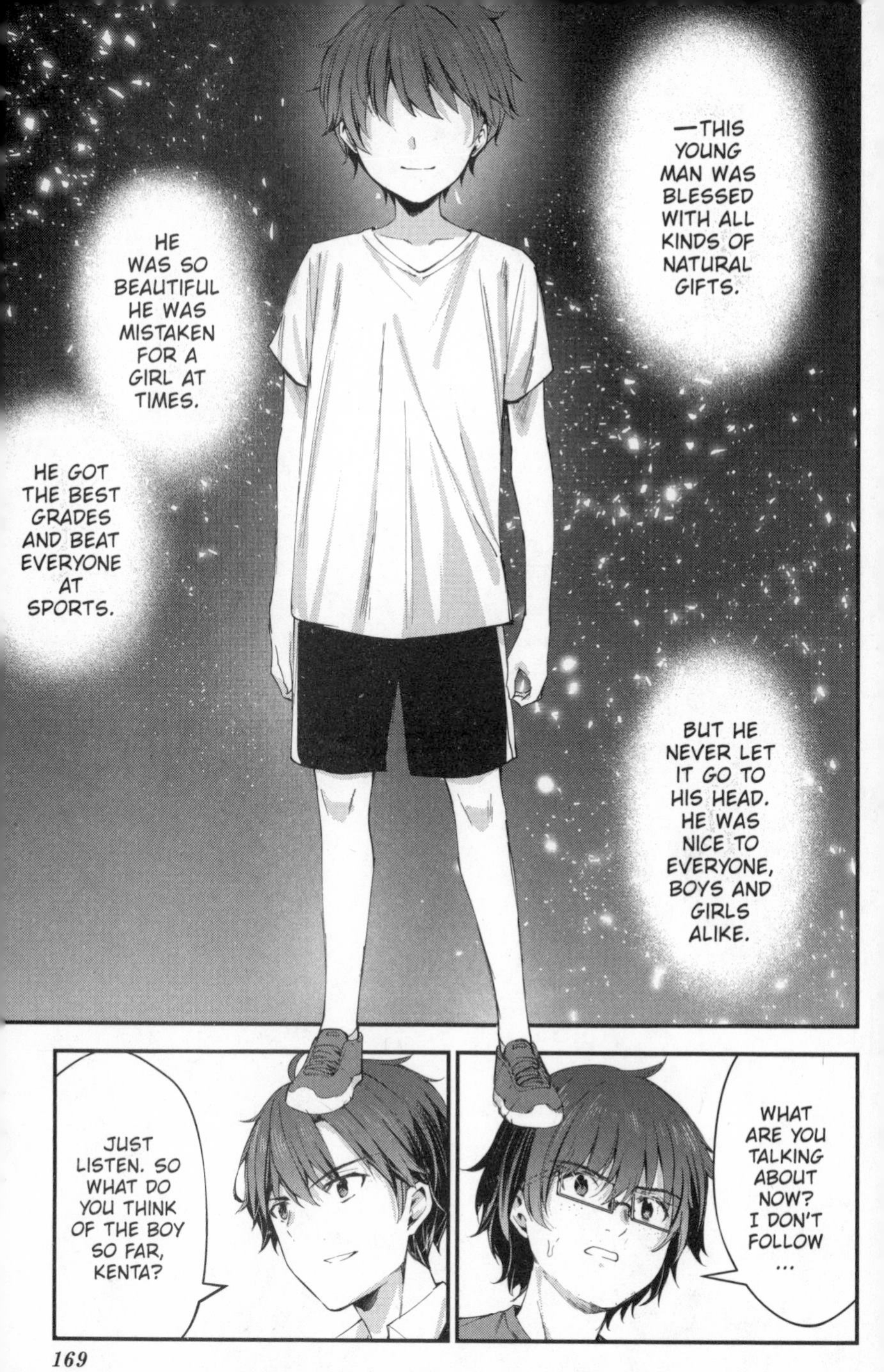
—THIS YOUNG MAN WAS BLESSED WITH ALL KINDS OF NATURAL GIFTS.
HE WAS SO BEAUTIFUL HE WAS MISTAKEN FOR A GIRL AT TIMES.
HE GOT THE BEST GRADES AND BEAT EVERYONE AT SPORTS.
BUT HE NEVER LET IT GO TO HIS HEAD. HE WAS NICE TO EVERYONE, BOYS AND GIRLS ALIKE.
WHAT ARE YOU TALKING ABOUT NOW? I DON'T FOLLOW...
JUST LISTEN. SO WHAT DO YOU THINK OF THE BOY SO FAR, KENTA?

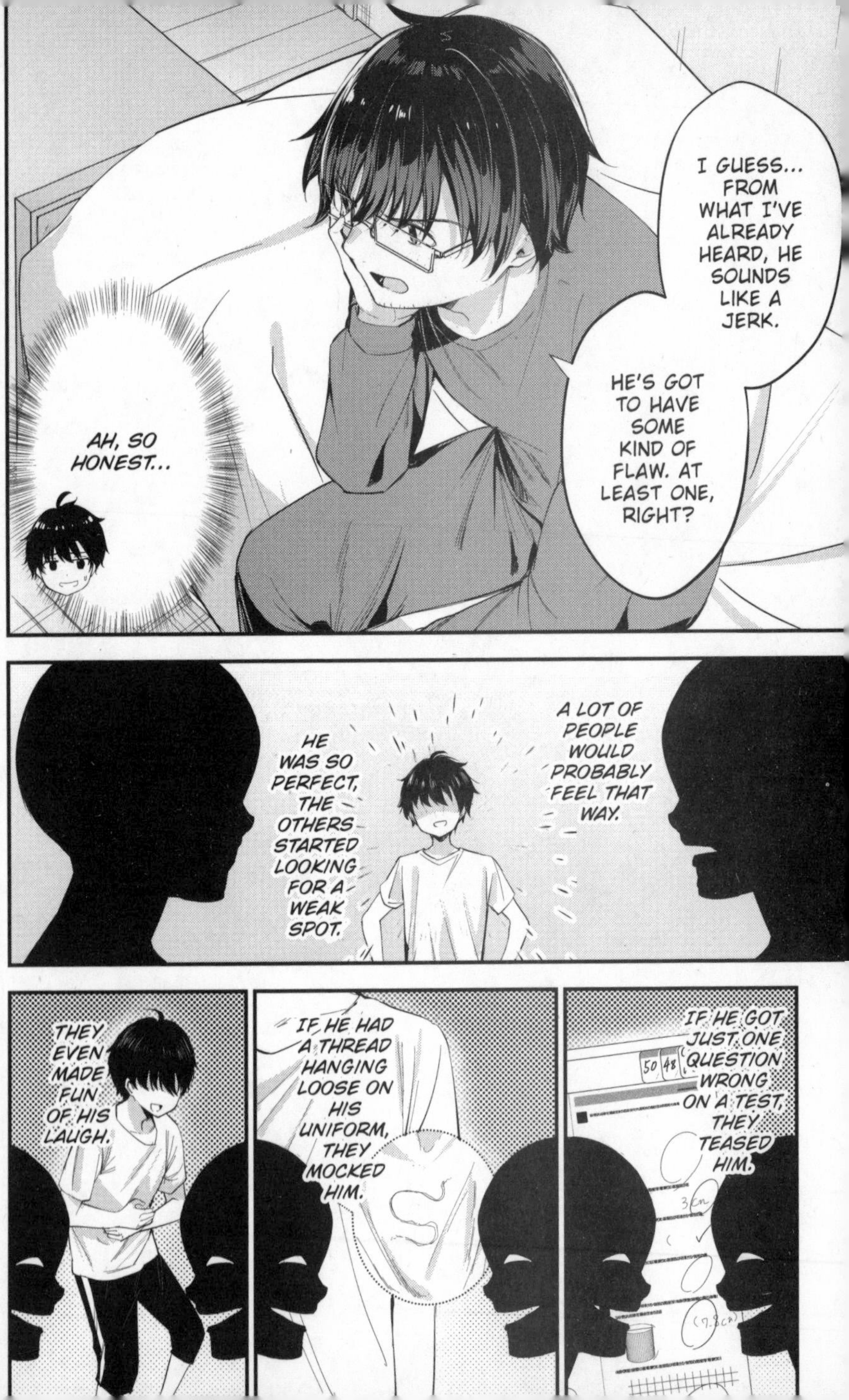
I GUESS... FROM WHAT I'VE ALREADY HEARD, HE SOUNDS LIKE A JERK.
HE'S GOT TO HAVE SOME KIND OF FLAW. AT LEAST ONE, RIGHT?
AH, SO HONEST...
A LOT OF PEOPLE WOULD PROBABLY FEEL THAT WAY.
HE WAS SO PERFECT, THE OTHERS STARTED LOOKING FOR A WEAK SPOT.
IF HE GOT JUST ONE QUESTION WRONG ON A TEST, THEY TEASED HIM.
IF HE HAD A THREAD HANGING LOOSE ON HIS UNIFORM, THEY MOCKED HIM.
THEY EVEN MADE FUN OF HIS LAUGH.

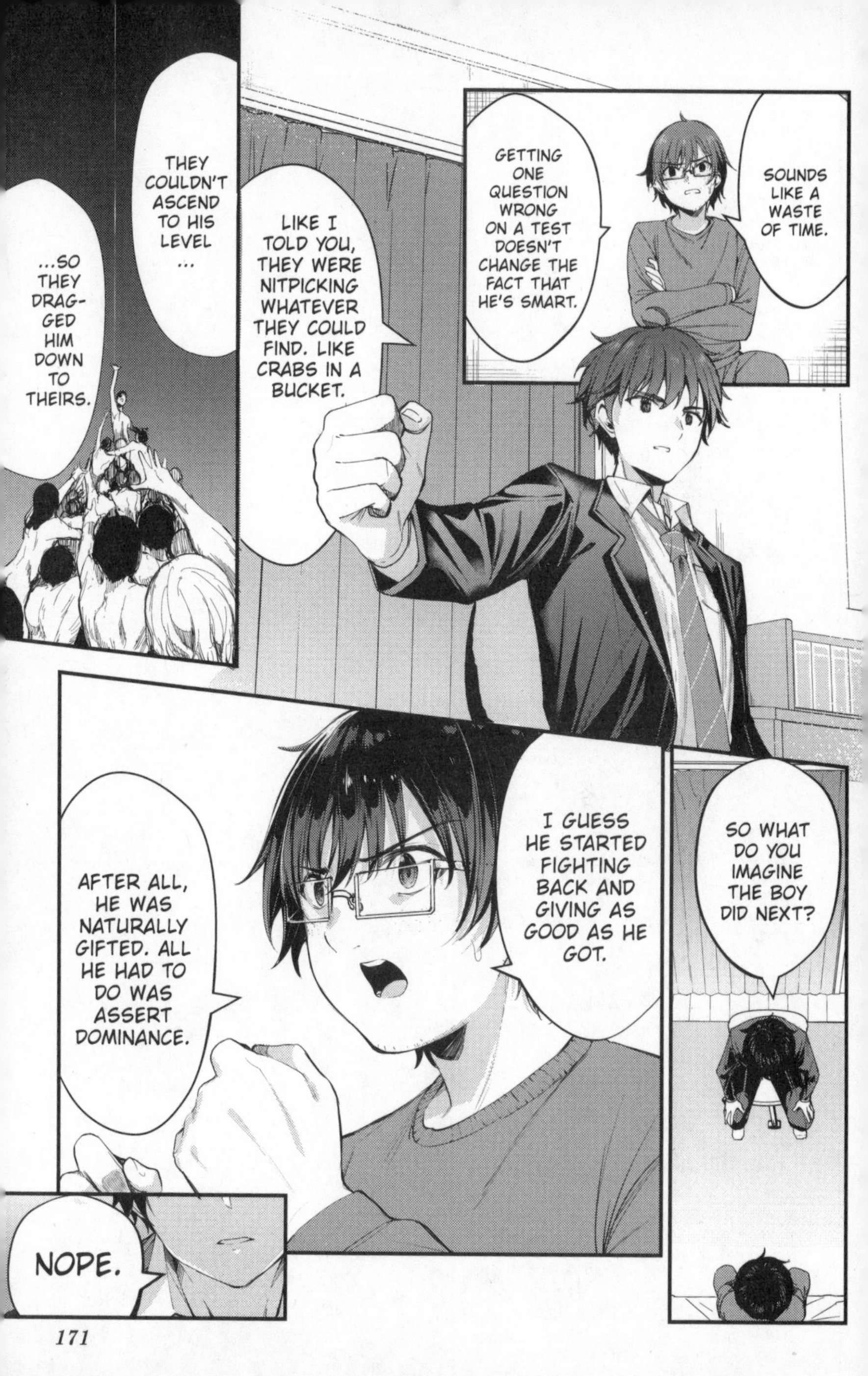

SOUNDS LIKE A WASTE OF TIME.
GETTING ONE QUESTION WRONG ON A TEST DOESN'T CHANGE THE FACT THAT HE'S SMART.
LIKE I TOLD YOU, THEY WERE NITPICKING WHATEVER THEY COULD FIND. LIKE CRABS IN A BUCKET.
THEY COULDN'T ASCEND TO HIS LEVEL ...
...SO THEY DRAG-GED HIM DOWN TO THEIRS.
SO WHAT DO YOU IMAGINE THE BOY DID NEXT?
I GUESS HE STARTED FIGHTING BACK AND GIVING AS GOOD AS HE GOT.
AFTER ALL, HE WAS NATURALLY GIFTED. ALL HE HAD TO DO WAS ASSERT DOMINANCE.
NOPE.

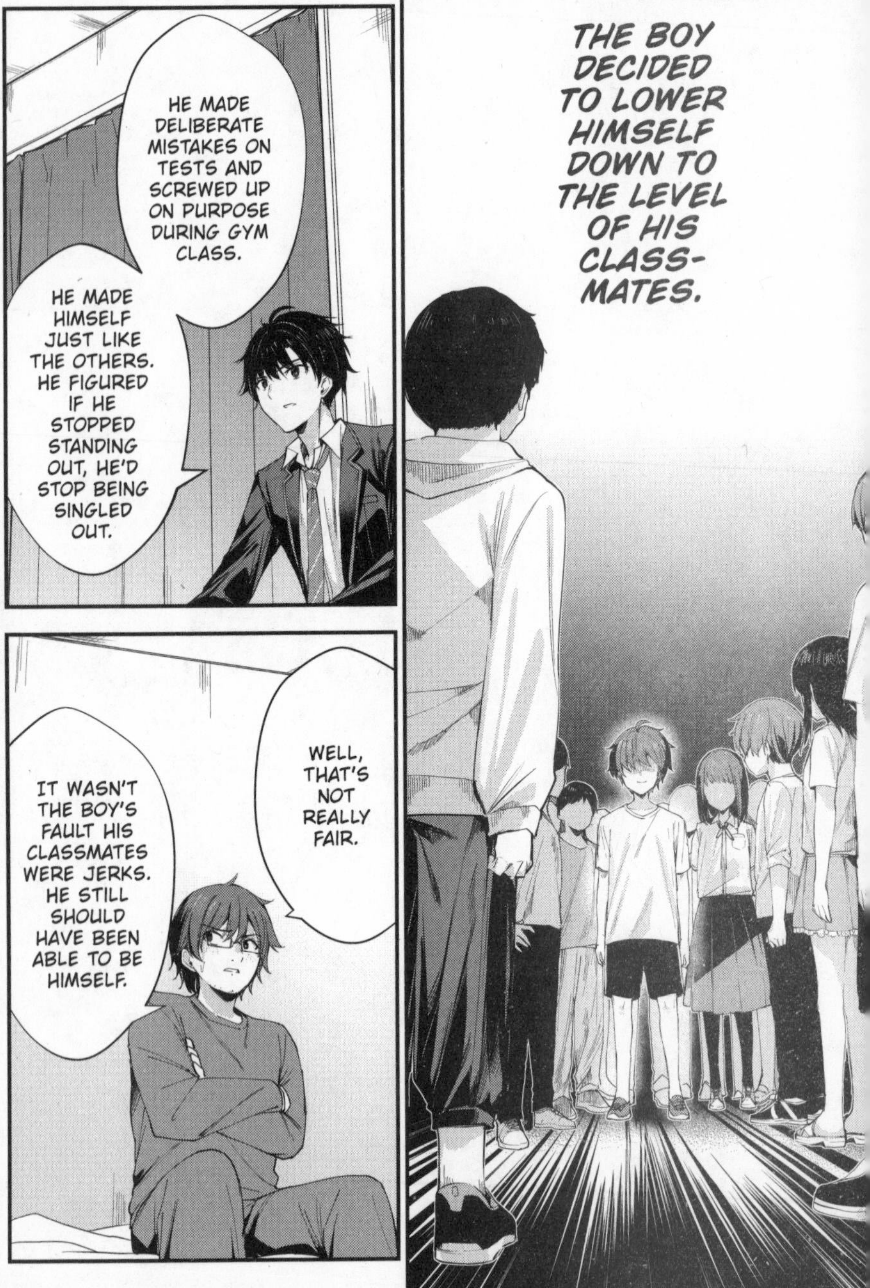
THE BOY DECIDED TO LOWER HIMSELF DOWN TO THE LEVEL OF HIS CLASS-MATES.
HE MADE DELIBERATE MISTAKES ON TESTS AND SCREWED UP ON PURPOSE DURING GYM CLASS.
HE MADE HIMSELF JUST LIKE THE OTHERS. HE FIGURED IF HE STOPPED STANDING OUT, HE'D STOP BEING SINGLED OUT.
WELL, THAT'S NOT REALLY FAIR.
IT WASN'T THE BOY'S FAULT HIS CLASSMATES WERE JERKS. HE STILL SHOULD HAVE BEEN ABLE TO BE HIMSELF.

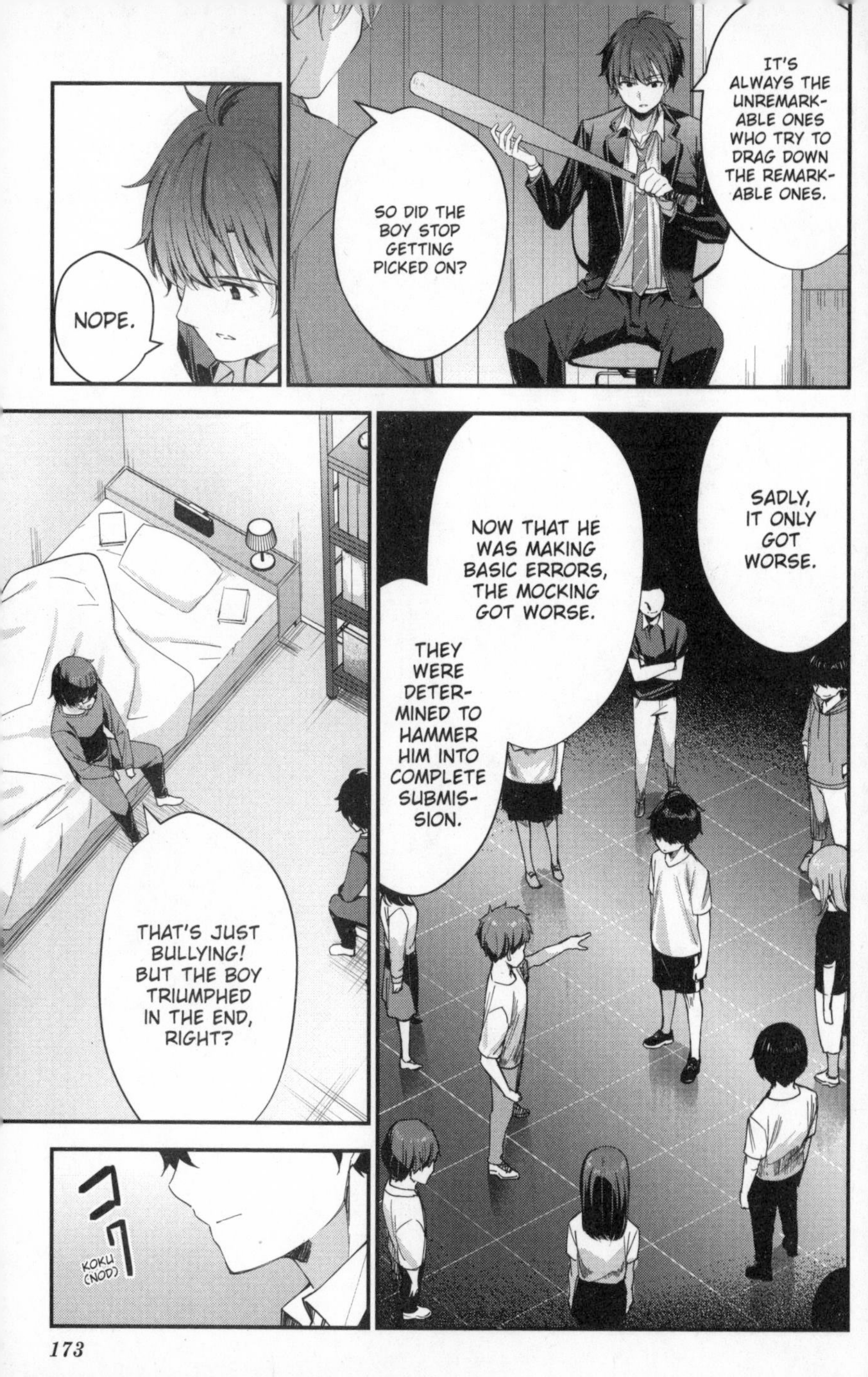
IT'S ALWAYS THE UNREMARK-ABLE ONES WHO TRY TO DRAG DOWN THE REMARK-ABLE ONES.
SO DID THE BOY STOP GETTING PICKED ON?
NOPE.
SADLY, IT ONLY GOT WORSE.
NOW THAT HE WAS MAKING BASIC ERRORS, THE MOCKING GOT WORSE.
THEY WERE DETER-MINED TO HAMMER HIM INTO COMPLETE SUBMIS-SION.
THAT'S JUST BULLYING! BUT THE BOY TRIUMPHED IN THE END, RIGHT?
KOKU (NOD)

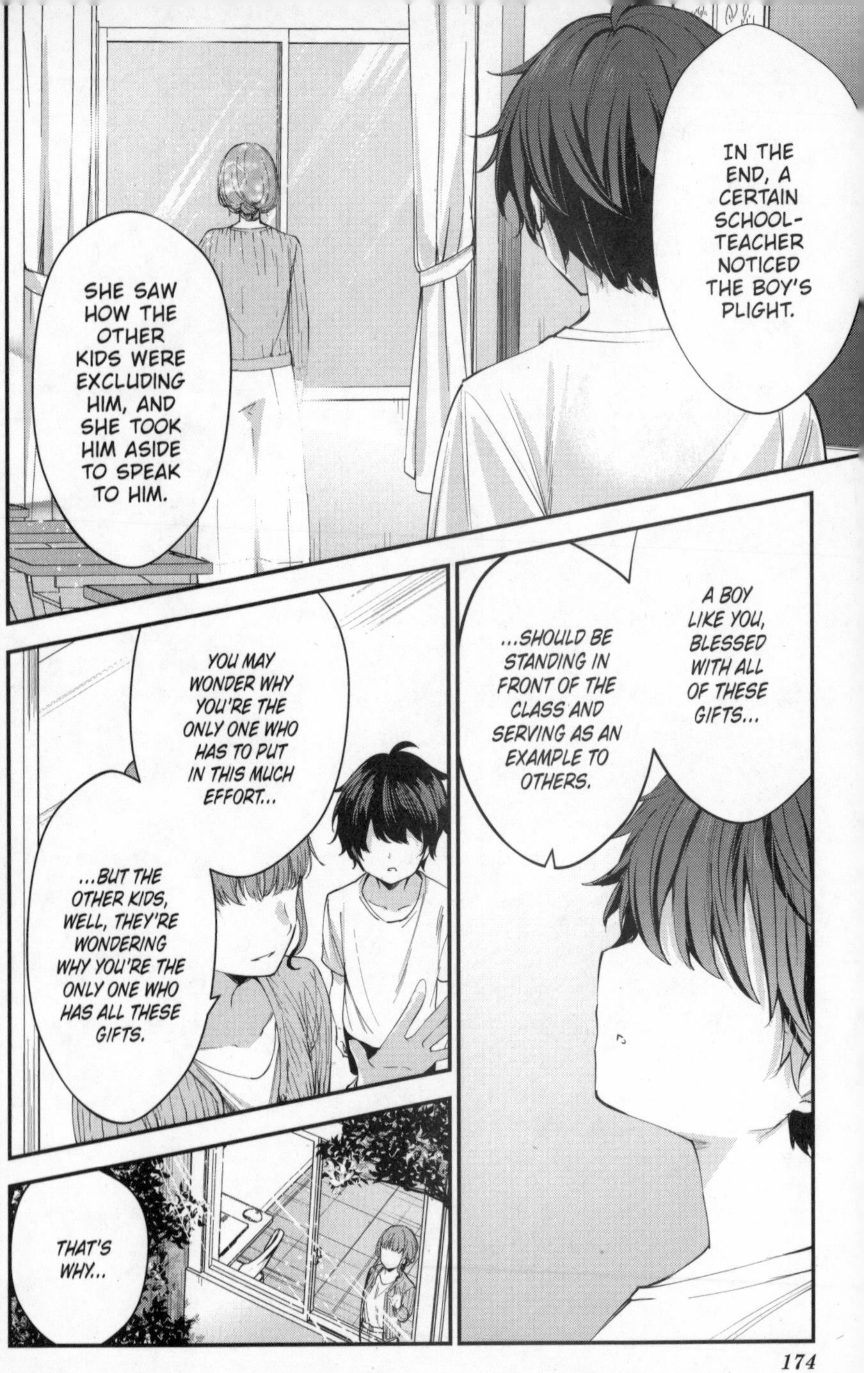
IN THE END, A CERTAIN SCHOOL-TEACHER NOTICED THE BOY'S PLIGHT.
SHE SAW HOW THE OTHER KIDS WERE EXCLUDING HIM, AND SHE TOOK HIM ASIDE TO SPEAK TO HIM.
A BOY LIKE YOU, BLESSED WITH ALL OF THESE GIFTS...
...SHOULD BE STANDING IN FRONT OF THE CLASS AND SERVING AS AN EXAMPLE TO OTHERS.
YOU MAY WONDER WHY YOU'RE THE ONLY ONE WHO HAS TO PUT IN THIS MUCH EFFORT...
...BUT THE OTHER KIDS, WELL, THEY'RE WONDERING WHY YOU'RE THE ONLY ONE WHO HAS ALL THESE GIFTS.
THAT'S WHY...

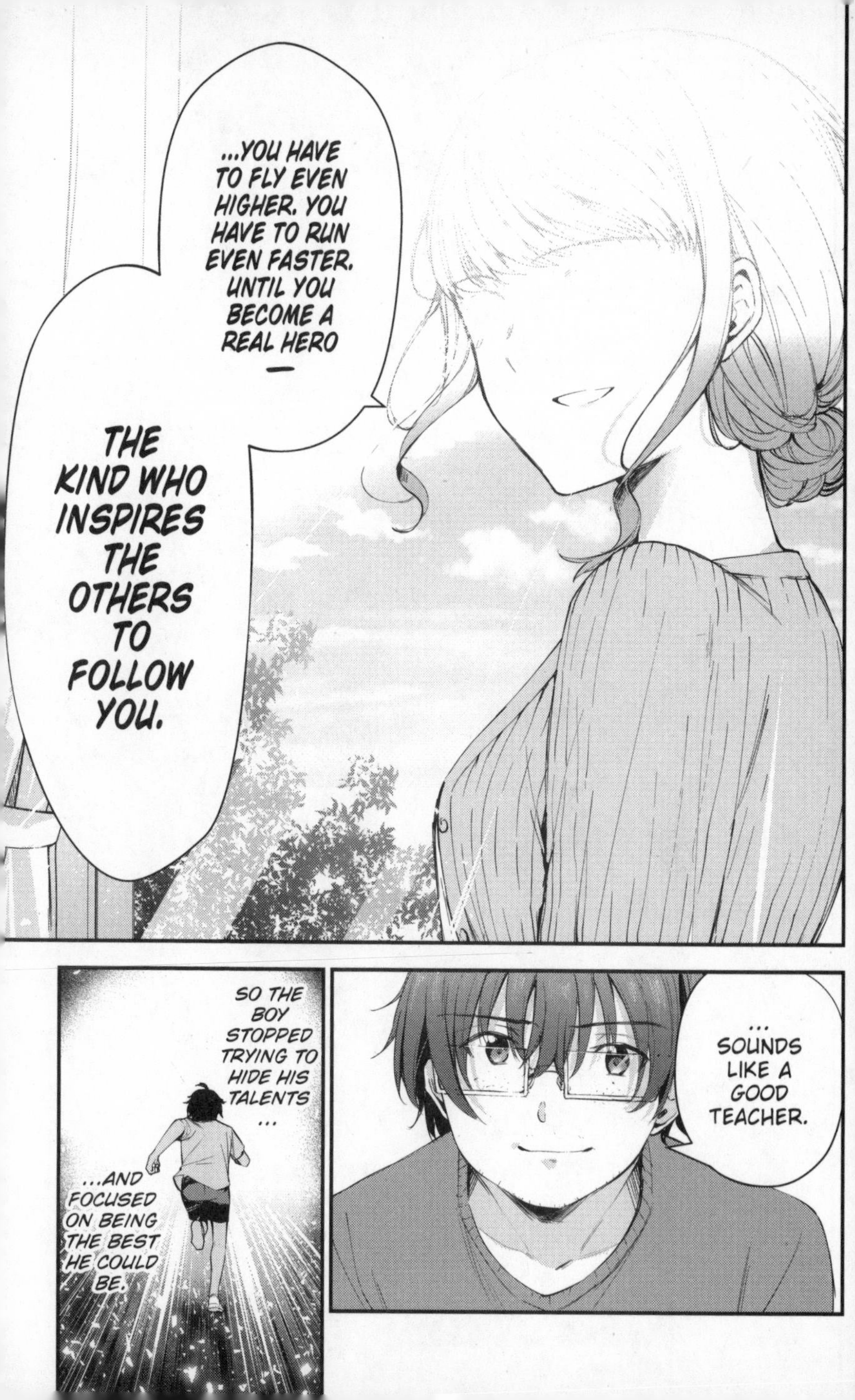
...YOU HAVE TO FLY EVEN HIGHER. YOU HAVE TO RUN EVEN FASTER. UNTIL YOU BECOME A REAL HERO —
THE KIND WHO INSPIRES THE OTHERS TO FOLLOW YOU.
... SOUNDS LIKE A GOOD TEACHER.
SO THE BOY STOPPED TRYING TO HIDE HIS TALENTS ...
...AND FOCUSED ON BEING THE BEST HE COULD BE.

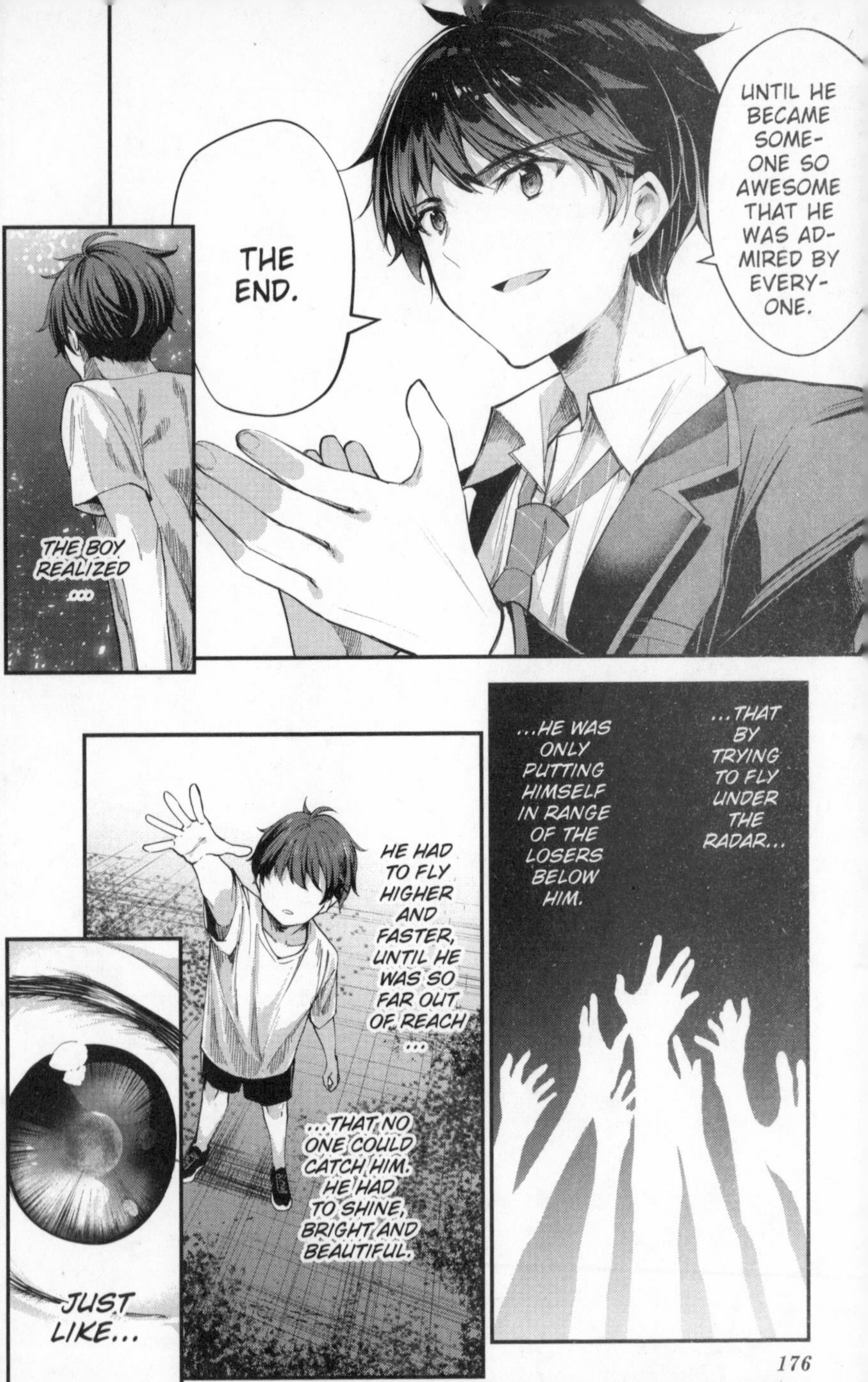
UNTIL HE BECAME SOME-ONE SO AWESOME THAT HE WAS AD-MIRED BY EVERY-ONE.
THE END.
THE BOY REALIZED...
...THAT BY TRYING TO FLY UNDER THE RADAR...
...HE WAS ONLY PUTTING HIMSELF IN RANGE OF THE LOSERS BELOW HIM.
HE HAD TO FLY HIGHER AND FASTER, UNTIL HE WAS SO FAR OUT OF REACH...
...THAT NO ONE COULD CATCH HIM. HE HAD TO SHINE, BRIGHT AND BEAUTIFUL.
JUST LIKE...

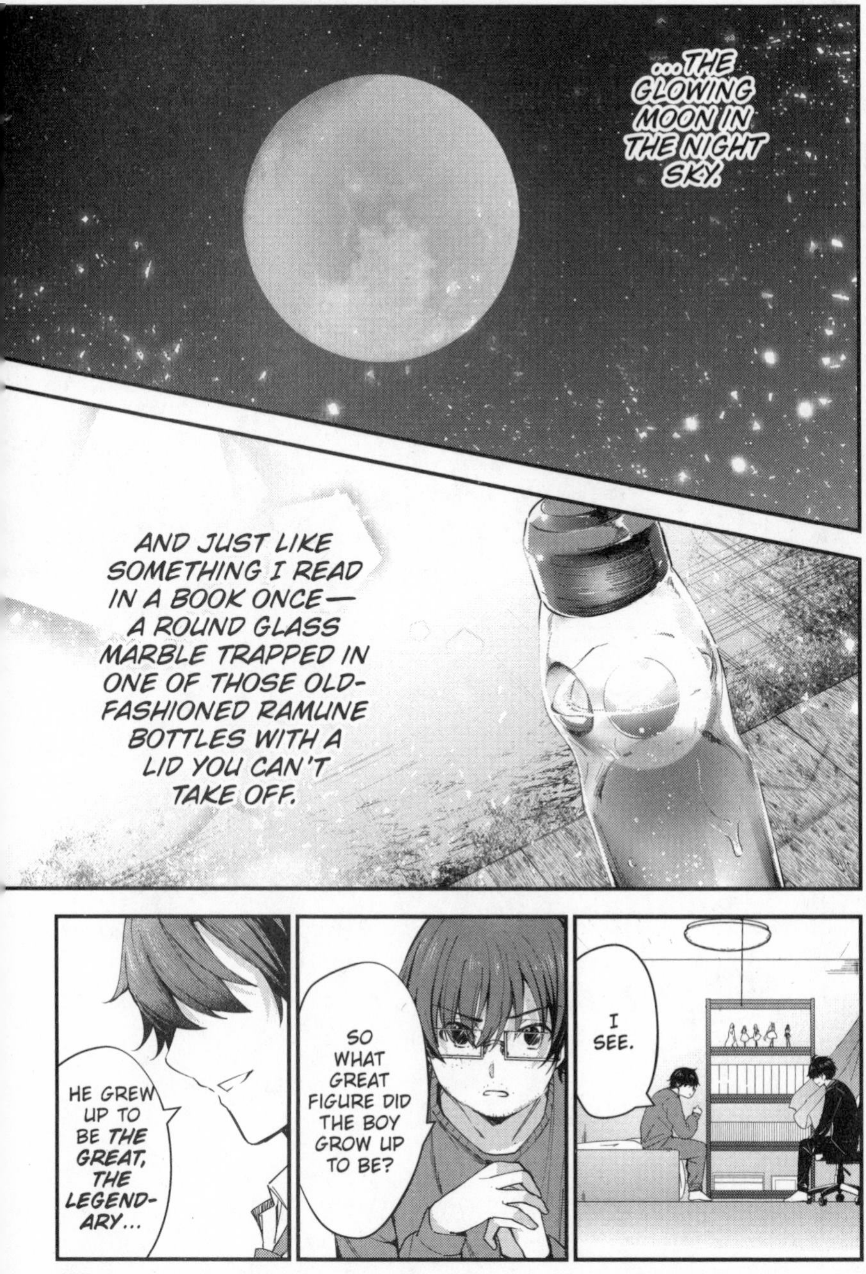
...THE GLOWING MOON IN THE NIGHT SKY.
AND JUST LIKE SOMETHING I READ IN A BOOK ONCE—A ROUND GLASS MARBLE TRAPPED IN ONE OF THOSE OLD-FASHIONED RAMUNE BOTTLES WITH A LID YOU CAN'T TAKE OFF.
I SEE.
SO WHAT GREAT FIGURE DID THE BOY GROW UP TO BE?
HE GREW UP TO BE *THE GREAT, THE LEGENDARY*...

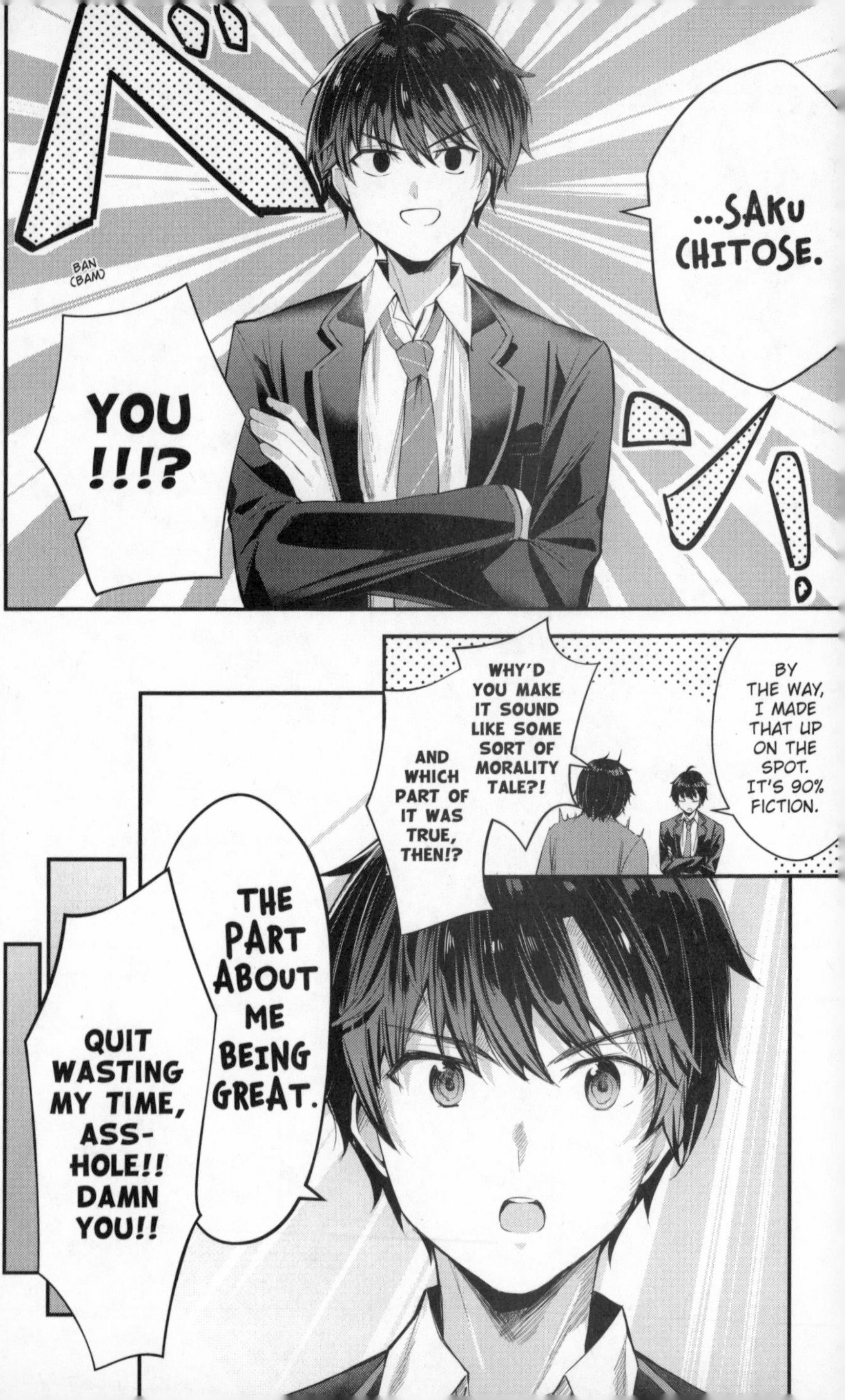
...SAKU CHITOSE.
BAN (BAM)
YOU!!!?
BY THE WAY, I MADE THAT UP ON THE SPOT. IT'S 90% FICTION.
WHY'D YOU MAKE IT SOUND LIKE SOME SORT OF MORALITY TALE?!
AND WHICH PART OF IT WAS TRUE, THEN!?
THE PART ABOUT ME BEING GREAT.
QUIT WASTING MY TIME, ASS-HOLE!! DAMN YOU!!

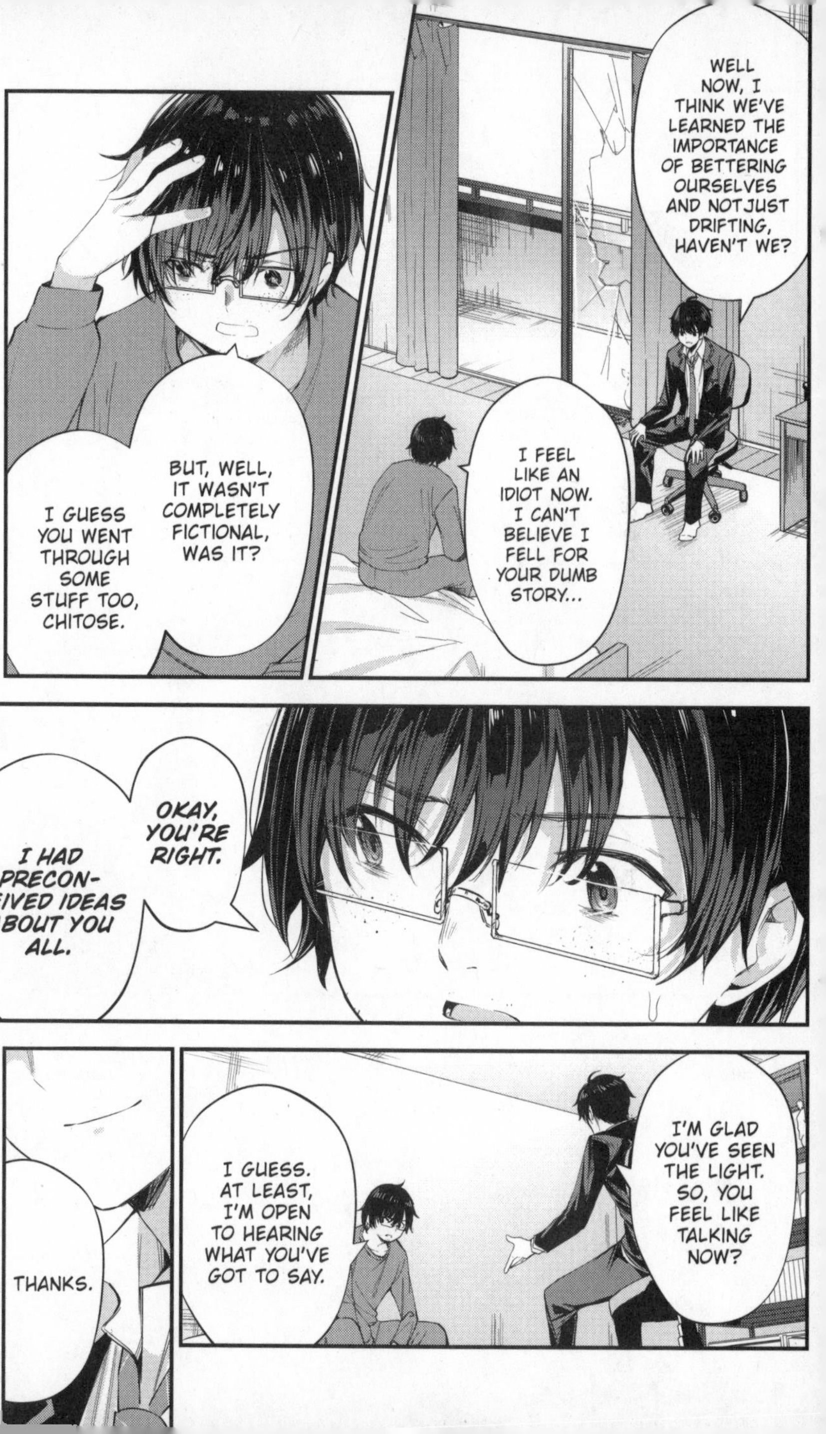
WELL NOW, I THINK WE'VE LEARNED THE IMPORTANCE OF BETTERING OURSELVES AND NOTJUST DRIFTING, HAVEN'T WE?
I FEEL LIKE AN IDIOT NOW. I CAN'T BELIEVE I FELL FOR YOUR DUMB STORY...
BUT, WELL, IT WASN'T COMPLETELY FICTIONAL, WAS IT?
I GUESS YOU WENT THROUGH SOME STUFF TOO, CHITOSE.
OKAY, YOU'RE RIGHT.
I HAD PRECON-CEIVED IDEAS ABOUT YOU ALL.
I'M GLAD YOU'VE SEEN THE LIGHT. SO, YOU FEEL LIKE TALKING NOW?
I GUESS. AT LEAST, I'M OPEN TO HEARING WHAT YOU'VE GOT TO SAY.
THANKS.

BOOK TITLE: I'M A HUGE OTAKU, BUT THE SLUTTY GIRLS ARE ALL UP ON ME?!

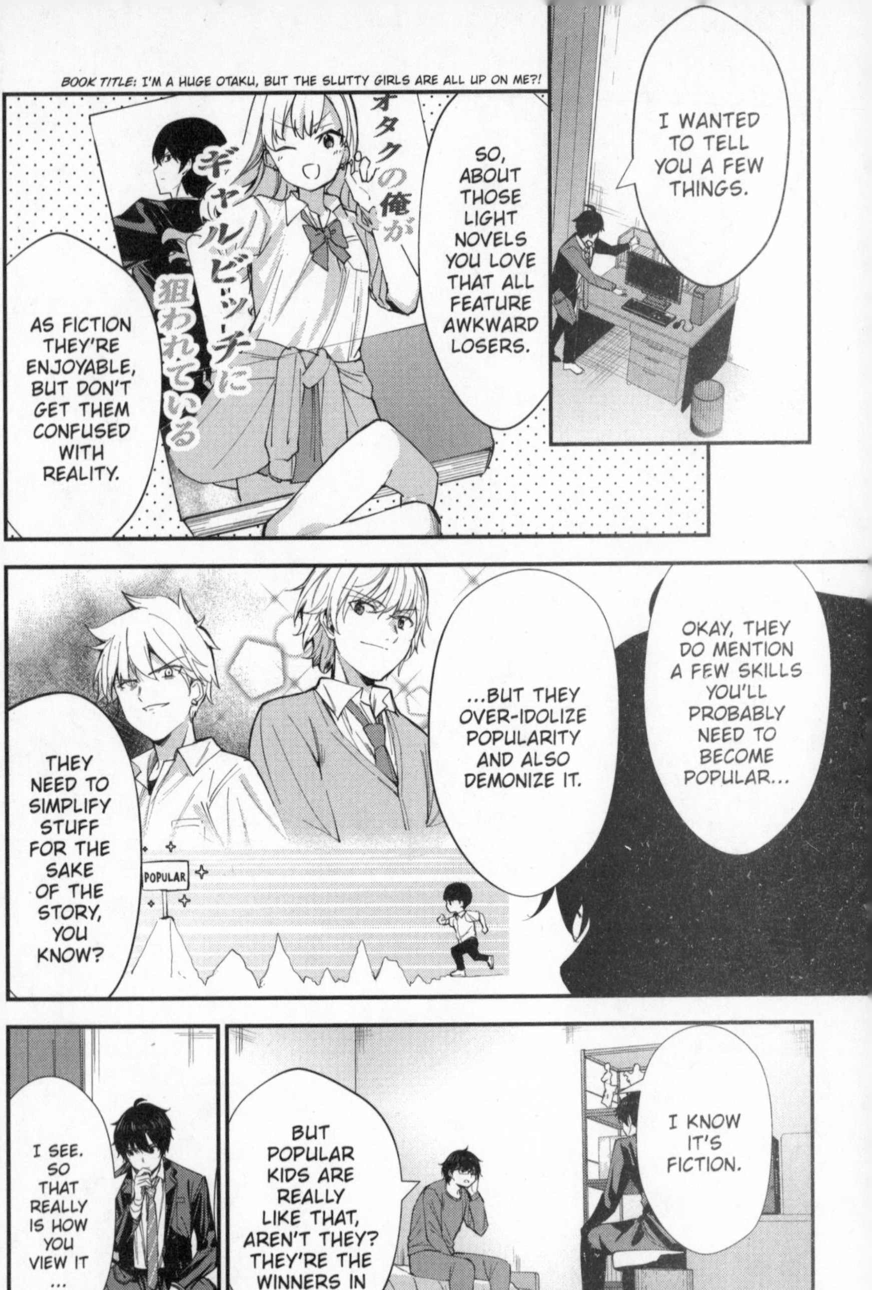
I WANTED TO TELL YOU A FEW THINGS.
SO, ABOUT THOSE LIGHT NOVELS YOU LOVE THAT ALL FEATURE AWKWARD LOSERS.
オタクの俺がギャルビッチに狙われている
AS FICTION THEY'RE ENJOYABLE, BUT DON'T GET THEM CONFUSED WITH REALITY.
OKAY, THEY DO MENTION A FEW SKILLS YOU'LL PROBABLY NEED TO BECOME POPULAR...
...BUT THEY OVER-IDOLIZE POPULARITY AND ALSO DEMONIZE IT.
THEY NEED TO SIMPLIFY STUFF FOR THE SAKE OF THE STORY, YOU KNOW?
POPULAR
I KNOW IT'S FICTION.
BUT POPULAR KIDS ARE REALLY LIKE THAT, AREN'T THEY? THEY'RE THE WINNERS IN LIFE.
I SEE. SO THAT REALLY IS HOW YOU VIEW IT ...

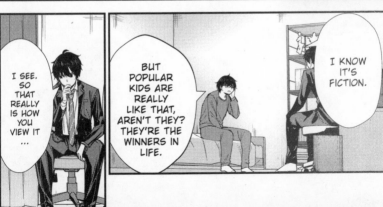

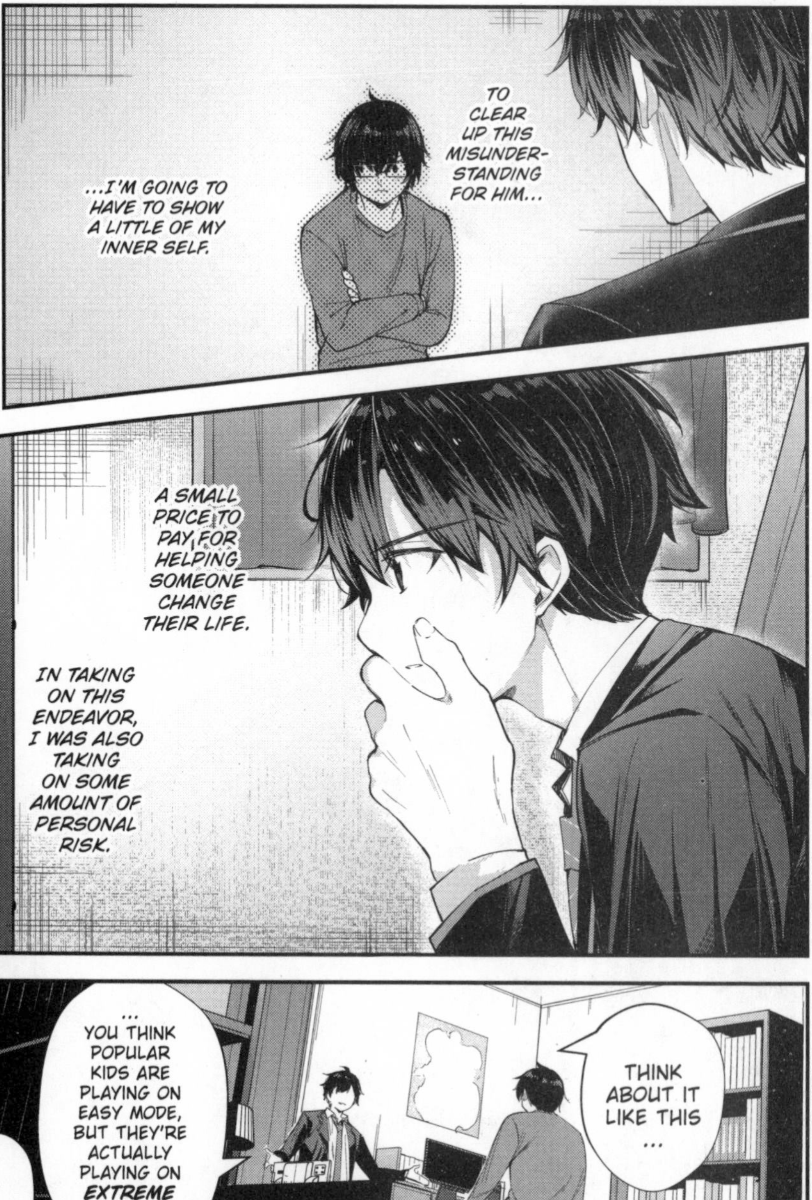
TO CLEAR UP THIS MISUNDER-STANDING FOR HIM...
...I'M GOING TO HAVE TO SHOW A LITTLE OF MY INNER SELF.
A SMALL PRICE TO PAY FOR HELPING SOMEONE CHANGE THEIR LIFE.
IN TAKING ON THIS ENDEAVOR, I WAS ALSO TAKING ON SOME AMOUNT OF PERSONAL RISK.
THINK ABOUT IT LIKE THIS ...
... YOU THINK POPULAR KIDS ARE PLAYING ON EASY MODE, BUT THEY'RE ACTUALLY PLAYING ON ***EXTREME MODE***.
?

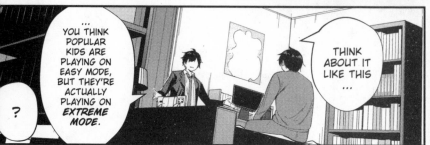

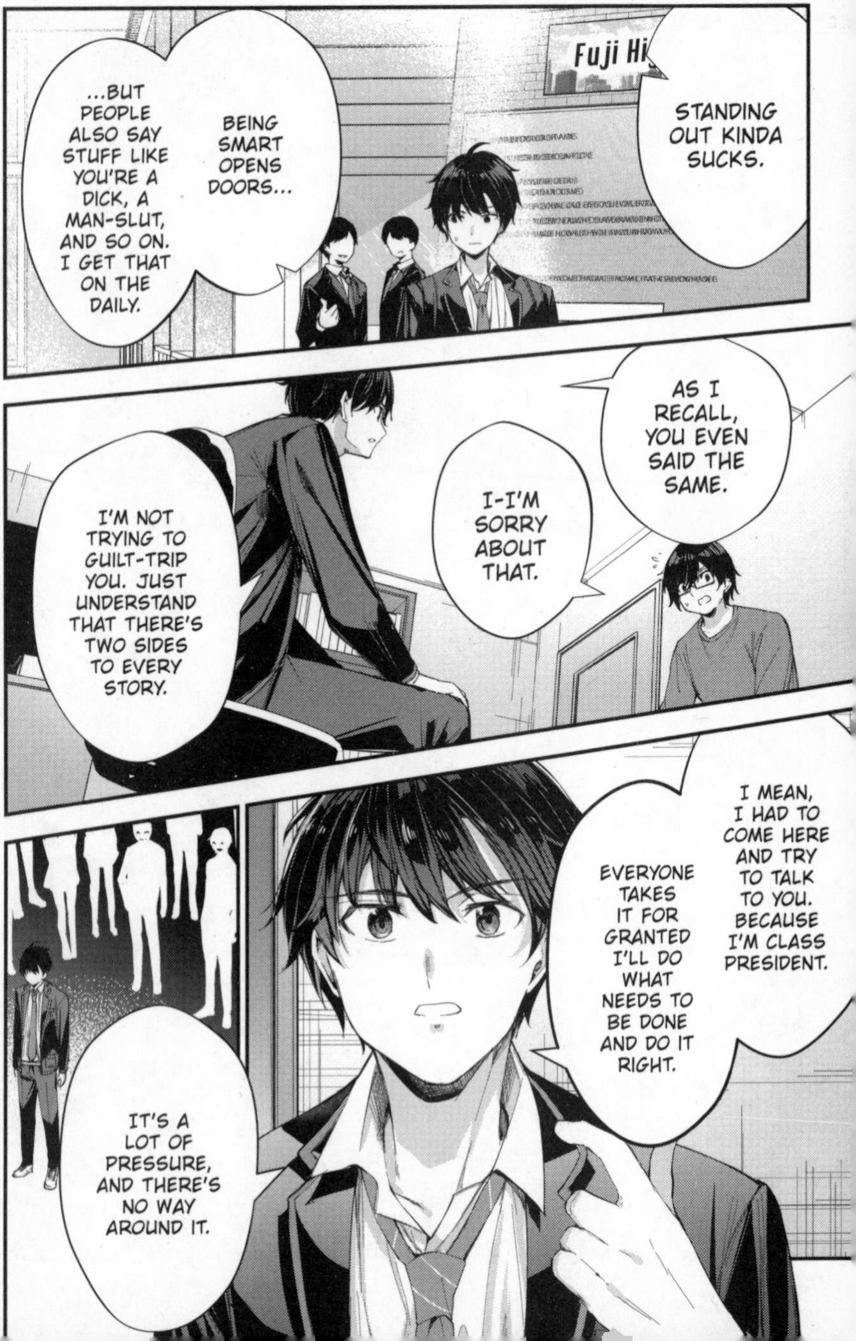
Fuji Hi
STANDING OUT KINDA SUCKS.
BEING SMART OPENS DOORS...
...BUT PEOPLE ALSO SAY STUFF LIKE YOU'RE A DICK, A MAN-SLUT, AND SO ON. I GET THAT ON THE DAILY.
AS I RECALL, YOU EVEN SAID THE SAME.
I-I'M SORRY ABOUT THAT.
I'M NOT TRYING TO GUILT-TRIP YOU. JUST UNDERSTAND THAT THERE'S TWO SIDES TO EVERY STORY.
I MEAN, I HAD TO COME HERE AND TRY TO TALK TO YOU. BECAUSE I'M CLASS PRESIDENT.
EVERYONE TAKES IT FOR GRANTED I'LL DO WHAT NEEDS TO BE DONE AND DO IT RIGHT.
IT'S A LOT OF PRESSURE, AND THERE'S NO WAY AROUND IT.

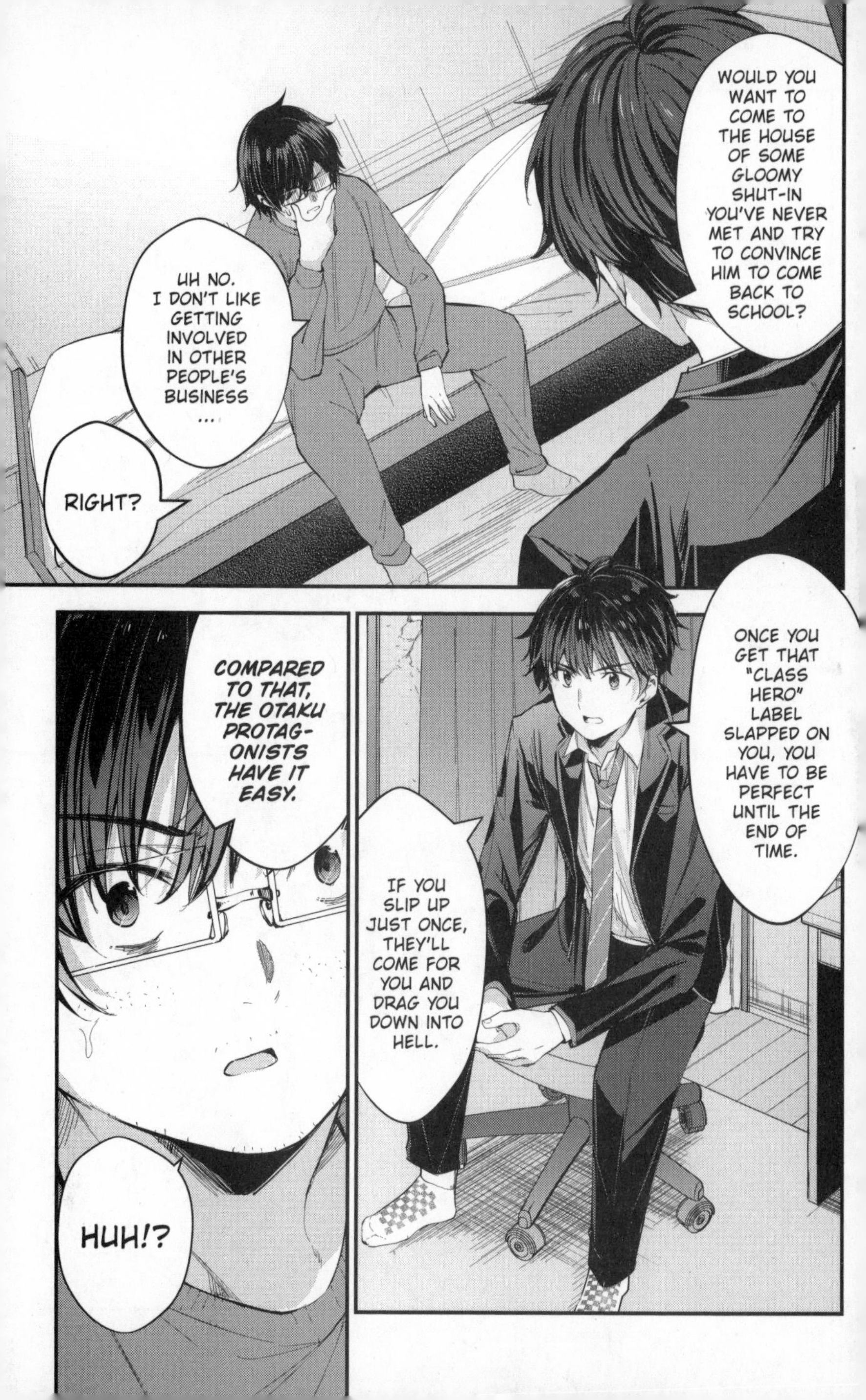
WOULD YOU WANT TO COME TO THE HOUSE OF SOME GLOOMY SHUT-IN YOU'VE NEVER MET AND TRY TO CONVINCE HIM TO COME BACK TO SCHOOL?
UH NO. I DON'T LIKE GETTING INVOLVED IN OTHER PEOPLE'S BUSINESS...
RIGHT?
ONCE YOU GET THAT "CLASS HERO" LABEL SLAPPED ON YOU, YOU HAVE TO BE PERFECT UNTIL THE END OF TIME.
IF YOU SLIP UP JUST ONCE, THEY'LL COME FOR YOU AND DRAG YOU DOWN INTO HELL.
COMPARED TO THAT, THE OTAKU PROTAG-ONISTS HAVE IT EASY.
HUH!?

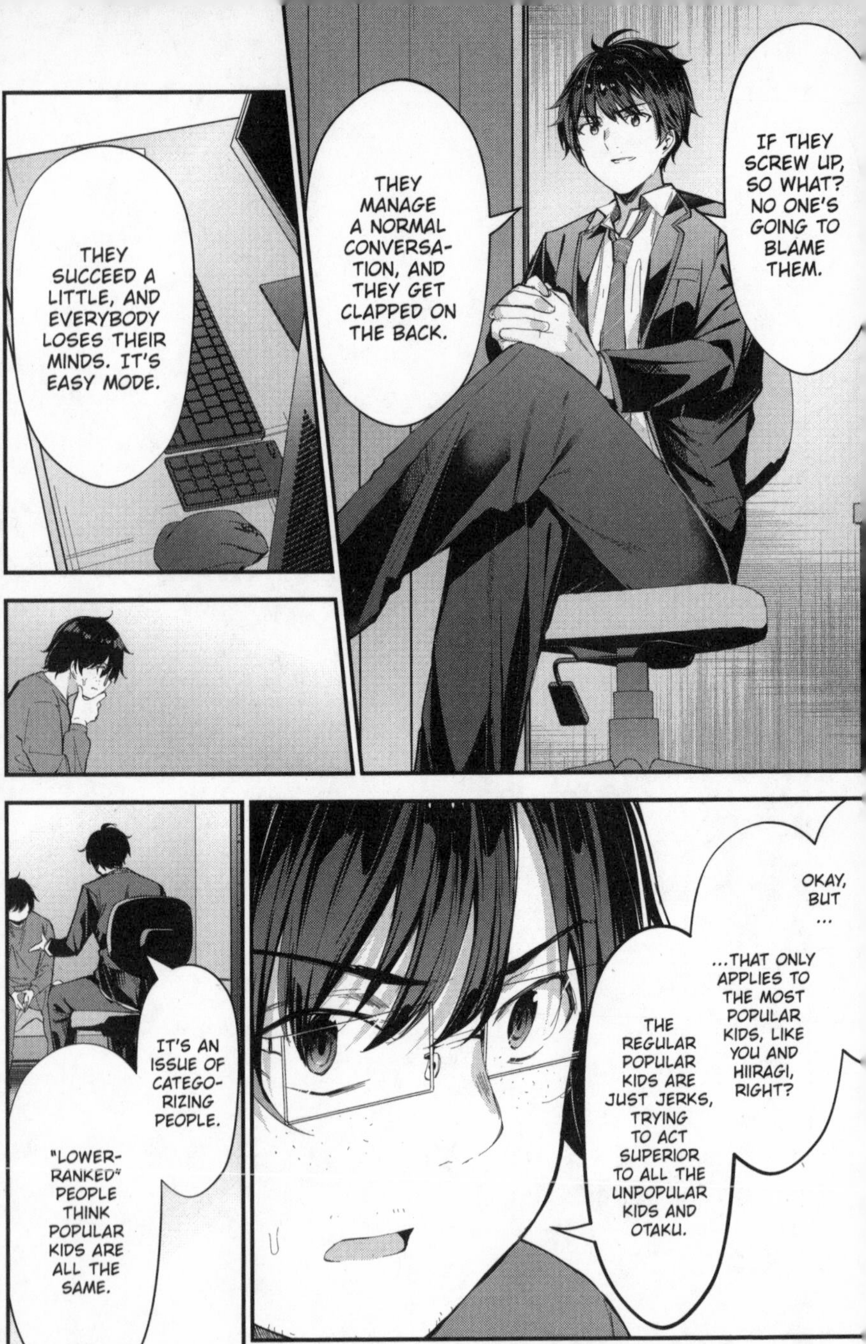
IF THEY SCREW UP, SO WHAT? NO ONE'S GOING TO BLAME THEM.
THEY MANAGE A NORMAL CONVERSA-TION, AND THEY GET CLAPPED ON THE BACK.
THEY SUCCEED A LITTLE, AND EVERYBODY LOSES THEIR MINDS. IT'S EASY MODE.
OKAY, BUT ...
...THAT ONLY APPLIES TO THE MOST POPULAR KIDS, LIKE YOU AND HIIRAGI, RIGHT?
THE REGULAR POPULAR KIDS ARE JUST JERKS, TRYING TO ACT SUPERIOR TO ALL THE UNPOPULAR KIDS AND OTAKU.
IT'S AN ISSUE OF CATEGO-RIZING PEOPLE.
"LOWER-RANKED" PEOPLE THINK POPULAR KIDS ARE ALL THE SAME.

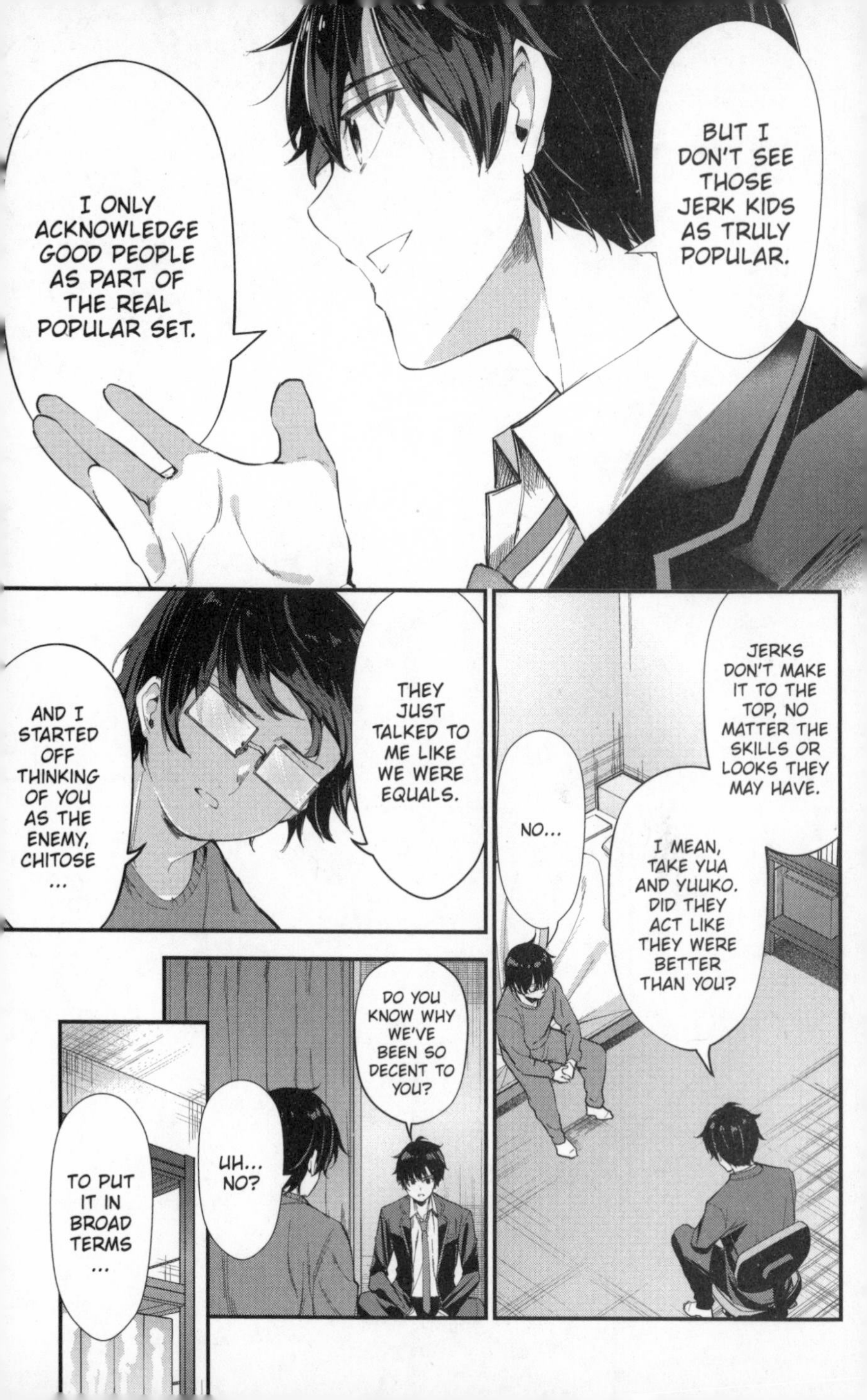
BUT I DON'T SEE THOSE JERK KIDS AS TRULY POPULAR.
I ONLY ACKNOWLEDGE GOOD PEOPLE AS PART OF THE REAL POPULAR SET.
JERKS DON'T MAKE IT TO THE TOP, NO MATTER THE SKILLS OR LOOKS THEY MAY HAVE.
I MEAN, TAKE YUA AND YUUKO. DID THEY ACT LIKE THEY WERE BETTER THAN YOU?
NO...
THEY JUST TALKED TO ME LIKE WE WERE EQUALS.
AND I STARTED OFF THINKING OF YOU AS THE ENEMY, CHITOSE ...
DO YOU KNOW WHY WE'VE BEEN SO DECENT TO YOU?
UH... NO?
TO PUT IT IN BROAD TERMS ...

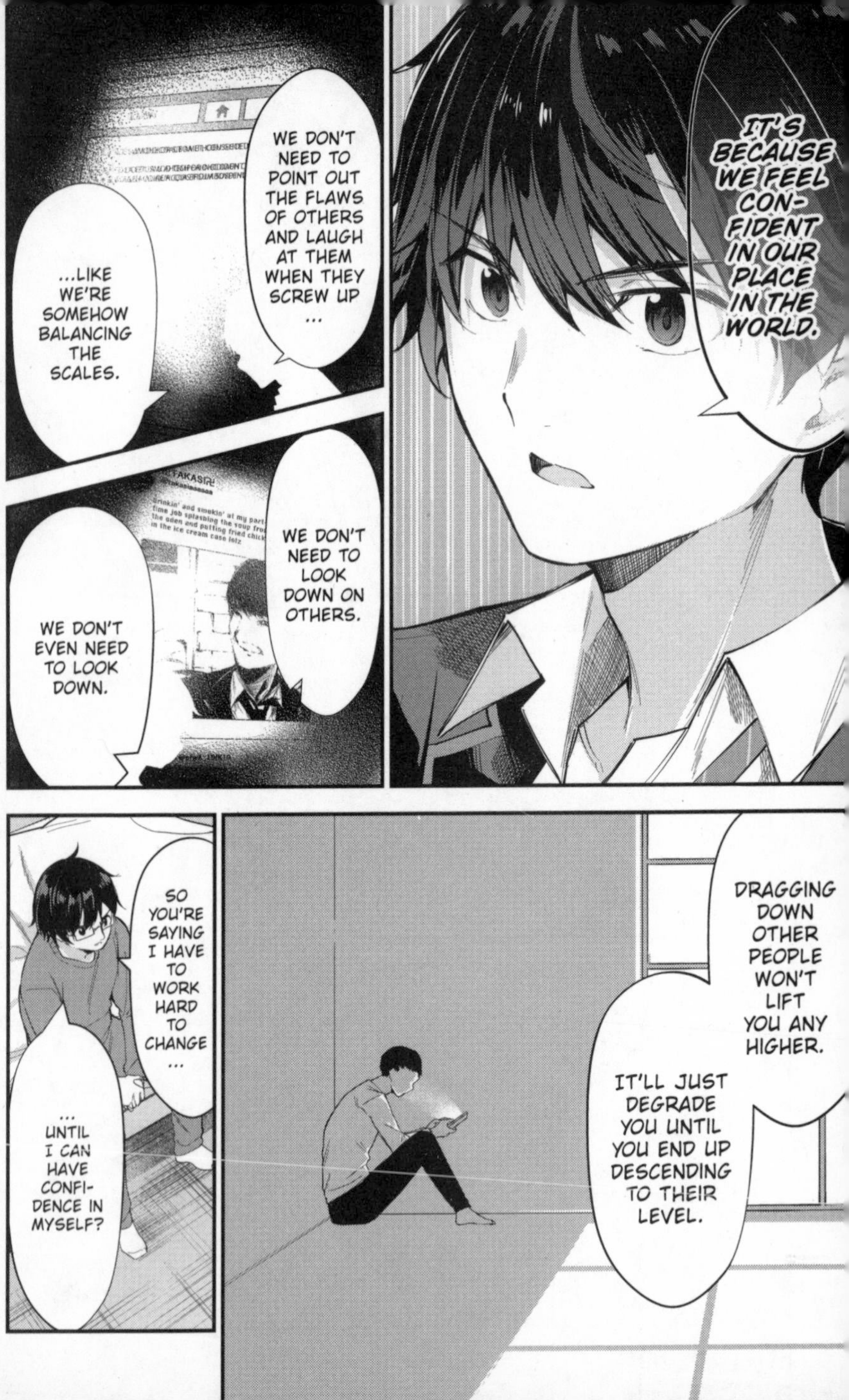
IT'S BECAUSE WE FEEL CON-FIDENT IN OUR PLACE IN THE WORLD.
WE DON'T NEED TO POINT OUT THE FLAWS OF OTHERS AND LAUGH AT THEM WHEN THEY SCREW UP...
...LIKE WE'RE SOMEHOW BALANCING THE SCALES.
WE DON'T NEED TO LOOK DOWN ON OTHERS.
WE DON'T EVEN NEED TO LOOK DOWN.
DRAGGING DOWN OTHER PEOPLE WON'T LIFT YOU ANY HIGHER.
IT'LL JUST DEGRADE YOU UNTIL YOU END UP DESCENDING TO THEIR LEVEL.
SO YOU'RE SAYING I HAVE TO WORK HARD TO CHANGE...
...UNTIL I CAN HAVE CONFI-DENCE IN MYSELF?

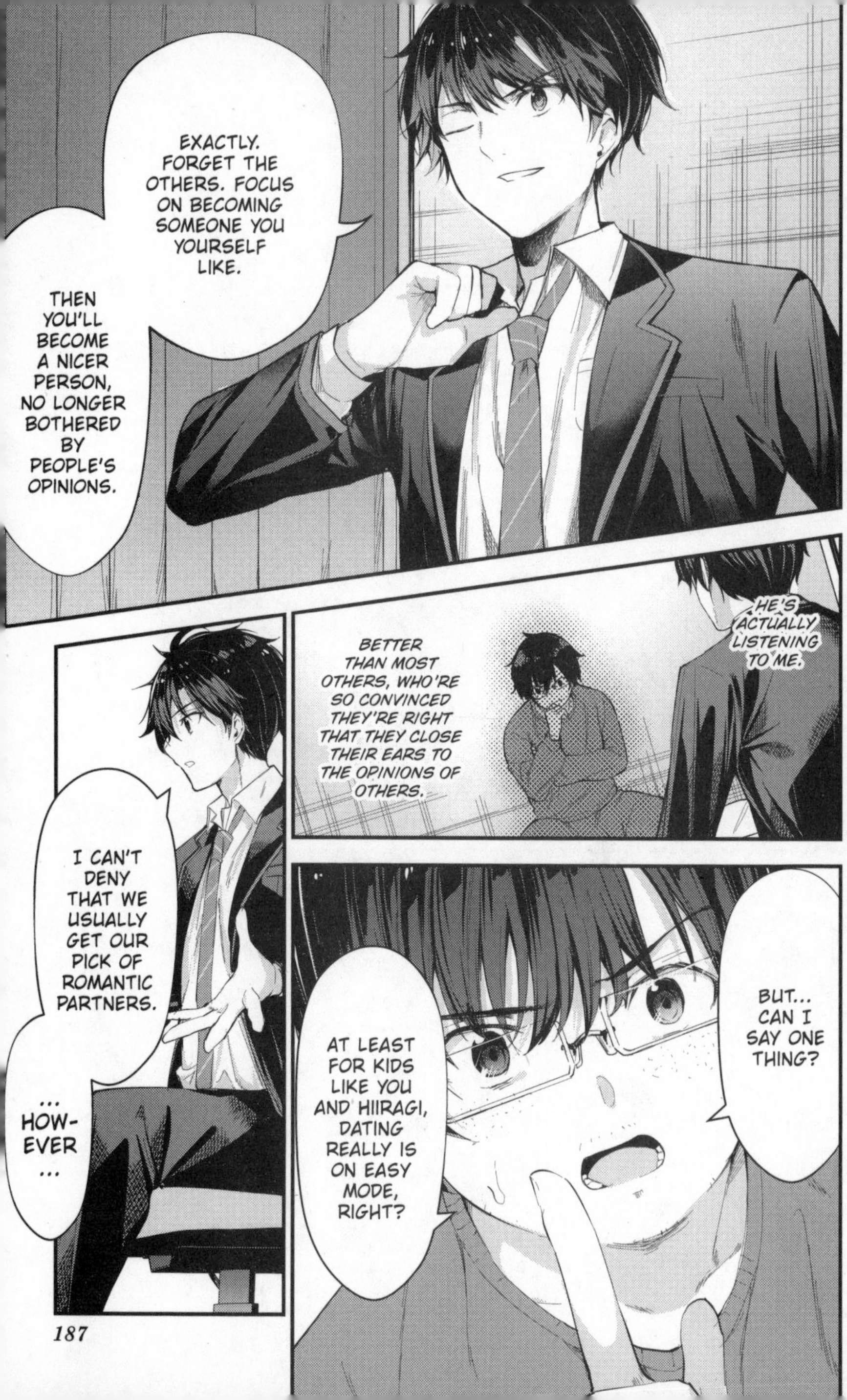
EXACTLY. FORGET THE OTHERS. FOCUS ON BECOMING SOMEONE YOU YOURSELF LIKE.
THEN YOU'LL BECOME A NICER PERSON, NO LONGER BOTHERED BY PEOPLE'S OPINIONS.
HE'S ACTUALLY LISTENING TO ME.
BETTER THAN MOST OTHERS, WHO'RE SO CONVINCED THEY'RE RIGHT THAT THEY CLOSE THEIR EARS TO THE OPINIONS OF OTHERS.
BUT... CAN I SAY ONE THING?
AT LEAST FOR KIDS LIKE YOU AND HIIRAGI, DATING REALLY IS ON EASY MODE, RIGHT?
I CAN'T DENY THAT WE USUALLY GET OUR PICK OF ROMANTIC PARTNERS.
...HOW-EVER...

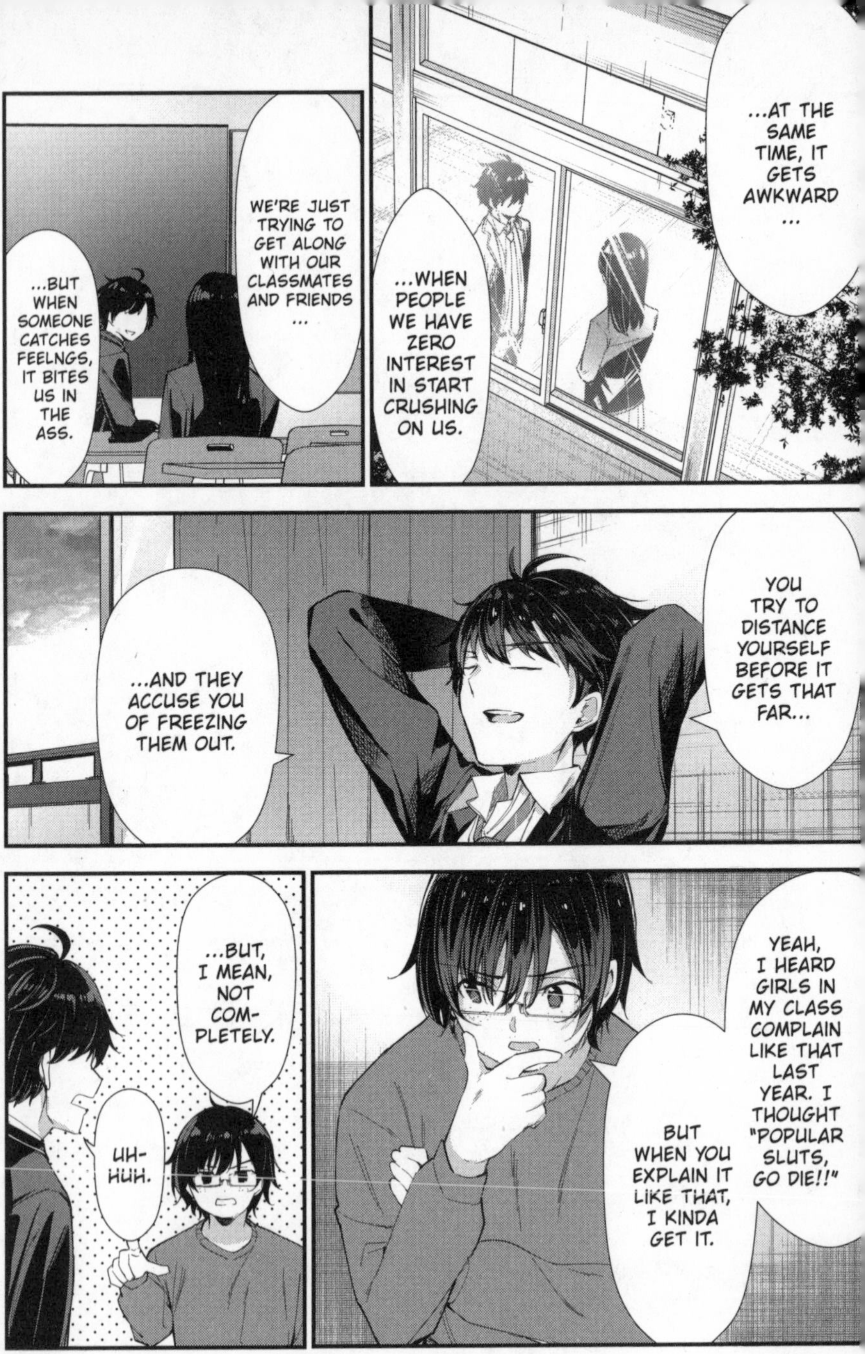
...AT THE SAME TIME, IT GETS AWKWARD ...
...WHEN PEOPLE WE HAVE ZERO INTEREST IN START CRUSHING ON US.
WE'RE JUST TRYING TO GET ALONG WITH OUR CLASSMATES AND FRIENDS ...
...BUT WHEN SOMEONE CATCHES FEELNGS, IT BITES US IN THE ASS.
YOU TRY TO DISTANCE YOURSELF BEFORE IT GETS THAT FAR...
...AND THEY ACCUSE YOU OF FREEZING THEM OUT.
YEAH, I HEARD GIRLS IN MY CLASS COMPLAIN LIKE THAT LAST YEAR. I THOUGHT "POPULAR SLUTS, GO DIE!!"
BUT WHEN YOU EXPLAIN IT LIKE THAT, I KINDA GET IT.
...BUT, I MEAN, NOT COM-PLETELY.
UH-HUH.

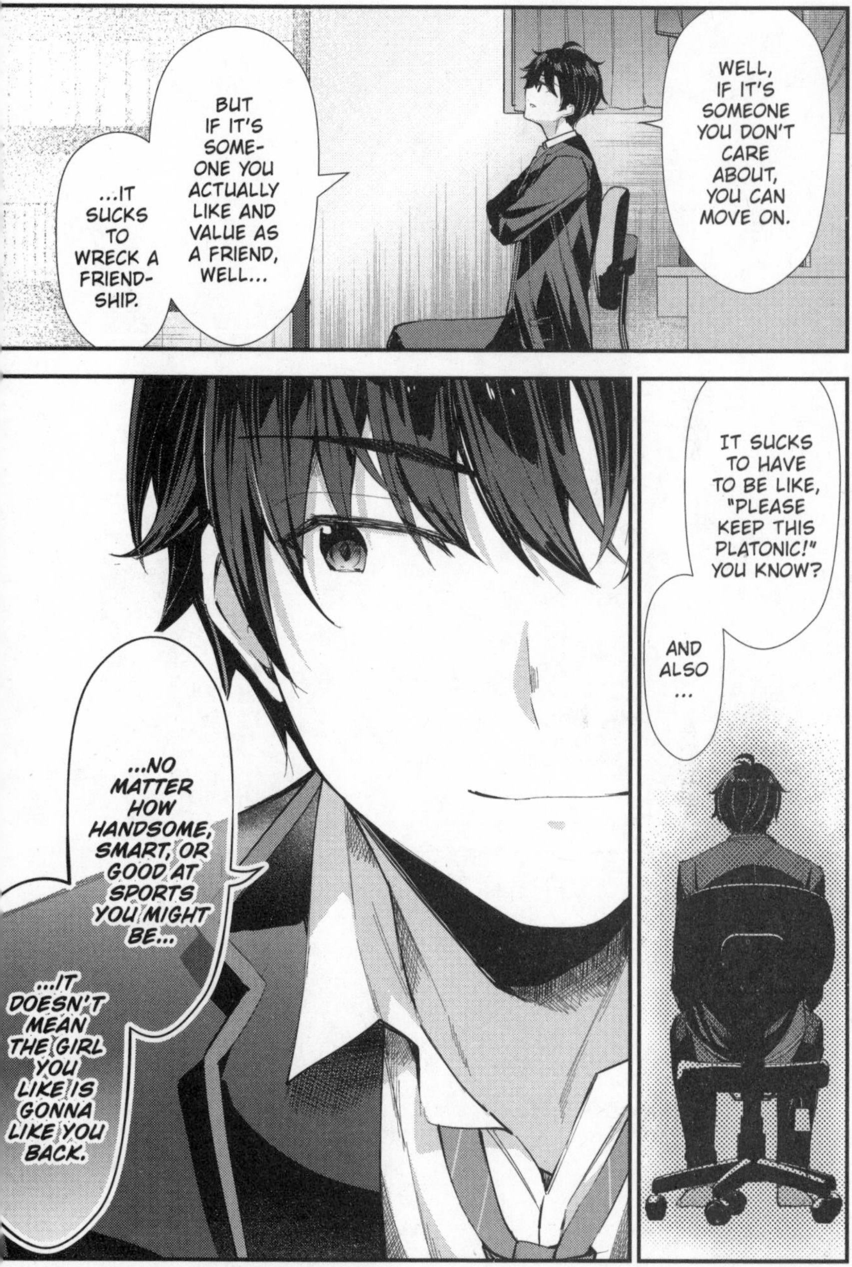
WELL, IF IT'S SOMEONE YOU DON'T CARE ABOUT, YOU CAN MOVE ON.
BUT IF IT'S SOME-ONE YOU ACTUALLY LIKE AND VALUE AS A FRIEND, WELL...
...IT SUCKS TO WRECK A FRIEND-SHIP.
IT SUCKS TO HAVE TO BE LIKE, "PLEASE KEEP THIS PLATONIC!" YOU KNOW?
AND ALSO ...
...NO MATTER HOW HANDSOME, SMART, OR GOOD AT SPORTS YOU MIGHT BE...
...IT DOESN'T MEAN THE GIRL YOU LIKE IS GONNA LIKE YOU BACK.

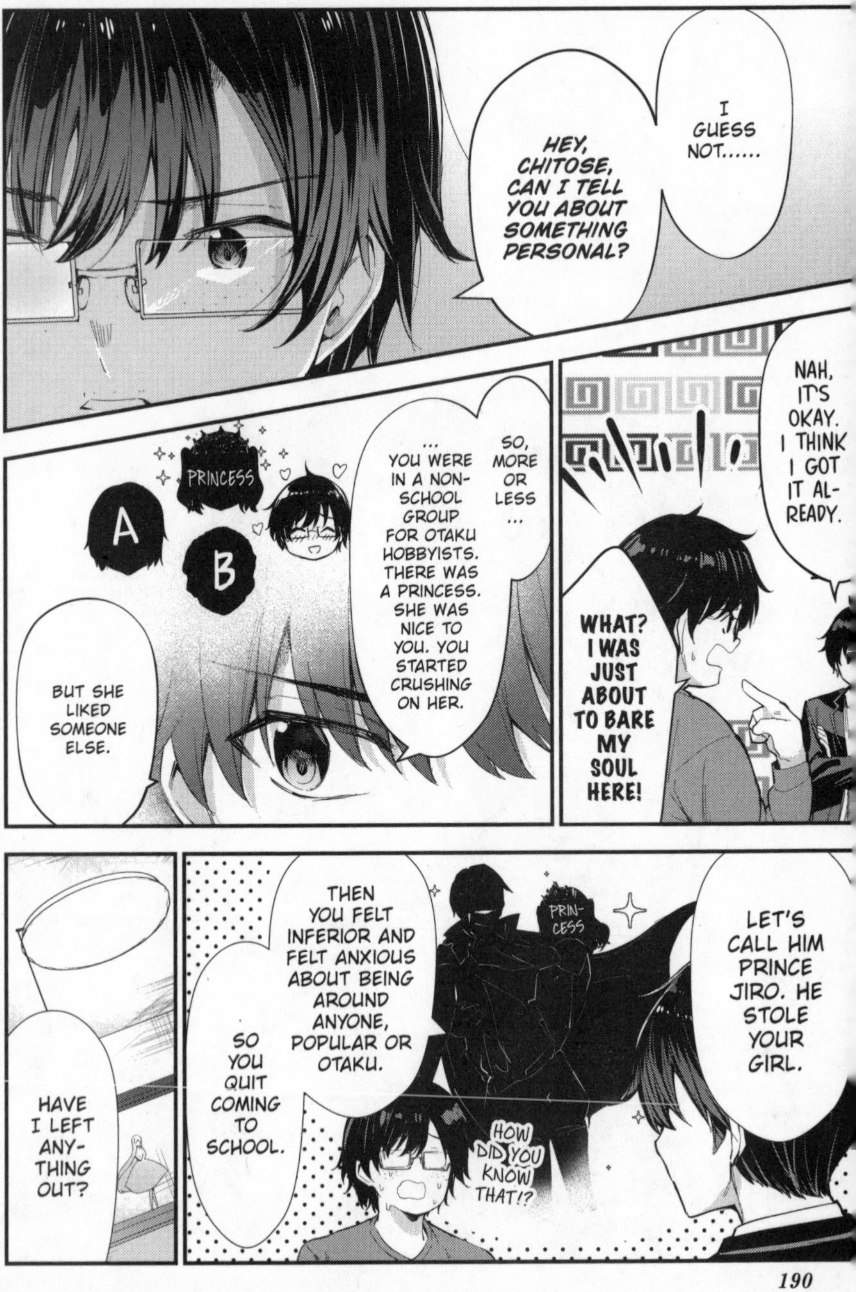
I GUESS NOT......
HEY, CHITOSE, CAN I TELL YOU ABOUT SOMETHING PERSONAL?
NAH, IT'S OKAY. I THINK I GOT IT AL-READY.
WHAT? I WAS JUST ABOUT TO BARE MY SOUL HERE!
SO, MORE OR LESS...
...YOU WERE IN A NON-SCHOOL GROUP FOR OTAKU HOBBYISTS. THERE WAS A PRINCESS. SHE WAS NICE TO YOU. YOU STARTED CRUSHING ON HER.
PRINCESS
A
B
BUT SHE LIKED SOMEONE ELSE.
LET'S CALL HIM PRINCE JIRO. HE STOLE YOUR GIRL.
PRIN-CESS
THEN YOU FELT INFERIOR AND FELT ANXIOUS ABOUT BEING AROUND ANYONE, POPULAR OR OTAKU.
HOW DID YOU KNOW THAT!?
SO YOU QUIT COMING TO SCHOOL.
HAVE I LEFT ANY-THING OUT?

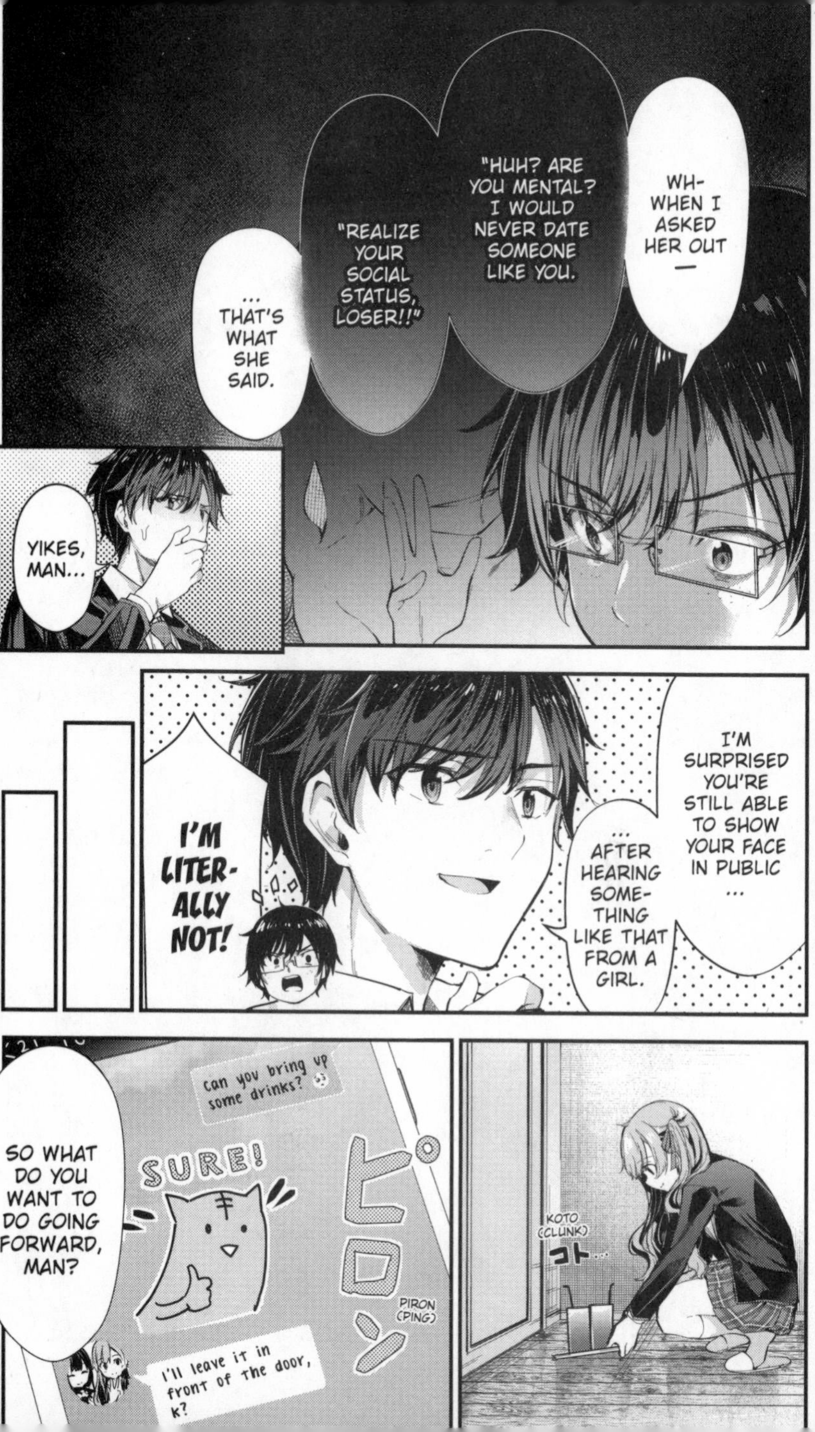
WH-WHEN I ASKED HER OUT —
"HUH? ARE YOU MENTAL? I WOULD NEVER DATE SOMEONE LIKE YOU.
"REALIZE YOUR SOCIAL STATUS, LOSER!!"
...THAT'S WHAT SHE SAID.
YIKES, MAN...
I'M SURPRISED YOU'RE STILL ABLE TO SHOW YOUR FACE IN PUBLIC ...
... AFTER HEARING SOMETHING LIKE THAT FROM A GIRL.
I'M LITERALLY NOT!
KOTO (CLUNK)
コト...
can you bring up some drinks?
SURE!
ピロン
PIRON (PING)
I'll leave it in front of the door, k?
SO WHAT DO YOU WANT TO DO GOING FORWARD, MAN?

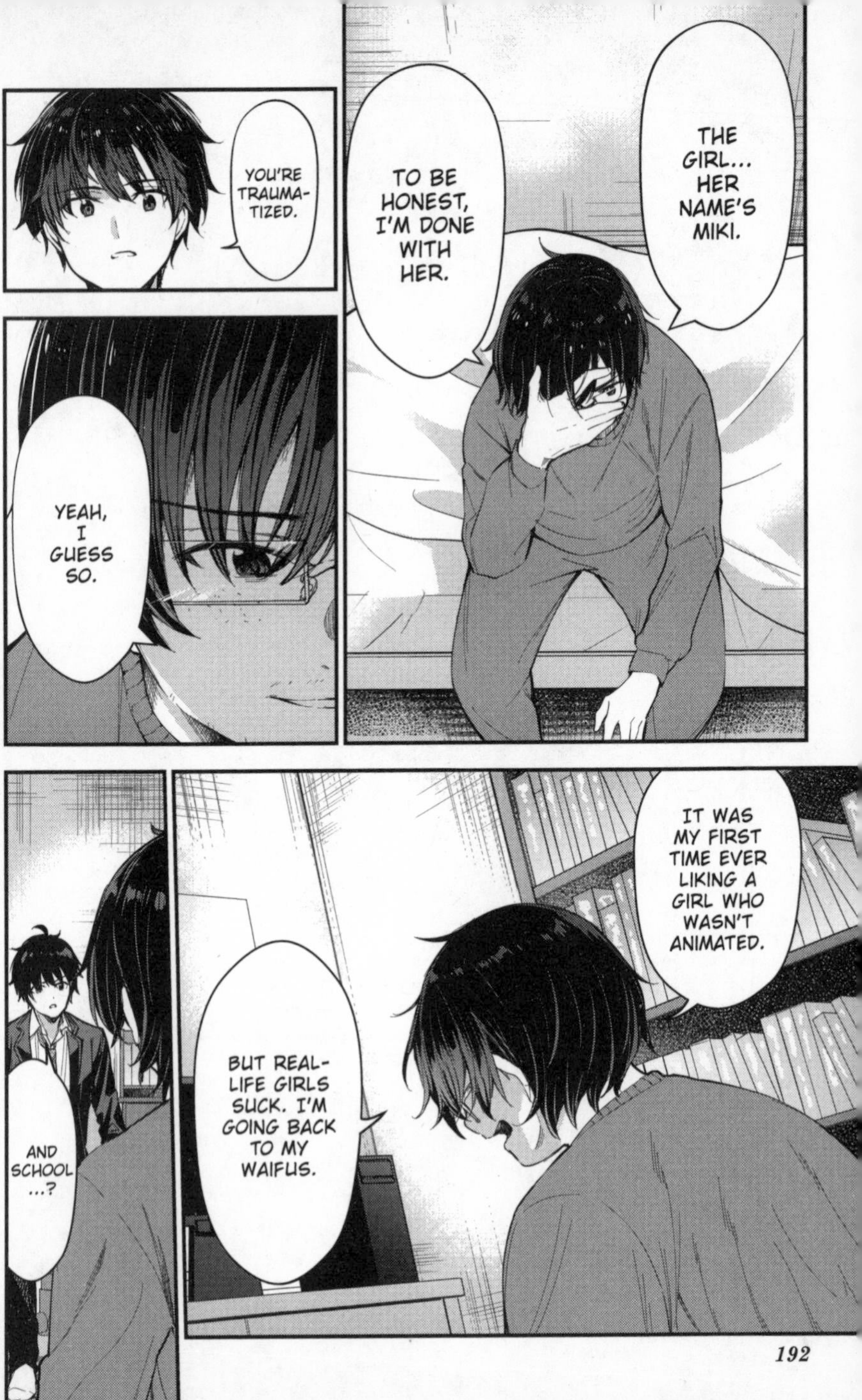
THE GIRL... HER NAME'S MIKI.
TO BE HONEST, I'M DONE WITH HER.
YOU'RE TRAUMATIZED.
YEAH, I GUESS SO.
IT WAS MY FIRST TIME EVER LIKING A GIRL WHO WASN'T ANIMATED.
BUT REAL-LIFE GIRLS SUCK. I'M GOING BACK TO MY WAIFUS.
AND SCHOOL ...?

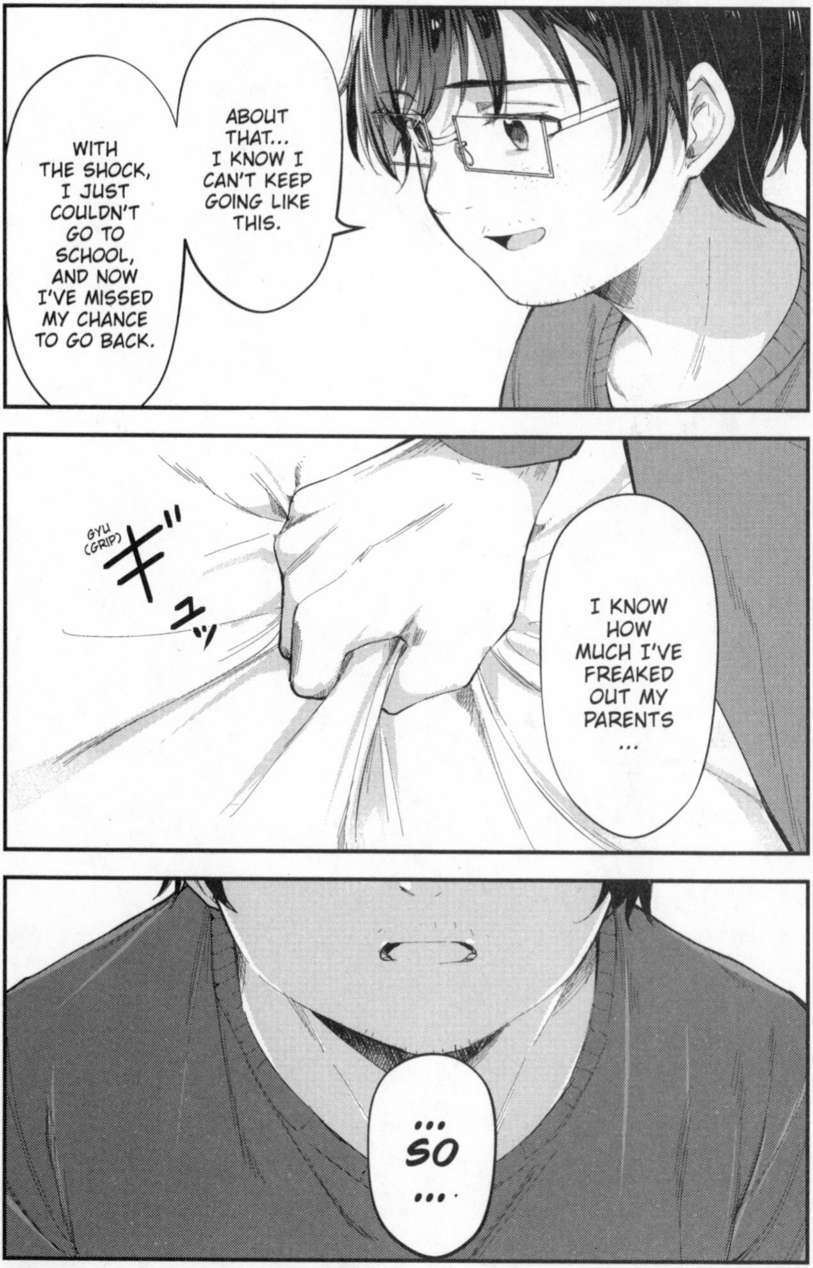
ABOUT THAT... I KNOW I CAN'T KEEP GOING LIKE THIS.
WITH THE SHOCK, I JUST COULDN'T GO TO SCHOOL, AND NOW I'VE MISSED MY CHANCE TO GO BACK.
I KNOW HOW MUCH I'VE FREAKED OUT MY PARENTS ...
GYU (GRIP)
ギュッ
...SO...

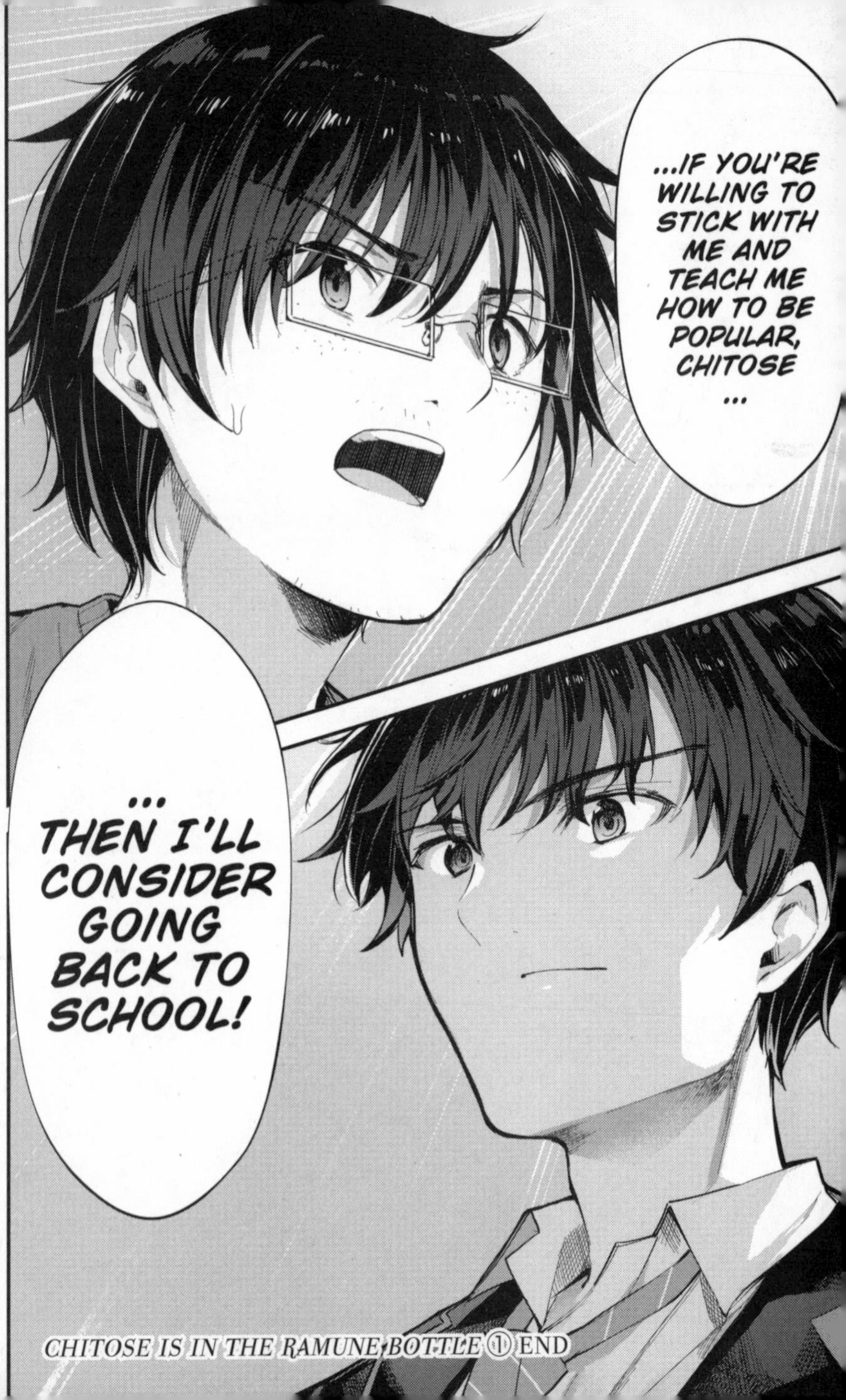
...IF YOU'RE WILLING TO STICK WITH ME AND TEACH ME HOW TO BE POPULAR, CHITOSE ...
... THEN I'LL CONSIDER GOING BACK TO SCHOOL!
CHITOSE IS IN THE RAMUNE BOTTLE ① END

BONUS MANGA: SUMMER DREAM

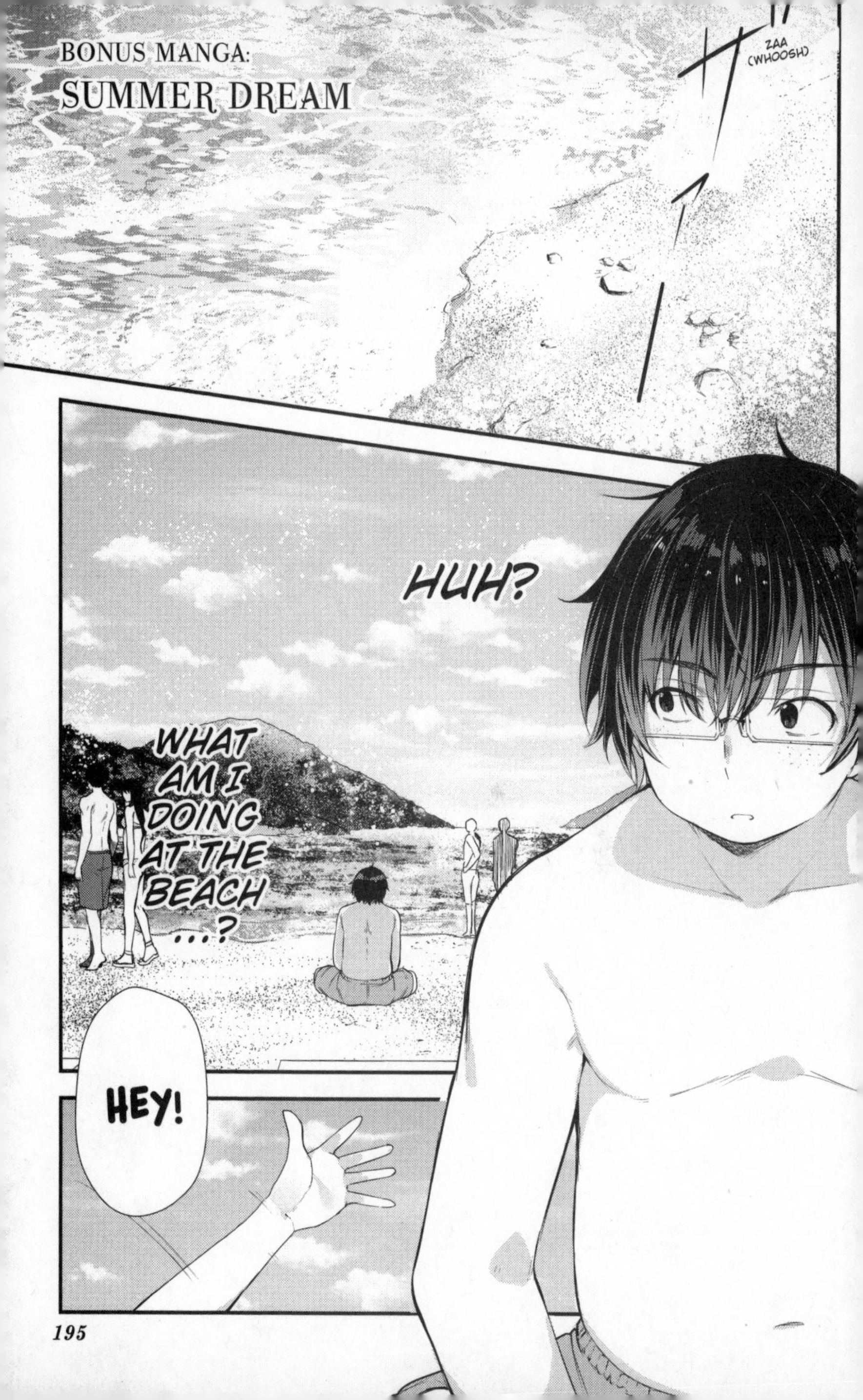
ZAA (WHOOSH)
HUH?
WHAT AM I DOING AT THE BEACH ...?
HEY!

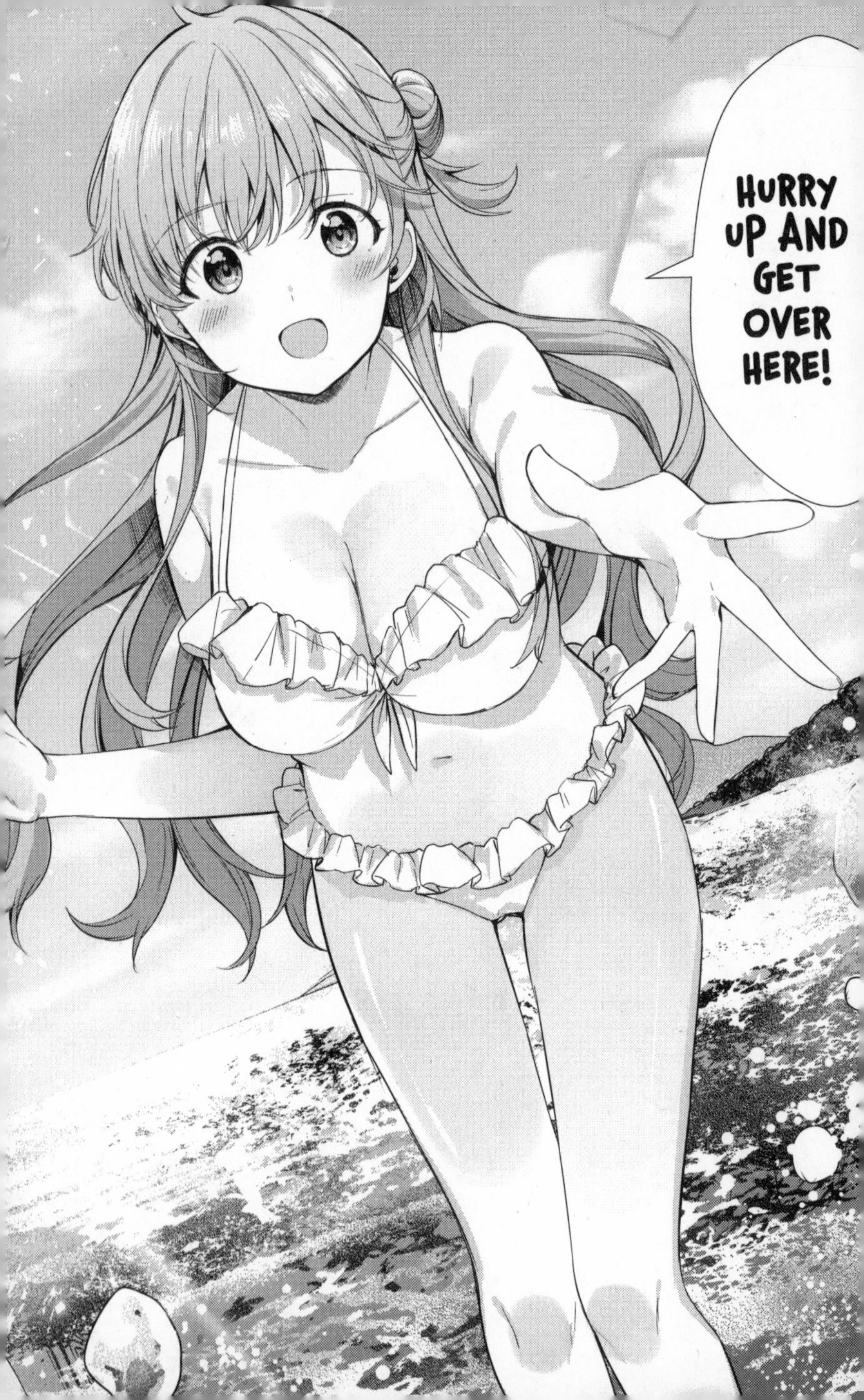
HURRY UP AND GET OVER HERE!

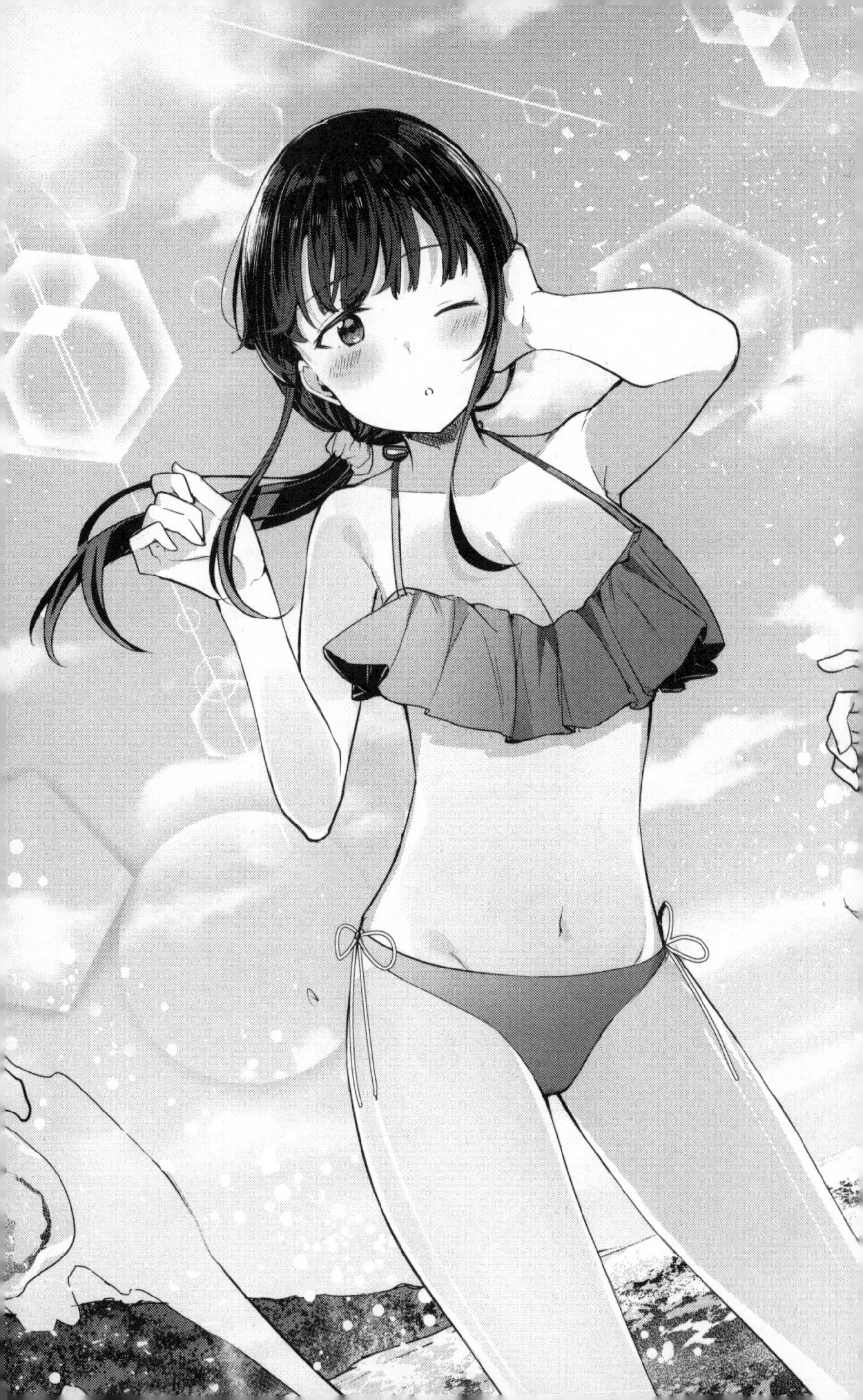

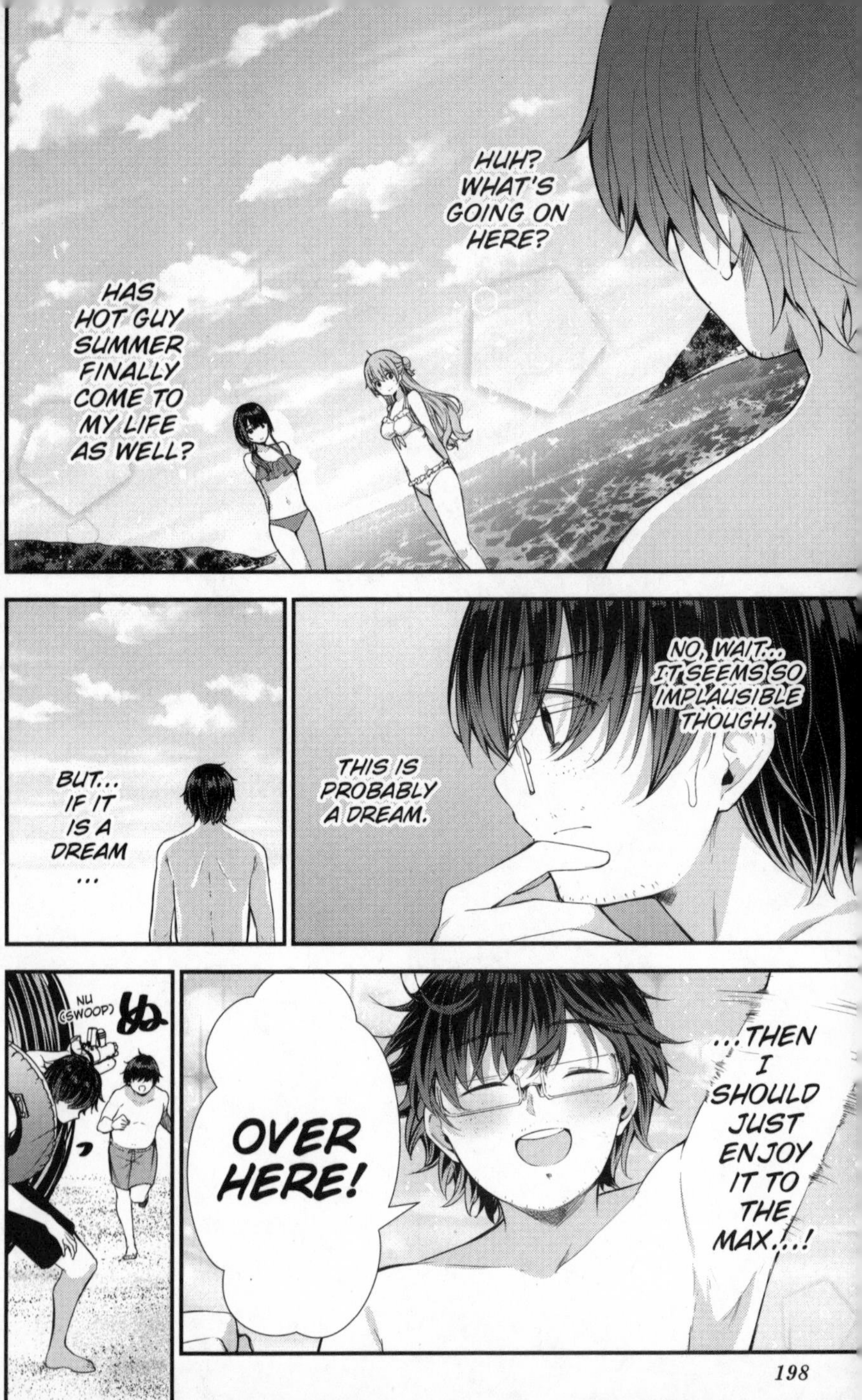
HUH? WHAT'S GOING ON HERE?
HAS HOT GUY SUMMER FINALLY COME TO MY LIFE AS WELL?
NO, WAIT... IT SEEMS SO IMPLAUSIBLE THOUGH.
THIS IS PROBABLY A DREAM.
BUT... IF IT IS A DREAM...
...THEN I SHOULD JUST ENJOY IT TO THE MAX...!
OVER HERE!
NU (SWOOP)
ぬ

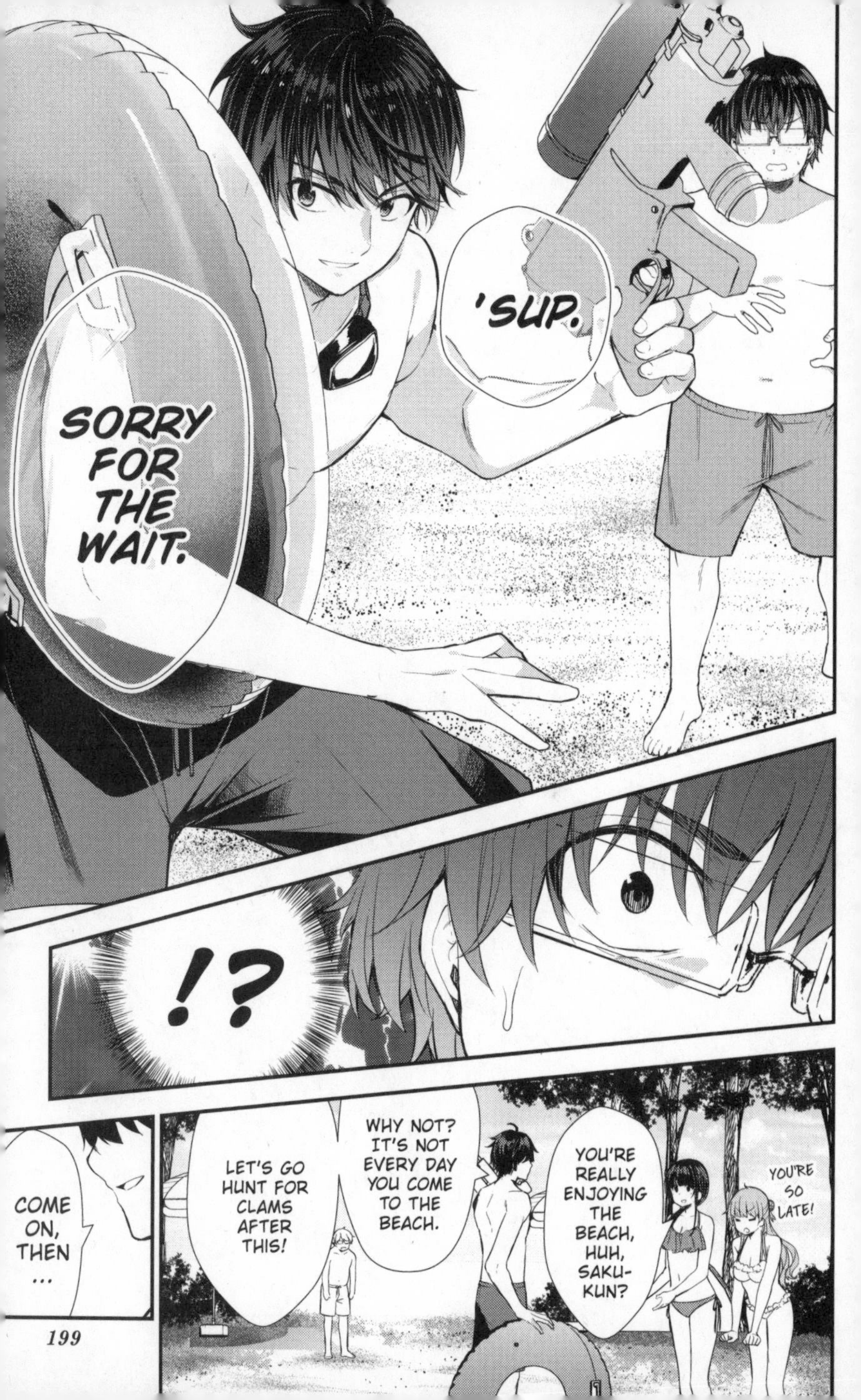

'SUP.
SORRY FOR THE WAIT.
!?
YOU'RE SO LATE!
YOU'RE REALLY ENJOYING THE BEACH, HUH, SAKU-KUN?
WHY NOT? IT'S NOT EVERY DAY YOU COME TO THE BEACH.
LET'S GO HUNT FOR CLAMS AFTER THIS!
COME ON, THEN ...

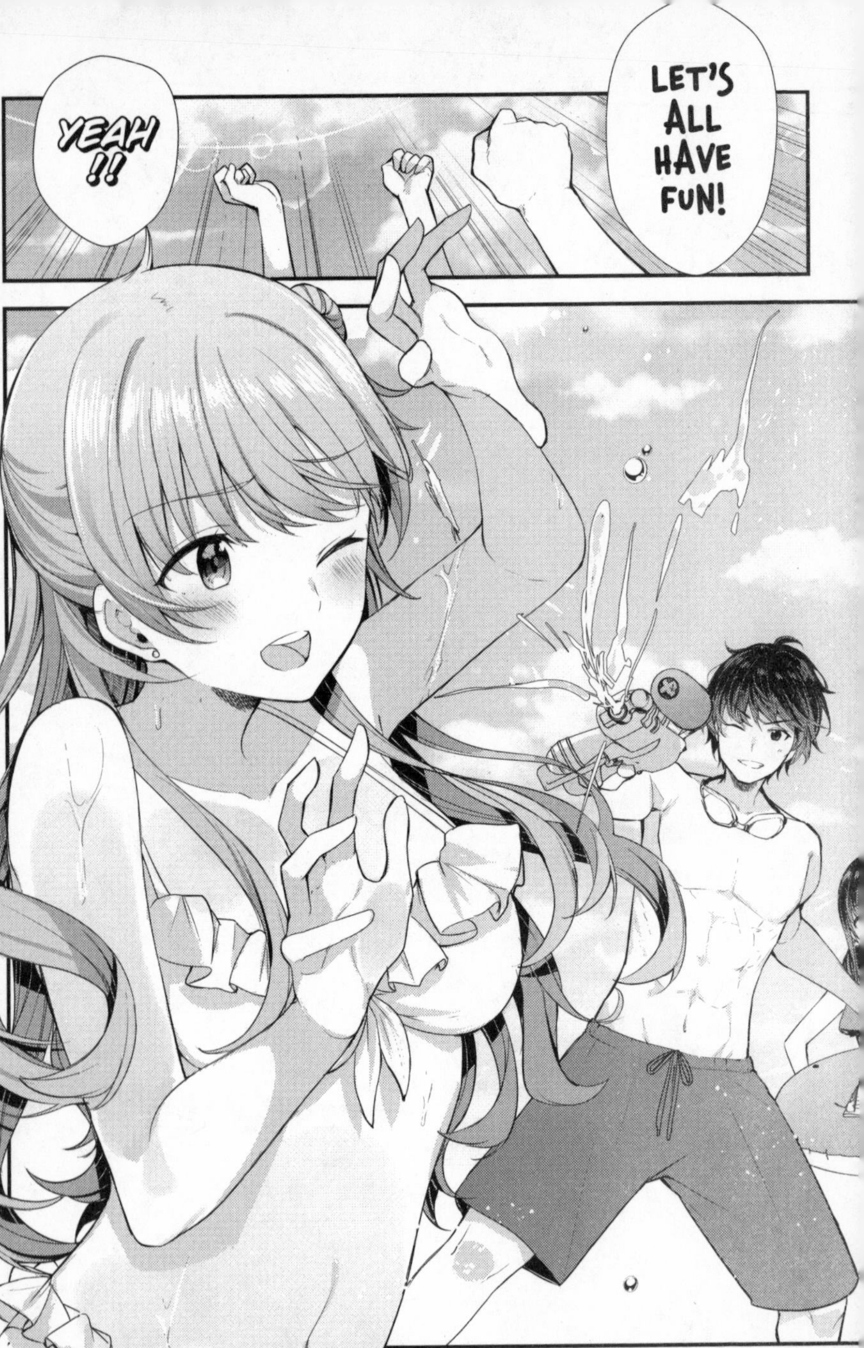
LET'S ALL HAVE FUN!
YEAH!!

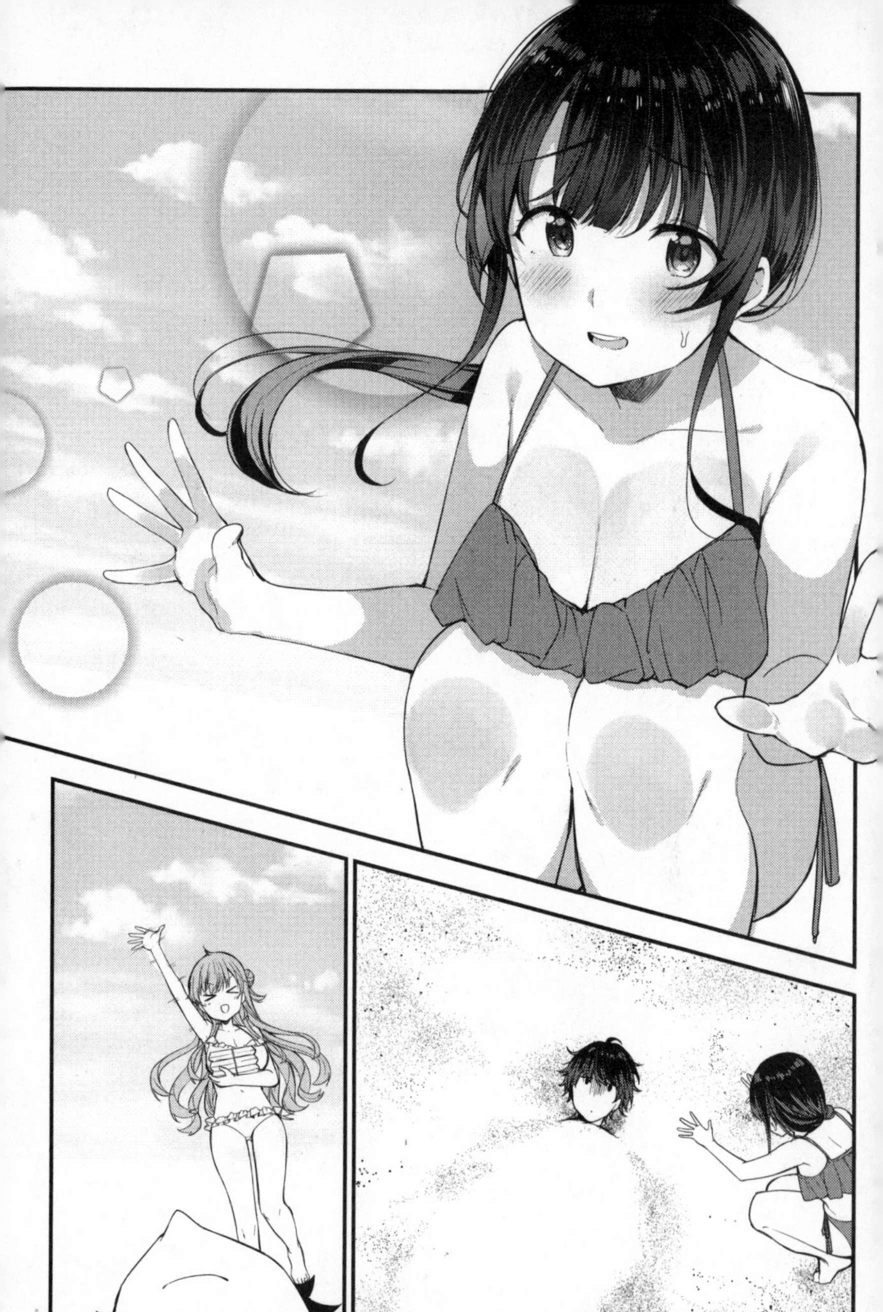

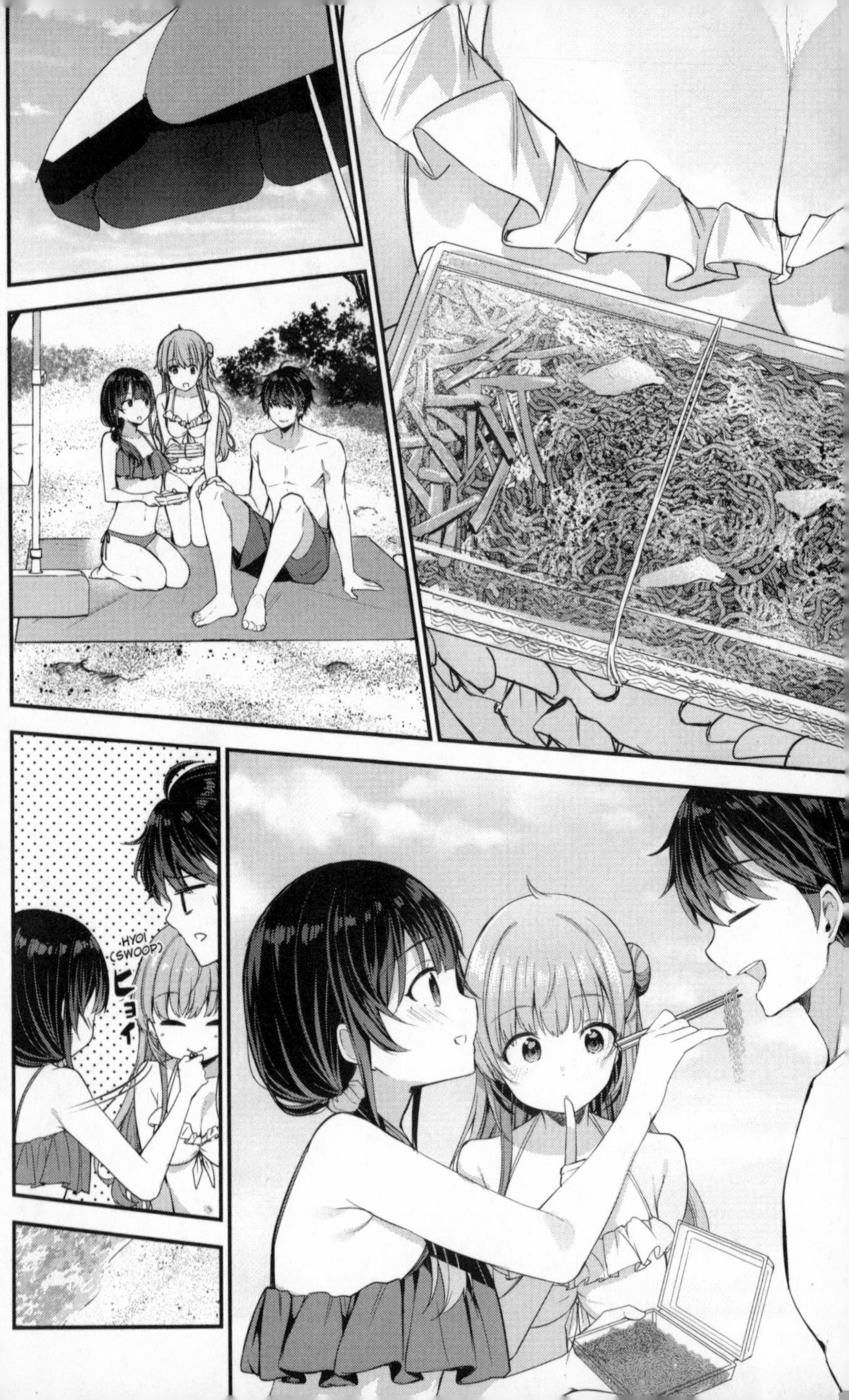
HYOI (SWOOP)
ヒョイ

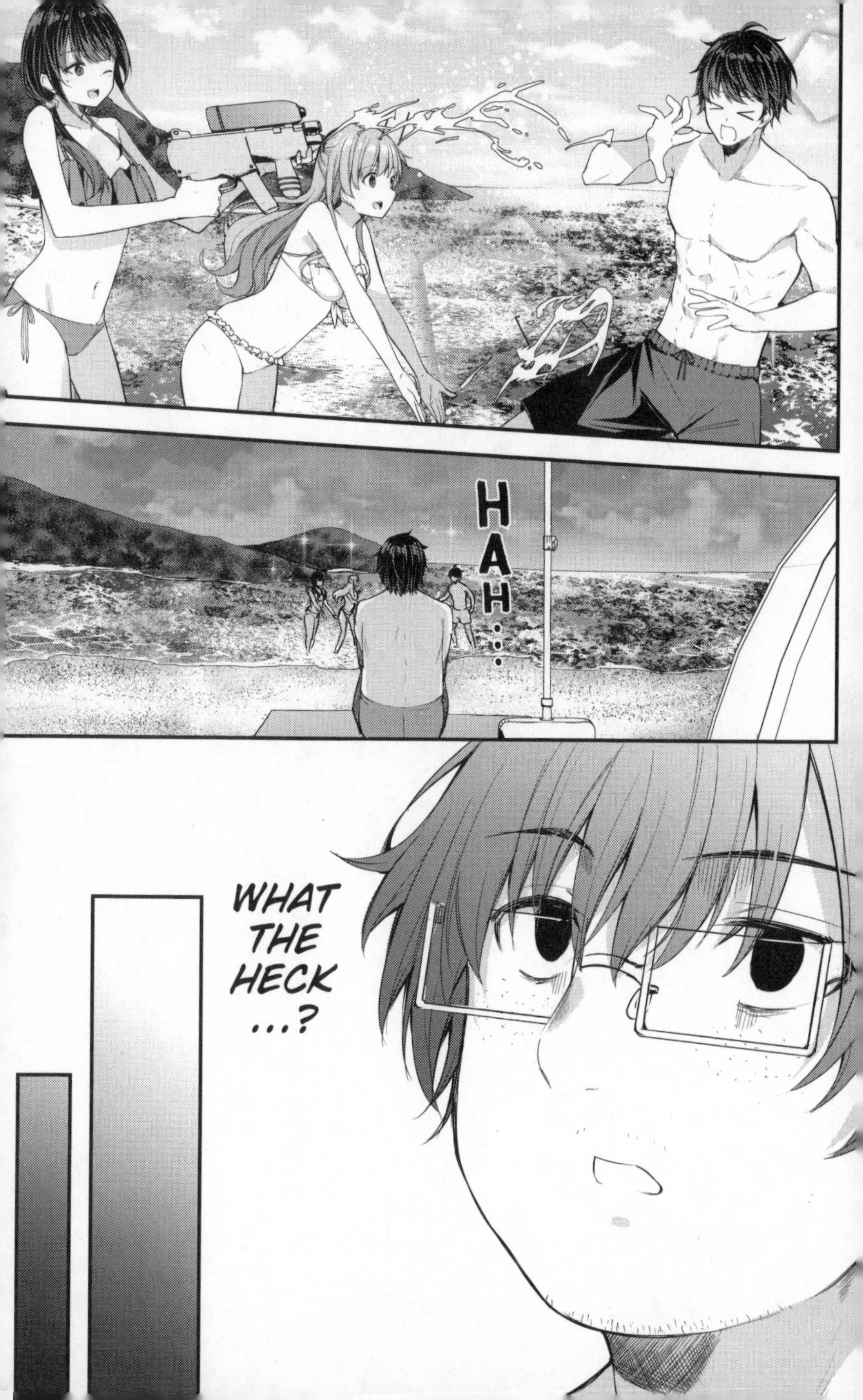
HAH...
WHAT THE HECK ...?

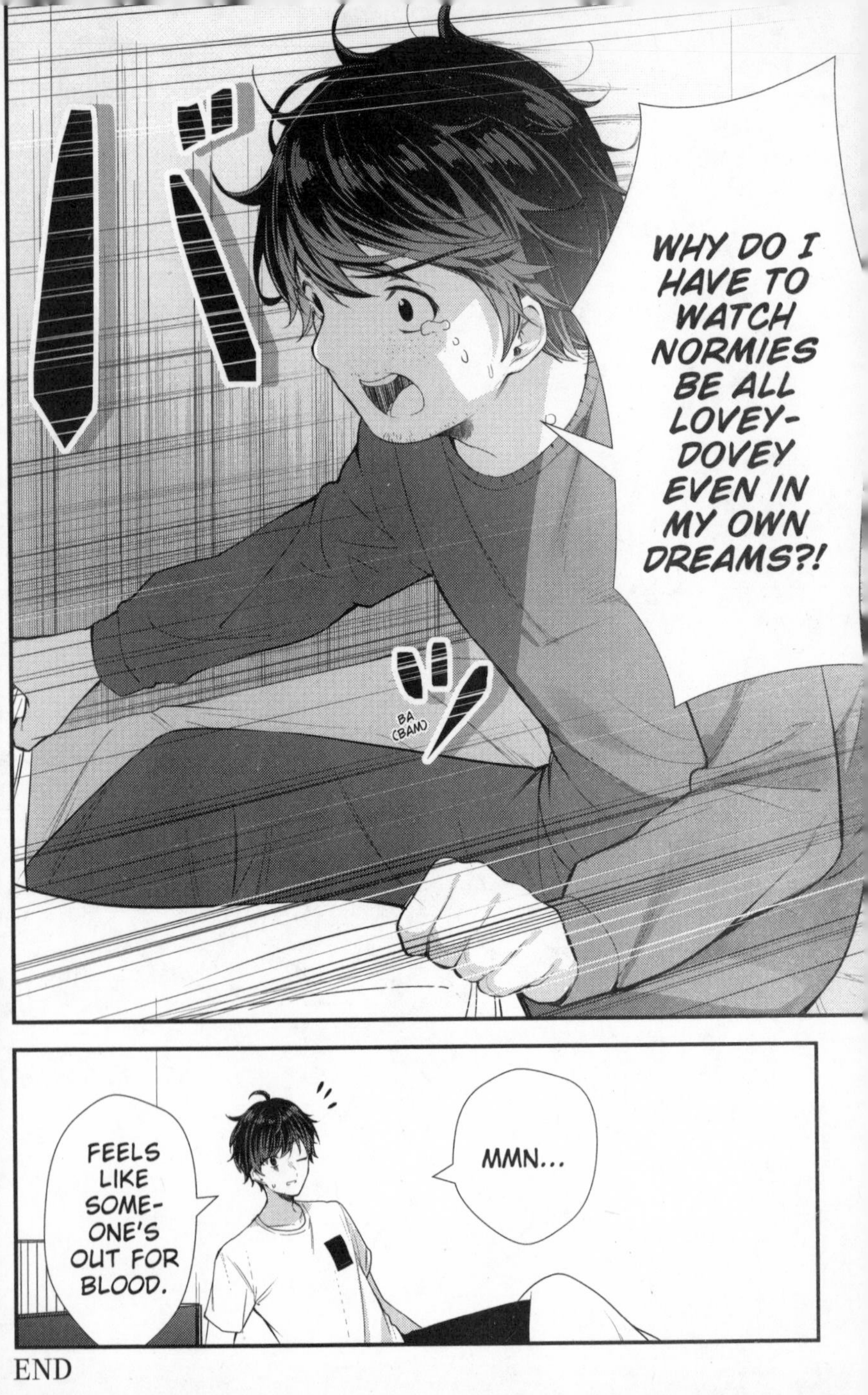
WHY DO I HAVE TO WATCH NORMIES BE ALL LOVEY-DOVEY EVEN IN MY OWN DREAMS?!
BA (BAM)
MMN...
FEELS LIKE SOME-ONE'S OUT FOR BLOOD.

END

Chitose Is in the Ramune Bottle

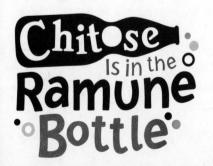

Translation Notes

Common Honorifics

-san: The Japanese equivalent of Mr./Mrs./Miss. If a situation calls for politeness, this is the fail-safe honorific.

-kun: Used most often when referring to boys, this indicates affection or familiarity. Occasionally used by older men among their peers, but it may also be used by anyone referring to a person of lower standing.

-chan: An affectionate honorific indicating familiarity used mostly in reference to girls; also used in reference to cute persons or animals of either gender.

-sensei: A respectful term for teachers, artists, or high-level professionals.

-sen: A shortened version of the honorific '-sensei'. This suggests that students have a very casual and friendly relationship with their teacher.

-nii-san/aniki and **nee-san/aneki**: A term of endearment meaning "big brother" or "big sister" that may be used to address anyone regardless of whether they are related or not.

No honorific: Indicates familiarity or closeness; if used without permission or reason, addressing someone in this manner would be interpreted as an insult or disrespectful.

Page 3

Three years: The Japanese school system is organized in such a way that their high school term is three years (what would be 10th, 11th, and 12th grade in the US), and middle school is comprised of three years (7th, 8th, and 9th grade equivalent in the U.S).

Page 14

Humanities track: The study of literature, arts, and history. Students in Japanese high schools are sometimes divided into different tracks based on their focus of study, such as science or humanities. This often reflects the profession they are aspiring toward.

Page 29

Straight man: Called *tsukkomi* in Japanese, one member of a comedy duo (the other being the "funny man" or *boke*) whose role is to misinterpret jokes or act more serious.

Page 57

Light novels: Also called *ranoberu*, short stories that are often adapted into manga or anime series in Japan. They have rapidly increased in popularity over the past few years.

Page 99

Normie: A slang term used by people of certain subcultures (like *otaku*) to describe people who are part of mainstream culture and generally follow more "acceptable" cultural norms.

Page 114
Otaku **culture:** *Otaku* is a slang term for people who are generally known as avid fans of something, such as computer *otaku* or camera *otaku*. *Otaku* by itself is typically used to refer to fans of manga and anime.

Page 116
Shounen **manga:** These are Japanese graphic novels typically aimed at young boys and men. Action and adventure are popular genres to advertise to this demographic.

Page 125
Shut-in: Also called *hikikomori*, these are people who have separated themselves from society by closing themselves off in their rooms and refusing to leave the house to attend work or school. This situation is an increasing problem in Japan, and many believe it to be a result of bullying or social anxiety.

Page 177
Ramune **bottle:** *Ramune* is a carbonated soft drink from Japan that comes in a variety of flavors. The glass bottles used a glass marble in the opening instead of a cap to trap the pressurized contents. A plastic device would come with the bottle, and it could be used to push the glass marble free and allow consumers to enjoy the beverage. It is impossible to open the bottle in order to remove the marble.

Page 192
Waifu: From the English word "wife," generally refers to a beloved character from manga, anime, or game. The term for male characters is *husbando*.

Short Story, Page 224
Roasted green tea latte: Roasted green tea or *houjicha* is a type of green tea distinct from other types (like regular steamed tea leaves or macha powder) because it is roasted at high temperatures, which produces a light gold color and unmistakable flavor.

Chitose Is in the Ramune Bottle

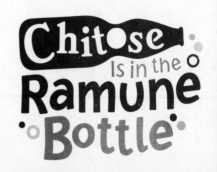

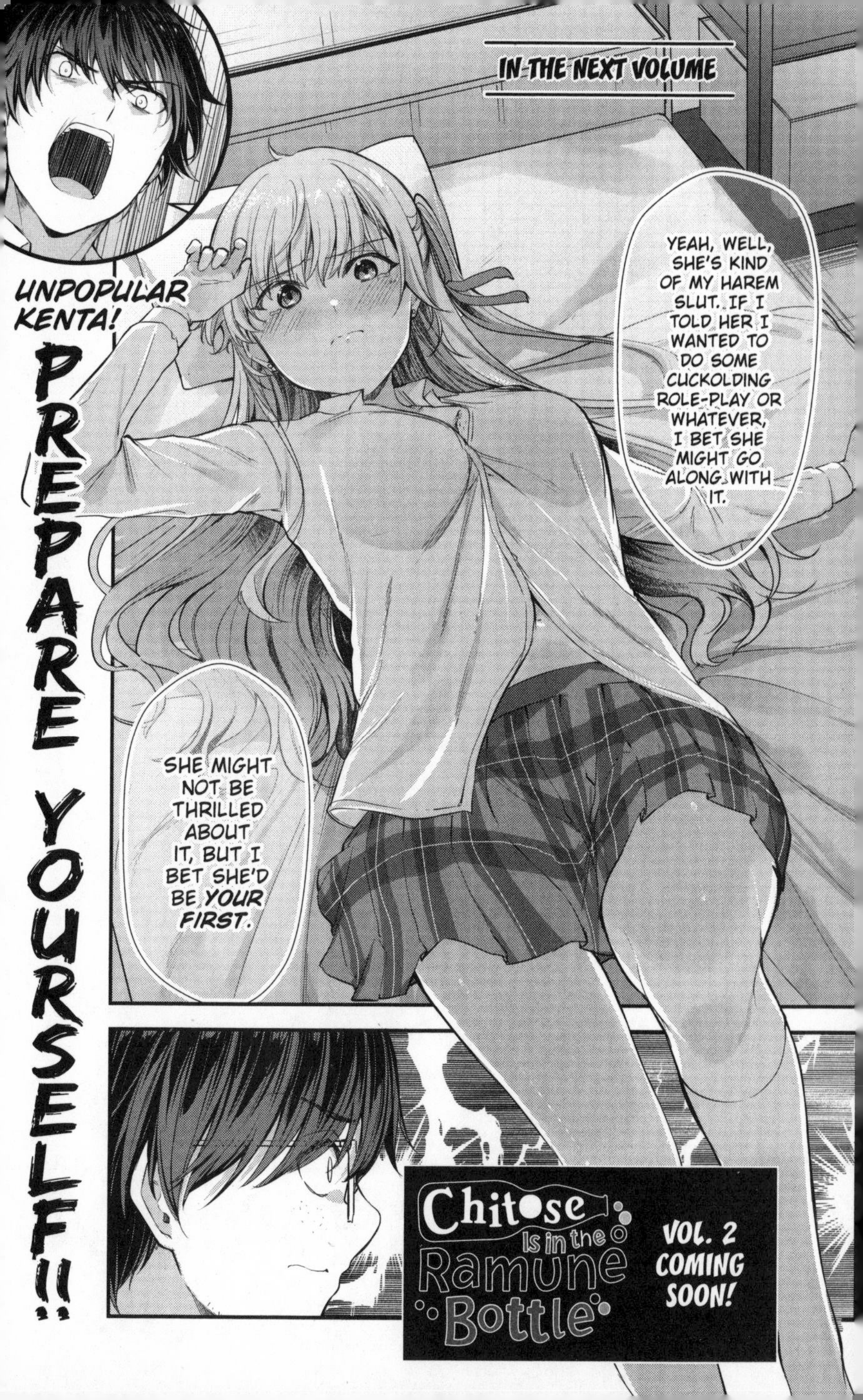
IN THE NEXT VOLUME
YEAH, WELL, SHE'S KIND OF MY HAREM SLUT. IF I TOLD HER I WANTED TO DO SOME CUCKOLDING ROLE-PLAY OR WHATEVER, I BET SHE MIGHT GO ALONG WITH IT.
SHE MIGHT NOT BE THRILLED ABOUT IT, BUT I BET SHE'D BE *YOUR FIRST*.
UNPOPULAR KENTA!
PREPARE YOURSELF!!
Chitose Is in the Ramune Bottle
VOL. 2 COMING SOON!

Chitose Is in the Ramune Bottle

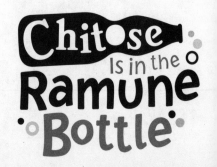

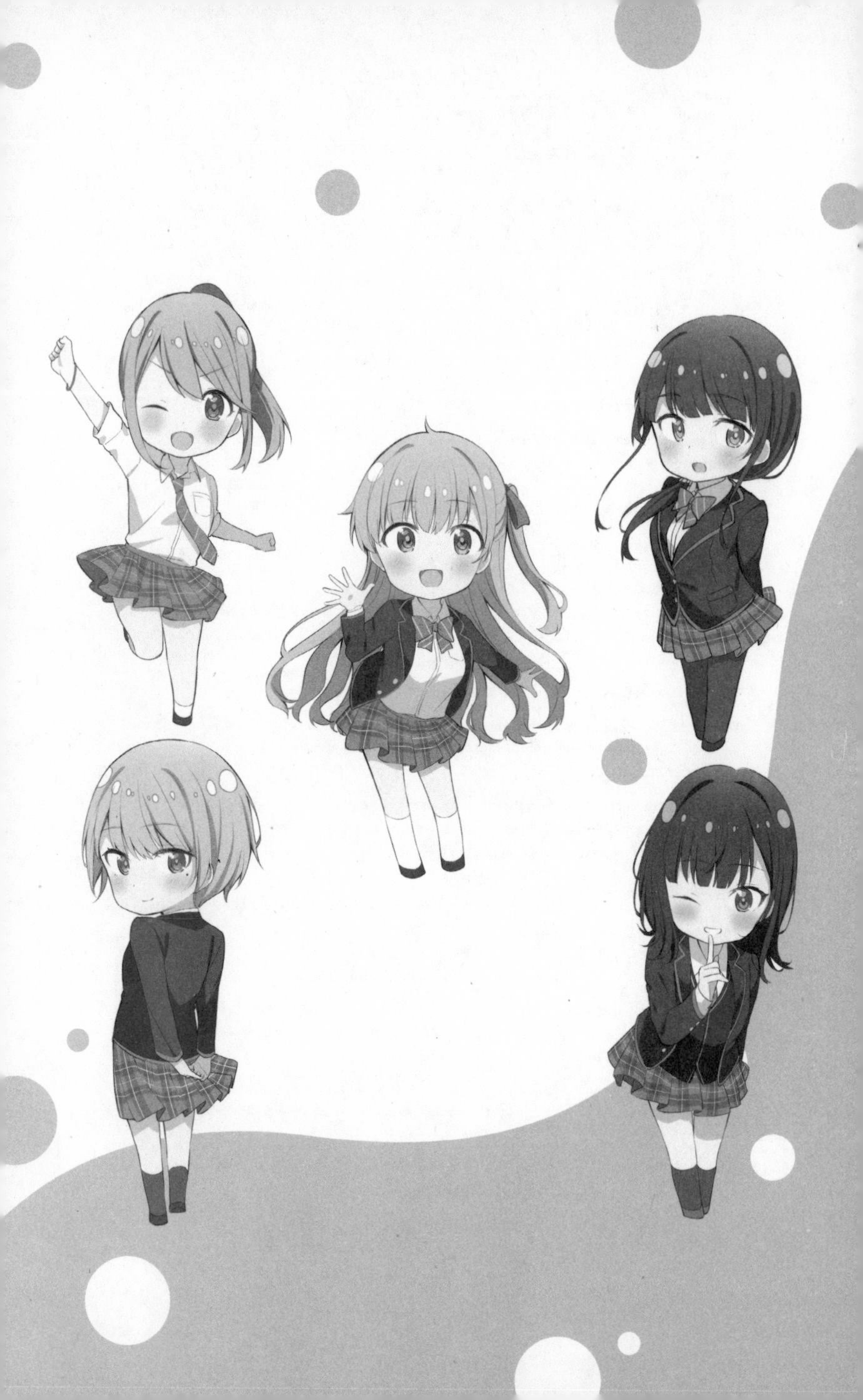

1

Original Story
Hiromu

Art
Bobkya

Character Design
raemz

Translation
Evie Lund

Lettering
Rachel J. Pierce

CHITOSE-KUN WA RAMUNE-BIN NO NAKA vol. 1
©Hiromu, raemz/Shogakukan Inc.(Gagaga Bunko)
©2020 Bobkya/SQUARE ENIX CO., LTD.
First published in Japan in 2020 by SQUARE ENIX CO., LTD. English translation rights arranged with SQUARE ENIX CO., LTD. and Yen Press, LLC through Tuttle-Mori Agency, Inc.

English translation ©2022 by SQUARE ENIX CO., LTD.

Yen Press
150 West 30th Street, 19th Floor
New York, NY 10001

Visit us at yenpress.com
facebook.com/yenpress
twitter.com/yenpress
yenpress.tumblr.com
instagram.com/yenpress

First Yen Press Edition: June 2022
Edited by Yen Press Editorial: Leilah Labossiere,
Won Young Seo
Designed by Yen Press Design: Andy Swist

Yen Press is an imprint of Yen Press, LLC.
The Yen Press name and logo are trademarks
of Yen Press, LLC.

The publisher is not responsible for websites
(or their content) that are not owned by the
publisher.

Library of Congress Control Number:
2022934292

ISBNs: 978-1-9753-4498-6 (paperback)
       978-1-9753-4499-3 (ebook)

10 9 8 7 6 5 4 3 2 1

WOR

Printed in the United States of America

Please flip to back to read an exclusive, new short story.

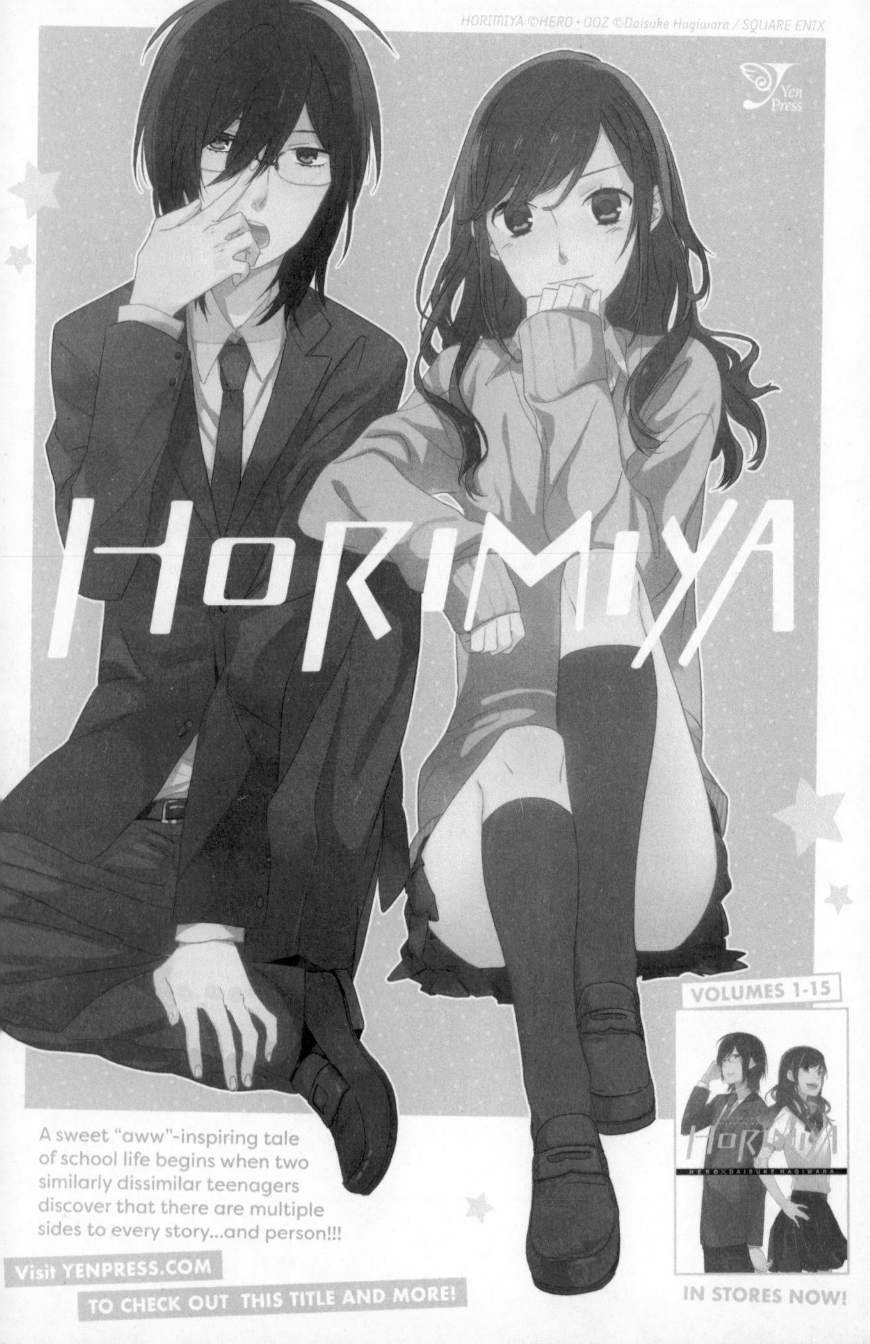
HORIMIYA ©HERO • OOZ ©Daisuke Hagiwara / SQUARE ENIX
Yen Press
HORIMIYA
VOLUMES 1-15
A sweet "aww"-inspiring tale of school life begins when two similarly dissimilar teenagers discover that there are multiple sides to every story...and person!!!
Visit YENPRESS.COM
TO CHECK OUT THIS TITLE AND MORE!
IN STORES NOW!

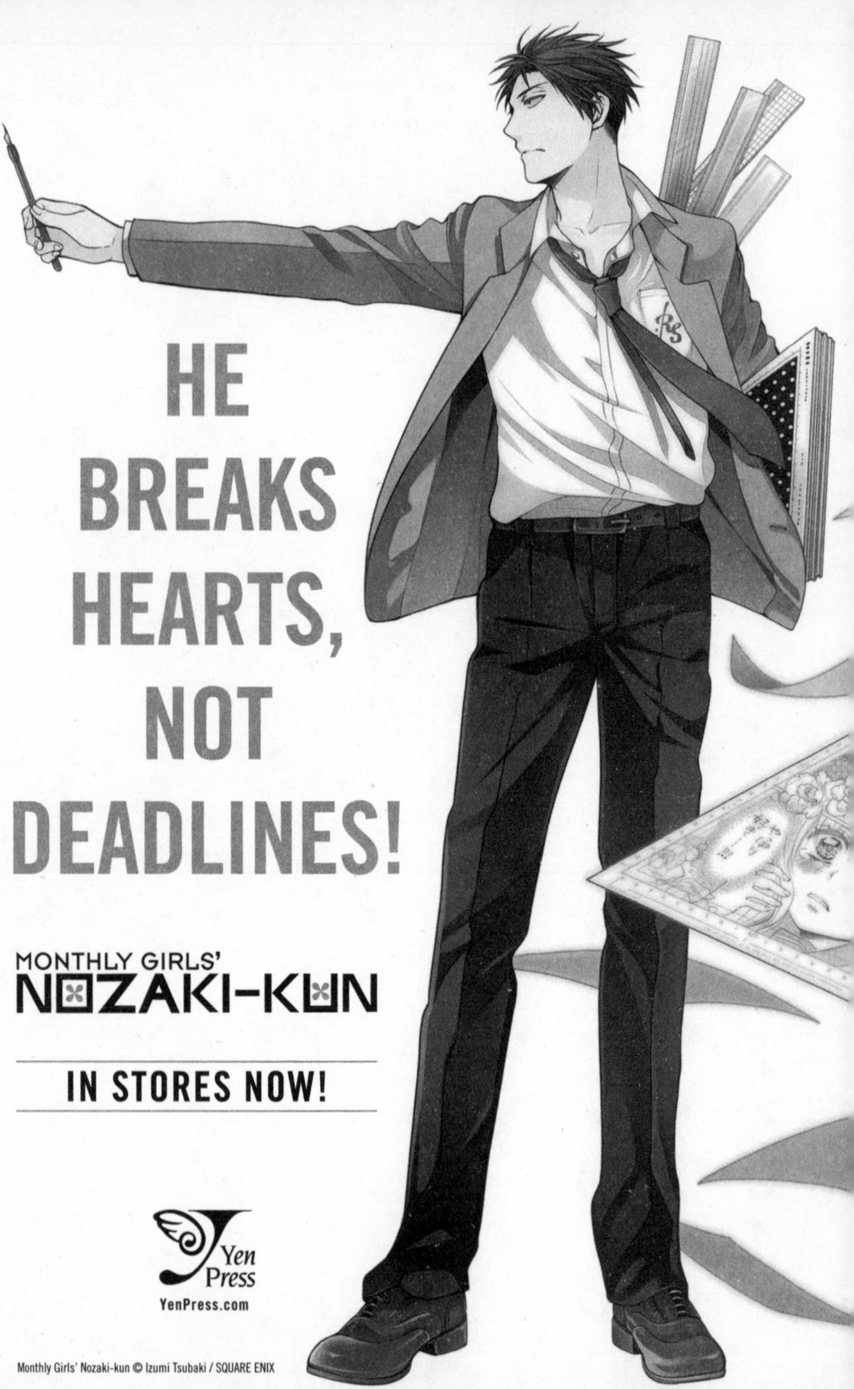

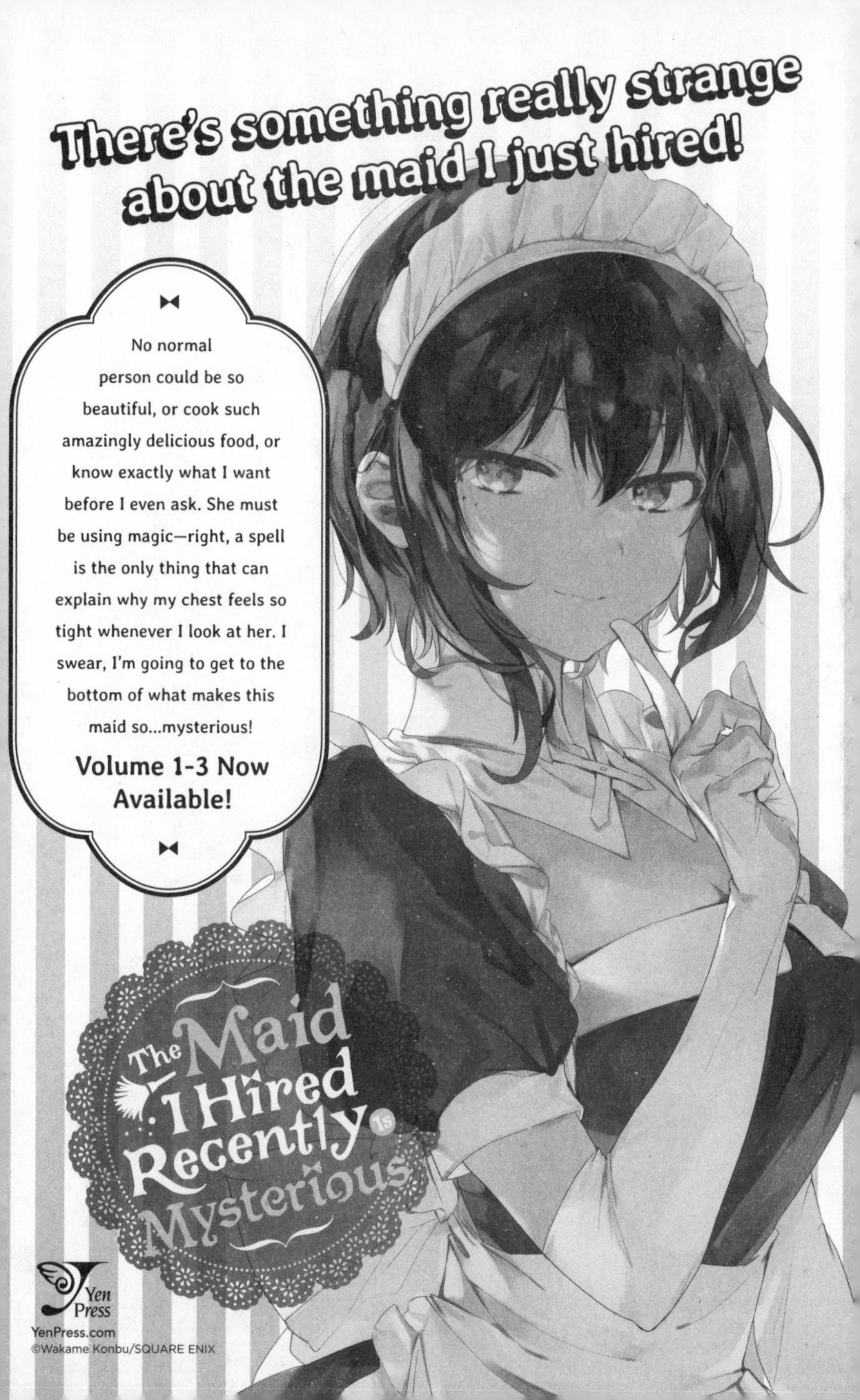
There's something really strange about the maid I just hired!
No normal person could be so beautiful, or cook such amazingly delicious food, or know exactly what I want before I even ask. She must be using magic—right, a spell is the only thing that can explain why my chest feels so tight whenever I look at her. I swear, I'm going to get to the bottom of what makes this maid so...mysterious!
Volume 1-3 Now Available!
The Maid I Hired Recently is Mysterious
Yen Press
YenPress.com
©Wakame Konbu/SQUARE ENIX

©Aidalro/SQUARE ENIX

VOLUMES 1-15 **IN STORES NOW!**

VOLUMES 1-16 AVAILABLE DIGITALLY!

Toilet-bound Hanako-Kun

At Kamome Academy, rumors abound about the school's Seven Mysteries, one of which is Hanako-san. Said to occupy the third stall of the third floor girls' bathroom in the old school building, Hanako-san grants any wish when summoned. Nene Yashiro, an occult-loving high school girl who dreams of romance, ventures into this haunted bathroom...but the Hanako-san she meets there is nothing like she imagined! Kamome Academy's Hanako-san...is a boy!

Yen Press

For more information
visit www.yenpress.com

PRESENTING THE LATEST SERIES FROM
JUN MOCHIZUKI

THE CASE STUDY OF VANITAS

CHAPTER 1

JUN MOCHIZUKI
THE CASE STUDY OF
VANITAS

**READ THE CHAPTERS AT
THE SAME TIME AS JAPAN!**

**AVAILABLE NOW WORLDWIDE
WHEREVER E-BOOKS ARE SOLD!**

www.yenpress.com

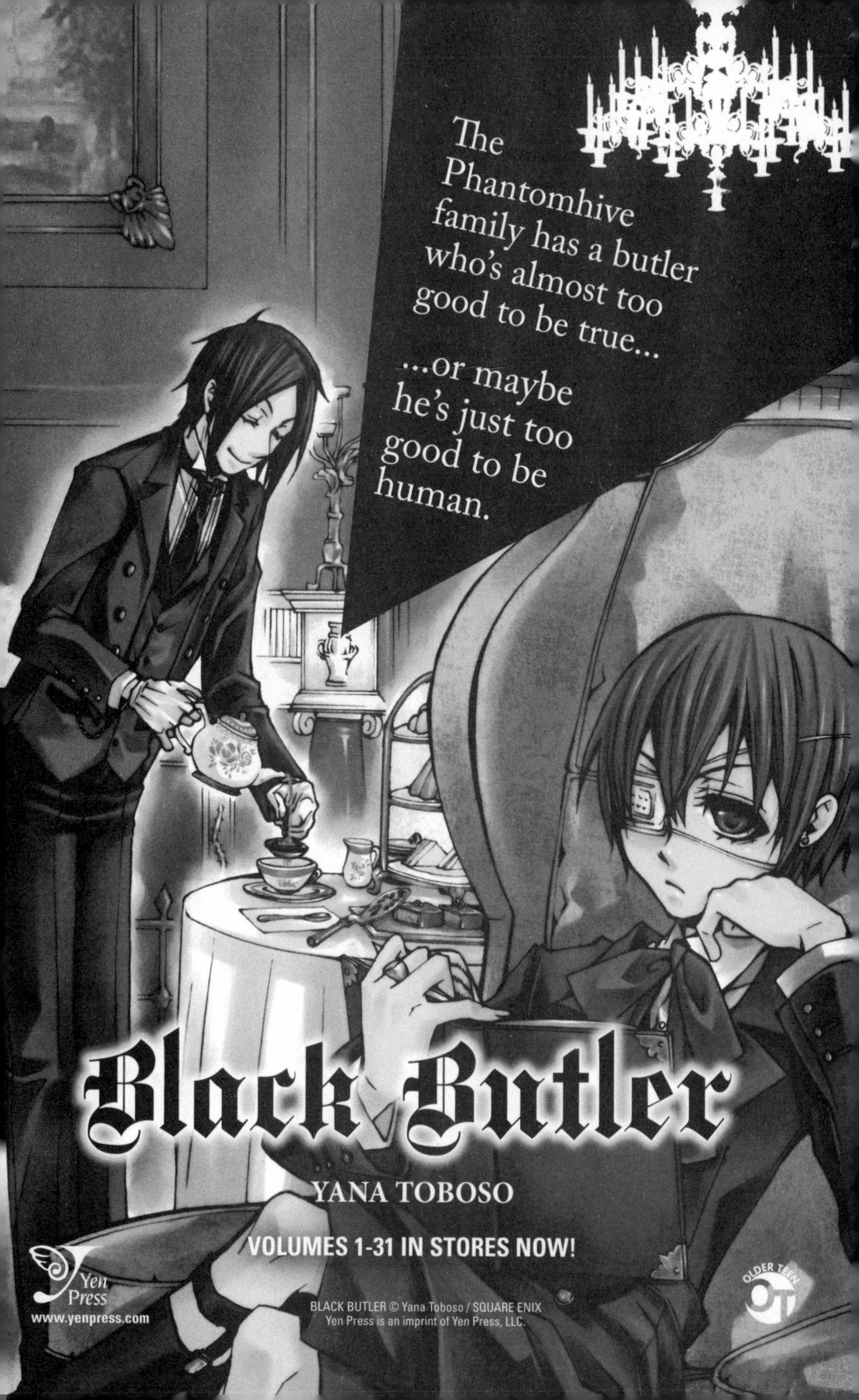
The Phantomhive family has a butler who's almost too good to be true...
...or maybe he's just too good to be human.
Black Butler
YANA TOBOSO
VOLUMES 1-31 IN STORES NOW!
Yen Press
www.yenpress.com
BLACK BUTLER © Yana Toboso / SQUARE ENIX
Yen Press is an imprint of Yen Press, LLC.
OLDER TEEN
OT

"I'd really prefer if you didn't make me relive that."

Yua blushed, and I couldn't suppress a burst of laughter.

Yua pouted just a little, but then she couldn't stop herself from laughing, too.

"Suppose…" I began. "Suppose Yamazaki comes back to school. I'll make him take back his words."

"Harem skank, you mean?"

"Yep. Then we'll fist-bump and be friends."

"Heh-heh. Then I'll have to give him a piece of my mind, too." The river water gurgled gently as it flowed past. From somewhere, a bicycle bell rang. The big round moon floating high above illuminated everything again tonight with a mellow glow. Were the curtains in Yamazaki's room still drawn tightly closed? If so, what a waste when such a beautiful evening was unfolding outside. The bag filled with light novels rustled in the breeze. What was going to happen next?

than you'd think." In fact, details that were supposed to be confidential had a way of finding themselves published on the underground gossip site. It was pretty depressing.

"I get more hate than most, so I'm more aware of it. But the truth is that everyone goes through it at least once or twice during high school, right?"

"Hmm, I guess you're right." Yua smiled wryly.

"Kenta didn't strike me as the type who really knows how to talk to people."

"Could it be that this is the first time in his life he's encountered this kind of issue? I mean, he got so defensive and aggressive against total strangers."

The main risk with this kind of thing is descending into self-hate. Or when being attacked directly by someone who clearly hates you, it can make you feel like you've been betrayed by a friend, and that leads you to be harsh with everyone you meet after that. Still, we barely got to talk to Kenta, so at this stage, we could only really guess.

Yua continued, her tone soft. "I'm amazed you have so much compassion for someone who said such mean stuff just after meeting you."

"Well, I'm used to being bashed. But to be honest…it does sting more hearing it in person." Still, I continued. "Sometimes you end up getting to know someone well even though the first impression was not good. **Like someone I could mention.**"

went down outside. Evening was approaching.

"Yua, I'll walk you home."

"Thanks. But I'm actually feeling a little tired right now." Well, that was only to be expected, I thought.

"Shall we stop somewhere for a drink?"

"Sure!"

My suggestion was a casual one, but actually there weren't a lot of cafés to be found in the sticks of Fukui.

We stopped at the convenience store, and each bought a drink; then we headed over to the riverbank to sit down.

It hit me all over again that spring was already here.

The cherry blossom trees weren't illuminated, but they still floated above like pink clouds, illuminated by the sparse glow of the streetlights. A cool breeze blew, still carrying the last traces of the winter chill, but it felt pleasant against my skin.

"Hey, Saku..." Yua spoke up, cupping her hot houjicha latte in both hands. "What did you think of Yamazaki?"

I slurped my iced caffe latte before answering.

"He's a pure-minded guy. That's what I thought."

"Pure-minded?"

"You've seen me get roasted, right, Yua? So you probably know this. But people aren't always nice to others. Someone you thought was nice might be bad-mouthing you behind your back. That happens more

"You remembered half? With him speaking that fast and everything?"

"Well, I already made up my mind to read them when he started listing the titles. I listened hard to memorize as many as I could." They were all titles that differed a lot from the books I usually read, so they stuck in my mind. Still, I could only recite one or two from memory. In front of the light novel section of the bookstore, I scanned the spines to see which titles looked familiar. Yua giggled lightly.

"This kind of thing…it's just classic Saku."

"I think you're referring to my awesome information retention skills here, which are at odds with my handsome face and prowess with the ladies?"

"And that, right there…that's classic Saku, too." I felt like she was exposing me here. Feeling a little awkward, I refocused my attention on the bookshelf in front of me.

*

In the end, I managed to find four of the light novel series Kenta had mentioned in the bookstore.

But they were all long-running series, with countless volumes each. My paper bag was bursting with twenty books. I couldn't exactly go back on my word now. But there were still six more series Kenta had mentioned. I was running up quite the expenses bill here.

While I was pondering over the books, the sun

Chitose Is in the Ramune Bottle
Bonus Short Story

On the way home from Kenta's house with Yua, we stopped by the large bookstore that was conveniently nearby. So I got turned away at the door, but that was only to be expected. Kura sent me—that was my official line—but that was really just my excuse, wasn't it? The way Kenta probably saw it, I showed up at his place, a man-whore he naturally didn't like, bringing a pretty girl with me to score points with her.

I tried to find out the truth, but in the end, all I did was rile him up a little. No doubt even now, Kenta was at home seething about popular kids and how much they suck. I wasn't even Kenta's friend or anything, but I'd made up my mind to find out more about his personal life. To that end, the very least I could do was try to read those light novels he mentioned.

"Thanks for coming along."

Yua blushed a little when I said that, looking slightly flustered.

"Oh, I don't mind at all. Only I can't remember a single one of the book titles Yamazaki mentioned. I'm not sure how much help I'll be."

"Oh yeah. I think I only managed to memorize around half of them myself."